THE KILLERS
DAYS&AGES

MARK BEAUMONT

OMNIBUS PRESS
London / New York / Paris / Sydney / Copenhagen / Berlin / Madrid / Tokyo

Exclusive Distributors
Music Sales Limited,
14/15 Berners Street,
London, W1T 3LJ.

Music Sales Corporation
180 Madison Avenue, 24th Floor,
New York,
NY 10016,
USA.

Macmillan Distribution Services
56 Parkwest Drive
Derrimut, Vic 3030,
Australia.

Every effort has been made to trace the copyright holders of the photographs in this book but one or
two were unreachable. We would be grateful if the photographers concerned would contact us.

Printed in the EU

A catalogue record for this book is available from the British Library.

Visit Omnibus Press on the web at www.omnibuspress.com

Contents

Introduction – On Top

From outside the stage door, the club seems to bulge. Sweat, steam and noise gout from the open door. The building buzzes with a heady, excited babble from within; squeals and chatter, a crush of bodies, past midnight in a shuttered corner of the city, wrapped in a clubland gauze of backlight, smoke, alcohol and adrenalin. A bouncer glares at you, loitering, checking your phone for a word from your contact inside.

Then an inner door opens, the noise crescendos, a triple-A laminate is flashed; "he's fine". You're bundled through a graffiti-coated backstage hell-warren, past a grotty closet of a dressing room where a flustered PA is badgering the promoter for tea for the singer (clearly not a rock'n'roll bunch tonight) and out into the crush of the club, pushing through a sea of sticky flesh. Eight hundred hyper-charged rock fans, amazed they made it into the hottest gig in town, unlike the hundreds left disappointed or begging for tickets outside. Eight hundred winners – there's a palpable celebration lifting the Highbury Garage, even before the band take the stage.

The second they do, around 1 a.m., pandemonium. They're dressed casually, wave modestly at the crowd and open with a couple of lesser-known tracks, but the floor erupts. Over an 11-song set, the band cuts loose, playing obscure satires on the exclusive American indie scene, the odd B-side and a cover of Tommy James & The Shondells' 'I Think We're Alone Now', kicking back, enjoying themselves. By the time their grinning, wide-eyed singer leads them through a handful of their most famous tunes to close, the wild and rapturous crowd are in drunken paroxysms, stumbling breathless into the silvery night, gasping about the gig of the century.

A white-hot underground cult band on the rise, you might think; fresh press darlings riding the hype with a sold-out club show, on the fast track to the front pages. Another hipster flash-in-the-pan, perhaps, feted until the next punk dog and pony show rides into town. But no, this is a band at the very pinnacle of their success. Two hours before this first-come-first-served late-night show, announced only this afternoon, they were headlining Wembley Stadium before 90,000 people, flanked by 50-foot lightning bolts and beaming through a song they'd written for the occasion, the gig they'd been dreaming of all their lives.

For this is The Killers, the gleaming pride of Fabulous Las Vegas, celebrating the battle finally won.

★ ★ ★

"This is *crazy*," says the same grinning singer, 10 years younger, the triumph of a Wembley Stadium after-show gig still just the stuff of his wildest Bono fantasies. "Back at home you see Elvises now and then, you might pull up next to one at a stop light. But not on a *trapeze*."[1]

The Brandon Flowers I first met at Glastonbury 2004 was just as wide-eyed and awestruck as the one fulfilling his life's ambitions at Wembley Stadium in 2013, but a decade more naïve: it felt for all the world like being handed a newborn rock star. Everything was a first — it was his first UK festival, and he'd certainly never seen any event as vast and outlandish as Glastonbury. It was his first time ever wearing wellington boots, not regular desert wear.

And as I led him across the site to a field called Lost Vagueness, Glastonbury's hallucinogenic homage to Vegas, he'd certainly never seen his hometown condensed into such a surreal festival freak show. An Elvis on a trapeze sang 'Burning Love'. Mexican hombres, Venetian gondoliers, Egyptian pharaohs, feather-clad Parisian can-can dancers and S&M Charlie Chaplins roamed a mini-casino set up in a velvet-lined cabaret tent. "It reminds me of Las Vegas at Christmas or something," Brandon smiled, sipping champagne from a plastic glass. "That's the only time it'd be like this. It's like Vegas, *Mad Max* style."[2] Pictures taken with reticent bassist Mark Stoermer around Lost Vagueness' roulette wheel – Brandon dressed down in a blazer and striped hoop pullover – I escorted Brandon and Mark outside to gaze up at the gigantic inflatable Little White Wedding Chapel on the far side of the field. "Oh man," Brandon gasped as a pair of dreadlocked cybergoths in full wedding regalia and spiked stack-heel boots marched jubilantly up the aisle, "Ronnie our drummer used to work at the Little White Wedding Chapel as a photographer. He actually had this goth couple get married there while handcuffed to each other. It was like ''til death do us part'. But this..."[3]

At which point, Brandon was hooked under the arms from behind by a gaggle of fifties laundry attendants and dragged off to have his hair fluffed with feather dusters and his nails buffed in a makeshift laundrette.

The next time I saw him – pampered, preened and prepped for stardom – he was gazing out from the tiny New Band stage at thousands upon thousands of fans racing towards the tent, piling into a crowd bulging 50 deep outside. The Killers were the word-of-mouth phenomenon of Glastonbury 2004; The Victims were starting to mount.

For a few years, as The Killers' star ascended from their UK explosion as The Best British Band From America to their vindication as desert rock heroes in their own right, I was locked in a battle of fashion one-upmanship with Brandon that he never knew he was involved in. Joining them on tour around Germany the following

9

month, The Killers' expansive electro-rock rattling stately Weimar reception rooms in Cologne and ravaged Berlin rock bars to sparse crowds, I was inspired by Brandon's slickness to smarten up myself. At a London photo shoot for the band's first *NME* cover, I loved the shirt Brandon had chosen from the stylist's rack so much that, at the end of the shoot, I bought it[*] and was wearing it when I next ran into Brandon at an *NME* Awards event, only to find him having graduated to a three-piece suit. The next time I saw him, having suited myself to the max for the occasion, he was wearing a military jacket with eagle feather epaulettes. Without ever telling him there was a contest, I admitted defeat.

As fashion, so band. Over the course of almost a decade, The Killers become gradually more grand, ornate and unmatchable. From meeting, lunching and playing with their heroes – Bono, Morrissey, New Order – they were soon their peers, headlining major festivals, gracing international magazine covers and selling a combined 20 million copies of their four chart-crushing albums. Among their own generation of breakthrough rock bands from the early years of the new century – The Strokes, The White Stripes, Franz Ferdinand, Arctic Monkeys, Kaiser Chiefs – they alone have attained the upper echelons of rock'n'roll, scaled the stadium league like a mild-mannered Kong. And they've done it without resorting to the rock'n'roll shortcuts of shock, sensation or (too much) spitefulness.

No, The Killers have become arguably the most successful 21st-century rock band on the back of a vaulting ambition, ceaseless commitment, laser-eyed intent and a touring work ethic that's almost split the band in two. That, and magnificent, heart-busting music that blends the dramatic with the melodic as only world-beaters can.

The Killers' story is Scorsese widescreen, Coppola epic. From the vampiric neon sleaze of downtown Vegas to the screaming hordes of Wembley via private jets, dinners with Elton and songs

---

[*] Having, ahem, "grown out" of this shirt, I'll happily accept bids for it...

of spacemen, murderers, nuclear tourists and cheating girlfriends, it's a billion dollar global blockbuster with four heroes you can't help but root for.

It's also a lifetime's gamble that paid off big.

Now kiss the dice and throw.

CHAPTER 1

Welcome To Fabulous Las Vegas

"I can remember my first house in Henderson, a little suburb of Vegas. We had a dirt... we were the only house in the neighbourhood that didn't have grass. It wasn't a conscious decision to save the environment, it was because we didn't have enough money to have grass. Somebody put a dollar in the mailbox with a mean note saying 'this is towards getting sod'. I remember it was a proud day my dad finally got the sod and him and my uncles and my brother laid it and my dad planted a small palm tree. I still drive by the house and that palm tree that was three feet tall when he planted it is 30 feet tall now. They just shoot up."

– Brandon Flowers' earliest memory

At 3 a.m., the phone buzzed like the devil's purr. The phone buzzes at 3 a.m., Brandon knew what that meant. He lifted the receiver like a lead weight.

"Hello, Gold Coast Casino, bellhop desk, how can I help you this morning?"

"Is that the cute one?" A woman's voice, drawling drunk and breathless. "Can you go buy us some condoms and bring them on up."

More direct than usual. Brandon wished he had a dollar for every time he'd been propositioned by female guests while shunting bags at the

Gold Coast, and the hookers that frequently rented rooms sometimes made pretty odd requests, although this was a first. But his job remit was clear – anything the guest wants, within reason, the guest gets. So 15 minutes later, condoms on a silver platter, Brandon knocked on the appropriate door.

And when the nude woman opened the door to him, what he saw inside blew his poor Mormon boy's mind.

They were at it on both beds, against the walls, on the floor; a full-blown orgy. "I was just like 'what are you doing?'," he'd say when telling the story years later. "They didn't try to conceal it or anything."[1] The woman paid for her purchase and invited him to join them when his next break came up. True to his nature, Brandon worked straight through that night.

What happened in Vegas stayed with him in Vegas. Though Brandon Flowers kept his distance from the darker side of the city, it was the neon sleaze and seduction of the Strip, with its fairytale castles, full-scale pirate ships, dancing fountains, faux Manhattan skylines and miniature Eiffel Towers, that enchanted and intrigued him, made him feel that the place was unreal, nefariously magical, humankind's dazzling hub of glitz and sedition. He loved the fact that the downtown strip bars, transvestite clubs and bail bond offices were open around the clock, just like the casinos, even though none of it was particularly his scene. He could smell the death and felony on the bulb-burned downtown sidewalks, and the intoxicated high-life on the roulette wheels and craps tables. Vegas fascinated and appalled him in equal measure, but driving down the Strip at night it felt like the most beautiful city on the planet.

Set adrift in the city of lights; it sure seemed like a long way to have come for a wide-eyed kid from Nephi, a town with no stoplights.

★ ★ ★

Vegas was Brandon Flowers' first home. He was born June 21, 1981, to Terry and Jean Flowers, a fine-boned couple of teenage sweethearts, together since they were 15 years of age and Vegas residents for almost

40 years* but Terry and Jean had moved up in the world to Henderson by the time Brandon was born. Brandon was the youngest of six children by a margin of 12 years. "I was a mistake!" he'd say. "One day at my parents' friend's house, their son explained it to me. I don't think my mom was very happy about that."[2]

Mistake or not, Brandon was a joyful addition to the household in Henderson. Nicknaming him Bray, his four elder sisters pampered him constantly, ensuring his hair was always immaculately styled and dressing him up as a showgirl or in rayon shirts in imitation of their favourite boy band, New Edition. Aside from the artfulness of make-up, Brandon got a valuable insight into the feminine perspective from listening to his sisters gossip. "I learned the difference between good girls and bad girls," he said. "I can tell the second I meet someone."[3]

Generally peaceful and family-friendly, Henderson had its eye-opening moments of darkness for the young Brandon. "One time, somebody got murdered and they dumped the body [across the street from our house]," he said. "My cousin Bobby made us all go and look at it."[4]

Terry Flowers was a heavy drinking man, a gambler too. He got it from his own father, who may well have got it from his father before him. Brandon was too young to remember any bad side of Terry's alcoholism, but he would remember his mother driving him to a nearby casino and trawling the aisles of tables, looking for his father to drag him back home.

Though his father was the dreamer of the family, a trait that rubbed off on young Brandon and gave him a spark of ambition that would drive him all his life, it was his mother who had seen several kinds of light. Jean was from a generation of Vegas kids that had been taken out of town on school trips and given sunglasses to watch the nuclear tests going off in the desert in the fifties and sixties. "They'd have parties," Brandon would say, "give people martinis and sunglasses and wait for it to go off, it's crazy. They'd take school-kids out to designated points in the desert to watch the explosions."[5] Jean was also the spiritual core

---

* Brandon would tell me that his family was from a "trailer park... in the desert".

15

of the Flowers family. Her husband was brought up Catholic but Jean was involved with the Church of Jesus Christ of Latter-day Saints, a Christian primitivist church founded by Joseph Smith in 1830 around a holy text entitled *The Book Of Mormon*, which Smith claimed to have translated from golden plates he'd discovered in New York State under direction from an angel, plates containing the stories of indigenous American prophets. Much doubt has been cast on the validity of Smith's story, the questionable methodology he used to translate the plates and even his character, but Jean Flowers was an unwavering believer. She'd regularly invite missionaries and preachers to the house to talk about Mormonism, and the ideas and strong family values of the religion percolated. When Brandon was five, his father had what he described as a revelation and converted, giving up alcohol abuse in honour of his new faith, and suddenly Vegas lost a little of its gleam for the Flowers family.

As a small child, religion hadn't yet struck a chord with Brandon, but his other lifelong fascination certainly had. As his mother drove the family around town, careful to steer clear of the sleazier corners, John Waite's AOR classic 'Missing You' would frequently grace the car's radio; by the age of three Brandon knew all the words and would sing along so well that his sisters would take him around to their friends' houses and have him perform it. A year later he'd added 'Sunglasses At Night' by Corey Hart to his performance repertoire. "Looking back, I understood pop music when I was four," he said. "[It was] an awful song but I could follow melodies and knew how they worked even then."[6] At five, hearing it booming through his brother's bedroom wall, he knew The Cure's 'Just Like Heaven' by heart.

Aside from bad teeth*, he also inherited his father's love of Elton John and Johnny Cash, and was entranced by the Eagles' 'Peaceful Easy Feeling', a song he'd always associate with the Nevada wastes. "I love the desert, so there are a few people for me who've captured that specific

---

* "It's an ongoing battle," he'd say, "both of my parents have terrible teeth so I'm doomed. Ever since he was 20 my dad has had dentures, and my mom has every tooth capped." Source: *The Killers: Vagabonds And Victims*, Jimmy Ramsay (Independent Music Press, 2005).

area," he'd say, "like the Eagles and Fleetwood Mac and even Jackson Browne sometimes. I'll hear that stuff and I'm just there. I hear it and… I can just see the sun going down in Las Vegas."[7]

When he hit five his parents took him to the Las Vegas Liberace museum, dedicated to the legendary flamboyant showman. Amazed by the flowing stage-wear and grandiose candle holders, Brandon found himself drawn to the museum's spot-lit centrepiece – Liberace's grand piano, its lid transparent and its every surface cast silver by thousands upon thousands of glinting rhinestones. Music, Brandon realised, was a world of unlimited glamour and riches. A life worth having.

He started six years of piano lessons and by the age of six, around the same time that he 'got' Mormonism[*] and had his first bike stolen[**], his natural talents were starting to emerge. Eventually he'd regale the family with basic takes on Bach and Elton John's 'Your Song' and 'The One', but from the off he saw the exploratory possibilities of the instrument. "My mom and my sisters all watched *The Young And The Restless* religiously," he said, referencing a popular CBS daytime soap set in a fictional Wisconsin village. "In the beginning they have that 'ding… ding, ding, ding, ding' piano part. And I figured it out on my own when I was six. My mom heard me get it and she was amazed."[8]

Slowly, showbiz pulled him in; perhaps he was dazzled by the sight of the sign for Sam's Town Hotel And Gambling Hall that he could see from his bedroom window.[***]

When Brandon was eight years old, the Vegas rat race got too much for Terry and Jean Flowers. They craved a quieter life, closer to their God. Selling up the Henderson house, they moved their family into the Mormon stronghold of Utah, to the religion's very own Jerusalem.

Nephi, in Peyton, was a tiny town of barely 3,000 souls, little more than a truck stop. A town where drivers waved at every passing car

---

[*] "Basic religion is the reason we have morals," he'd tell the *NME Yearbook* in 2004.

[**] "I had it for four days and then somebody stole it," he told *NME*'s Tim Jonze in December 2004. "But I guess I'm happy that someone got a nice bike."

[***] Alternatively, Brandon may have lived across the street from Sam's Town on his return to Vegas at the age of 16.

as there were no strangers, and eight in every 10 inhabitants were Mormons. Where entertainment for kids stretched little further than watching friends wrestle in the dirt of the trucks. Director Herbert Ross found it the perfect backdrop to act as the town of Beaumont in his film *Footloose*, the story of a small town where religious authority figures ban dancing and rock'n'roll, since the Mormon faith frowns upon such wild youthful exploits as alcohol, tobacco, body piercing, tattoos and pre-marital sex. A safe haven – Jean no longer had to fret about her kids getting kidnapped 24 hours a day – but for a chubby pre-teen like Brandon with a fascination for music and no particular interest or ability in football, a sport that the town revolved around, it was a tough place to fit in. "[I] never really got over [the culture shock, but] I liked the freedom of being a kid in a small town,"[9] he said. "[It was] a total culture shock, the exact opposite of Vegas. I mean, I wasn't necessarily a city kid but I knew I wasn't like them."[10]

As he settled, Brandon got into the usual scrapes. He dabbled in ouija boards, until the board told him he would die on his birthday. And when he was nine he procured a pellet-firing BB gun at Christmas and shot a bird (which he regrets to this day), and accidentally himself. "It was during the first Gulf War, and my dad brought back pictures of Saddam Hussein to shoot at," he recalled. "So I was shooting at one of them one time and I ran forward to it immediately after I'd fired to see how good a shot I was, but it ricocheted off the shed and came back at me square in the head. I learned my lesson. I almost lost my eye that Christmas!"[11]

Called an 'incomer' at school because of his non-native status, Brandon sought solace in his family. His elder brother Shane, 12 years his senior, become his role model. Shane was a handsome young man and a good dresser, the guy who took Miss Nevada to his high school prom and was offered scholarships to colleges. Watching his success made Brandon feel that, for him too, anything was possible. "Everything he did, I wanted to do it too,"[12] Brandon said, and that included playing golf (Shane, like Brandon, had been a child prodigy golfer) and guzzling left-field culture. Shane would show Brandon films or play him music as what Brandon would describe as "a gift from my brother, [an] imparting of some kind of knowledge, a passage rite for me. It was music and certain films that he would introduce me to. Films like *Caddyshack*."[13] Brandon particularly remembered watching the Paul Newman and Tom Cruise pool hustling movie *The Color Of Money* with Shane. "This one was kinda out of the ordinary, I guess," he told me. "I love the soundtrack, Warren Zevon, Robert Palmer, Don Henley and stuff like that. It's a combination of the whole vibe of that movie I love. And *At Close Range*, the Sean Penn movie. The way that movie looks and the way it's lit is inspirational to me. That can be just as powerful as a great song."[14]

But Shane's most vital gift to his younger brother was a keen adoration of British and Irish bands. Shane's room was a shrine to The Smiths, The Cure, Depeche Mode and U2* and Brandon would sneak in when Shane was out to listen to his records. It was a deception Shane encouraged – he'd shown Brandon videos of The Smiths, The Rolling Stones' *Gimme Shelter* and U2's *Rattle And Hum*, filling him with the allure of the British and Irish music scene. "My brother wouldn't listen to anything that wasn't from the UK," he said, "and from the age of 12 I followed him[15]," he said. "When I was growing up in Las Vegas, England just seemed so far away: a genuine fantasy-land. There was something untouchable about the music – larger than life. It was so different from what the Americans were growing up with. And it became irresistible to try to emulate, even down to adopting an English accent when you sang."[16]

In those videos Brandon studied the way that Bono and Mick Jagger owned the stage. "I'd get so excited seeing them as a kid. It was something I had to try for myself."[17] His addiction to British music grew although, again encouraged by Shane, the first cassette album he convinced his parents to buy for him was a greatest hits collection by The Cars.** "I was 12. It was a rainy day. I made my mum and dad listen to it for two hours straight all the way home from the store. My

---

* One day, when Shane failed to show up for the funeral of his great-grandmother, Jean went into his room and tore every poster in half, knowing that was the worst possible retribution she could inflict on him.
** Brandon also procured a tape of The Psychedelic Furs around the same time.

parents are cool."[18] Singer Ric Ocasek became a hero of Brandon's and the track 'Just What I Needed' was his favourite song for a while. "It worked for me – 'It's not the perfume that you wear/It's not the ribbons in your hair' – it's similar to The Strokes in its simplicity. It's perfect."[19] "That song was just so cool to me, and it had such a big impact. It made that town more tolerable, and it made that town cooler, and it didn't matter. It was really profound[20]," he said. "When I listened to The Cars' 'Just What I Needed' or 'Double Life,' it made me feel like the coolest person alive – which I wasn't – and it was an escape."[21]

Brandon needed ways to make Nephi seem cooler. His weight issues were affecting his confidence and self-image, and would cause him self-doubt throughout his teenage years – he refused to go swimming for fear of people seeing his body, always thought people were looking at him and would imagine every laugh in every restaurant was aimed at him. His love of golf and increasing adoration of Morrissey and The Smiths, New Order, Depeche Mode, The Psychedelic Furs, Elton John, U2, Talking Heads and even new romantics Duran Duran* at a time when all the other kids in his Peyton school were buying wholesale into grunge, increasingly made him a loner. "I grew up in an era when Nirvana and Korn were the big things. All my classmates were into them, but they sounded like trash to me. No tunes, no melodies, no style," he said.[22] "I can't tell you how many times I've been called a 'faggot' for liking the Smiths."[23]

Brandon's school friend Wyatt Boswell** remembers the schoolyard strife Brandon endured. "He never had a girlfriend the whole time he lived there. [Nephi] is a little farm town that thrives on football, so he was seen as kind of 'off'. 'You play golf? You listen to Elton John?' He caught a lot of shit for that."[24] He often found himself on the receiving end of homophobic abuse. "You can either go the 'I'm not a fag' route," Brandon said, "or you can think 'oh, whatever'. I was all for

---

* Brandon would describe Duran Duran's debut album as "awesome... they have great songs, sometimes danceable and a great combination of rock and pop". Source: *Attitude*, Martin Aston, July 2004.
** Wyatt would go on to be a Killers guitar tech.

'oh, whatever'. I didn't care what they thought."[25] He even got a little stick for it at home. One day his father came into his room to find him dancing around to a tape of camp UK pop outfit Erasure. "You like that kinda music, huh son?" Terry noted, and walked out of the room. Little did any of them know that Brandon was so deeply heterosexual that his first crush was on Tina Turner, having been gobsmacked by the hirsute raunch of her 'What's Love Got To Do With It' video.

The thing was, Brandon felt music far more deeply than his schoolmates. He recalls a fourth grade teacher who'd fought in the Second World War performing an old battle ballad in class. "He explained about 'I'll Be Home For Christmas' and what it meant, with all the soldiers coming home from war. Then he sang it, without a piano or anything. He was crying his eyes out. And I was tearing up as well. I was really young and really emotional. I'll never forget that. What a sweet man."[26]

Alongside a fascination with sci-fi[*], as he entered his teens, music increasingly became a refuge. At 15, his mother's gifts of the odd cassette no longer keeping up with his voracious appetite for music, he started working at a fast food restaurant called Taco Time where his mother and two of his sisters also worked, in order to make money to buy more records. He still needed his mom's help to get hold of the music though – it was an hour's drive to the nearest record store in Provo. At Flying J he browsed the racks for the first album he'd buy with his own money, and chose *Songs Of Faith And Devotion* by Depeche Mode; he liked their "bubblegum" early stuff and would be rather shocked by how dark and devilish they'd become by 1996. But, at $5 on cassette, *Songs Of Faith And Devotion* would become one of Brandon's proudest possessions.

That same year he attended his first gig, The Cure on the tour for their 1996 *Wild Mood Swings* album, and wore eyeliner for the first time for the occasion – he was bundled into a bathroom by a girl and plastered in the stuff, but felt comfortable wearing it, liked the sensation of belonging. Beginning to shift some of his teen weight, Brandon

---

[*] Brandon's lifelong love of sci-fi was instigated by seeing a movie called *Fire In The Sky*, the 1993 story of a logger abducted by aliens in the White Mountains of Arizona.

started taking a certain pride in his appearance, particularly now he had new teeth. Genetically he'd inherited a poor set and when he had braces fitted at 14 he didn't take care of them too well; when they were taken off, chunks of tooth came off with them. At school he was teased for having food stuck in his teeth when in fact his smile was pitted with holes. So he had veneers fitted, and with a bright new smile came an inkling of confidence.

As the CD age took hold of the Flowers family and Shane flew the nest, Brandon was gifted Shane's entire cassette collection and his music world expanded – Britpop acts like Pulp crept in, the more artful grunge of Smashing Pumpkins. And more and more he adored Morrissey, plastering his bedroom walls with his posters and singing along to Smiths cassettes in the car with his mother.* The line "I love the romance of crime" from 'Sister, I'm A Poet' struck a chord and turned Brandon's thoughts to writing his own murder fiction, and he was hooked on Morrissey's videos. "I liked the way Morrissey was, onstage," he said. "The way he performed and owned the audience – the way people wanted to touch him. That led me into music."[27] "It wasn't like I was really into the miserable side of it all," he'd say, "I actually think they're some of the best pop songs ever written."[28]

On Halloween 1997, Brandon had the first of several audiences with his hero. Shane took him up to Salt Lake City to watch Morrissey play at the Saltair Pavilion. The set that night was short on hits and dominated with material from Morrissey's recent solo albums *Vauxhall And I*, *Southpaw Grammar* and *Maladjusted*, but Brandon went crazy, lost in what he'd soon be calling the most thrilling experience he'd ever had. "I'm taking my kid brother to a concert," said Shane, "but the moment Morrissey came on Brandon was off, down the front, going wild. I'd never seen him like that before."[29]

At school he'd couch himself in UK rock, prowling the halls in headphones, lost in his imaginary Salford. "I thought I understood it

---

* His mom already knew every word from watching Shane go through the same obsession and would regularly be found whistling 'Unhappy Birthday' or 'Girlfriend In A Coma' while cleaning dishes; "That was kinda weird," Brandon claimed.

all but I probably didn't. I created a world for myself that was kind of a virtual Manchester. I wore the clothes and walked the walk."[30]

It wasn't only elation and solace that Brandon got from music. It stoked him too. "When I hear good music, ever since I was 13, it made me jealous," he admitted. "I wanted to do something that good. I didn't realise what it was when I was 13. I loved the songs but there was something in me that was a little tinge of jealousy."[31]

Brandon boasted a fiercely competitive nature. If Shane's example had made Brandon feel he was destined for greatness from an early age, his elder brother's settling into family life and a regular job in his twenties spurred Brandon on to even headier ambition. He also took his competitive streak onto the golf course, never quite matching his brother's achievements but hitting a handicap of five at his peak, good enough to consider a future as a pro. In later years he'd be glad he didn't take that route, since he hated the sweaters, and even out on the links his mind was still on music. "Even when I was out there I was always singing songs," he remembered, "and I couldn't wait for my mom to pick me up so I could play my tapes in the car."[32]

Long before he turned to writing songs himself, they started gathering. In eighth grade he developed a fixation on a school friend called Andy, a sports star of the football field and the toast of Peyton. "If you're a loner, there are always going to be people that you want to be, even if it's just for one day,"[33] Brandon would later muse. "I wouldn't say that I was an outcast at school, but when you're at school, it's always the case that the more athletically gifted kids, the popular kids, are somewhat glorified, and that frustrated me a bit."[34] The feelings of admiration and aspiration that Andy stirred within him would linger, gnaw.

As would the troubling events in the life of his uncle Jonny. A cocaine user, Jonny was the black sheep of the family, and in 1996 his behaviour reached a nadir. Gripped in paranoia, he became obsessed with George Orwell's novel *1984* and somehow convinced himself that aliens were trying to climb through his TV set to steal his semen. His solution was shocking and tragic – he took a gun and tried to shoot off his own testicles. Thankfully he missed, but was hospitalised with a gunshot wound to the abdomen. Jonny would eventually recover from his paranoia, but the incident rocked the Flowers family and would stay with young Brandon long into adulthood.

Slowly, his rock star future was unravelling for him.

But no rock star ever came from Nephi.

★ ★ ★

In his father's truck, the croon of Elvis drifted from the FM stations like a siren call from his glistening roots. He bought a copy of Frank Sinatra's *The Main Event*, a live album from 1974. Sinatra was singing of old town Chicago, yet something about it oozed Vegas, churned homesickness, tore at the showman within him. "Something about that sound made me want to be back in Vegas."[35]

At the age of 16, the bright lights drew him back home.

After six years in Utah, having been forever 'grounded' by the ethics and values of the Mormon community and with his parents' blessing, Brandon returned to Vegas to finish high school. He lived with his aunt Joyce and a cousin of his own age in a house on the outskirts and enrolled at Chaparral High School, out on Annie Oakley Drive in a district called Paradise. "It was the most fun I'd ever had," he said. "Sixteen in this town? That's the dream."[36] He felt more comfortable here and, once he got his first car – a Geo Metro – he enjoyed skipping school, squeezing his 6ft 4in cousin into the passenger seat and "raising hell in that car"[37]. But his innocent Nephi years had ill-prepared him for Vegas' inherent iniquities. He'd overhear girls sitting behind him in English class dreaming of reaching 18 so they could start stripping. "That's one of the sad things about Vegas,"[38] he'd lament.

The prostitution, strip joints and gangs of Las Vegas burned Brandon's retinas* – though the city's motto was 'whatever happens in Vegas stays in Vegas', he always preferred the billboard that had been erected by a Christian group reading 'God Knows What Happens In Vegas'. But he was far more seduced by the myth and legend. "I romanticise,"

---

* "Never had a hooker!" he'd proudly exclaim to *Boyz* magazine in 2004.

he said, "I live with the ghosts of Elvis and Frank Sinatra. It seems so glamorous. They were American men who don't exist any more."[39] He got a fake ID, a pierced ear*, a taste for Marlboro and beer and a driving licence and hit the Strip, in thrall to "Frank Sinatra and the glamour and having a Cadillac".[40] "It's a beautiful city at night – so many colours, all the casinos... there's always something new opening on the Strip," he'd say, glisten-eyed. "It's there to partake of if you want. The nightclubs and the gambling casinos."[41] His drives through the overblown Vegas night filled him with the sheer enormity of show business: "You'd drive by Mike Tyson's house and there'd be posters for magicians and Tom Jones everywhere. It was just normal. If you thought about being onstage, it would be a big show. How else would you do it?"[42]

It was on one such night time drive that Brandon had his How To Be A Wallflower moment. And his world shifted star-ward.

After high school, Brandon had shunned the idea of college in favour of taking a job as a caddy on one of the many golf courses that encircled the Chaparral High School. "First time I drank alcohol was in that place," he said. "I was 16, it was called Aftershock."[43] Before long he had a steady girlfriend and was earning extra cash as a busboy. Over the coming years he'd work in several Vegas restaurants; his first ever public singing performance was at a Christmas party for staff at a French bistro he worked at in the Aladdin Hotel**, doing Oasis' 'Don't Look Back In Anger' on the karaoke machine set up in a Thai restaurant.*** But it was while working at Spago, an Italian restaurant in Caesars Palace, serving chicken or fish to Bernie Taupin and Celine Dion, that he waited on a personal icon. In October 1999, he turned up at his table to find none other than Morrissey waiting to order a mushroom pizza and Earl Grey tea. Utterly awestruck, and not put off by the way Morrissey ignored

---

* Brandon had his ear pierced in an establishment that would one day become a strip club called Precious Slut.

** Unbeknown to Brandon, both Ronnie and Dave were working in the same mall at the same time.

*** This is the only time Brandon has ever sung karaoke.

his gushing declarations of fandom, Brandon stole and kept the mug his hero had drunk from.[*]

But he kept up his studies, taking two courses at a community college, and it was on his way home from class, wide-winged on an overpass above the I-95 freeway, that a song came on the classic rock station he'd tuned to that seemed to send him airborne. "I'd never heard it before and at first I thought it was Bob Dylan just because of the way he sang the verses."[44] The song was 'Changes' and its singer one David Bowie. As soon as he could reach a record store, Brandon hunted out the album *Hunky Dory*, and was consumed, inspired, driven by it. "It raised the bar on everything I had ever heard," he said. "It's the working man's album and blue collar is never uncool. It was recorded during the time when Bowie was becoming a father; there are so many artists that lose their edge after having children but Bowie did not. 'Queen Bitch' should've been written by an 18-year-old full of cum and coke."[45] "The strange thing is I knew the bands I loved – like Morrissey and Depeche Mode and Duran Duran – were all influenced by him but I'd never sought Bowie out. That was really enlightening for me... *Hunky Dory* made me commit to being in a band."[46]

Bowie led Brandon to The Beatles, and then back to the golf course, where he'd met a fellow Smiths fan, a film student nine years his senior called Trevor Gagner. Sharing his love of British music and spotting the same fire in Brandon's eye, Trevor introduced Brandon to Lou Reed's 'Perfect Day' and suggested they start a band together, a suggestion which, Brandon thought "was ludicrous to me, it seemed so far-fetched".[47] Crazy or not, Brandon agreed.

"Trevor liked everything that I liked, from Morrissey to New Order," Brandon said. "And he knew stupid facts, such as Morrissey's birthday, like I did. We always dyed our hair black and drove around, plotting revenge against people – like how one day when we were on the cover of *Q* we'd drop a stack of magazines on their doorstep... before Trevor I never knew I was creative. It's not that he told me I was, but it was Trevor who convinced me to be in a band."[48]

---

[*] Brandon still has this mug safely stored away in his home safe.

Trevor became another role model to Brandon, his best friend and a man he'd credit as having "shaped my life and made music happen."[49] Together they recruited a girl singer called Billie Schubert to form an electropop trio initially called Subversion; by 2000 they were writing songs together, Brandon helping towards the construction of the tunes, playing melodies on piano, and Billie penning the lyrics. Inspired by the Pet Shop Boys* and Depeche Mode, Subversion's first and only release was a song ironically called 'The Victim', included on a compilation album *Electricity – An Electropop Sampler* from Ninthwave Records late in 2000. Built on synthetic electronic pop beats and adorned with death ray noises, this tale of a doomed affair owed clear debts to PSB's 'Go West' and Eighties rave culture, but it was Brandon's lush synth phase underlying the track that would become a trademark.

By the time the band came to record their second demo session of two tracks at the studio of engineer Brian Hazard at the start of 2001 they'd renamed themselves Blush Response, a name taken from a track on the *Blade Runner* soundtrack which also, fittingly, happened to be a kind of make-up. Also, Brandon's position in the band was looking increasingly untenable. First of all, financially: the band needed funds to pay for the out-of-town sessions and Brandon was unable to contribute. With Billie and Trevor unwilling to pay for his hotel and food for the trip, Brandon didn't even play on the two songs he'd helped write, 'I'm Not A Saint' and 'Your Sinister Heart'. In his absence, his parts were built up in the studio by Hazard, who also sang Brandon's backing vocals. As a result, these tracks had less of Brandon's sonic touch to them, although there's an ambitious melodicism to the tunes, early glints of his grand pop nous.

Though Brandon claims "we never played out",[50] other Vegas sources state that Blush Response played two shows with Brandon on synths and backing vocals, once at a private party and a second time on New Year's Eve 2000 at the Aladdin Hotel. The band was where Brandon

---

* Pet Shop Boys were another of Brandon's formative influences – the line "I never thought I would get to be/The creature I was meant to be" from 'Being Boring' was his favourite lyric growing up and Brandon has been quoted as believing that PSB's Neil Tennant should have his face carved onto Mount Rushmore.

learned to write songs, discovering how chords fit together and how hooks sank into the psyche, but it was also where he discovered he was no backroom svengali. He watched Billie from behind his synth stand and felt that same sense of jealousy he'd had when he'd first heard Dave Gahan, Morrissey or Bowie. "I was a lead singer trapped in a keyboardist's body," he said. "I was living a lie!"[51]

Reports differ on the circumstances of Brandon leaving Blush Response. According to Brandon himself, Billie and Trevor decided they'd never get a deal based in Vegas and moved to LA in search of that elusive contract while he stayed behind, knowing he was restricted in his role in the band and needed to be a frontman. Hazard, in an online article, claimed that Brandon was asked to leave the band around February 2001, shortly after the second demo session and some months before the rest of the band left for LA, ejected because he couldn't add to the Blush Response coffers.*

For a while after Blush Response, Brandon flailed. He had his drunkest ever nights out, hammered on gin in downtown nightclubs, convinced he was going to die – "I can remember the next day, if I could have spoken I would have said, 'Take me to the hospital'."[52] He made a demo with another band, edging his way ever closer to the centre-stage microphone. Each member took turns singing a particular tune, each of them worse than the man before. "I went into a little closet and when I came out the singer obviously didn't like the fact that I was better than him," Brandon remembers. "For them it was hard hitting the notes, but it just came naturally to me. And I loved it."[53]

Ditching his busboy job, he signed up as bellhop at the Gold Coast, a coral of rodeo rings and Wild West saloon bars populated by hookers and gamblers, run by a rich cowboy out on West Flamingo Road, in the shadow of the Rio. From behind his desk he watched high flyers and lowlifes mingle – one night a wallet-lifting hooker ran across the hotel lobby, past the high rollers throwing chips into the roulette's vortex,

---

* However it happened, the split was somewhat acrimonious; in 2010, Brandon would claim that Trevor refuses to speak to him, although internet rumours suggest that Trevor has since attended a Vegas awards show with The Killers at Brandon's request.

her patsy of a client racing after her, still zipping his fly and tripping over untied shoelaces. Calling into the hospital later to check on his mother, who'd gone there with a heart complaint, Brandon saw the same guy, wheezing into breathing apparatus and nursing bruises from the hooker's stiletto heel. "What are the odds of that?" he'd say. "The hooker took his wallet and tried to ditch him. He obviously had health problems. But that's Las Vegas."[54]

On quieter shifts he booked helicopter tours along the Strip or over the Grand Canyon, carried the suitcases of the tip-happy whales and stag suckers heaving into town. Once in a while, he got to chat to Morrissey's guitarist, Boz Boorer, who attended the hotel's regular rockabilly conventions. He spent his wages on CDs, keyboards and a four-track and hit the major gigs whenever he could. When U2's Elevation tour rolled into Vegas' Thomas & Mack Center on November 18, 2001, Brandon was there to gawp at Bono "reapplying for the job of the best band in the world" on his heart-shaped stage. And earlier in the year, on May 11, Brandon was at the Joint venue at the Hard Rock Hotel to see Oasis play on their Tour Of Brotherly Love, unknowingly standing mere feet away from a guitarist that would help make him a superstar.[*]

Watching Oasis made Brandon desperate to start a band of his own. Ambition at its steaming peak, he now only needed the emotion to drive it. And that would soon come in the most devastating fashion possible.

One morning, headed for the Gold Coast without a tie to his name, he stopped off at his girlfriend's apartment to pick up one he'd left there. He knew she was screwing someone else before he even got out of the car. Across the street, her car was parked, touching bumpers with another. It was a well-known signal of romance among the youth of Vegas.

Crushed and filled with agonising mental images of his girl with another man, Brandon crumpled: "It was painful and I really felt like I was gonna die."[55] A few nights later he saw the two of them, his nemeses, together in an English pub. "I was asleep and I knew

---

[*] Not only was Dave Keuning also at the same gig but, by chance, this writer was there too, reviewing for *NME*.

something was wrong," he said. "I have these instincts. I went to the Crown & Anchor and my girlfriend was there with another guy."[56] "I guess I should have done something but I'm not a violent person, but it really affected me. I would physically throw up... jealousy is a terrible, terrible experience."[57]

Unable to confront his desolation, Brandon ran. He fled back to Nephi, to the bosom of his family, to nurse his wounds. All the while his resentments festered, he tortured himself with the carnality of the affair. The knowledge of the two of them together, dress unzipping, flesh bared. His pain needed an outlet. It needed to be roared out of him.

He returned to Vegas a knot of determination. Las Vegas had three weekly papers, and he scoured the Musicians Wanted ad sections of each for several months, hunting out any like-minded musical soulmate. The Strokes and their New York underground explosion hadn't made the slightest dent on America yet, and particularly not in the Nevada desert; these were the demon days of nu metal, of Limp Bizkit and Korn bestriding the *Billboard* chart like puerile, baseball-capped Colossi, and the ad sections were a deep, dark mirror of the national airwaves. Shredding guitarists sought whiny-voiced singers, the breadth of the Vegas rock scene. 'Must be into Tool and Sevendust' read every single ad. They were disheartening times for a Brit-obsessed pop kid in Nevada, dreaming of Being Bono.

Then, like so few Vegas hopefuls, Brandon struck gold.

A small box marked for the attention of singers. 'Looking to start or join a band? Influences: U2, Pumpkins, The Beatles, Oasis.'

Brandon called relentlessly until his destiny answered him.

CHAPTER 2

When You Were Young

"It's me lying on a pillow in the living room of my first home staring at my mom."

— Dave Keuning's earliest memory

Deep in the desert, many hours' drive back from the wreckage of his dashed LA hopes, Vegas drifted out of the heat-haze through the Greyhound window, an oasis of lights and temptation. Dave Keuning eyed it like a lifeboat. Past the sign reading 'WELCOME TO FABULOUS LAS VEGAS', the city grew, glamorised. The highway into town felt like a yellow brick road; the palm switches and tropical beaches of Mandalay Bay, the glinting jet pyramid of the Luxor, the gigantic gold lion perched at the gates to the MGM*. Fantasyland, 500ft tall and oozing success and seduction.

Downtrodden from finding LA too expensive to play backdrop to his musical dream and hitting the long bus ride back to Iowa, Dave saw a fresh chance of escape. As the bus pulled into a Vegas coach station and hissed open its doors for a rest-stop, Dave grabbed his guitar and wandered off into the Vegas glow.

---

* The biggest bronze statue in the United States.

When the bus left, Dave simply forgot to get back on.

At least, that's the cinema version of how Dave arrived in Vegas in 2000. The way he tells it is a little less filmic. "My first trip to Vegas, I never even saw the Strip," he says. "I had a job in Iowa that only required me to work every other weekend and I squeaked by on noodles and lived with my friends. So I decided just to go and explore the West Coast; San Francisco, LA then through Vegas, then come home with maybe the idea of moving there because I really wanted to move to LA. I had decided to take the Greyhound bus and I decided to explore with no plans or anything. I would never do that again, it was an awful way to do things. I had to find hotels on the spot and I had to find Greyhound buses on the spot or whatever. But I was gonna take the bus all the way from LA back home to Iowa and it was so awful that I got off at Vegas and stayed the night because there were cheap hotels downtown near the bus station, which was nowhere near the Strip. I just saw the downtown. I then flew back home on my credit card and that was the end of that trip. But taking the Greyhound bus for more than a day, I wouldn't wish that on my worst enemy – it was that bad. You can't sleep. It was 10 hours from LA to Vegas and it should take four or five."

Back home, Dave did his research. "I considered moving to New York or Los Angeles," he said, "but they're two of the hardest places to move to when you're just starting out in a band. I did some research and found that Vegas was, like, a third of the price. So I thought, 'well, it's close to Los Angeles, and it's a pretty cool place'. And I moved there."[1]

Celluloid-worthy or not, when Dave hit Vegas he reinvented himself. Goodbye Dave Brent Keuning, university dropout, reluctant plumber's apprentice and failed Midwest hair-rock sensation. Hello Tavian Go, enigmatic guitar wizard of the New Vegas scene.*

★ ★ ★

* Dave would use the name Tavian Go in interviews during the early part of The Killers' career; he'd rather forget about it now.

Dave was a kid from nowhere with a lot to forget. Born to Chuck and Sandy Keuning on March 28, 1976, in a world of fresh-built artifice 20 miles out of Des Moines, Iowa – famed as the hated hometown of Slipknot, and pretty much nothing else. In 1847, Reverend Hendrik Pieter Scholte and his family had fled Holland under threat of persecution from separatists. But landing in the US by steam ship alongside 800 fellow Dutch immigrants he wasn't ready to give up all memory of his homeland. Midwest land was plentiful and cheap in 19th-century America, so Scholte snapped up 18,000 acres of Marion County, Iowa for $1.25 an acre and built himself a new Amsterdam right there. Buildings sprang up based on Dutch architecture, windmills decorated the edges of town; Scholte called his vision Pella, after the refuge of Jerusalem's Christians in the Roman-Jewish War of 70AD, and his 800 countrymen made it their home from home.

Almost 150 years later, the Keuning family joined them.

With Dutch tradition written deep into the Pella bedrock, it was a clean, quaint, kid-friendly sort of town. Once a year every child at sixth grade or lower, including Dave, would wear clogs to school for the Tulip Time parade at Pella High School. Such kitsch never really appealed to Dave; he was into sci-fi as a pre-teen – getting an ewok village for Christmas when he was six was, he'd claim, "the sex"[2] – and if there was music involved, it intrigued him all the more.

"I first heard [David Bowie's 'Space Oddity'] when I was in kindergarten," he remembered. "For whatever reason, my friend Adam Barker had a David Bowie tape. I was a huge *Star Wars* and *Star Trek* fan. Still am. When I was six, there was not that much that I could relate to, but I understood that Bowie was talking about space stuff. Maybe he was talking about drug stuff, but I thought he was talking about space stuff."[3]

Unlike Brandon Flowers, Dave failed to defy the draw of pomp rock. On a trip to summer camp from his high school in his early teens, a 12-hour drive from Iowa, the stereo played 'Classic Queen' the whole way there and back, and Dave was indoctrinated. He found himself wrapped up in Brian May's guitar, ignoring Freddie Mercury's lyrics to concentrate on the intricacies, sonics and fripperies happening behind.

It would be years before he'd realise that his obsession wasn't the norm, that other people listened primarily to the singer, or only watched the frontman at live shows.

Like every Midwest kid, Dave was swamped with hair metal fans at school. Aerosmith, AC/DC, Mötley Crüe and, later, U2 were the sounds that rang through his halls through the eighties and seeped into his stereo. It was a sound he yearned to emulate. In his early teens he was a video games enthusiast – "[I was] the Nintendo wizard of the town," he said, "people phoned me at home to ask me how to get to the next level of Mario Brothers and I didn't know who these people were!"[4] – but at 14, at the dawn of the nineties, he sold his video games, bought his first guitar and threw himself into the study of it, filling the house with noise. "When I first picked up the guitar," he recalled, "naturally I was interested in music with loud guitars. AC/DC, Aerosmith and Mötley Crüe is just what I was drawn to first and those were the kinds of bands that made me want to learn to play the guitar, 'cause I was excited to play along with those songs. It's not as fun necessarily to play along with other stuff."[5] "He was pretty determined to try and master guitar," his father, Chuck, told the local press. "Of course, like most parents, we had no idea he'd carry it this far."

At school he joined the Pella High School Jazz Band in his second year; at home he filled his five-CD disc-changer with solos he could learn to copy. The bands he formed to try out his skills each added their influence to his tastes, evolved his listening habits. His first was in eighth grade, a covers band howling out tunes from his favourite metal bands. Then, from 1992 when Dave hit 16, he was guitarist in Pickle, a Christian rock band based in Newton, 20 miles north of Pella. A cross between Nirvana and Rush, Pickle introduced him to *Nevermind*, The Smashing Pumpkins' *Siamese Dream* and U2's *The Unforgettable Fire* and *Achtung Baby*, which he dutifully loaded into his stack of solos.

"I changed my way of thinking," he recalled. "Like, 'Oh, maybe I should start to give other bands a chance'. So I did and I guess a lot of people did in that era... I didn't like to go out much back then but it was the most fun in the world for me to do a 20-song jam with the CD player. And for five years *Siamese Dream* was always in the CD changer.

I think I can play the 'Cherub Rock' solo almost note for note. I'm 99 per cent of the way there. There are a couple of backward tape effects in there that I'm not so sure about."[6]

According to his bandmates, despite being shy, quiet and impossible to rile to a high temper, Dave was already 99 per cent of the way to guitar god status. "Dave was just like a monster on guitar at this early age," said drummer Keith Nestor, now working as a pastor at Christ United Methodist Church in Davenport. "He was really, really good."[7] "He always had a real knack for coming up with original riffs and original arrangements to songs,"[8] added bassist Kyle Reynolds. And for Dave himself, Pickle was a steep learning curve. "It was cool to be part of something positive," he said. "They were great musicians. They helped me get better. They taught me a lot of new things."[9]

For four years Dave played with Pickle, enjoying the prog-grunge indulgence of it even if he wasn't particularly in tune with the religious message. His immersion in Smashing Pumpkins and Nirvana's music became all consuming, to the point that he played them to death, studying every note. "I exhausted the Smashing Pumpkins and Nirvana," he said. "Eventually I had to just move on and start listening to other stuff."[10]

Pickle earned themselves a name on the live circuit; not a difficult task since bands were few, scenes sparse and the region dominated by the eventual rise of masked local horrorcore nine-piece Slipknot, a carnival slasher-flick freak show who built their nefarious furies around the hells of their hometown. "My best friend from high school is now in one of the Slipknot spin-off bands," Dave would say years later. "The circle of musicians is that small. Des Moines is not that big a town. Everybody knows somebody in Slipknot. I don't really like them to tell you the truth but they did say something once that I understood, 'The boredom of Iowa is what made us this way!'"[11]

Graduating from Pella High and shifting up to Kirkwood Community College out to the east of Pella towards Cedar Rapids and Iowa City, Dave also graduated from grunge to electro-goth – New Order and The Cure were his new jams. "When I discovered The Cure for the first time ... I had heard of 'em a little bit but by the time I was into 'em, they already had like 17 albums out," he said. "It was like, 'Oh wow, there's a whole body of work here I haven't even tapped into to listen to'."[12]

As with the hair metal of the eighties and the grunge of the nineties, Dave's new obsessions seeped into his playing. He learned new ways of utilising his amp and drew the space and atmospherics of The Cure and New Order into his developing personal style. Around the same time, Sigur Rós became his new favourite band and he discovered the work of Johnny Marr, studying the unique fretwork patterns of 'Reel Around The Fountain', the malevolent reverb of 'How Soon Is Now?', the acoustic airiness, major seventh chords and sheer diversity of the Smiths legend. His mind, and technique, expanded.

"Without the boredom of growing up in [the Midwest]," Dave explained, "I probably wouldn't have got into music as much as I did. That was one good thing about the winters there. I used to stay in and listen to Morrissey and stuff, in that town I was the only person who listened to that kind of music."[13]

While his bedroom guitar studies thrived, his further education faltered. From Kirkwood, Dave enrolled at the University of Iowa, leaving Pickle and trying to launch a succession of bands with his new Iowa City contacts. Nothing clicked; new bandmates lost interest or moved away. Dave felt stranded at university and dislocated in Iowa. In the pre-internet age, word of great new bands was slow to reach the Midwest and no local scenes were springing up; he felt removed, out of touch.

To combat his itch, he tried drastic measures. Dropping out of university after a year, he took jobs instead, but found the daily grind unrewarding. The nadir of his Iowa alienation came when his father kindly offered him a job at his plumbing and central heating firm, a job for life if he wanted it. Chuck meant well, but Dave needed more. "Eventually I just said to myself, 'this can't be it. This can't be, you know, how it ends'," he said. "So I decided I had to get out."[14]

"I don't know if anything pushed me over the edge," he says. "I was always focused on starting bands and I had tried in and around Pella. I had worked trying to get a couple of bands going there but Iowa's small enough that I kind of knew what was available in Des Moines,

Cedar Rapids and Iowa City – those would be the three big cities to play in. In fairness, there was opportunity there, but I didn't feel like anything was clicking with any of the people that I met. I knew what was available. It wasn't like New York or LA, where there's thousands of guys – there was probably, like, less than a hundred. And they had all formed bands, and I kind of knew what was out there."

So Dave booked his ticket on the Greyhound tour out West, the start of his search for a new home base. In its wake he found that New York and LA, the accepted utopias for the budding rock star, proved too pricey, but one stop-off on his trip – by chance or design – echoed the fabulous pizzazz of the new persona Dave was about to transform himself into, as blink-fast as a Luxor illusionist.

Fabulous Las Vegas.

"I wound up in Vegas because I just wanted to get out of Iowa and try to get something going somewhere else," he says. "I thought 'What the hell, this'll be an adventure, and if I move back after a couple of months, I will at least have done this crazy thing where I moved out to Vegas for a little bit' – that's kind of honestly what I thought. And my parents were horrified, and rightfully so. I feel bad about how I did that, how that whole thing went down. But I just wanted to go on an adventure. I packed all my stuff in a U-Haul; furniture, everything. I had my car towed behind; it was a big deal. So I moved out, and I just remember driving through Colorado thinking, like, 'Am I crazy? Am I sure about this?' It was very scary. I didn't know anybody in Vegas, not a single person. And I didn't have a job waiting for me. I had saved some money, so I had the first couple of months paid for."

★ ★ ★

Stepping out of the U-Haul, Dave gawped.

"It was a big culture shock when I first moved there," he'd say. "Vegas is really different to the Midwest. It's not just the gambling, I gambled for the first week and got it out of my system and then never went back. It's just a really amazing place. There are strip clubs open literally all the time, you can go there at eight o'clock in the morning if you're bored. There are girls and things to do. You've got dance clubs, gambling, it's always open. It's such a pretty city as well. When you fly into Vegas at night I think it's one of the most beautiful cities you'll ever see. You come over this mountain and it's this sprawling city of light and you can see the Strip and it's full of colours… It's getting a lot more sex-themed in a lot of places and I think that's taking away from some of it, but it'll always be there, the tackiness. The way that clubs and dance music and everything is, there's so many clubs like that now. It's getting crazy. Some casinos have three dance clubs and they're all hip places."[15]

Launching himself into Las Vegas, Dave set about building a new life. First stop, the seedy end of town, where police tape split the streets and sirens split the night. "I found an apartment I could afford," he said, remembering the run-down place behind the Desert Inn he decided to call home.* "It was pretty awful by most people's standards, but I liked it. It served my needs."[16]

He got a series of jobs – first at Best Buy for a year, then polishing and selling silver goods in a store in the newly opened Aladdin Hotel. Straight off the bat, Dave started advertising. Month after month, in the Musicians Wanted sections of *Las Vegas CityLife* and *Las Vegas Weekly*, he was there, crying out for fellow musos into Beck, The Beatles, The Smashing Pumpkins, Oasis and U2. He found himself a girlfriend to form the core of the band with him, but otherwise his ads drew "retard after retard" to auditions, and certainly no one who shared his hatred of mainstream rock radio and the love of eighties music he was developing via Vegas radio.

"I love heavy music," he explained, "but you see, I had fallen in love with a radio station in Vegas that played nothing but eighties music. That had a real profound impact on me. All the other stations were playing… Creed and Limp Bizkit – these faux heavy bands and nu-metal-type things. I'm not trying to put them down, although I guess

---

* Dave eked out a pretty meagre existence in his apartment at times; The Killers' manager, Robert Reynolds, remembers visiting him to find him eating rice mixed with tomato ketchup, since they were the only two ingredients he had in the flat.

I am, but they weren't my cup of tea. I liked groups that didn't just plod along on one idea throughout a song."[17]

"From '99 to 2001, I just didn't like anything that was on the radio. I was just like, 'I can do better than this'. And as it turns out, I was sort of right."[18]

Eighties radio bolstered his addiction to The Cure, New Order and The Smiths, a fix he wasn't getting with his current band. The prickly practice of dating his bandmate didn't work out either: "Moral to the story: don't get involved with girls in your bands."[19] The band fell apart and, though he was constantly writing music, all of his subsequent attempts to get a new band together came to nothing. His ads became fewer and further between; by mid-2001, he'd simply given up.

Then, almost two years into his foray into the Vegas scene, another kick. The US economic downturn that began in March 2001 and was eventually deepened in the wake of the September 11 attacks hit Vegas harder than most cities, feeding as it does on optimism and extravagance. As the decade drew on, malls were left deserted and huge repossessed houses stood empty as the sub-prime mortgage market collapsed; Vegas slumped, and minimum wage workers like Dave were first to go. The Aladdin resort bombed, taking Dave down with it. "I lost my job," he recalled, "and I was, 'well, I might as well make another effort to start a band'. I was always trying to start bands but had given up for a few months. I was like, 'I'm gonna try and start a band now that I had time'."[20]

Around August 2001 the ads reappeared, and the freaks returned in force. One try-out had his arms tattooed with the names of numerous family members who'd died. Knuckle-headed rock fans dominated, and those who favoured UK music almost exclusively liked Radiohead and thought that was as deep as anyone needed to get. "I had one guy who called and wanted to do something along the lines of Three Doors Down, Tool and Staind, who I hate."[21] He'd virtually given up, and having only one line for both phone and internet almost stopped his dreams coming true. "I put an ad in the paper that said 'looking to start or join a band? Influences: U2, Pumpkins, Oasis'," Dave said. "That's when Brandon called. I was on the internet at the time, so my line was busy. It took a week to actually get hold of each other."[22]

Brandon Flowers had called the number three times before he got hold of Dave, and was close to giving up himself. Eventually an email got through: 'I'm 20 years old, I'm heavily influenced by Bowie and Oasis and you seem like the only one in there who seems close to what I'm into', Brandon wrote.

And when they finally connected, the connection was strong. Brandon made a perfect first impression. For one thing, he wasn't a total weirdo. He'd made sure to turn up to meet Dave wearing Clark's Hush Puppies, as that's what Oasis wore, and the pair instantly bonded over the U2 and Oasis gigs they'd both been to in town. Once Brandon started throwing some of his musical ideas around, Dave was even more impressed. "We knew we could make the kind of music we loved but make it tough sounding."[23] He could tell there was something special in Brandon, something primed for success.

And within weeks the pair would have the song that would put their name in lights.

One afternoon, shortly after their first introduction, Brandon took his keyboard over to Dave's apartment for their first rehearsal, his recent break-up churning for a release. As they began to throw ideas around, Dave played him a verse he'd been wrestling with; a tripping Johnny Marr-esque, high-end guitar riff that bled into a driving chord sequence, more intricate and inventive than other pieces he'd written. An airy riff and pounding rhythm that seemed to ache to the same beat as Brandon's heartbreak. It sounded defiant, redemptive, his chance.

Dave gave Brandon a tape of the part he'd written; Brandon took it away and returned with a chorus he'd added, and some lyrics he'd half-written, half-spat: "Now they're going to bed, and my stomach is sick/And it's all in my head but she's touching his chest now/He takes off her dress now/Let me go". The lyric could have been ripped from the most anguished page of Brandon's personal diary, picturing his ex with the guy she'd left him for in agonising detail and laying bare the turmoil he was suffering, the green-eyed monster gnawing at his soul. "Jealousy, turning saints into the sea," he sang, "swimming through sick lullabies, choking on your alibis". The perma-positivism of his Mormon upbringing wouldn't let him wallow though; the chorus reached a peak of defiance, determined to brave the emotional tornado, learn one of life's harshest lessons and emerge wiser, stronger, unbroken. "Destiny is calling me/Open up my eager eyes because I'm Mr. Brightside".*

"I remember the day we had 'Mr. Brightside'," Dave would say. "I had given him a tape and I kind of had the verse part worked out and the pre-chorus worked out on that original riff. Then he came in and just played it down and he had the chorus and I played along to the chorus and it was just like instantly we both loved it. It was like actually fun for just the two of us to play. It was like, 'Let's play that again. That was fun'. It felt good."[24]

It didn't take Dave too long to realise they had a hit, that Brandon was a hugely talented songwriter and the perfect match for his own skills. What's more, their mutual ambition gleamed bright as Brandon's beaming smile.

"I think it was the second day me and Brandon ever practised together," Dave said. "We were just hanging out afterwards and I said 'So you want to be big?' and he said 'Oh yeah' and I said 'Good'. And it was never discussed again. Some people don't want to be big, but I only wanted to do music. He was the same."[25]

"Brandon and I were on the same page. I had to get that out of the way because there are musicians – plenty of them that I've met – who would laugh at that idea or that goal, like 'Oh, you think you're gonna be all big some day?' or 'Why even try?' That's our goal, and there's nothing wrong with [not wanting] to be big and just playing around town – that's different. We just wanted to take it as far as we can get, wherever that would be."[26]

From the off, Brandon envisioned his new band competing on a national scale. "I never considered myself part of the local music scene. We weren't trying to write songs better than anyone in the town. I was more worried about The White Stripes and The Strokes."[27]

---

* "I wouldn't be here if we hadn't written 'Mr. Brightside'," Brandon would say some years later. "I have no regrets. And they've split up now so I hear. She knows she fucked up." Source: Q, Michael Odell, December 2004.

These were challenging targets to set sights on. In 2001, The White Stripes and The Strokes were the alt-rock A-list, the new millennium's indie press darlings, the saviours of alternative rock'n'roll sweeping nu metal aside with a blast of blues rock squeal or garage punk clatter. Between them they'd rejuvenated a guitar rock scene that was gasping its last and inspired a new generation of wasted pretty boys modelling leather jackets and super-skinny women's jeans. The new wave of narcotic punk was gathering – Kings Of Leon from the preacher churches of the South, The Yeah Yeah Yeahs and The Rapture from the art funk Brooklyn basements to the east. To compete with such stellar names of the 21st-century cult rock underground would take dedication, hard work, eye-catching style, undeniable songwriting genius and a hefty chunk of luck.

Spurred on by the rush of self-belief, they wrote and rehearsed relentlessly. Every day, as soon as he clocked off from the Gold Coast, Brandon would head to Dave's tiny apartment. "I didn't have a job for about three months," said Dave, "and he'd come over and I'd just wait for him to get off work and we'd get together and write. I had a keyboard and he brought his own keyboard… It came pretty easily 'cause he was good at playing keyboards spontaneously and I was good at accommodating him."[28]

Over those first few months, lightning struck often. Their earliest material showed great melodic promise and vaulting synth-rock ambition in emulating The Cure, Oasis and contemporary alternative US cult acts, and acted as exorcism and therapy for Brandon's emotional hell. 'Under The Gun', a fuzzy, rough-hewn buzzsaw rock number, took the basement brittleness of The Strokes and lashed it to the dustland desert Americana that Brandon and Dave had grown up on. It throbbed with devastation and heartbreak – "kill me now" went the addictive, repetitive pop chorus – but also introduced a cinematic noir fantasism that would come to characterise Brandon's lyrics. He cast his cheating, lying love interest as an angel with "her halo and wings" but also "a criminal mind", entrapping a lovelorn victim and sending him into surreal, dreamlike agonies: "crashing cars in his brain/Keep him tied up to a dream… now he just wants to wake up". Dropping in other such filmic images of glamorous desolation ("stupid on the streets of London/James Dean in the rain"), 'Under The Gun' was the first sign of Brandon's ability to sketch and flesh grand crimes and dramas with his words.

'Desperate' was a far plainer and more direct proposition. Drifting out of emotive piano chords redolent of Elvis Costello's maudlin docker ballad 'Shipbuilding', the mid-paced Oasis-like groove that followed, bedecked with Dave's free-soaring guitar work nodding to Manic Street Preachers' 'Motorcycle Emptiness' or Oasis' 'Don't Look Back In Anger', was a portrait of a broken-hearted wretch racked with unbearable loss and anguish. "Send me away, I'm here on my own", Brandon sighed, lost for a way to turn, his confusion and insecurity evident in the contrasting lines "I'm better off like this" and "I wish I was myself again". It was, and would remain, Brandon's most open-hearted, soul-baring lyric.

The songs wrought from Brandon's break-up just kept coming. Another, 'Replaceable', was a twee indie pop tune built around piano-set synths and a melody reminiscent of Ben Folds at his most grandiose. Here, Brandon struggled with the ennui in the fallout of his relationship, meeting up with his ex out of duty, despite feeling powerless and manipulated by the situation. "Pick you up later on/ What to do?/It doesn't matter 'cause you get what you want," he sang, "will you call me on occasion, if you like it or not?" The pain of the betrayal was still sharp as he twitched "he looks a bit like me" and has to confront the stark truth that he was "replaceable", and his bitterness was palpable in lines like "you watched me die at least a thousand times/But it's great to hear you're doing fine". Ultimately though, as with 'Mr. Brightside', revenge and one-upmanship were the light at the end of his dark emotional tunnel, biting back with a snarled prediction: "soon you'll find you're all alone/You call me on the telephone/Who'd have thought that you'd regret/All those evil things you said". There were the first signs of Brandon coming to terms with his hurt here, too, particularly in self-aware phrases like "burning bridges, wasted hate" and the central sentiment "now as friends, we say goodbye/I think there's something in my eye".

It was lucky Brandon exorcised his angst while he was still suffering. Within weeks of writing out his heartache he met a girl called Tana, a designer at Betsey Johnson's fashion label. On their first date, Brandon took her to a late-night record store and ushered her around the aisles, gauging her knowledge of key artists – Leonard Cohen, Bowie, his beloved Smiths. When she picked up a Bowie album and told him she had the UK import, their future together was secure. Even though Tana's mother warned her off dating a grown man with a Morrissey pillowcase.[*]

With everything suddenly going so right, it's no wonder Brandon and Dave wanted to make a swift rush for the big time. Their songs sounded far better than the rubbish they were hearing on the radio and they seriously believed they'd be shooed onto the playlists like pop royalty. "I thought we had pretty good material," Dave admitted. "If it ever saw the light of day, I thought it might do good. I was a believer."[29] All they needed now was the light of day.

And for that, they'd need further recruits.

Feelers were put out around the – very limited – Vegas scene for a rhythm section and produced several knock-backs from players they were interested in. Luckily, help was very close at hand. Dave was sharing his apartment with one Dell Neal, a guitarist in his thirties from St. Louis; the two of them had toyed with starting their own band with Dave on bass, but nothing had come of it. Dell had been hearing the ideas come together through the cracks of Dave's bedroom door, and liked what he heard. "Brandon was a real amazing writer," he said, "and Dave was an awesome guitar player. Brandon would come to practice with ideas, pretty much have the whole song mapped out on the keyboard. I was really impressed, because he was so young, and he was really in tune with music and with writing... One day Brandon asked if I wanted to play bass. He said, 'Well, you play guitar, can't you play bass, too?' I was like, 'Why not, I'm not doing anything else, really'."[30]

---

[*] Brandon's penchant for mascara was fine with Tana's mother though; she'd been out with guys into The Cure and the inevitable eyeliner herself.

Dell Neil had such a dull ring to it for a glamorous synth-rock bass god, though. So Dell took on his grandmother's maiden name. He would be Dell Star.

You couldn't throw a stick across Dave's apartment and hit a percussionist, though, so Dave's ads went out to the local papers and alternative press once more, this time aimed specifically at drummers. Matt Norcross, two and a half years in Vegas, saw one and, though he was into Tom Petty and Black Crowes, he was also intrigued by the Cure and Oasis references in the ad. "At that time, rap-rock and nu-metal were all around," Matt said, "so when I saw a band trying that European sound, I decided to give them a call."[31]

Matt's ill-fit with Dave and Brandon's aesthetic might have been clear from the second they opened Dave's apartment door to him; Matt had turned up wearing a Goatwhore T-shirt. Still, having played him a few of their formative songs, they took him on without hearing him tap a single cymbal. "It was good," Matt recalled. "Dave and Brandon had their [stuff] together. They had a plan from the get-go. I guess they figured as long as I could keep a beat, I was in. Who knows if I was ever intended to be the long-term drummer?"[32]

Within an hour of starting their first rehearsal as a full four-piece, up in Norcross' place in the Lakes – to the west of town by Lake Sahara – they'd settled on a name. Discarding an early suggestion of The Genius Sex Poets*, they would be The Killers, after the band of lithe young rock'n'rollers standing in for New Order before a huge video screen in the video for 'Crystal'. This faux band didn't only represent everything pert, beautiful and talented about the music scene – traits they planned to emulate – it also spoke to their obsession with electronic pop with strong links to the British eighties and, since it clearly didn't suit such gentle souls, their sense of mischief.

"We were talking about that video," Star said, "and Brandon asked if we'd seen it. I was like, 'Yeah, it's badass.' And he said, 'Can we use it?' And we were all like, 'I don't know ... is it even a good name? It's cool,

---

* A name which they comically printed on the bass drum used in the US version of their video for 'Mr. Brightside'.

but are people gonna assume we're a metal band or a hardcore band?' But it was the best name we could come up with. It's good, and it's simple."[33]

"I like the contradiction," Brandon said, likening the juxtaposition to that of seventies glam heroes T. Rex. "Tyrannosaurus Rex was the biggest creature ever, yet Marc Bolan was five foot one."[34] "It's so good that we thought for sure somebody, some little band somewhere, somebody's gonna have it."[35]

No one had it. And thus The Killers leapt out of the screen, straight into the studio.

With Brandon and Dave itching to get their first few songs on tape, it was only a matter of weeks before Star and Norcross found themselves in Kill The Messenger Studio in Henderson, recording four songs – Dell and Norcross played on 'Replaceable' and 'Under The Gun'; Norcross on an additional two tracks, 'Desperate' and 'Mr. Brightside'; the rest of the recording was covered by Brandon and Dave. The CD was raw and unrefined, but worth sharing with the local scene, The Killers thought. They burned a limited number, made their own artwork reading simply THE KILLERS* and sent or personally handed them to notable Vegas names – radio DJs, record shop owners, venue promoters, fellow musicians.

Marco Brizuela, the manager of the Big B record store near the University of Nevada, Las Vegas (UNLV) where Brandon would go to buy records and get recommendations for new acts to check out**, was among the first to hear it. He'd been handed a copy by his bandmate in a band called The Bleachers, Joe Maloney, one of the Vegas scene players who'd turned down a place in The Killers when asked. Maloney had been given the CD in the Crown & Anchor pub by an excited Dave, and the pair were swept along by his confidence. Back at Brizuela's place they dropped it in the deck, and sat unimpressed. "I liked 'Mr.

---

* And including the contact numbers of both Matt and Dave.

** It was Brizuela who suggested Brandon might like Suede, only to have the singer rush back after his first listen to buy up the band's albums, overwhelmed with love for them.

Brightside' a bit, but I didn't think much of the other tracks," said Brizuela. "They sounded to me just like The Strokes or Oasis."[36]

To The Killers themselves, on the other hand, the demos sounded like the future. And it was time for them to start slaying.

★ ★ ★

Café Expresso Roma was a down-at-the-heels coffee and cigarette stop-off for Converse-clad Vegas hipsters, right across the street from the UNLV out on South Maryland Parkway. Part of a chain, it had long since gone to seed, which attracted the students turned off by glossy commercialism and turned the place into Vegas' artistic hub. Run by a student DJ by the name of Ryan Pardey, it played The Strokes, Flaming Lips and Modest Mouse records by day and hosted low-key shows by night. Its open mic night was the coolest in town, the only place to showcase new acoustic tunes to a discerning crowd.

So there Brandon and Dave found themselves in January 2002, twitching edgily at the back of the room, Brandon glancing around for somewhere to throw up from nerves without hitting anybody, waiting for their turn to be called. "It was full of snobbish coffee house listeners," Dave said, "and they called our names 'Brandon and David up next' and we walked from the back of the room with everyone watching us and they just handed me the guitars. It was so uncomfortable."[37]

It was the very first time Brandon and Dave had ever appeared on a stage together, and Dell was there to give his support. "You could tell Brandon was nervous," he said.[38]

The set was a disaster. The duo played two songs, a formative version of 'Mr. Brightside' and 'Replaceable', but the brutal honesty Brandon poured into these songs, the interpersonal intricacies of the psychological post-romance roller coaster, were doubtless lost on the hipster crowd at Café Roma. Choked with nerves, Brandon's voice broke a couple of times until he simply stopped singing, stared into his keyboard and concentrated on playing his synth parts. "That was our most nerve-racking gig ever," he recalled. "We stayed and finished it but all the way through I was thinking 'OK, I'm never going to do this again'."[39]

Scorched by the spotlight but undeterred, they sought out shows where the rhythm section could give them moral and musical support. After six months of solid unemployment, Dave had landed a job at Banana Republic in Caesars Palace by this point and had become a master shirt folder in a matter of days; he filled his wardrobe with his staff discount and cleaned it by striding confidently into the nearby Paramount Hotel, acting like a regular guest and handing them his laundry. But the band were at the forefront of his mind so, showing a strong work ethic for such a low-paid job, he negotiated flexible hours with a manager who understood the inconstant lifestyle of the struggling musician, that he needed random evenings off at short notice to play shows. And he'd not been slacking in distributing the demos either. The CDs had begun to circulate by the start of 2002 – local radio station DJs picked it up and began to give spot plays to 'Under The Gun' and 'Desperate', strangely considering 'Mr. Brightside' in some way less radio-friendly, and venue owners agreed to give them gig slots. The full line-up of The Killers made their live debut on February 12 at the Emergency Room Lounge on Decatur Boulevard, a locals bar that hosted Tuesday night jam sessions, run by a manager affectionately known as Grumpy. The plain brick wall behind the stage would eventually be decorated with a huge mural of Lennon, Hendrix and Henry Rollins, but that night the crowd were just as colourful – drunks and bikers, as far as the eye could see, fuming for fist-fights. As the open mic compere introduced them – as "Killers, no 'The'" – and they launched into opening numbers called 'Newsman' and 'The Future'*, Brandon awkwardly prowling the stage without a keyboard, the band smelled trouble. "We were playing indie, eighties-style rock in front of a bunch of bikers," Star recalled. "We thought we were gonna get our asses kicked."[40] Amazingly, the bikers liked it, and the band grew in confidence as the set went on. "The Killers sounded almost Iggy Pop-y then," said onlooker Corlene Byrd. "Melodic, but also jangly and messy, in a good way."[41]

---

* These tracks, and many of the songs from these early Killers shows, were never recorded outside live videos.

Leaving their biker crowd baffled, bemused and not a little excited at the eighties electro-freak scene they'd just witnessed, The Killers handed out free copies of their demo and instantly set off something of a local stir. A few weeks later, on March 2, they played their second show at Tinoco's Bistro for a night billed as The Ritual. The Ritual was a sprawling concept of a club night – there was a goth rock and industrial room, areas dedicated to Spanish rock and darkwave music and a Britpop section, where the DJs had such a broad idea of Britpop that they dropped everything from The Smiths to The Boomtown Rats. "It was a gothy, dark party," Star said. "First, we think we're gonna get our asses kicked by a bunch of bikers; now we're gonna get our asses kicked by a bunch of goth kids."[42]

Into this wild stylistic mash were dropped The Killers, a crowd of 100 esoteric rock kids and Mike Prevatt, arts and entertainments editor at the local paper *CityLife*. Mike had heard word of this strange new force on the circuit and wanted to see the British pop invasion of Vegas with his own eyes. His face dripping with eye shadow, glitter and mascara and full of the terror that gripped him before every one of those early sets, Brandon caught Prevatt at the door to explain that it was early days for The Killers and to press him for feedback after the show. Having watched the band play a short set at 1 a.m. featuring 'Mr. Brightside' and 'Under The Gun', lapped up by the goths, Prevatt gave his feedback in print. "A live band called The Killers offered some melodic garage rock that sounded like The White Stripes gone New Wave," he wrote in his March 14 lounge-scene column *Fear And Lounging*. "They play [the Ritual] periodically."

The tip worked wonders. The Killers' third gig on March 16 at the Junkyard club near the Sahara Hotel on Eastern Avenue was rammed with an enthusiastic crowd, heating a stage with a ceiling so low the lights could have burned off the band's hair. Seeing the power of press first hand sent Dave into a frenzy. At the end of March, three copies of the demo CD went out to the Vegas local papers – *CityLife*, *Las Vegas Weekly* and the *Las Vegas Mercury*. Far beyond their wildest expectations, one of them reviewed it. "Normally *CityLife* doesn't review demos," the review read, housed on a page of the paper devoted largely to blues, punk and trad rock bands from Vegas. "However, The Killers' recent three-song sampler provides a great opportunity to talk about them, as they are one of the most intriguing new bands to kick up dust locally. The Killers, thankfully, don't come across like any other band in town. The newbie act marries pop styles of British music with the lo-fi fuzz of modern indie rock, which is to say these guys don't listen to radio or even very many local bands. This is exemplified in 'Mr. Brightside', the band's best and most popular song, which leads off this demo. It's energetic, New Wave garage – a feel-good Strokes-esque anthem that ranks as one of the best local tracks in a long time. Odd though, that the song hasn't received local radio airplay, and the other two on this demo have. However 'Under The Gun' – another catchy, retro-pop gem – and 'Desperate' – a mid-tempo ballad that takes cues from Oasis, without the rip-off feel of peer act Psychic Radio – are welcome inclusions on what amounts to a sign of extremely promising things to come."

Their first forays out of Café Roma's indie enclave and into the wider world of the Vegas gig circuit were eye-opening, in a disconcerting way. The lounge venues were full of what Brandon would describe as "chubby guys wearing baggy pants, goatees and tattoos, listening to Slipknot"[43] and the acts they were supporting were all hardcore, emo and nu metal rip-offs. "It's a lot to do with the radio," Brandon would explain. "The radio's just not very good there. There's a lot of emo and punk kids, but not very tasteful at all. They don't play The Strokes; they don't play Coldplay. They'll play a little bit of The White Stripes now and it's like, wow!"[44] The metal audience simply didn't know what to make of The Killers, dressed up in scarves and mascara, Dave looking a confrontational sight with his bottle blond hair and occasional deployment of a feather boa. "He looks a lot like Marc Bolan," said Brandon, "he has a good physique – he can pull it off."[45]

At one particularly terrifying show, on March 26 at a venue called Boston[*], they felt the sharp end of the locals' animosity. The Killers were scheduled to open the night, but the second-on band, Cutlass, had other ideas. "We're in the back of the Boston with our gear," said

[*] The fourth ever Killers gig.

Norcross, "and Cutlass starts telling us they're going on before us."[46] When Dave argued back, the horde of gangstas that the other band had brought along en masse to watch them stepped in, threatening him with a rusty screwdriver until he complied with their demands. "We almost got in a knife fight over it," Dell remembered. "Who fights over the second slot?"[47] "They had all these Bloods with them in the crowd," Dave said. "Midway through their set they pointed at them and said 'Hey guys, the real killers are over here'."[48]

Such, you might argue, are the consequences of taking on an ironic hip-hop/hardcore moniker, or of Brandon's flamboyant onstage attire. "I was always into jackets with jeans and vintage T-shirts," He'd explain, "but then the beloved Strokes came along. So I had to find something else. I chose a more dandy kind of route."[49]

It was a tendency that sat uncomfortably with Norcross. While Brandon would trounce across the stage in his blazers and glitter and Dave would strike guitar god poses beneath his blond curls, Matt would be sitting at the back in football shirts and jerseys. "We always wanted to play a fashionable style of music and look fashionable, too," said Star. "Matt wasn't really into that... Matt wasn't really into eighties rock, glam rock. With him it was more Southern rock, the Black Crowes. I think it just wasn't the right fit. And he really wasn't into the fashion part of it. Brandon had a pretty specific idea for how he wanted the band to look. Some of my fondest memories are of Brandon doing Dave's hair and make-up before a show."[50]

"I'm just a jeans and T-shirt guy," Norcross would argue. "And it wasn't like we had band meetings where they said, 'Okay, here's L'Oréal No. 4 for everyone.' If the way I looked was a problem, how hard would it have been for them to say, 'Hey man, could you wear a skinny tie when you're onstage with us?'"[51]

Matt's technical limitations were starting to hamper the band, too. In May, The Killers headed out to the Green Valley home studio of a local engineer called Scott Bray, planning to lay down a second demo of two new songs, 'Beg Your Pardon' and 'Tiny Techno Tease'. Unfortunately, the tracks were never completed, possibly because Norcross was, in his own words, a "green drummer... When we were recording, I had trouble locking into a click, so they were probably frustrated with that. They never really said anything, but I think they wanted a more electronic drum sound, like in New Order."[52]

As Norcross moved in with his fiancée in a place north of Flamingo and the band began rehearsing in his new garage, the underlying tensions were unnoticeable. "It wasn't like we were best buddies,'" Norcross said, "but I wouldn't say we were complete strangers, either. We joked around and BS'd and all that stuff… We did photo sessions, and I don't recall it being like, 'We're The Killers, and Matt go stand over there with this bush in front of your face'."[53]

The band were facing external as well as internal issues, too. As the initial buzz around them faded a little, they struggled for shows outside of the Vegas lounge scene, battling disinterested metal fans and promoters who'd never heard of them. It strengthened their resolve and self-belief, but made them feel like outsiders in their own city. Brandon's nerves began to kick in in earnest, quivering his voice. "Our first shows were probably very boring," he'd say. "Yet I wanted to do it so desperately. My brother would constantly be watching old rock concert movies like *Gimme Shelter* and I'd get so excited seeing them as a kid. It was something I had to try for myself. At first, though, I was just concentrating on not throwing up! So it was hard. And I'm so self-conscious that it's always a struggle to let the bad thoughts fly out of the window and let the music live through me. When that happens, though, it's the best feeling in the world."[54]

Their inexperience shone through on occasion: one memorable night at Tremorz nightclub on May 15, an all-ages show in a strip mall close to the university, their set fell apart almost in sympathy with the venue. The place was a wreck – the ceiling and floor had both caved in, the tiny crowd of around six shared a solitary toilet and the stage, essentially just a tiny riser, was lit with only fluorescent lightbulbs and bookended with a cheap PA the bands had had to hire in themselves. With nerves shaking Brandon's voice well out of key, the sound guy's experiment with a Strokes-like tin-can effect on the vocals making him sound like a deep sea diver choking to death and technical gremlins shorting out equipment at every turn, their set was a tough listen, climaxing in a lengthy electro-disco instrumental piece reminiscent of eighties New Order. Few were impressed, apart from the drummer in the evening's support band Daphne Major. He was a guy named Ronnie Vannucci, Jr.*, and though his bandmates in Daphne Major considered The Killers' eighties fixation cheesy, Ronnie dug it. "I actually like their songs," he told his gang, "I think they're really good."[55] He wouldn't approach the band that night, but he'd remember their name.

The Tremorz show would be Norcross' last gig with The Killers. A few days afterwards he received an email from Dave. "'You're not in the band any more', basically, 'we're gonna move on with someone else'," he recalls with little regret. "It wasn't like I was Pete Best, like I just got kicked out of The Beatles. I didn't know the band I was in was destined for greatness. I was like, 'Damn, I just got kicked out of this band; I need to find another band.'"[56]

And The Killers needed to find another drummer.

★ ★ ★

Brian Havens – 16 years old, swarthy of look and fresh from spiritual questing – was stacking shelves at Virgin Megastore in the Forum Shops in Caesars Palace when he heard a tapping, half-drumbeat, half impatient tattoo. He looked up; a stylish looking guy was drumming on the floor with a pen. They laughed at each other, and got talking. "We started talking about bands we liked," Havens said, "and he asked, 'Do you play music?' He said, 'I've got a band, and we're looking for a drummer,' and he gave me his number. I've dreamt about that moment over the years. It's like a movie, and the pen tapping the ground sounds like a heartbeat."[57]

The teenage Havens was a natural dreamer. He'd fostered fantasies of rock stardom alongside his elder brother, Johnny, since childhood – they'd even got as far as forming a primitive band to play their school assembly. When that had failed to take off, he'd dropped out

---

* Ronnie claims this wasn't the first time he'd seen The Killers play, but caught them first at the Junkyard club.

of Durango High School in his second year to take what he called a two-month "soul journey"' along the West Coast and work with his mother's humanitarian organisation, Wings Of Love. For the time being, though, reality had bitten, and he was working the aisles at Virgin Megastore to get by. But even here, other-worldly things could happen.

He turned the slip of paper in his hands. Brandon Flowers – sounded like some kind of crazy stage magician.

Still, Havens wasn't going to spit in the eye of fate. So, downtown, behind the Desert Inn, he too came knocking at Dave's door. During his initial once-over he was given a copy of The Strokes' debut album, *Is This It*, and told "This is what we're going for, only better." "It was magic and I knew it," Havens said of his first rehearsal with the band, up at Havens' home in the Lakes. "From the first time we played together it was clear that it was good. The *it* factor was completely there."[58]

With only a few weeks to go before his first show with his new band, Havens worked frantically to learn the songs from a tape of Norcross' drumming. He felt out of his depth at rehearsals, but was determined not to let The Killers down. By the May 30 show at the Boston, Havens was as ready as he was going to be but, as the band struck into the swirling gothic intro of opening track 'Japanese Soldier', he was utterly terrified. "I was incredibly nervous," he said, "sweating so much it was hard to hold onto the sticks... I remember thinking, just let the songs breathe; it's not about the new drummer coming out with a 20-minute drum solo."[59]

As the show wound its way through a host of tunes now long lost – the frivolous pop of 'I've Got This Feeling', an instrumental called '007', synth ballad 'I Think I'm Falling Apart', the Beatledelic 'Humour Me'[*] – Havens' style added import and grandeur to The Killers' sound. "If you listen to when Matt was in the band and when Brian was in the band, you can hear a difference," said Star. "Brian was more experimental, and with him we sounded a little darker. He was really

---

[*] 'Humour Me' was Dave's favourite song of those early sets.

young, but he was good. I thought, 'If he's drumming like this at 16, he's gonna be really awesome'."[60] *

Keen to fit in, and noticing that only Brandon was using his real name in the band, Havens decided he needed a stage name too. He plumped for the faintly ridiculous moniker of Buss Bradley. "I had a concept," he explained, "a bus ... like, ride the bus ... be spontaneous ... with two S's to give it more flair ... and Bradley just sounded good with it."[61]

As the child of the group, Buss fit in just fine. Brandon would take him under his wing – as the baby of his own family he was pleased to have someone to pamper. "One night Brandon came up to me with the eyeliner and said, 'At least let me put three dots on your cheek,' So I wore three dots at that show," he chuckled. "[And] I remember one day I was working, and Brandon came into the store. We had a show that night, and I said, 'What are we gonna do until then?' He said, 'You know, buddy stuff.' It was an intro into a lot of things for me as far as what a band really is and what it means to have that circle."[62]

A gang again, The Killers spread their fire wider. They hit the Junkyard, Gameworks, the Crown & Anchor, anywhere that would have them. They supported Hot Hot Heat, the Canadian indie rockers preparing to unleash their monster hit 'Bandages' upon the world, when they passed through Café Roma, and their own local crowd grew just as fervid and passionate, a mini Vegas cult, set apart from the metal mainstream.

They even chanced their arm out of town. With Dave hiring a minivan to transport the gear and Star driving himself and a sleeping Bradley out West, The Killers hit LA for their first show outside Vegas, at the Gig-Hollywood on Melrose. LA, as is its way, shrugged them off without a second thought – the venue was virtually empty and the sign outside read 'THE KILLER'. "The place was beautiful, the sound was so good. It just sucked nobody was there," Bradley sighed. "We went

---

* Corlene Byrd, who had by this time become an avid follower of the band, shot video footage from the evening, culminating in a scene of the band hanging out in the venue's parking lot after the show with a tall blond guitarist from a fellow Vegas band called The Negative Ponies, by the name of Mark Stoermer.

up and down the street trying to get people to go to the show," said Star. "It didn't work."[63]

Back in the cradle of Vegas, the band shifted rehearsal spaces again, to a room in an office complex by the Desert Inn that Bradley's mother helped them secure for free through her manager friend, and over the summer of 2002, they concentrated on compiling a greater raft of songs. As Dave began to share Brandon's love of Depeche Mode and Duran Duran, their electronic malevolence crept into The Killers' songwriting, their synths sizzling with dark dance-floor pounds, and a tune called 'Somebody Told Me' began to take shape. Lighter and more languid, a sharp volley of synth notes and swirling atmospherics converged on a melodic rock saunter reminiscent of The Cure, which they called 'On Top'.

And, perhaps most promising of all, a guitar riff that began life on Brandon's keyboard as part of an attempt to emulate Lou Reed; he imagined a louche Lou muttering the chorus in a flippant, throwaway manner. "He said 'Can you put this on guitar?'," Dave explained, "and I was like, 'Yeah, of course', and that's how that went. 'Mr. Brightside' was more influenced by me, or whatever. But that one was mostly Brandon; he put that together."[64] The riff gave way to a marching pop verse far removed from the lip-biting anguish of 'Mr. Brightside', its sense of profound confidence, optimism and ambition offset with elements of insecurity and emotions hardened – "I wanna shine on in the hearts of men," it went, "another head aches, another heart breaks/I'm so much older than I can take… I need direction to perfection." And if its brazen chorus demanding "don't you put me on the back burner" wasn't ecstatic enough, it broke down into a volcanic gospel interlude swirling around a repeated line, "I've got soul but I'm not a soldier." Here was Brandon's internal ethical dilemma laid bare: as a good Mormon boy he struggled endlessly with the temptations of alcohol, drugs and women constantly orbiting the world of a rising rock band, and while his spirit was strong, his flesh was sometimes weak. "You're not always going to be perfect," he'd explain. "For me it was more of a religious thing. Going through this phase in my life of … believing what I believe and being thrown to the dogs, to the rock'n'roll world … Because even when I slipped I still believed what I believe."[65]

They called the song 'All These Things That I've Done', a nod to the song's redemptive final lines: "While everyone's lost, the battle is won/ With all these things that I've done." And it marked another step on their long road to greatness.

Meanwhile, Daphne Major's Ronnie Vannucci had made contact with Brandon since catching them at Tremorz, and the two had become casual buddies, chatting on the phone regularly, Ronnie giving Brandon as much advice on how to push forward with the band as he could. Ronnie would no doubt have mentioned The Killers to the gaggle of musicians he shared a house with in Vegas, including the highly respected multi-instrumentalist Ted Sablay, a man considered the best musician in Vegas, who also wrote music journalism for the *Las Vegas Mercury*. Come July, Sablay had secured space in the paper for an interview with the band, and he found an excited Brandon in defensive but ebullient mood. "A lot of people think eighties music is a horrible thing," he blurted, all of his frustration built up over months of hunting out acceptance from a sneering rock scene finding release. "I mean, if you're labelled a seventies-styled band, that's okay. But when you say eighties? I don't know – people have a weird thing about it."[66] Sablay himself agreed. "Flowers has a point," he wrote, insightfully, "sounding like Led Zeppelin – or rather, re-creating their sometimes overwhelming masculinity – is still more acceptable than musically borrowing from the Greed Decade. However, The Killers' version of the eighties has less to do with Aztec Camera and 'The Politics Of Dancing' and more to do with The Smiths and The Cure. If anything, The Killers take cues from bands like The Faint and Cursive, who quote the eighties on their way to making new, interesting music."[67]

Quizzed on Brandon's camp stagecraft – he'd strut around the stage and place his hands on his hips while singing – and their androgynous stage-wear, the band were similarly unrepentant. "It makes people maybe unsure," Dave said. "There are standards that we're not completely in. But it's not like we're an L.A. band, like Orgy, who look like girls." "So far, people have been really good about it," Brandon added. "No one's called me a faggot or booed me off the stage – yet."[68]

57

Brandon flirted further with androgyny over coming photo shoots. When *CityLife* offered the band a major chunk of local press – the newspaper would collaborate once a month with music website LVlocalmusicscene.com to profile an up-and-coming local act both online and in print simultaneously, and their August 2002 edition fell at The Killers' feet – the band arrived at the Mermaid café in the back of the tiny Mermaid Casino one Monday evening, ready to glam themselves to the max. Dolling themselves up in make-up and scarves, they took control of the shoot from the off, asking to be photographed lounging on the boho sofas. The *CityLife* photographer Bill Hughes complied, then took them outside for some shots in front of a nearby lake where Brandon, as the camera whirred, grabbed hold of the hand that Bradley had draped affectionately over his shoulder, and struck his campest pose ever.

It would be one of the last signs of affection between Buss and The Killers. At gigs, Bradley would peer out through the lights and get a heart-wrenching reminder of his inner Havens. His brother, Johnny – who he still regularly jammed with back home – would be at every show, cheering him on, but it only had the effect of reminding Buss that he'd always dreamed of hitting the big time with his brother at his side. "He'd come to our shows," he said, "and every time I'd look into the crowd and see him, my heart would sink because he wasn't up there with me."[69] Buss felt the pull of the familial cord. "I had every opportunity to commit myself to [The Killers], but I didn't," he said. "I wasn't into it enough and they saw it, they felt it, and I'd go to sleep every night knowing that they knew it… I knew what the band required, and I never did it."[70]

When Buss finally did make up his mind to give his all to The Killers, within a week of the *CityLife* interview, it was too late. "I finally decided, there's an opportunity here and I'm fucking going for it," he said. "I called Dave to say, 'I'm in', but even as I told Dave that, I could tell something was wrong."

What Buss sensed was Dave struggling to tell him that, in the midst of his wavering, they'd already snapped up another drummer: Ronnie Vannucci, Jr.[*]

---

[*] Dave had been complaining to his workmates for months that the band couldn't find a steady drummer.

"He'd seen us play a few times, and I think he started to see the potential," Star said. "I think Brandon and Dave started to feel like, 'Well, if he's interested, we've got to have him'."[71]

"Lo and behold, Ronnie's already been playing with them," Buss, now plain old Brian Havens once more, recalled, with no hard feelings. "I'd just decided I was ready, so to get shot down like that… But I've never lied and said it was some awful separation. In that same conversation, I told Dave I understood and wished the guys the best. They needed to move on. If they hadn't done it, they would have been cowards."[72]

The Killers had their stick-toting showman. The grinning, gurning man of a million rhythms.

And a man with a devilish past.

Dave Keuning, March 2014

Do you have any memories of growing up in Iowa?
I was born in Pella, raised in Pella. I would go shopping in Des Moines occasionally with my mum and grandma. Pella was a Midwestern small town. Typical small-town schooling, pretty clean, friendly, but kind of a strict town. Everybody is religious and most people go to church, so there's a fairly clean influence on the town, which is not a bad thing I guess, now I'm a little bit older, but when I was growing up I didn't like it.

What were you like as a child?
I could say a lot of bad things about me. I was kind of antisocial for some periods of time. I spent a lot of time in my room just practising the guitar because I wasn't a great people person from the ages of 12 to 17.

What were your musical awakenings?
I'd say I was influenced by Michael Jackson. He was massive when I was a kid and I thought he was great and I bought his stuff; I bought other stuff, too, like Billy Joel, and that was the first stuff I was listening to. The Stones were an influence of mine, as much as I was into Aerosmith, Mötley Crüe, AC/DC and U2. I was definitely into the Stones right away because *Sticky Fingers* was one of my first tapes and I was trying to figure out stuff on that and *Goats Head Soup*. I was trying to learn songs off those. When you first pick up a guitar you want to listen to music with lots of guitar.

Where did your sci-fi interest come from?
Come on, that's all over the place! *Star Wars*… I've always loved that – I still do. I was a nerd.

Was it a secure family setup?
Yes, it was good times and it was secure, my parents never got divorced or we never fought that much. I had one brother who was four or five years older. He left behind a few cassettes that maybe influenced me, like The Beatles' greatest hits and things like that. I kind of inherited some of his collection when he went to college.

What sort of holidays would you take?
We went down to Kansas City a lot and Chicago, St Louis, those sorts of towns that were close by. Long drives.

You got into classic rock in your early teens – was that about fitting in at school or was it an escape?
That was early nineties; I don't know, that's the music I liked. It wasn't to fit in but I did have a couple friends who were into the same thing with me. We would go to Aerosmith concerts together. I saw the Stones when they came to Ames but they don't come to Ames any more. They sold out the football stadium though, there were, like, 70,000 people there. That was on the Voodoo Lounge tour. One of the best concerts I've ever seen in my life to this day.

Were the Stones one of your first obsessive musical loves?
Yeah, they were mixed in with those other bands. All of Keith's playing, just great, great stuff. I think my brother had *Hot Rocks* and I went out and got my own cassettes, like *Sticky Fingers*. *Sticky Fingers*, *Goats Head Soup* and *Tattoo You* were the ones that stood out for me.

Why do you think you weren't great with people?
I don't know. I'm still not really a great people person. I just like to be in my room listening to music or playing guitar. I've grown up a little bit but I wouldn't say I'm super outgoing or anything.

Were you popular at all? Was there female interest?
There was. I dated. I had a girlfriend in seventh grade, that was my first girlfriend. Then I kind of didn't date anyone all through high school or college. That just sounds pathetic. But it fuelled me practising guitar and stuff. I was too shy, too awkward. I would always find a way to screw up any date or possible date in a hundred different ways. I'd just do something retarded.

What made you decide to sell all your video games and buy a guitar at the age of 14?
I don't know. It was a smart move because – I have video games now, but they can be a time vortex and you can lose track of time. I got rid

of mine and practised. I remember I was grounded at the time. All the more time in my room, practising.

Was that a sign of growing up?
I guess so. When I delve into something, I get obsessed with one hobby at a time. For a while it was Nintendo, then it was guitar – I was obsessed with that in the beginning; I'd practise for seven hours a day.

It seems there were years where you'd just sit there playing along with a CD changer.
Well it's fun playing along to a disc player. I'd make a programme of 20 songs that I knew how to play and sometimes do a playlist of songs in a certain tuning, like Nirvana are usually in E flat tuning. Some of the Smashing Pumpkins' stuff is E flat, a lot of The Beatles' stuff is E. I would just play along, or sometimes I would just solo over a song. It's really more of a guitar player recommendation than anything, but that's how I spent a lot of my weekends.

How did you come to join Pickle at 16?
My guitar teacher in Pella, whose name is Chris Hopkins, he was my guitar teacher for three or four years, they asked him and he recommended me because I was one of his better students. We didn't play that much, we played maybe once a month for a good year and then kind of stopped for a little bit and just played once a year for the next three or four years until I moved out of state.

How did you feel about the religious slant of the whole thing?
It didn't bother me at all. A lot of people out there would maybe want to poke fun at it or something, but my parents loved that aspect of it. I was actually in another band before Pickle called Send You Screaming, taken from a racehorse name. I was only in that band for a few months and those guys were nice – it was kind of my first band. It was more along the lines of eighties metal at the time, which I was into. I went from classical rock, I loved the hair metal bands in the day,

and then I moved on to grunge and from there new wave, one year at a time. My parents approved of the band from Newton more than the other band.

So that's why you stayed?
Yes, 'cause I didn't want to get crap and they were great musicians, the Christian band.

What were the gigs like?
Wild. One was different than the next. I mean, sometimes we'd play a church basement, sometimes we'd go to Iowa City and play in a bar, and that's a college town that I spent some time in because we had a friend there who knew how to get some gigs. That was a college crowd and they didn't know what to think. It was all original music – Send You Screaming was all covers of Ozzy Osbourne, Pearl Jam and other stuff. But this was all original music, this Christian band, and it was pretty fun. That's what I wanted to do, play original music. So that was a good experience.

Did you contribute any music to it?
Yeah, right away we wrote together and I had some stuff that we were using; they were good to write with. I was the youngest and they were just solid – solid bass player, solid drummer – it was good to be around them, it was a good influence on me. The other guitar player was really good, too. I was still sloppy, I had some refining to do, but I liked to come up with original stuff back then, original guitar riffs and so forth.

What was your time at Kirkwood College like?
I was just happy to be in college whether it was for the right reasons or not, and so I went to Kirkwood. The first semester I actually took college really seriously and I got a couple different A's in different classes. I don't think I ever got an A in college, that's why I had to go to community college because my grades sucked. I tried hard that first semester and then second semester I got sidetracked hanging out with my roommate because we didn't really know each other the first semester. The second

semester was a lot of fun and then the second year I decided I wanted to take music classes. So I was taking a lot of music theory classes, music history classes; I loved that sort of thing and I excelled in those because I was avoiding the harder classes. Then the third year I went to Iowa. I played in some combos at Kirkwood, just for the community college thing. I remember I played bass.

Why did you drop out of university?
I went to the University of Iowa after Kirkwood. I didn't actually get a degree at Kirkwood, I just went there for two years. I decided I wanted to go to Iowa because I had lived in Iowa City for a little bit one summer and I had friends there, and it's a much funner town. So I lived with my friend there for a year but the schooling was harder and a lot more expensive. That would have been fine if I was really committed to it but I wasn't committed to it, I just wanted to be in a band. I was a music major for one semester and there were some of the snootiest people I've ever met in my life on that music programme. They're all studying to compose; there's not much you can do with a music degree except teach music or learn composing techniques and that was not my world. I loved classical music and I still do, but the people there were very snooty, it just was a shitty experience, the whole thing.

So you dropped out and you did some jobs.
I worked for a telemarketing company where I'd try to sell Discover Cards to people and push them on people at home. I hated myself because I hate telemarketing, but at the time I needed money. I loathed myself for doing it but I did it anyway. You read off a script so it can be done if you're not a people person, but I didn't do it with a whole lot of enthusiasm. Then I was also a security guard for a retirement home for old people. I would basically go around and lock doors at night – I did that every other weekend. I loved that job because it wasn't dangerous, I would just go around and lock doors when everybody was asleep. They had a piano in the lobby so I would practise, or I'd go down in the basement and shoot pool by myself, or I'd ride around in the security truck. I enjoyed it.

Was being offered a job at your dad's mechanic firm the impetus for getting out?
No, in fairness to my dad that's not exactly the story. I always had that opportunity. Back in Pella I worked for my dad from a very early age on and off through high school. I wouldn't say I disliked it, I would just say that some people are mechanically inclined, like they can fix a car and nobody even told them how to do it. I'm the opposite of that and I think I knew that, but I still thought that maybe I would do that someday and learn how to take over his business. He had a very successful business – it was no small-time thing – so it was a good opportunity for me, it just wasn't meant for me. My older brother was great in computers at a very early age so he's working with computers right now and so it worked out for him and me, and my dad has come to peace with it now, like "I guess this is what everyone else was meant to do".

When you arrived in Vegas, was your apartment quite squalid?
It was not good. If you want to live by the Strip, 'cause that's where the Aladdin was, there was only one block that had three different apartment places, and the one in the far corner was really good, the one in the middle was pretty good and the one on the left side of it was not very good. I stayed in the middle one with my girlfriend for a little bit, and then when we broke up, I moved into the shitty ones next door. But their rent was cheap, and I managed to live there for a little while. They're torn down now, and now it's a parking lot for the Wynn.

What happened to the band you were in with your then-girlfriend?
It was fun for a while, we actually worked on music a lot when we first met. And then when we became a couple, we really didn't practise that much. She was a keyboard player. When you're in a relationship, you don't have as much free time, so when we broke up I had free time again. I got laid off, then 9/11 happened, and then it was even harder for me to find a job. After 9/11, Vegas was – significantly less people went there, and people were getting laid off left and right. It was at that point where I put out the ad, 'cause I had a ton of time to kill. And thank God; I've always been good at saving money, whether it was to move or have a

little backup plan in the savings account. So I had that, which allowed me to live there for a few more months and just look for band members, and that's when I met Brandon. I lived off ramen noodles for a long time.

How did you write the 'Mr. Brightside' riff?

Just before I had met Brandon I messed around and came up with that riff in my closet. I was playing in my closet because I had a microphone set up in there and all of the clothes drowned out the sound – it was a pretty good setup. I would play in the closet and then later when I worked with Brandon he would sing in the closet, like a vocal booth. I can't control my neighbours or my roommate or cars honking so we would make little demos and use that as a sound booth. I was just playing my SG in the closet and then stumbled onto that riff.

Can you remember what you thought when you first opened the door to Brandon?

He was fairly normal and nice. I was like, "Yeah, okay". And I wasn't, like, scared of him or anything. Not that I was scared of all of them. But he was just different. I can't remember the first conversation. I'm not really a great conversationalist. We just focused on music a lot. I had a keyboard already for the first time we met and he played on my cheap Yamaha keyboard. I think it was the second or third little get-together that he brought over his own keyboard and left it, so I knew he trusted me with his keyboard. We just started playing and jammed around – it was easy.

Did he have any songs then?

'Desperate' was one of the first things he had. That was the first few months though. The second practice we worked on 'Mr. Brightside'.

A lot of those early songs were about Brandon's break-up – did you feel like you were being a therapist for him?

We were both getting out of relationships, not just him, so it was good timing on both of our parts to have met and hang out a little bit. We went out a few times to some bars, not a lot, but once or twice.

What can you remember about the first Café Roma show?
There were a few Café Roma shows – some of them were horrible. We opened up for Hot Hot Heat once, that was a fun show and that was really early on – nobody around town knew who we were. It was later when the good Roma shows came, when we packed them in. There were some good ones and bad ones. In the early days I was breaking strings and making mistakes.

What happened when you were threatened with a screwdriver at The Boston?
It was just this guy in a band, they were kind of rap metal – that was big in Vegas, this tough attitude bullshit thing. They had to pick up their girlfriend from a strip club or something and they didn't wanna go on last. It's all The Boston's fault because they don't pay the bands dirt and there was nobody there in charge. There was, like, one bartender for lots of customers. It was chaos. Hell, there were probably bands that could have just showed up and played and fought their way onstage. It was a fairly easy place to get a gig but there was no one there, apart from maybe the sound guy if they had one that night. So it was left for the bands to sort it out. He basically pulled out a screwdriver and said "We're gonna go on first". He didn't have to say it. I wasn't gonna get stabbed over that.

CHAPTER 3

Mr. Brightside

"Birth. Man, it was hot in there. And I used to go out in the garage when I was little and play on the refrigerator and the washer-dryer and sing songs, we had a little Spinet piano that was out in the garage. The garage was my haven, my Abbey Road. I used to go out there and tinker."
    – Ronnie Vannucci, Jr.'s earliest memories

At times it seemed like Ronnie wanted to beat up the entire house. For hours, he'd be out there, locked in the garage, hammering on the washer, the fridge, the clothes dryer, the old beaten-up piano his aunt had given him to hammer away at, anything that shook the building. While all the other six-year-olds were out riding bikes or playing ball games, Ronnie would be lost in his own world of white goods rhythm.

"I'd make tapes," he said. "I still have those tapes somewhere. I had a great song called 'Creatures In The Night' which was basically a rip-off of Donna Summer's 'She Works Hard For The Money'. I'd always be really embarrassed because I'd be like 'boom, boom', in concert, and then my mom or dad would come out and startle the hell out of me."[1]

Ever since he was born – on February 15, 1976 – music was in Ronnie's blood. "I was their firstborn," he said, "so it was like, 'I don't know what to do! Stick some headphones on him!' And I just liked sounds. Everything from the process of pulling out a piece of vinyl and putting it on to watching the vinyl for where the next song started."[2] The Vannucci household was full of Stax records: Otis Redding, Sam Cooke, Booker T. & The M.G.s' 'Green Onions'. "I went to sleep to that stuff," he'd say. "That was my dance music."[3] His father, a Vegas bartender and "a pretty weird dude, although he's calmed down some"[4], fed him jazz, The Beatles, Steely Dan and Dylan in his Ford F-150 truck, which accidentally turned young Ronnie on to Tom Petty. "I was in the truck as a little kid," he said, "and I heard *Damn The Torpedoes* by Tom Petty and I thought he was Bob Dylan too. I can really remember being in Vegas and it was so hot and the stereo was loud and I was drumming on the side of the truck. Even before that, when I first heard 'American Girl', I just freaked out. At that moment I couldn't decide whether to play drums or guitar, but I knew I had to do something. It was a totally pulverising feeling."[5]

Even the truck itself became a percussive instrument for Ronnie. "I'd roll the window down and the body was steel and it had a good snap to it when you hit it."[6]

The beats soaked into his soul, seeped out through his fingers, rattled the garage. The only thing his parents could do to save their laundry room from total annihilation was buy him a drum kit. "I was around six years old and my parents were like 'We've got to get this kid some fucking drums, he's just hitting everything'."[7]

It was a cheap set, bought that Christmas from a heroin addict who needed fast cash. Not wanting to leave anyone out, Ronnie's two younger brothers received instruments too, and Ronnie instantly set about fulfilling his short life's ambition of being the Michael Jackson of his own family band, roping in his brothers and a cousin to form The Vannucci Five. With only four members.

Unfortunately, none of his relatives showed the slightest spark of musical talent or interest in being the next soul pop superstars. So Ronnie – already something of a loner, growing up on the sparse outskirts of Vegas in a neighbourhood that gradually built up as he got older – struck out on his own. His parents got him private drum tuition from an old Vegas lounge drummer – "In Vegas you have access to a lot of older musicians, old cats who played in the Rat Pack era"[8] – and, still only six, he became the youngest musician ever to play in a Vegas band, taking the sticks for a version of 'Play That Funky Music' in a lounge at Caesars Palace. He played his first full gig at the age of nine and come the fourth grade, he was conquering talent competitions with his skin skills and his musical horizons were exploding. His interest in British indie rock was sparked when his babysitter gave him a mix-tape of eighties music such as The Smiths and The Cure, as well as some lessons in love. "She was my first kiss too," Ronnie said, "she made out with me. I remember it like it was yesterday."[9] His first cassette album was *The Head On The Door* by The Cure and, from there, he dug into Britpop, punk and Depeche Mode – by junior high he was bleaching his hair blond, getting a loose perm and wearing white leather combat boots in tribute to Martin Gore.

An alt-rock prodigy, there was still magic in Ronnie's life. One Christmas, aged 11, when his family had moved up into the woods of Northern California for a few years to escape the Vegas sprawl, his parents woke their three sons up at 4 a.m., yapping excitedly about how they'd heard Santa Claus landing. Outside, in the snow, the boys found sleigh tracks and hoof marks, but no footprints anywhere near the scene. "To this day, they still insist that they had nothing to do with it," Ronnie would say years later, "and they insist it really was Santa. Dude, I'm 30 years old, and I'll tell you right now, it was fuckin' Santa!"[10] Another Christmas soon afterwards, his father took him driving through the desert as a rite of passage, only for the pair to break down out in the wilds and meet a real-life St Nicholas. "It was really cold and we had to sleep on the floor. We got rescued on Christmas Day and paid $500 to get towed back to Vegas."[11]

A foray into his junior high school's jazz band ended badly – he quit the band citing creative differences – and for a time Ronnie shunned the drums in favour of the guitar his father handed down to him. Over his time at two separate Vegas high schools, Clark and Western, Ronnie tempered a keen interest in sports by playing in various bands while tutoring other kids on drums; his first band, Purple Dirt[*], took him

---

[*] Including a guy who would one day become Ronnie's dentist.

nowhere, others took him to wedding halls and desert parties, learning the art of the jobbing muso from scratch and having his eyes swiftly opened to the true nature of his hometown. "Vegas isn't about fucking coffee or vegetarian meals," he said. "It's about staying up late, gambling away other people's money and seeing your English teacher working in a strip club."[12]

When it came to girlfriends, Ronnie was a drifter. "I'm just not the clingy type," he said. "I liked all these girls but I still wanted to spend time with my friends. If it had been just one I would've been like 'Oh, whatever'. But this was happening again and again with different women, to the point where I started to think I had a problem."[13]

Graduating to the University Of Las Vegas to study percussion on a classical music course, Ronnie joined the marching band on snare, marching alongside a trumpeter by the name of Mark Stoermer. But it was outside class that his musical exploits were really taking hold. Ronnie was becoming a famed name on the Vegas local band scene; word of his talents had got around and he was considered among the best players in town, and one of its wildest onstage personalities, gurning, grinning and pouting through gigs like a desert Keith Moon. "I look up to a lot of older drummers," he'd say. "I first started out by getting into a lot of drummers like Buddy Rich, Gene Krupa, Joe Jones and other jazz drummers. Of course I went into my rock'n'roll phases – particularly sixties rock'n'roll – like Keith Moon, John Bonham, Mitch Mitchell, who is probably one of my favourite drummers from that era."[14]

He floated through a variety of local bands but his main gig for much of the early century was with Attaboy Skip, a ska band in the vein of The Mighty Mighty Bosstones but with twists of pop and metal who knocked out covers of the 'Ghostbusters' theme and Twisted Sister's 'We're Not Gonna Take It' around the bars and lounges. This lounge lizard life he coupled with a sideline as a wedding photographer at the Little Chapel of the Flowers, where couples would burn up to the door on Harley Davidsons to be married to the strains of fake Elvises singing 'Blue Hawaii'. Or worse. "The best service we ever had was this pair of attorneys," he recalled. "They came in mock courtroom clothes. It had a real S&M vibe, because they were cuffed and bound. They were obviously into kinky shit."[15] "Everyone had black latex underneath their normal wedding clothes. And when they started to exchange rings, the groom pulled out a pair of handcuffs and the minister said 'You are now sentenced to life. With each other'."[16]

At the chapel, Ronnie had run-ins with his co-workers – he argued with a driver over an alleged $15 debt and his boss, David Foote, was his nemesis. "We were locked in a power struggle of cool. He thought he had much cooler hair, but he just had cooler hair."[17] But at home, things were far more harmonious. Ronnie lived in an immaculately clean commune of musicians, including Ted Sablay, a metal guitarist called Shay Mehrdad, devoted ska punk Bronson Mack and an indie singer called Ann Yu. The garage was stuffed with amps, PA gear, timpani and an enormous marimba; cable TV was a constant background buzz; junk food the staple diet; and the house stereo pumped out Costello, Waits and Cohen, the sort of intellectual, poetic music that Ronnie had developed an extensive knowledge of by his early twenties.

The musicians in the house would regularly jam together in various guises (Expert On October was another of Ronnie's early bands) playing impromptu gigs at house parties and at PT's pub, a redneck bar up in the north of town near the Nellis Air Force Base. They'd host parties full of local musicians and artists – a videographer called Jesse Harvel was a regular, as was a tall and charismatic classic literature student and evening poker table grinder called Michael Valentine, a member of a band called Romance Fantasy. At such gatherings they would swap word of the latest hot acts in town and gossip about which bands had failed to secure a major label deal or had their album shelved, a regular Vegas band pitfall that instilled a deep-seated distrust of the music industry. Ronnie's place was the closest Vegas had to a scene HQ.

When Ronnie first saw The Killers he began passing on what few grains of rock'n'roll wisdom he could to Brandon, to the extent that, over the summer of 2002, Ronnie – a self-confessed "music Nazi" – became a close and valued advisor to The Killers and, as issues grew with Havens, their number one choice as the ideal replacement drummer.

The band were in urgent need of advice, too. A management firm called Steifel Entertainment had expressed an interest in taking The

Killers on. Steifel was big business; it had represented Prince, Guns N' Roses and Brandon's beloved Morrissey. But the band had no idea how to go about negotiating a contract. So Ronnie found them a lawyer in the shape of an old bandmate of his called Robert Reynolds, who was now working at Skadden, Arps, Slate, Meagher & Flom LLP, a law firm in Times Square, New York City.

"I went to NYU law school, then later did some high profile music litigation, NBA trademark work and false advertising claims," Robert says today. "It was a large law firm but it didn't represent bands. I had played in a band with Ronnie and a guy from [Utah rock band] Neon Trees when we were younger. I got a record deal for this bluegrass band out of Utah that I liked and Ronnie heard about it. Then the day came when Ronnie says 'Hey, there's this band called The Killers, I think I'm going to be their drummer, what do you think?' and he sent me the demo. I flipped out over 'Mr. Brightside', I was convinced this was going to be huge. So I flew out from New York to Las Vegas, went into Ronnie's garage and my brother and I sat there and they played their songs. I said 'I want to be your lawyer'. I remember Brandon saying 'Why do we need a lawyer, we don't hardly have any fans yet!' I said 'I'll just work on spec and when you make money I'll make money'."

"One of the first things I did [with The Killers] was negotiate the [Steifel] contract," he continues. "We couldn't get terms that the band and I were comfortable with and we didn't think they were right for the band." Convinced that the band were destined for great things, he soon quit his New York firm and moved to Las Vegas. "Looking back, quitting Skadden was a crazy thing – it was prestigious and the highest-paying firm in America at the time. I loved that job. Great people, great work, an amazing gym, cafeteria, car service home at night, you name it. I cut my salary to one-third the salary when I moved to Vegas. All I could think about was that The Killers were going to be huge, and I wanted to do whatever I could to help make that happen."

Then, in August, a major breakthrough struck. An A&R scout from Warner Bros. in San Francisco by the name of Braden Merrick contacted the band. "At the time I was doing A&R for Warner Bros. Records," Braden remembers today, "and my boss at the time, this woman named

Paula Moore, she gave me this budget to hire a bunch of scouts. One of the states I was supposed to cover was Nevada, so I reached out to this gentleman named Jeff Higginbotham who had built this website in Vegas called LVlocalmusicscene.com. We were talking and it sounded like he had the local scene there pretty dialled in. He goes 'Before you hire me, check out this list of bands that I'm gonna feature on my website' and of the bands he sent over the first band I saw that jumped out at me from the list was called The Killers, because I thought it might've been an Iron Maiden cover band! I clicked on that link and there was a very rough version of 'Mr. Brightside' up there, I think it was maybe five minutes long or something. I was like 'Wow, this is pretty hooky'. I said 'Jeff, you've got great taste in music, let's work together'. So he would report directly to me and that's how I got turned on to the band."

Braden first made contact with The Killers via email. "I reached out to whatever the email address was on that website and I think Dave or maybe Brandon was the first to respond to me. It was 'Hey, what's going on with your band, are there any shows coming up, do you have any more material you can send me?' So they sent me this CD, which I still have to this day. It had three or four songs on it, 'Mr. Brightside' and some other songs that were never released, a song called 'Desperate' and another song called 'Replaceable' which I always tried to get Brandon to revamp but he just wasn't having it."

Originally from San Francisco, then in his mid-thirties, Merrick had a good track record behind him – at his previous position as a scout at A&R site redbutton.com he'd found and passed on many bands to majors for a finder's fee, and having played in a punk band in San Francisco in the nineties and gradually worked his way into the industry side, he certainly knew his way around the business. His offer was simple: as a scout he couldn't offer the band an instant deal with Warners, but he could certainly push them at the label and encourage the label bigwigs to see them for themselves. But, he strongly advised, they should ditch the rhythm section first. "Early on I thought, when you listen to those recordings, the drummer's timing was really bad and I wasn't too sure of the bass," Braden says. "Other people may have given them the same advice."

Brandon and Dave turned to Ronnie Vannucci for advice, but also with an ulterior motive. Both Attaboy Skip and Expert On October had come close to landing a record deal but negotiations had collapsed at the closing stages, so Ronnie had tips on dealing with labels for the ambitious Flowers. In return, they told him they'd been grooming him as a Killer for three months, now they wanted him in the band.

And Ronnie was a believer.

"One day I got a call from Dave and Brandon," he said, "one of those weird three o'clock in the morning conversations. And Brandon says 'Well, why don't you just do it?' Brandon's lack of tact sometimes is really cool."[18] "I didn't even want to be in a band when I was approached. I was studying classical percussion at UNLV. I quit the course two months before my recital. I guess sometimes you have to heed the calling. My parents kind of freaked out but they're cool now. They're proud I think."[19]

The Killers Mk 1 played its final show at the Crown & Anchor that August, a British expat pub with no in-house PA, no monitors and no interest in watching them. With the band unable to hear each other, Brandon left the stage to roam among the disinterested crowd, falling into drinkers and turning the vibe against them. Their cover of Oasis' 'Champagne Supernova' was met with boos, even from a largely British crowd, and a sour note hung in the air.

With Havens ousted and Ronnie installed in his place, the sour air lingered into the rehearsal room. Ronnie set the band up in the garage of his shared house, much to the annoyance of the three or four other bands who already rehearsed there, who now had to kick aside Dave's guitar pedals to get to their own practice equipment[*]. And in the first rehearsals, all air conditioning broken and the place sweltering in the late summer heat-haze, The Killers failed to instantly click.

The problem, it would transpire, was Dell's. He liked Ronnie just fine, but they didn't gel as an even-handed rhythm section. "I knew he was really trained," said Star, "and I was still really new to the bass, so I was probably a little bit intimidated by that."[20] The clash aggravated a

---

[*] "I was like 'Get this going-nowhere eighties crap out of here!'" said one disgruntled musician in Jarret Keene's biography *The Killers: Destiny Is Calling Me*.

sense of unease and uncertainty about his role in the band that Dell had been feeling for a while. "Something was missing," he said. "I'd moved out of Dave's apartment after we'd started the band, so I wasn't around him as much. I was just at a point where I wasn't even sure if I even wanted to be in a band, or maybe I wanted to be in a different kind of band. I wasn't sure I wanted to go too pop."[21]

At the same time, Dell was undergoing anxiety issues and personal problems that made him question whether it was the right time to be dedicating himself to the band. "Personally, it was just a bad time for me," he said. "I was really struggling. I was working as a lab tech at Southern Nevada Optical; I remember it was a slow day and I was pacing back and forth, trying to decide if I should make the call [to quit]. I finally called Dave and told him I just didn't think it was gonna work out any longer. I told him I was just really stressed out – from personal life, from being in the band – and that I felt like I was having a nervous breakdown. He said, 'I don't want you to be in bad health because of the band, but are you sure you've made up your mind?' And I said, 'Yeah, I just don't think I can do it.' It was a really disappointing day for me."[22]

A pivotal day for The Killers, though. As much as Dell leaving was a blow to the band, it paved the way for the final piece of their puzzle to slot into place.

★ ★ ★

"I was probably two years old and I was in front of the TV, I guess I was at my parents' house in Houston – I was born in Texas but then grew up in Vegas – it must've been something like Solid Gold, a weekly music show. I remember hearing this disco, it might've been Donna Summer, this song called 'Hot Stuff'. I think it was that because it's definitely something disco, synthesizer with these girls with feathers, almost Vegas showgirls, but we weren't in Vegas, I was just watching this on TV. And then my mom was telling me it was time to go to bed or something. I always remember I first snapped into consciousness, like thinking 'Where am I? Where did I come from? Boom' and I remember seeing these dancing girls and I think it was Donna Summer."
– Mark Stoermer's earliest memory

77

The heat of the fight still hung in the arena, the crowd roar at the knockout punch faded to a blood-sated buzz. The fighters recovered in the locker rooms, stitched their cuts, bandaged their bruises, gave their samples. And, ahead of the surging crowds, a bike courier charged from the backstage compound, weaving its way onto the highway bound for the hospital. In the ice box on the back, Mike Tyson's urine sample, streaked with blood.

On the biker's headphones, the Stones. Ducking between traffic along Vegas' grand neon boulevards, ferrying his medical cargo of boxer's samples or body parts for transplant between hospitals by bike or car, Mark Stoermer would always listen to the classics – U2, Paul McCartney, The Who, New Order. "First of all, it's not as gross as it sounds," he'd say. "Most of the time it's in bags. The best thing about it was I had a lot of free time. So I'd buy all the Rolling Stones albums and listen to them in the car. Study them because I was so bored."[23]

It was all part of Mark's intense self-training. As lead guitarist in local bands Habit Rouge and then The Negative Ponies in his time off, and a towering figure on the Vegas rock scene at 6ft 5in, Stoermer was keen to hone his skills and emulate the greats, and Keith Richards played like a demon. So every chance he got, as he buzzed the Nevada freeways of 2002 with his gruesome packages, he listened and learned.

It had been a lifelong study. Born Mark August Stoermer on June 28, 1977 in Houston, Texas, to an Australian father and American mother, both doctors – the family moved to Vegas when Mark was just three – Mark had picked up the trumpet as a child, inspired by his father playing in a big band. Though he was a prodigy at taekwondo, reaching the child's version of a black belt by the age of 10, and had always planned a rather more highbrow future as an academic or a lawyer, he was given a guitar and took to it like a natural, and also learned to play bass in his early teens at Chaparral High School, while still playing trumpet in the school's jazz ensemble. Fellow jazz player Tommy Marth was among the few friends he had at school. "I definitely was shy," he admitted. "I only had a few friends but I had music. I would listen to albums every day in their entirety, just sit there with headphones on and escape to a different world."[24]

He bought his first bass having saved up his lunch money for a whole year in order to buy a skateboard, then swiftly discovered he was useless on it, so sold it for a bass he'd keep secret. "It was weird," he said, "I left it at my friend's house and my parents didn't even know. I had a bass for four years. It's hard to explain why... I was being kind of private about it."[25]

Back then his main musical interest was hip-hop, and he became a big fan of NWA and Public Enemy, but with the advent of grunge in the early nineties he discovered Nirvana and worked his way backwards towards The Beatles, The Who and Pink Floyd. "Pink Floyd were one of the bands that got me into music when I was 12 or 13," he said. "I'd listen to *The Wall* and *Wish You Were Here*. Roger Waters is one of my favourite bassists and inspired me to play. The lyrics are cool, too."[26]

Mark's playing style on the bass wasn't that of the Neanderthal thunker. Like his bass heroes – Roger Waters, Paul McCartney, John Entwistle, Hendrix's bassist Noel Redding – he used a pick to play, giving his sound a more defined and resonant tone. "I feel that bass is a half melodic and half percussive instrument," he'd say. "It's best when it fits right in the middle but still gives something interesting to the listener."[27]

But bass wasn't his main love. Even when he graduated to the University Of Las Vegas to study philosophy[*] and play trumpet in the marching band, he kept up music classes, sometimes in the same study group as Ronnie. And as he immersed himself in the Vegas rock scene it was as a guitarist, The Negative Ponies' bearded blond focal point.

Over the summer of 2002 Mark had become a big fan of The Killers. He'd heard and loved their demo and was a regular at their shows. He saw them improving as they wrote more songs, and was particularly excited when he heard that a drummer of the stature of Ronnie Vannucci was set to join. "[Ronnie was] the best drummer in Vegas," Mark said. "When I heard he was going to be in the band, I knew it was going to be really good."[28]

---

[*] Mark was inspired to take philosophy by Robert M. Pirsig's 1974 classic *Zen And The Art Of Motorcycle Maintenance*.

He was also on hand when the band was clearly struggling for a regular bassist. In the month or two after Dell quit, The Killers had several people stand in on bass, including Aly Unna, who'd go on to join The Objex. Auditions came to nothing, and bassists came and went on a whim – the band would settle on a player then ditch them soon after. Ronnie was keen on getting Ted Sablay into the band, having played with him in Attaboy Skip and Expert On October and knowing he was considered the best musician in the city, but Ted had been burned by the false promises of record labels too many times before, thought The Killers too retro for his tastes in this punk-pop age and had dedicated himself to his medical degree. And anyway, Ronnie's bandmates had their eye on a different player: Mark Stoermer.

As late as September 2002, Dave was complaining in local press interviews that they had no permanent bassist, but Ronnie had dropped hints to Mark that he'd be welcomed if he wanted to make the shift from guitar to bass. In October, Mark took the role, albeit tentatively. The Killers wasn't his band and he'd always dreamed of being the guitarist and songwriter in his dream act. He wasn't sure The Killers would make it but his friends convinced him to give it a try on a stand-in basis. Who knew where it would lead him?

And so Mark joined the rehearsals in Ronnie's heatbox of a windowless garage, the temperature hitting 120 degrees the one time they measured it. Mark was wary of being the quiet one in the band: "We were thrown together and maybe became close in the process, but it wasn't that we were ever a natural fit, personality-wise,"[29] he said. "I think we clicked because the three of us brought a certain wisdom to the band, the wisdom of experience, I guess, while Brandon brought the conviction that we really could go somewhere; the guy never faced rejection his whole life."[30]

But the songs were the reason he came to decide to stick with the band. "You could tell that there were good songs there," he said. "And that special something it takes..." "[When they were] little dwarf versions of what we have now, Brandon wasn't afraid to just get up there and just do it," Ronnie would add. "You need that when you're trying to get something off the ground. As far as the drive goes, Brandon was never half-assed."[31]

"The heat may have got to our heads, definitely," Ronnie said. "But it's always been kinetic with us – we wrote some songs in 10 minutes."[32]

When the heat in the garage got too much, The Killers split. Around December, Ronnie sold the house, and the band leaned on their old friend Ryan Parday at Café Roma for help. Ryan agreed to let them use the coffee shop to write and rehearse once the open mic nights had finished for the night; he fed them the leftover sandwiches and coffee and they played until way past midnight. They even played a short residency at the café – three gigs between December 2002 and January 2003, much to the distaste of the indie hipsters and grunge fiends that frequented Café Roma. They sniggered and sneered at this pop band infiltrating their space with their catchy eighties choruses and deeply uncool interest in appealing to a wider audience. "They just never seemed to fit in at Roma," said one anonymous musician. "They wore make-up and scarves and played a synthesizer instead of a glockenspiel, which is what, for instance, Death Cab for Cutie played on certain songs. Acoustic guitars were really big that year. A lot of us just thought that Duran Duran had invaded the place, and we didn't understand why Ryan liked them so much."[33]

At Roma, The Killers began to feel ostracised. They were called loners and freaks, considered sell-outs before they'd sold a single thing. And it stung. "In America,'" Mark would tell me, "indie has turned into an oppressive regime where you only wear trucker hats, listen to Pavement and hang out in coffee shops and turn your nose up at anyone that'd ever aspire to being on the radio. In America you have the two extremes, the mainstream and the anti-mainstream, which is just as close-minded. There comes a point when you ask 'When is it about the music instead of judging people on how cool they are?'"[34]

"I understand a lot of the indie thing," Brandon said, "but if you ask me what my favourite bands are, I'd say The Beatles and U2 and bands that were not indie bands... I want as many people to listen to the songs as possible. We don't just want the hip, cool kids liking us. We're not afraid of people enjoying our songs... We were shunned and made fun

81

of because we were obviously writing these big pop songs. And then it was like 'What, so you want to sign to a major label? Do you want to be a corporate whore?' I can't stand that mentality and I couldn't stand it even before I was in a band. In America, [indie artists] hide behind the fact that they are able to write a good pop song. They'll veer away from it right when you think it's about to get good just because they don't want it to be too obvious. We're all fans of big songs. I love hits."[35]

The result of this animosity was The Killers' first satirical song. Entitled 'Glamorous Indie Rock & Roll', it set out to parody the pompous, insular and sniffy indie fans that were casting knives at them from beneath their trucker caps across the Café Roma counters. To a plodding beat that slowly rose to defiantly epic proportions, Brandon painted a comic, cynical portrait of the enemy loitering in the "coffee shop with a cause" – "Two of us, flipping through a thrift store magazine/She plays the drums, I'm on tambourine/Bet your bottom dollar on me/It's indie rock and roll for me". Mocking the emo fraternity for their straight-edge ethics, purity rings and vows of pre-marital chastity, he went on: "No sex, no drugs, no life, no love/ When it comes to today", but ultimately offered the indie sneerers an olive branch. "Stay if you want to love me, stay," he suggested, "oh don't be shy, let's cause a scene". There was, Brandon was claiming, a New Vegas scene to be built beyond the limited boundaries of wilfully underachieving indie rock.

If anything, The Killers gained strength from being called fakers for their glimmering pop hooks and theatrical onstage flourishes. "I don't think great bands come out of great music scenes," Brandon would say. "I don't need some local person to inspire me." "Being outside a music scene helped us," Mark added. "Bands in New York and LA are inspired by each other but they are limited too, because they have to fit into that scene."[36]

"[There were] no other bands for us to worry about," Brandon would insist. "The only band I saw as rivals were The Strokes. We always wanted to be popular. All our favourite bands got popular – U2, Duran Duran, Oasis – I don't see anything wrong with wanting people to like your music."[37]

A stronger unit in their defiance at being shunned by the Roma scenesters, before long The Killers Mk 2 were ready to hit the circuit again, determined to prove themselves. Parday helped book them shows across the city – at the House of Blues, the Skillet Café and The Rock – and they approached their second incarnation with a degree of seriousness. Immediately, the step up in quality from their new rhythm section and intense rehearsals put them at the top table of Vegas rock.

"We were playing in small bars," Brandon recalled, "and although it wasn't apparent we were going to sell four million records, we was getting to people in a way other local bands weren't. You're never sure how big you are going to be, but in our heads we knew."[38] "They were always going on last after all the other bands who didn't sound anything like them had played, so the crowds weren't the greatest," remembered local musician PJ Perez. "More often than not though, they'd win whoever was there and get asked back."[39] "We practised while the other bands were doing those shitty tours," Brandon said. "And we wrote better songs."[40]

It wasn't long before Mark dedicated himself fully to The Killers cause, and dropped out of his philosophy course. "I was doing well [at college]," he said, "getting decent grades, then we started playing gigs in town and after one opening show I was sitting in class bored and I thought 'I don't want to be here because this isn't what I need to be doing right now'. I dropped out the next day. It was maybe a cocky thing to think, we weren't even signed or anything, but I just saw it happening."[41]

Dave had also used this rehearsal period to hone his guitar style. The writing of 'Somebody Told Me' had defined the sound he was after with The Killers; that alluring pop sedition. "Even before 'Somebody Told Me'," he said, "just as soon as I found Brandon, I had never really found anyone to explore this side of me until I met him. So we were on the same page there and definitely weren't into anything that was going on at the time."[42]

The glowing reviews continued to trickle in. "Like no other noise in the city of lounge acts and covers bands," wrote the *Las Vegas Weekly* in September, "The Killers… prove that there is hope for a music scene that is oft-criticised for lacking originality and stamina." The stars seemed to be aligning. By the start of 2003, The Killers felt they were ready to take on the music industry.

Unfortunately, the music industry had other ideas. Back in San Francisco, Braden Merrick had been busy hustling The Killers' demo CD around the various offices of his label, garnering little interest. He had convinced one VP to go see them live, though. "I think the band were playing at some diner that had live bands," he says. "I sent this executive out to see them named Troy Wallace, who was famous for signing Filter, and he called me back and said 'Dude, it's really early days but they're a really cool band, keep me posted on them'."

There was only one thing for it. Merrick would have to go drag this band out of Vegas with his own bare hands.

★ ★ ★

Dusty from the desert drive, Braden Merrick stepped out of his car as hungry for success as the biggest whale of the poker rooms. The Vegas lights gleamed with glory; like a gambler with an inside tip, he knew he was onto a sure-fire winner. "I went to Vegas not to bet everything on the tables," he says, "but to bet everything on a band."

Merrick had driven 10 hours from San Francisco to Vegas in January 2003, with a local producer riding shotgun for advice, to witness his first Killers slaying. Braden's friend Corky Gainsford – a drummer with the Blue Man Group – had organised the band a gig with his old band, Petrol, at the Junkyard on January 18. Braden was concerned when he got there; the Junkyard hardly seemed set up for show-stopping. A dark dive of a bar, the guitars were feeding through amps and Brandon's notoriously uneven vocals emanating from a weak and fuzzy PA system. Come the show, though, Braden was convinced these ambitious pop showmen were bound for brighter lights. "They play this set at the Junkyard and you hear 'Jenny Was A Friend Of Mine' and 'Somebody Told Me' and you're like 'oh my God'," he enthuses. "I was sitting at the bar just getting so excited. You could just see it, where this thing could go if we had the right producer to make this record.

"That night there was a lot of excitement. They seemed to be excited I was there. After the show we had had a dinner at some diner inside the Hard Rock, and I was just talking to them: 'Hey, I gotta be involved with you guys somehow, if it's not as an A&R maybe it's a manager role or a producer role, because I think these songs are incredible and you guys look amazing – the live show's a little rough but that can be improved upon with a tour, you guys will learn'. I felt like we all got on pretty well. Brandon was a little shy but you could see, through the conversations, his ambition. He was reaching out to quite a few people then. I remember having a conversation with Paul Berrow, who managed Duran Duran from day one, asking me 'Are you gonna sign this band because I keep getting emails from this Brandon kid about wanting me to manage him and his band. I like the demos but they're not quite up to snuff, I need to know if you're gonna sign this band or not'."

Robert was in charge of putting together the band's contract with Braden. "'We all loved Braden because he was so charismatic," he remembers. "Working A&R, he was also connected with the labels and at the time we felt those relationships would help land a record deal."

In the meantime, with such promise and possibility beginning to cohere, The Killers needed to rid themselves of the Roma snipers.

So they took to housebreaking.

★ ★ ★

"If you pull the doors hard enough they just open," Ronnie told his bandmates, "they make this big crack."[43]

The doors were to the Alta Ham Fine Arts Building at UNLV, a 2,000-square foot rehearsal space on Ronnie's campus built for the use of the college's hopeful musicians. Into Alta Ham The Killers would secrete themselves most nights, hurrying in their instruments and amps at midnight and rehearsing and writing until dawn. "We record all the rehearsals," Ronnie said. "There hasn't been one practice when we haven't come up with something we could use in a song. Ideas blossom in 10 to 15 minutes, stuff like 'Smile Like You Mean It'*. We're a very prolific band."[44]

At sun-up they'd split for their day jobs, but even then the new line-up had grown so close that they'd still want to hang out during the day. During one shift at the Gold Coast, when the rockabilly convention had brought Morrissey's guitarist Boz Boorer to town once again, Brandon was entrusted with Boz's bags for safe keeping while he went for a drink. "I shouldn't have done it, and I still feel bad," Brandon said, "but I went through one of them. I just wanted to see what Boz was listening to."[45] Inside, Brandon found a plastic bag full of CDs. "One of the CDs said 'The Album', and it had all the tracks [from *You Are The Quarry*] on it. I knew they were making a new record and I recognised the song titles." His first thought was to share his find with his new bandmate. "I called Ronnie and he was going to come and burn it because it wasn't out for months. But I put it on the CD player at work, and it was only the music, not the vocals, so I called Ronnie back and told him not to bother."[46]

Meanwhile, Ryan Parday had wangled them a doozie of a residency. He DJed regularly at a transvestite bar called Sascha's in an area called The Fruit Loop out by McCarren airport, "the dark side of Vegas" famous for its gay bars. Sascha's was an oddball hangout but pretty cool – local kids, drunks and trannies would gather there for its cabaret feel, its decent food and its 6 a.m. licence. Ryan had started bringing friends in to DJ alongside him during his slot, and now he convinced the owners to let him put on a band. The Killers first played there on February 23, but by the summer Ryan had got the band a monthly slot at the club's Sunday night eighties party starting on June 29, their very own Vegas residency.

From the off, playing to cross-dressing waiters, emo kids, tramps and students, they were a hit. "We would always have a really good turnout and a good time," said Ronnie. "We always got funny looks at first because we're a Vegas band and Vegas bands aren't very good – they're a bit behind."[47] "It was a cool place to play, on Sundays," Brandon

---

* Elsewhere, the band have claimed they wrote 'Smile…' in eight minutes flat.

added. "Drag queens would come watch us. The club tried an indie-rock thing, but the scene didn't last long."[48]

Sascha's became Tramps, Tramps would eventually become Trans, but The Killers were a steady fixture. Every month they'd fight off the horny transvestites and pull a bigger crowd. They'd play to rooms of 300, drawn to their subversive pop attitude and their new numbers oozing dark criminality. A trilogy of murder songs telling the story of a frustrated, drunken lover, a wicked plan, a tussle on a rainy promenade. It was Brandon's grandest lyrical achievement yet.

It began with the clatter of a bar room, the jabber of a confused, whiskey-addled mind. Then a gritty glam groove struck up, swaggering and steaming, and a vision of broken solitude swam into splintered focus. "Shaking like the devil when she lets me go," Brandon sang, casting himself as a discarded alcoholic drinking himself through a break-up, "got a new place and now it's so much better... oh Jennifer, you know I've always tried, before you say goodbye". As the dejected sot's situation becomes brutally hopeless – "who's that other boy holding your hand?" – he sinks into the bottle to drench his sorrows, and begins slurring his revenges. "I love you endlessly, but darling don't you see I'm not satisfied until I hold you tight," he sang, his passions rising as the bar room pop bounce grew to a dark cinematic sweep, "but you ain't got time for this, and that wrecking ball is ringing..."

This was 'Leave The Bourbon On The Shelf', the first chapter of Brandon's murderous triptych. In the next, the edgy, propulsive and furious funk pop 'Midnight Show', his leading man's worst intentions were being played out. Luring his ex-girlfriend into his car with promises – warbled like a breathless Morrissey – of stargazing on blankets at the midnight drive-in show, instead, racked with lust and despair, he drives her out into the desert and "took my baby's breath beneath the chandelier of stars... and watch her disappear into the midnight show", creating his own real-life crime thriller denouement. Only Brandon really knew how his anti-hero dispatched his ex and disposed of her body but all he'd say was that there was water involved, but no drowning.[*]

---

[*] It's widely supposed that the killer strangles Jenny and throws her body into the sea.

'Midnight Show' would end with brooding funereal strings; then, the sirens. Emerging from a squealing electronic squall and the whirr of helicopters – the sounds of the murder scene, the dredging of the lake, blue flashes on police tape – came a dark, brooding disco funk groove, as taut and tense as a dance-floor garrotte. Over it, handcuffed to an interrogation room table, our protagonist desperately protesting his innocence. "There ain't no motive for this crime," he bawled, breaking under questioning, "Jenny was a friend of mine." His story didn't seem to match up: "We took a walk that night, but it wasn't the same/We had a fight on the promenade out in the rain/She said she loved me but she had somewhere to go." Still, the evidence against him was as yet flimsy, and he knew his rights, knew no formal charges had been brought and he'd be free to go.

The Jenny murder trilogy also sprang from Brandon's hurt and anger at being cheated on, but expanded his cinematic vision into a full-blown noir plotline. "'Leave The Bourbon On The Shelf' [is] about a couple breaking up; all the boy cares about is keeping the whiskey they bought," he'd say, and of 'Jenny...' he'd explain, "it's okay making the decision to split up, but when somebody finds somebody else, it's terrible; it's the worst feeling in the world."[49]

Brandon saw the big screen in 'Jenny...', but Ronnie heard something even bigger. "I said I can see 'Jenny Was A Friend Of Mine' being played in stadiums. I might have said Wembley. Or any big stadium. It just felt like a stadium song at the time!"[50]

The trilogy added a frisson of danger and filmic allure to The Killers' sets at Trans, and the crowds kept flocking.[*] The optimism in the band was lifting, buoyed further by the occasion of Ronnie's marriage to his childhood sweetheart Lisa, in May. Meanwhile, Merrick called in March with fantastic news. Signing a production deal with the band, he'd arranged for them to fly to Berkeley, near San Francisco, where

---

[*] At one point around this time, The Killers forged their first link to the UK when they supported The Libertines in Vegas, who were on an American tour despite singer Peter Doherty being in prison. "I feel really sorry for Pete," Brandon would say, "I'm assuming it's a lot better with him." Source: *NME Yearbook*, Tim Jonze, November 2004.

they would record a new set of demos at the Oakland home studio of Green Day's one-time manager Jeff Saltzman.

"I was asked to be a guest on this commercial alternative radio station called Live 105 in San Francisco," says Braden, explaining the origin of the sessions, "and they had this programme on there for the five o'clock drive home called Fast Forward, it was about an hour-long show. They'd asked me to be on because I was the local Warner Bros. rep and they also invited this guy on the air known as Jeff Saltzman, who was famous for managing Green Day and being the lawyer for The Offspring and Rancid, bands like that. We had had such a good time on the show, he hit me up and said 'If you've got any bands, I've got this studio, just bring them by and you can record them for free'. So I initially sent Jeff the demos and he wasn't too sure about it, I really had to force his hand. He helped me arrange some financing to fly the band out and put them up in Berkeley, and we started the sessions. I was brought in as a co-producer with Jeff. My primary role was to help the band with their arrangements of those songs. It was all independently financed with our own time and pretty much Jeff Saltzman and the band's money. We were pretty much doing it all on spec in hopes that the band would get signed."

This was a big step up from Kill The Messenger Studio and the band had by now compiled almost an album's worth of world-beating material to showcase on the sessions. Alongside the likes of 'Jenny…', 'On Top', 'Mr. Brightside' and 'Glamorous Indie Rock & Roll', they'd completed work on their eighties electro-disco masterpiece 'Somebody Told Me', a sizzling four-to-the-floor sensation reminiscent of Duran Duran and recent New York electroclash acts like Fischerspooner and The Fever, given an extra androgynous twist by Brandon following having his eyes widened during those long nights at Tramps.

"It was about all of our experiences playing there and in all the clubs," he'd say, "the strip clubs and everything that goes on in Las Vegas. I'm sure it had an effect."[51] Hence this tale of a dance-floor hook-up revolved around the gender-melding chorus line of "Somebody told me/You had a boyfriend/Who looked like a girlfriend/That I had in February of last year". "[It's] the story of trying to meet somebody in a club," Brandon explained. "It could be a strip club or a dance club. It's really just a play on words but it gets people confused. That's good. The androgyny means we appeal to boys and girls. That's really important to us."[52]

Though the whole song throbbed with a salacious sexuality and the scent of late-night clubland seduction, Brandon was particularly proud of the song's opening line, "Breaking my back just to know your name". "It's a great ice-breaker," he said. "I think of it as the ultimate pick-up line. If I was a girl I would think that it's very clever if a boy came up to me and said that... I think the girl would melt."[53] The Killers' parents melted for 'Somebody...' too. "'My dad likes it," Dave said. "He's from a small town in Iowa and he likes church music but 'Somebody Told Me' is his favourite song [of ours]. That's when I knew it had to be good!"[54]

Braden Merrick has memories of the sessions, spread over several months, going very well. "It was really cool because the first three songs we worked on were 'Mr. Brightside', 'Jenny Was A Friend Of Mine' and 'On Top', and the way we had built the session was we wanted to have the band play their songs live then we would play them back and go 'Y'know what, this part of the song sounds more like a hook or a chorus' so we would rearrange the material. The band were such quick learners they would learn the new arrangement and sign off on it, they were like 'Yeah, this feels good, this feels right'. Once we decided on the arrangement we'd go in and track to a click the drums, bass and guitars. Ronnie would do multiple takes on the drums and we'd build the perfect take. But Ronnie was such a good drummer that we didn't need to comp the perfect take from multiple takes. Once we got the foundation laid then we would do overdubs of any creative ideas. Brandon would be like 'Hey, I got this great keyboard riff' and we were like 'Fine', because when you're in the studio you want to lay down every idea and once you get to mixing you can pull back those ideas. So then we got to the vocals and Brandon got into the vocal booth, got comfortable and started laying down some amazing vocals, because he heard the playback on these sessions and realised 'This is what I always wanted to sound like, this big, huge U2, Duran Duran, Blur-style rock.

At that point we were making demos that became the album, but there was such a good creative exchange going on, we trusted each other because we got results."

One memorable piece of magic that occurred during the sessions was when Dave hit the recording booth to confront the riff to 'Smile Like You Mean It'. With its wails of "Dreams aren't what they used to be/ Some things slide by so carelessly", it was a song built around the misty wisp of nostalgia – of naive mistakes, glorious sunsets* and houses of youth now occupied by whole new families – Dave had yet to come up with a suitable solo to gel the mood of the song. So, hitting his trusty flange and delay effects pedals for the huge sound he liked, he bent out a willowy five-note refrain on the spot. "I didn't know what to do on that song," he said. "It was just a spur of the moment thing I think I did in the studio. I still hadn't worked it out and that was the one that stuck on the record. I never was sure if it was good, honestly."[55] **

Ronnie played down Saltzman's role in the recordings. "We constructed all the songs and mostly did everything ourselves," he said. "There wasn't a lot of production involved. It was almost like a live show or rehearsal. No songs were more than three takes."[56]

"Jeff seemed in a great rush and would convince everyone that early takes were fine," says Robert Reynolds, who was also at the sessions. "Because the band knew the songs well before coming in, this worked. Those *Hot Fuss* songs have a rawness to them which came, in part, from the speedy recording process."

Many of the seven or eight tracks that The Killers emerged with from the Saltzman sessions were near-perfect takes and a fine showcase for their impeccable songwriting: "When we heard the playback – we got some rough mixes done by Mark Needham – it just sounded incredible," recalls

---

* The confusing line "Looking back at sunsets on the Eastside", Brandon would later explain, refers to being in the east side of Vegas while watching the sunset.

** Dave's uncertainty about the riff would linger until he heard a version of the track recorded by The String Quartet on their classical tribute to *Hot Fuss*: "the 'Smile Like You Mean It' solo came up with string players playing it and I was like, 'Wow, it is a good solo'. That was the first time I thought it was cool." Source: *Ultimate Guitar*, Steven Rosen, November 14, 2012.

Merrick. But some were a little dense and splashy, leaning a touch towards pounding rock rather than emphasising The Killers' synth pop panache. A tune like 'Believe Me Natalie'*, for example, was driven by a thumping tribal beat rather than the ethereal atmospherics the tune demanded, since it concerned more salacious tragedy. The fictional Natalie was a young girl killed by the party; in the narcotic swirl of the disco scene she falls in with a class A crowd, injecting HIV from a shared needle. "It's about the last days of disco, how AIDS brought it crashing down," Brandon would explain. "I was born in 1981 so I don't remember it. There was some cheesy music but I think a lot of good things then, especially bands like The Cure, intertwined dance with rock. I guess it's tragedy that draws us to this subject matter. It makes for a good song, a different song."

Braden was contractually obliged to send the new demos to Warner Bros. first, and the response was lightning fast. "Immediately I got a call back from my boss saying 'Braden, here's a budget, I want you to fly the band to Los Angeles, we have to showcase them because I've sent [the demos] around the building and everyone is freaking out in the building'," he says. "This meant Seymour Stein was going to be there, all the heads of A&R, Tom Whalley, who was the head of Warner Bros. Records. So I let the band know this info and we were all freaking out with excitement."

The Warners showcase was set for a space called SIR on Sunset in LA, an instrument rental facility opposite Amoeba Records. The band prepared for this potentially life-changing audition by renting a rehearsal space in San Francisco and preparing their five-song set right down to the clothes they'd wear and the light show they'd use. They even videotaped the rehearsals to watch back, looking for ways to hone their performance. They wanted nothing to get in the way of securing a record deal.

---

* The demo version of 'Believe Me Natalie' included different lyrics from the finished song, the line: "There is an old cliché/Under your Monet painting/Remember the arch of roses/Right above your couch" originally reading "There is an old cliché/ Under your Monet, baby/Remember we used to make out underneath that couch".

When the day came, however, the Warners reps failed to see the same magic that Braden and Robert Reynolds saw. "I remember Tom Whalley, the president of Warner, almost curled up in a foetal position while he listened to the set," says Reynolds. "Afterwards he said to his A&R guy, right in front of us, 'I don't hear any hits'."

"Personally I thought the showcase went really well," Merrick says, "five songs, they crushed it, it sounded amazing. But based on past showcases I've been at, usually when the president is the first one up out of his chair to go and talk to the band, he's trying to send a signal like 'We're not gonna do this deal'. The reason I got a few days later was 'Why would we want to sign another band where the front guy plays keyboards when we just signed Hot Hot Heat?'. My argument was, 'Well, we have six singles' but it didn't matter. When I had to deliver that news to the band, they were totally gutted, as was I. But that led to another round of showcasing. Once my company passed, I could then shop it elsewhere and try to find a different home for them."

One man in the Warners showcase had had his mind blown, however. Alex Gilbert was a UK A&R rep for East/West Records; Braden had met him at the South By Southwest industry festival in Austin in March, played him the Killers demos and hadn't had Gilbert off his back since. "I first met Braden at breakfast at the Four Seasons hotel in Austin, Texas," Gilbert says. "Braden was working for Warner Bros. at the time and we had a Warner Music get-together, a corporate breakfast meeting. At the end of it this guy, who I'd never met before, said 'What sort of music do you like?' and I said 'Shit that could sell bucketloads of records' and Braden said 'I think I've got a band that you'll like'. Then I was listening to the second Biffy Clyro record and during the listening process someone put a CD under my door, and that CD went into the discman purely because I was confused by the Biffy record. I remember hearing the opening riff to 'On Top' and thinking 'Fucking hell, that's a killer riff'. The next song I heard was 'Mr. Brightside' and the third was 'Jenny Was A Friend Of Mine'. Those were the first three songs that anyone in the UK ever heard. I remember being in a haze and coming round and realising I'd been playing these three tracks on rotation for two hours. It was 'This is the best demo I've ever heard in my working professional time'. I then tracked Braden down and he told me he was trying to organise a showcase for the US label."

"Alex Gilbert would not leave me alone," says Merrick, "he was like 'This is the best band I've ever heard, I want to try to sign this to East/ West Records'." Despite being barred from the Warners showcase by Braden's bosses, Gilbert snuck in anyway. "At the time, my label 14th Floor's affiliation was with Atlantic Records so I wasn't allowed to attend the showcase because it was set up through WB," Alex explains. "So I had to lie to everyone in the company that I didn't work for Atlantic Records, I worked for Warner Bros., and as the doors were closing I snuck in right at the end. I met Brandon Flowers before the showcase and when Braden introduced me to him as an A&R man from the UK he was slightly awkward, and he went 'It's really nice to meet you, why haven't you signed Morrissey?' I remember Brandon falling off the stage during the showcase or losing his footing. They were terrible, really awkward, but I remember Ronnie standing up all the time and thinking that was really cool, but what was striking about them was how much of a frontman Brandon looked and Dave was playing an Explorer, a very rock guitar in a band that sounded like Duran Duran, and I thought that was fucking hilarious. And I thought they had the best bass player in modern music – Mark's bass parts were incredible on that first record. We came out of the rehearsal room and there was a rumour that Madonna was rehearsing there in one of the rooms. I remember Brandon, Ronnie and maybe me running round SIR trying to get a look into Madonna's rehearsal room. I remember thinking that this kid was so excited about seeing Madonna, he had this incredible passion for pop music."

"He flipped out," Braden says, and the two had lunch at the Standard Hotel in West Hollywood the following day. Gilbert brought along the singer in a band called Longview that he was making a record with; Longview were managed by a guy named Ben Durling in the UK, who'd just landed a role at a fledgling record label called Lizard King. Little did Merrick know that, before too long, these names would mean the world to him.

Swiftly, word of this glitter-storm from Vegas spread. Demos went out to more labels, many of which failed to hit their mark. "Braden thought it would be cool and mysterious to send all the demos without the name of the band on them or any other press kit information," said Reynolds. "A couple of A&R guys later said that those demo CDs were just thrown away." Nonetheless, via word of mouth among the small A&R community emanating from the initial excitement at Warners, interest began to trickle in. Merrick booked the band into a showcase at another annual industry event in Chicago called MOBfest and there was a flood of RSVPs from A&R people from across the industry. Maverick, Columbia and American Recordings all sent representatives; of the 120 people The Killers played to in Chicago, the majority were from record labels. Right after the show I got mobbed by this guy Anthony Bland, who worked for Rick Rubin's label American Recordings. He was like 'What are you doing tomorrow? Let's do a dinner, I wanna take the band out for lunch or something'. That was the band's first proper industry lunch. That was the beginning of quite a long courtship between us and American."

Another LA showcase was set up, this time for legendary producer and Def Jam founder Rick Rubin himself. "I thought it was an amazing showcase," Merrick laughs, "because Rick showed up, he didn't say much, he kinda had his Luke Skywalker, *Star Wars Episode 4* tan yoga pants on and a big white T-shirt, and he sat on the floor of the showcase cross-legged and rocked back and forth on his ass during the whole thing. Then he got up, put his sunglasses on and left the room. The band was like 'What did he think?' I'm like 'I have no idea!'"

Rubin passed, as did Madonna's label Maverick following its own showcase with The Killers at the Viper Room at which the entire staff showed up, including chairman Guy Oseary. "I talked to every single label," Reynolds recalls, "some called Braden, some called me, I called people, everybody passed, nobody's interested, and I'm thinking 'What in the heck am I doing? I just quit my job to do this, this is crazy'. I couldn't understand why these labels who were supposed to recognise great music didn't see what, to me, was so obvious." But The Killers weren't the sort of band to be disheartened too much by this flurry of slammed doors. Ronnie had been in the same situation several times before and Dave and Brandon had the confidence of lions. And besides, wheels were turning, far away, they had no idea about.

Back in the UK, having failed to get East/West Records interested in signing the band, Alex Gilbert had handed the Killers demos to Ben Durling at Lizard King. "I came home and Warners flatly refused to let me sign the band," Gilbert says. "I was a kid at this point, I didn't know what politics were, whether anyone had spoken to the American label, and I certainly had no clout to call up the American label and go 'I think you're wrong, I'd like to sign an American band in the UK'. So what I tried to do was build profile for the band to get to a point where there was a load of heat round them so I could then go to my boss and say 'Look, there's a ton of heat'. That's what he told me to do, 'If you believe in it, make it happen and then come back to me'. The first person to hear it in the UK was Ian Baker at XFM and Ian started infiltrating them into XFM. Ben managed this band that I represented called Longview and he'd started at this tiny indie called Lizard King. I said to Ben 'You should work with this band and put out a single, build some heat on this band'. I didn't tell other A&R people about them because I wanted to sign them and I didn't think they'd do a deal with Lizard King, I thought they wanted to be on a major."

Recently founded by Martin Heath, an ex-president of Arista UK, with the help of his financial partner Dominic Hardisty, Lizard King was on the lookout for new acts to fill its roster. "The first two songs I heard were 'Mr. Brightside' and 'Somebody Told Me'," Durling said, "and they weren't too dissimilar to what's on [*Hot Fuss*]. I thought it was a pretty obvious thing at the time. The whole eighties revival was starting to rear its head in the UK and The Killers were potentially a perfect fit. Bands like The Strokes and the White Stripes had also made it cool to be American again, so the timing felt really right. They have such strong, catchy songs and such great lyrics that everybody at the label was confident [they] would be successful."[57]

"I started getting calls from Ben and he sent over a contract," Braden recalls. "Even though that label, at the time, had only put out maybe one release, or a single and an album and hadn't had any success, it was great to see somebody that was willing to take this risk based on the music alone and seeing our photographs and whatnot. So it was pretty exciting. I called the band and said 'Look, this is how Kings Of Leon and The Strokes have done it, they were pretty much broken in the UK. It seems the UK is paying attention to American rock bands, this may be the way to go for us, let's go where we're wanted, here's this indie label willing to stick their neck out on the line. There's no advance but they've guaranteed us tour support and marketing, so let's go over and do this'."

The terms of the deal went back and forward between The Killers' team and Lizard King, Robert Reynolds locked in "very bitter battles" with the label over the duration of the contract and the territories it would cover.

"We didn't love their roster," Reynolds says. "I thought 'This is not a good label for a band that has to be huge'. But the deal was great, and the people involved worked hard and really believed in it. After some intense negotiations, we ended up not having to give them any future options for other territories and for other records. It's unheard of. Nobody says 'We'll give you a one-record deal and if it explodes, we get nothing'. We also got to choose our own press and radio people. The Killers had the songs and we got good press and PR people and a label in the UK that was able to get it on the radar of *NME*. This made all the difference. Looking back, we owe a lot to Martin Heath, Dominic Hardisty, Ben Durling, Siona Ryan, Rachel Hendry – who still works with the band – and the rest of the Lizard King team for giving us the opportunity we needed."

The label was understandably keen to release the band's records outside the UK and have the option of taking on further albums, but the band's side were adamant – five-year licence, one album only, no option, UK territory only. The Lizard King album would be a one-off; from there the deals could get a whole lot bigger.

So Lizard King signed The Killers without ever meeting them or seeing them play live, the second band they'd ever signed. In July, the band inked their first deal; sure, it was with a tiny label half a world away, but their global takeover would have to work one territory at a time. And as a band born with British souls, the UK seemed the perfect place to start.

★ ★ ★

Their celebrations were tainted by a certain tragedy. Jason Rugaard, the drummer with The Negative Ponies and a close friend of Mark's, died that year of thyroid cancer, and The Killers honoured him by playing his memorial show at the Palapa Lounge in the Palms Casino on July 14. It was a deeply sad point for Mark – not only had he lost a friend, but The Negative Ponies were no more.

Ronnie had his own gut-wrench to face, too. "The week we got signed, they phoned me up and asked me if I wanted to audition for the Blue Man Group back in Vegas," he said. "I was so disappointed! I loved that show. I'd seen it so many times I practically knew it anyway."[58]

In the UK, Lizard King set about promoting The Killers in earnest. They sent promos of the demos to influential alternative DJs like Steve Lamacq and Zane Lowe, who began giving 'Mr. Brightside' spot plays, and the music press quickly caught wind. Word of The Killers' Brit-slanted brilliance seeped into the UK, pricking the interest of those corners of the UK scene that kept a constant, twitching ear to the ground for great new music from around the globe. Braden began booking the band shows in the UK for September; clearly, it was time to go to the source.

In the meantime, Britain came to them. In their first ever piece in international press, they were photographed for the *NME* amid the swarming casino lights of downtown Vegas. It was a big day for The Killers – very few copies of the *NME* made their way to the big record stores in Las Vegas but these were the guys who would always snap them up. "We were very nervous and excited," Brandon said, having known of the magazine since childhood, from the copies his brother would pin up in his room. To him, this was his first chance to sit up there on Shane's bedroom wall alongside his heroes. "We all knew about *NME*, so it was a big deal for us. We'd only played two shows outside of Vegas, so to all of a sudden be doing a photo shoot and interview with *NME*, it was important."[59]

Interviewed in a casino lounge surrounded by lookalikes – Cher, Adam Ant, Slash, a dozen Elvises – The Killers played up their glamorous slant. "Our lives are pretty much like that movie *Casino*," said Ronnie. "I'm the only guy that works in my store who's ventured into the dressing room with a client on more than one occasion," smirked Dave. "When they see something good and new they just fly off the handle,"[60] said Brandon, trying to explain why they'd caused such hysterical reactions in Vegas as being threatened with screwdrivers and hit-on by underage fans. They read, all told, like the most exciting new band on the planet.

The Killers' final US show before they fled to foreign shores took place at Tramps on August 31, 2003, amid a buzz that Rick Rubin was planning to hit town to watch the band again that night. Whether Rubin showed up or not, The Killers set out to prove to Vegas how much they'd grown. "Christ, this band has come a long way from their sorry-ass performances around this time last year," wrote Jarret Keene, reviewing them at the sweltering, rammed show, noting Brandon's mascara melting down his face in the heat. "Now the band plays the tightest, slickest, most vicious set of pop tunes I've heard in Las Vegas in the two ho-hum years I've covered this scene. Somebody is grooming these guys for the big leagues, and the effort has clearly paid off. Most of the old, crappy numbers are gone, replaced by unhappy, shiny, infinitely superior ones... the guys are even starting to resemble rock stars, what with Ronnie gasping for breath as he punishes his kit; Dave, his blowout 'fro in full effect, slashing and raking his guitar; and Brandon facing off with the front row ladies as they touch his magnificent jacket. This much is clear; The Killers kick butt."[61]

And with that, they set off to kick ass the world over.

Mark Stoermer, April 2014

What were your first musical interests?
Really young, first time ever? Music from films really affected me early on, the theme from *Rocky*, the theme from *Star Wars*. Both were films that came out the year I was born – I remember getting the chills to the music from *Star Wars*, that was the first real musical impact. And going back to *Rocky*, *Rocky III*, 'Eye Of The Tiger' – that was the first single I ever bought when I was only six.

Those are fairly brass-heavy songs; is that what led you towards picking up the trumpet?
Maybe. My dad played trombone and he also played guitar. He was a doctor but an amateur musician, sometimes semi-professional. He put himself through school playing music. I played the trumpet because we had a trumpet in the house and I was told I could pick the clarinet, the trombone or the trumpet. I picked the trumpet. I would've rather played the drums.

What are your parents like?
My dad was a doctor, he's retired now, and my mom was a nurse. My dad is actually German, born in Germany pre-World War II, so older and foreign. My mom is from America, grew up in Arizona. They're very different in that way, different culturally and in temperament. My dad is pretty serious – the time I spent with him was to have German lessons or history lessons. The German lessons didn't go that far because I never really learned it. The time that we had together wasn't playing sports or anything, it was "Sit down, it's time for your German lesson", or music lessons too, actually. Music lessons, German lessons or history lessons was our one-on-one father and son time. Looking back, that's not terrible – at least it's time, and I think it's shaped my appreciation for different things, whether it be music or culture, at least to some degree I had a little bit of that from my father.

Was it a middle-class upbringing?

Yeah, I'd say middle class. I grew up in a one-storey four-bedroom house in a middle-class neighbourhood. I think my father had financial ups and downs but in general we didn't have it hard. I wasn't going to a private school, I went to public school, which was free. We weren't going on vacations all the time to Europe or anything like that, so I'd call it middle class, fairly average but not struggling too much. There was a period where my father went back to Australia and my parents separated. He left when I was 17 and between 17 and 22, when he was gone, was the end of my high school and the whole of my university stage. That was a little bit different – I was living with a single mother. They never divorced but they separated for about five years and my father wasn't even in the country. Around that time it was probably a little less middle class, it was maybe almost pay-check to pay-check with my mom, but we did fine.

How did the change affect you?

It's one of those things you don't realise while it's happening, but I'm sure it did affect me. I just went on with my daily life and went to school. I wasn't aware that I was thinking about it but it's around the time I discovered rock music and bands, it's when I discovered Nirvana, and Nirvana opened the door to basically everything rock to me. I didn't really listen to rock until I was 14 – I was more into hip-hop. I didn't have anyone showing me the music from the seventies or the eighties, but for whatever reason, when I discovered Nirvana I was also attracted more to The Beatles and Jimi Hendrix and Led Zeppelin – going backwards and playing all of that at once. I would listen to an album a night with my headphones on, and that's when I bought a bass and teamed up with a neighbourhood friend that I was in bands with until the times of The Killers.

Why did you keep your bass playing secret?

Well, it wasn't a secret, I just didn't bring it home and I didn't talk about it. It was a secret but if I'd have been asked, I would've talked about it. I'm a private person maybe, especially then. Maybe fear, being judged a little bit. My family wasn't a very rock'n'roll family. My mom listened to some pop music and country but my dad was jazz and classical and

101

I felt like I was maybe doing something not accepted by delving into the rock world.

Why were you shy as a child?
I'm not sure but I've had a theory: I used to talk a lot when I was really young and I thought at some point I was told to be quiet so much that I just clammed up.

Did you grow up with any other family?
I have a half sister and a half brother. I grew up with my half sister but my half brother was from my father's side, who was from Australia – I didn't even know I had a half brother until I was nine years old and he lived with us for one year when I was nine and one year later when I was 17 for a brief bit. He left the house and my dad left the house at the same time, then it was just me and my mom. My half sister and half brother are both the same age, they're both eight years older than me. I haven't seen my half brother since then. He once sent me an email in 2005 when he knew we were coming to Australia but when I replied the email was no good. He had a falling out with the family and went his own way. I have relatives in Australia because my father's family moved there when he was 17, so I have cousins and aunts there, and he's distanced himself from the family. I'm aware that that's there, but every family has a story.

You'd say you wanted to grow up to be a lawyer; was that a real ambition or something you felt you were meant to do?
When I was asked when I was six years old "What do you want to be when you grow up?" I always said "a lawyer" and I didn't know why. I wondered if it was just because I felt like my dad was a professional so I should be a professional, but I didn't think of it that way, that was always my answer. I thought about being a lawyer when I was younger and then by the time I was at university I didn't know what I really wanted to do, but I wanted to study philosophy because of all the courses I took, that was the one that attracted me the most. People said "What are you gonna do with a philosophy degree?" and I thought "I don't really care, I wanna learn this and if I have to do something I could possibly teach,

I could possibly go get a law degree with this kind of degree, too". Those were the backup professions I was thinking of when I was going to university, but by then I wanted to be a musician. I think I wanted to be a musician by the time I was 14 and I didn't fully admit it to myself until I was probably 20.

Did you feel you were heading down a conventional route that wasn't you?
Not exactly. I maybe thought it when I was younger but by the time I was 14 I did not want the conventional route. I knew, whatever it was, I don't want what everyone else is doing. At a young age I saw a lot of people doing things that they hated and I feel like I'm very lucky that I don't have to do that. Around that age that was my goal – I don't know what I wanna do but I wanna do something that I love doing. It could be a few things.

The music you were into – hip-hop, Nirvana and so on – was quite angry or angsty in tone. Was that a reflection of your feelings at the time?
Maybe, but I think it's also more that that was the times, that was the music that was out. It was that it was sincere, not that it was angry. I was turned off to the hair bands, although I have more of an appreciation for some of that stuff now in so far as there's some good songs in almost any genre, right? But I always saw guys with guitars as being kinda contrived and cheesy – at a young age I thought that – and that's why things like Public Enemy appealed to me. There's a bit of an angst thing there too, but it wasn't only because of that. I felt something genuine with it, and it doesn't mean you have to have angst to be genuine. It's also the melodies in the songs.

How did you develop your interest in art house cinema and art?
I think it developed over time. I'm interested in art but I'd like to know a lot more. If I have a side interest, I agree that's film and some literature and philosophy. That started to develop at 17 and 18 when I started reading things like *Zen And The Art Of Motorcycle Maintenance* and *Brave New World* and dabbling in Plato and Nietzsche and things like that, like a lot of people do when they get to college. That brought in my

perspective, then – I don't know if it's totally related – but it possibly led to my appreciation of films that go a little bit deeper, have multi-levels of meaning. I first got into David Lynch films and Woody Allen. I started with directors that I really loved almost everything they do, and then I'd get all of them. Then it was Ingmar Bergman, then it was Fellini and then I started getting lists of the AFI Top 200 and I'd go through the ones that interested me the most. Currently I'm going through this other list of the 1,001 Films You Must See Before You Die. I pick and choose directors and genres, but it definitely started with a handful of directors that I just watched their entire catalogue.

Can you remember the first time you saw The Killers?
Yes. I'm pretty sure that it was a small gig at this place called Money Plays where they kinda played behind a wall – the wall comes about waist high to me, which is pretty high I guess! It was half a wall they were playing behind. I came down because my friend who I learned to play bass with – the friend I left the bass over at their house, we were friends for about 10 years, he passed away at the beginning of the band.

Your partner in The Negative Ponies, Jason Rugaard?
Yeah – The Negative Ponies were essentially the same band as a high school band that we formed when I was 17, but it reunited with me on guitar and the guitar player on bass. It was almost a variation on a band that was together, like, seven years before that. We'd tried to start five or six bands in Las Vegas and I'd learned to play with him. But to go back to the first show I remember of seeing The Killers, I'd received a demo from Jason, who lived around the corner from me. He brought home a demo. Brandon and Dave were pretty smart, they did something I'd never thought of or saw happen on the Vegas scene, they started handing out demos around town with the original 'Mr. Brightside' on it before they ever played a gig. That was circulating for a month, almost building the hype machine. That was unusual back then, I don't know if it's usual now but it's different with the internet, how a band would start to promote themselves now. The internet was available but it was more word-of-mouth still, even then. So Jason got the demo from his

work; he worked at a music store. I think the original drummer of The Killers handed in that demo. He loved it, he said "You've got to hear this band, it's rough but the songs are great". He played it to me and I agreed there was something to it. You could tell that it was very unpolished, but that was kinda cool about it. And you could tell there was something special about these songs and this was not like any other band, definitely not in Vegas. You hear influences, but also they had songs that there was something to them, some kind of magic there. So we go to that place Money Plays and I remember standing five feet in front of Brandon. Later he said he remembers that gig and thought "Why are these two scary-looking dudes at a Killers show?" We probably weren't what he'd imagine would be fans of The Killers, some guys that looked like they were in a grunge band or something. But the bottom line is, I always liked different kinds of music.

Do you remember meeting them?
I remember meeting Brandon but that was later, probably the third or fourth time I saw them play. We began to play shows with them too, The Negative Ponies would play shows together with them. I became friends with Dave first – I remember I had his phone number and we talked about music a little bit. The first conversation I had with Brandon was at a show they played at another Vegas place called The Boston, we were discussing nineties Britpop. We both liked Oasis and we talked about that a little bit then I'm like "What about The Verve?" and he's like "No". I was like "Really? I like The Verve" and he was like "No". He wasn't having it if I tried to bring up anyone but Oasis.

How were you asked to join?
Me and Dave were talking all the time and at one point they were thinking of having a second guitar player. I was playing guitar in The Negative Ponies and he was like "We're thinking of having a second guitar player, would you be interested?" I was like "Yeah, I think it would be good". But when he asked me that I also said "but I also play bass", because I knew that something wasn't right yet with the rhythm section. I don't want to be rude, but it wasn't there. I threw that out there, knowing that maybe

one day they'd be getting a new bass player. Maybe a month after that I was at my mother's house here in Vegas when I got the call from Dave. "Remember when you said you play the bass? Well, we need a bass player right now because we changed our rhythm section. We're gonna have a new drummer, his name's Ronnie, and we need you to come down and play bass for these next couple of gigs". I didn't know Ronnie personally but he was the drum star of town because he was in every band that ever had a shot – Attaboy Skip, the ska band that almost got signed, or Expert On October, the indie band that almost got signed. By Vegas local standards, they were big, so everyone in the scene knew who Ronnie was because there weren't many good drummers. When he told me that, I remember getting the chills. I think it was because I just know that if I'm playing the bass and Ronnie's playing the drums, this is gonna be good. I remember our first practice, it was like nothing before. It was rough still, a little bit, by our standards today but there was definitely magic in that line-up. Me and Ronnie's first gig was the same day. Some people seem to believe that Ronnie joined first – maybe technically, but that can also be disputed because he was in about five bands for another year! But the real story is, our first gig was the same day at the Junkyard. I think I also played with The Negative Ponies the same day.

Was that a special show?

It was special for me. Back then, what was crazy is the band and Brandon were writing so many songs that every gig there were five new songs. Every set was different – even if the show was only three or four days later there were new songs in the set and other songs were thrown away. I really wish that there was a pre-*Hot Fuss* album but then it would've had 'Mr. Brightside'. There were at least 10 songs that were good enough that were never recorded ever, they're just lost in history. There definitely could've been a pre-EP or album that would've been different but it would've had 'Brightside' and could've changed everything in a different way. Then we did a couple more, we played at the Cooler Lounge at Las Vegas – there were two or three gigs that we played together and I was totally into it and wanted to do it but because of my high school friends, we already had gigs lined up and they were doing two a week, almost.

In the next couple of weeks we had three more gigs and I think two of the three fell on days that I had gigs with The Negative Ponies, because I was trying to balance both for a while. I wasn't gonna just leave the other guys hanging. I was thinking "That's probably at its end anyway but if we have gigs booked I'm gonna fulfil the commitment to that". So I was like "I wanna play with you guys but I can't do these gigs". They went "Well, we might have to try out other bass players" – I forget who said that, I think it was Dave probably – "and if you're cool with that we're going to try some other people". I think they did maybe four gigs without me and two were with a girl in town and one or two were with another guy. I saw the one where they had a girl bass player, I came to that show. At the end of that show we all went out to eat and they basically said "You gotta be in the band" and I said "Yes". So I was kinda in before me and Ronnie's gig the same day, I had the spot, but then I guess I risked it because of commitment to my prior band – these are high school friends. But they asked me back because they recognised the magic that was there as a group. There was something special, and they felt it.

Were The Tramps gigs your training ground?
Yeah, it was crazy. Besides a few exceptions – and I think Ronnie was in every band – there was no band getting the kind of buzz we were getting once we had the full line-up. When it wasn't the full line-up I already liked The Killers, the early Killers, but there were a lot of haters, "Oh, they can't play" sort of thing, and there was some truth to that. But you've gotta see through that and see there's good songs and there's a frontman who has something special as well, which are a big part of a rock band. Sometimes we'd have 200 people at a show and that might as well have been 2,000 for the Vegas local scene, because usually local bands played to their friends or three people sometimes. We were starting to play to full rooms even if we just played last week. In Vegas, where people are really jaded and there never really was a scene, that was unheard of, and here we were in the middle of it. I didn't know where it was going but I knew something was happening. I thought "Maybe we'll do this for a few years – we're definitely good enough to be on the radio even if we won't get on the radio".

How did you find the Saltzman sessions?
By the beginning of 2003… none of us could afford to do a demo back then, this was before home demos where you could make one cheaply, because someone with a laptop and Logic these days can almost do a quality demo for free in their house. This was still in the days when you needed to go in a studio for sure. We were getting quotes, and to do five songs was $2,000, and that might as well have been a million dollars back then. We were all broke or had to spend our money on rent. It was when Braden Merrick basically offered us – "I have a guy that I work with that can get a bit of recording for you". We had no choices so we took it and he recorded us for free, but on spec that he would get producer points and basically be the producer. We went up there to Berkeley and recorded three to five songs at a time. Usually we'd go for the weekend. We did a session in March and another one in May and another one in June. By then we're doing showcases. By May, we have about six or seven songs that go on *Hot Fuss* and maybe a couple of them are the B-sides, and that really is the album. Fast forward to October when we signed to Island Def Jam, we went and recorded a few more with Jeff Saltzman and added it to the bunch. We basically remixed it and handed Island Def Jam the demos that we did with Jeff Saltzman. In my opinion the sessions were very efficient. What he brought to the table was putting a time limit on everything because he was watching the clock, but I think that's good in retrospect, from what I've experienced in the studio afterwards. He was like "Two, three takes, that's good, we're moving on!" He wouldn't let us redo things except for once or twice. We'd do everything very quickly, we'd cut most of the tracks to three songs in one or two days and the vocals were done on another day and then you have three songs and you mix them. The whole album, if you added up all the days we were in the studio not including mix days, was done in maybe two weeks, but spread out over six months.

Was it disheartening getting rejected by all of the labels you showcased for, or did it give you a sense of determination?
A little bit of both. The first one was the scariest thing ever. We did the Warner Bros. showcase and we had everyone from the Warner Bros.

family in LA at S.I.R. Studios on Sunset, and we also had the guy who signed Madonna and Talking Heads from Sire in the room and people from Elektra. So you have about 30 A&R plus record execs in the room staring at us and we'd hardly ever played a show out of Vegas. I think Brandon and Dave had played in LA once, somewhere really small. So it was terrifying and when they turn us down we feel like "Well we gave them all we got, that doesn't make any sense". It was kinda grim for a while because then we did Chicago MOBfest and every label was there — it was the Chicago version of SXSW at the time — that was in June, and everyone turned us down. The first time, although it was scary and we got turned down, it wasn't that bad, but by June it was starting to get like "Maybe we're kinda blacklisted". It was almost that way, and what brought us back to life in that game was that back at that Warner showcase the A&R for Warner UK was there. He showed it to Warner UK, they didn't like it but then it got handed to Ben Durling, our A&R for Lizard King. It was probably by July that we heard from those guys, that they wanted to sign us and do a two short-tour deal to go to the UK.

Dave Keuning, March 2014

Can you remember the first time you met Ronnie?
He would come around to shows because he was in local bands too; he saw us and we even played a show with one of his bands. He was good, [but] I have nothing bad to say about the other guys. Ronnie is a pretty good drummer and the other guys have their strengths and weaknesses, too. Ronnie fit with us better than the other guys – I hated getting rid of the other guys, it was hard. I'm not good at doing those kind of things.

Ronnie said you called him at 3 a.m. to join.
Maybe it was 3 a.m., I don't remember it being that late. At the time we were always up late anyway. I was always a late-night person.

Can you remember that conversation?
Yeah I do, it was pretty straightforward. We had already talked to him several times, he was kind of trying to talk to us but not trying to join at the same time. He would say "I think you're a great band, and if you wanna jam at all just give us a call" – that kind of thing, I don't remember the exact words. He never said "Hey I think you should get rid of these guys". He was already in three bands, but they were bands that weren't super busy.

You then had a complete nightmare finding a bassist?
I wouldn't say we had a complete nightmare. Del was my roommate at the time, he was also in a band and then he quit but he remained friends. Then he called me out of the blue one day needing a place to live. I said he could live with me, so he lived with me for a little bit. He was our first bass player for almost a year.

You already knew Mark from playing with The Negative Ponies as well?
Yep, Mark was with The Negative Ponies, a band that I liked. I just wanted him in the band one way or another because he was a great guitar player and he could play bass, too. We toyed with the idea of him

110

being the other guitar player, but we liked him on bass more so we erased that idea.

How did you manage to rehearse in the university all night and still make it to your day jobs?

You do what you have to, if you wanna play loud with bass and drums and you don't want the neighbours to bother you. Banana Republic didn't give me that many hours. I only worked four days a week. I would survive on very little sleep. It was a great room. It was totally private and meant for music, with no neighbours. We would carry in the stuff in the middle of the night then carry it out and go home.

What were the most outlandish Tramps gigs?

They were only outlandish because of the setting. I saw on one of these music TV stations where they give fun trivia facts, one of them was like "The Killers got their start at a transvestite bar" and I was like "That's not really what happened". It was a gay bar but nobody went there on Sundays, so our friend Ryan talked to them and he said "Hey, can I DJ on Sunday night and I'll advertise and get people down here". So Sunday night was like indie night. For about nine months, it was the coolest place in town. We played there, other bands played there, they got around the 21-year-old thing and there were a lot of 18-year-olds there. So it was win–win until it got shut down. They found out 18-year-olds were drinking there and it was over. By then things were happening for us, we'd had labels actually see us at Tramps before it got shut down.

What can you remember about showcases in LA?

It was a really unnatural, intimidating process, and we did quite a few of them, like five or six. They all stand with their arms crossed and their chest out, "Show us what you got" type attitude. I just remember being turned down by all of them. I do take some joy that some of them regret that opportunity. It was just really uncomfortable. Some of them were nicer than others. They seemed almost obligated to have us come down. It seemed like they weren't paying us attention at times. Some of them didn't want 'Mr. Brightside', because they didn't know it was gonna be a big hit. One of our showcases thought 'Indie Rock And Roll' would be a big single.

Was it disheartening when you kept getting rejections?
It's hard to call it disheartening because we never actually got turned down, we just got strung along. We were always in limbo, hoping. We never got formally turned down by these people. I was just kind of working at Banana Republic hoping that one of them would say yes for quite a while. It was Lizard King that were the only ones that gave us an offer, so we took it.

What did you think of the Saltzman sessions?
The Saltzman sessions were great, I wanna give him more credit than I did at the time. He works fast and he doesn't have a lot of patience. We were still working jobs, we had to take time off. It wasn't like we were gonna argue with anyone. He would often say "Don't worry, these are just demos". I know we finished at least five songs which I thought were gonna be demos and they stayed. It would only take three of four days to make three or four songs. We had to work fast. It's fine, it's kinda cool it worked out. At the time I was frustrated.

CHAPTER 4

Runaways

"It wasn't like a genius plot to rule the world or anything. It was more like America didn't like us at first. They kinda rejected us. We tried to play and get signed and all that. We played a few other cities. But in England, it's almost like they like new music more."

— Dave Keuning, 2005[1]

Britain — to the four breathless young Las Vegas kids stepping off the plane clutching brand new passports — was satisfyingly miserable. The food was awful: "People say the food in England is bad," said Brandon, "and it is. But now that I've eaten a limp cheese and tomato sandwich, I can feel the world that bands like Blur are talking about. There's an authenticity to bad British food."[2] The accommodation was squalid: they slept four to a dorm at the Columbia Hotel, a legendarily bedbug riddled and down-at-the-heels flop house favoured by low-end touring bands on tiny budgets.* "You've got an avocado-green shag carpet, green tub," laughed Ronnie. "I remember throwing up in the bathtub, kid's shit."

---

* The Columbia Hotel was such a regular stop-off for bands that Oasis shot the sleeve of their 'Cigarettes And Alcohol' single in one of the bedrooms.

The venues, too, stank of grimy history. The Dublin Castle pub in Camden, with its nicotine décor, beer-sticky carpets and lavatory stench, was a grubby pit compared with the slick Vegas casino lounges, but to The Killers, arriving for their first show in the UK, it was Mecca. They knew of its history as the spawning ground of generations of British indie rock acts, they gawped at the wall-mounted photos of Blur playing in the tiny back room. Its grit was glamorous, its grim scent perfume to their nostrils. "The smell and the way it looked," said Brandon, "it was everything I wanted an English pub to be."[3]

Everything about Britain, in fact, lived down to their expectations. "We had this romantic notion of the UK before we arrived," Brandon said. "It's so small and yet so many amazing bands are British, it's unreal. The Beatles, Oasis, Blur, Franz Ferdinand, they just keep coming!"[4] "I was still very young when we started out, and I think I was still searching for a lot of things, and my own identity being one of those. I was obsessed with British culture and music, and then somebody put me on a plane and stuck me there, and I realised that you can fantasise about something as much as you want, but the reality is never going to be what you expect."[5]

"When we came to London," said Tana, hitching along for the ride, "Brandon insisted on eating at Pizza Express because he had read that The Edge always eats there."[6]

Their Dublin Castle show on September 16 had been booked by Simon Williams, an *NME* alumnus who ran Fierce Panda Records and the Club Fandango night that the band was to play. "I can recall putting the show on on the back of a Lizard King promo which was totally brilliant," Williams says, "exemplary shiny alt pop from beginning to end. The show wasn't too shabby either but like a totally superficial A&R arse I really didn't like the bassist – far too smooth for my shambolic indie tastes. I think it was a pretty hot ticket."

It was indeed; the radio plays from Lamacq, Lowe and XFM's John Kennedy had sparked a minor buzz around the band, stoked by several small previews in the national press. *The Sunday Times* ran a snippet in its New Kids In Town section, describing The Killers as "T Rex and Ziggy-era Bowie at their most blowsy and histrionic; Psychedelic

Furs in the vocal department; and Duran Duran for the cheesy synth parts."[7] Hence, Williams' club partner Andy McLeod recalls "queues out the pub stretching down Parkway. They tore the roof off and 'Mr. Brightside' seemed to be on repeat on the Dublin Castle jukebox for the rest of that decade. It's the gig that most captures the indie boom time for me." Richard Cassar, who was managing two other bands playing the 100-capacity back room that night, remembers a rammed venue. "For The Killers the place was indeed packed, left to right, front to back, packed with people," he says. "There weren't so many people in attendance for the bands before or after, maybe 40 or so."

"Brandon wore a bow tie," says another attendee, photographer Kate Booker, "and was dressed like he was going to sing Sinatra or something. They started the set with 'Jenny Was A Friend Of Mine' and that literally gave me goose pimples and almost blew the sound too as they were so loud. I'm pretty sure they did a cover of a Smiths song as I remember talking to them about it afterwards – Brandon said that he was crazy nervous that night and not well."

"When The Killers started," Brandon explained, "I was very aware that I wasn't ready and it was scary. I was on these famous stages I'd read about as a kid and I started to feel I was getting too big for my breeches. It made me want to learn to try and be better."[8]

The band themselves talk of a rather more sparsely attended Dublin Castle show. "There were about 50 people there," said Brandon, "[but] it was a big deal to us."[9] "We'd done regional shows in the US but nobody gave a shit," Ronnie added. "Then we came and did this show and it felt like somebody finally cared."[10]

Aside from drinkers from the main bar drawn by the sound of electro-rock magnificence leaking through the swinging door, the crowd at the Dublin Castle consisted mostly of those in-the-know: cutting edge indie fans, A&R, label reps and key industry players, including their new UK press publicist Rachel Hendry, a radio plugger named Stuart Bridgeman and most of Lizard King. "Being so early it was mainly industry heads who were there," said Siona Ryan from Lizard King's A&R team, "including quite a few A&R people who weren't sure if they were signed or not."[11] "I remember we had a pretty heavy guest list from industry," says Braden, "it wasn't super busy but there was an *NME* writer that gave us a live review, which was great, we were hoping for that, that was our goal; to leave England with a live review in the *NME*." The review, by Tim Jonze* enthused "*NME* can't remember the last time a band arrived on these shores as perfectly formed as The Killers… this might be their first gig outside the US but they're already sensational. Best of all is forthcoming single 'Mr. Brightside' which propels itself into the stars with a synth-enhanced chorus so joyous it could persuade The Cure's Robert Smith to risk all his chips on red (hot band). Right now few bands are safer bets than The Killers."[12]

The Killers' first UK tour was short and insalubrious. The day after the Dublin Castle show, they played another legendary Camden dive, the Barfly, for a night put on by the Rough Trade Shops group. That night Dave, who'd left the Tavian Go persona he'd been using in the press back in Vegas for good, received a further knock to his rock star fantasy when he turned up at the stage door only to be turned away by the manager of the support band, who didn't know who he was. Yet the club was besieged, hundreds of fans left ticketless outside. "It was completely rammed," says Braden. "At that point the word had gotten out and an Island Def Jam person had flown out just to see that show. It was mayhem."

One reviewer who had managed to get inside described the scenes: "Beating out fat, obese tune after fat, glitzy tune, their hometown Vegas glamour dribbles all over the minuscule stage. Reactions are riotous… tonight simply breaks the mould; jiggling industry types abound, the supposed 'cool observers' at the back."[13] No mention, though, of Brandon falling off the stage, having had one too many pre-gig beers.

On the 18th, The Killers played to a crowd of around 60 at the central London Metro club as part of the charmingly titled Club Motherfucker night and finally, on the 19th, they appeared Upstairs At The Garage. Though these shows were tiny, the fact that there were hundreds of people in his spiritual home of London desperate to see his band made Brandon play up to his wildest rock star fantasies onstage, taking on the

---

* Tim would also crop up in The Killers' first video for 'All These Things That I've Done'.

persona of the cocky Vegas showman almost for protection. "The ego thing was somewhat real but it was never completely real," he'd tell me later, "it was a little bit of a façade, a little bit of a front for how insecure I felt. We don't come from New York or London or LA. Dave's from the Midwest and I grew up in Utah. We're just a different kind of band and all of a sudden we're getting popular in London, the coolest city in the world, and we were like 'This is not what we're cut from'. So I puffed up my chest and spread the feathers, that was my reaction to that."

To capitalise on the buzz, Lizard King released a limited edition single of the demo of 'Mr. Brightside' in the UK on September 29. The song had been freshly adorned with the sound effect of shuffling cards to highlight their Vegas roots, and came backed with 'Smile Like You Mean It' on the 7-inch vinyl version and by 'Smile…', 'On Top' and 'Who Let You Go?' on the CD. A grinding glam slam of a tune, 'Who Let You Go?' was Brandon at his most sexually charged, lusting after a woman he can't believe hasn't been snapped up with no small degree of self-assurance: "So tell me that's fantastic/And promise me you'll always sigh/I find it so romantic/When you look into my beautiful eyes/And lose control". The tune built to a slinky strut reminiscent of prime Suede, Brandon uttering a sultry "ooh" like a cross between Brett Anderson and Barry White. Here, buried at the end of their limited-edition debut EP, was proof that The Killers had twist with their shout.

'Mr. Brightside' wasn't chart eligible as only a thousand copies were pressed, but for that very reason it was an instant collector's item. The *NME*'s review of the record was typically enthusiastic: "If you will, the flip side to The Strokes," wrote Rob Fitzpatrick. "The Killers steal so smartly, and with such mind-boggling variety, that they demand the most surreal references. How about a pock-marked, teenage U2 suddenly realising what an awesome racket they could make? The coked-up Manhattan wank-fantasies of a 'Queen Bitch'-era Bowie? The aching, pre-teen yearn of Hot Chocolate's 'It Started With A Kiss' and the hollow-eyed disdain of prime Psychedelic Furs? Whatever, 'Mr. Brightside' sounds as massive and magnificent as impossibly filthy, drugged-up sex with strangers. 'Destiny is calling', sings the ridiculously named Brandon Flowers… and you can't help but think it probably is. Ambition, sex, noise; no filler, these Killers."[14] "Once in a blue moon such a single arrives," write *The Times*. "The old shiver up the spine is present for sure… three minutes and forty-one seconds of synth-pop perfection." Unsurprisingly, with this sort of press weight behind them, the original 'Mr. Brightside' single sold out in a week. Lizard King printed up another couple of thousand copies; those too sold out in a blink.

The British buzz made a serious impact back home. "Ironically," Robert Reynolds recalls, "a few A&R people Braden or I had sent the EP to and corresponded with that had initially passed, after the big press in the UK reached back and asked me 'Can you send me the new songs? I love them'. I'll admit that I enjoyed explaining that the songs were identical to what they had heard before and at that time didn't consider strong enough. They refused to believe it. They said 'No, no, no, these are new ones, I love these' and I said 'Nope, they're the same exact songs, the same recordings. You didn't like it, man!' That was the value of UK press at the time. The only difference between what they heard before was that we got *NME* press. America said 'Hey, The Strokes and The White Stripes, they're getting love over in England and we in America are behind the curve, the UK knows what's next'. This gave The Killers the leverage they deserved."

Braden had been keeping the US labels keen via the band's website, thekillersmusic.com. "I put up a photograph of the band logo and all the little victories we were getting along the way with a date stamp," he says. "I put up one free download on the site, it was 'Jenny Was A Friend Of Mine' and then just my email address." The site attracted the attention of Sarah Lewitinn, the assistant to Rob Stevenson at Island Def Jam, who had downloaded 'Jenny…' and passed it on to her boss. Stevenson went crazy for the song, began calling Braden about the band non-stop. And, such is the pack mentality of the A&R world, when one major label starts courting an unsigned band, the others start chasing too.

Island Def Jam is a subsidiary of Universal Records, and by the time The Killers got back from Britain with a glowing report from the Island Def Jam representative in their wake, Universal's other labels had got the Killers scent. "We had so many labels within the Universal system fighting for the band," Braden recalls, "but there is a policy in Universal where labels can't out-bid each other, they can only match whoever was first putting an offer in. So we received an offer first from Rob Stevenson, and he had never seen the band live. He was simply reacting to the buzz and the music itself. On the other hand, American Recordings had seen the band live several times, they put their offer in after Island Def Jam. Then Universal came into play and all of a sudden Island Records' head Nick Gatfield flew into Vegas, we had a meeting with him. Universal Republic flew to Vegas, we played craps with Monte Lipman and his whole gang. There was a real courting going on."

"The bidding war got strong," says Robert Reynolds. "We had two label presidents standing side by side, fighting over the band. People invited us to dinner and made some great pitches. Braden was good at being non-committal. He'd just be like 'Yeah, yeah, whatever!'. This all worked to our advantage and the labels started coming out."

The Killers felt destined to sign with a Universal group label, home to their beloved U2, but as the auction for their signatures became more feverish, Braden felt it wise to bring another major in, in case the Universal offers fell apart through in-house fighting. "There was all this courting going on and all this confusion being developed among all the personalities and the band's affections," says Braden, "and I thought, if that implodes I better bring in another company. So I got Columbia Records involved just in case, and we had Matt Penfield come up to Ronnie's garage and that's how the band showcased for Columbia. Then we ended up doing a dinner with Columbia at some place in the Bellagio Hotel, or Hard Rock, one of those hotels. You know what really hurt Columbia's chances? Tim Devine turns up with a board game of Siegfried and Roy, and this was just a week after one of the guys from Siegfried and Roy had his neck bitten out by their pet tiger. So Tim shows up to Brandon like 'Hey I just got you a gift' and grabbed his fork and starts stabbing Roy's photo in the neck and growling like a tiger. Brandon looked at me and he got really offended by Tim Devine's move. I thought it was hysterical and classic of just meeting's gone wrong."

Robert Reynolds remembers some other big A&R gaffs. "We had one label showcase where the main A&R executive, who I won't name, spent the entire set time in another room playing video poker. I kept walking back and watching him play. It was pretty frustrating."

The Killers' next showcase gig was set for the CMJ conference in NYC, an annual A&R hogfest which regularly saw label reps and journalists jumping cabs across Manhattan to catch dozens of bands a night from a packed and varied schedule of new bands from across the States and beyond. Getting on the schedule is tough enough, getting noticed even tougher, yet labels flocked to Don Hill's venue on October 22 for the showcase for the American Society of Composers, Authors and Publishers (ASCAP) where The Killers would be playing. The chase had reached fever pitch: "We had Universal Republic and the whole American gang and they were leaving gifts for us in our hotel room," Braden laughs. "I don't know how they broke into our hotel room but there were all these gifts from the label, like clothes and packages of music, champagne, food baskets and stuff like that. We were just all scratching our heads like 'How did they get into our room, aren't you supposed to have permission to do this'?"

The gig itself – arguably the most important of the band's career so far – struck a technical iceberg. Before a crowd of around 75, mostly industry faces and a few lucky fans that had managed to get in, the band threw themselves into a showcase they were convinced was their biggest shot yet at landing a major label deal. But Dave's guitar kept cutting out, foot pedal problems destroying his parts. At the end of the set, Dave walked straight offstage, out the back door and kept walking. "I just walked straight,"[15] he said, off into the city, sure he'd screwed up the band's hopes of a deal and his own life in the bargain. "The band played about five or six songs," says Braden. "I thought the band played a pretty strong set, but Dave took off and disappeared somewhere, we couldn't find him. It was hours later that he actually showed up at the venue and everyone had since taken off, but I stuck around waiting to find Dave and I saw him really upset outside, he was just worried he blew our chances of getting a deal so they could quit their day jobs and live out their dreams of being a rock band."

Dave walked until he was too cold to walk any more, ignoring his phone chattering away in his pocket. Little did he realise that the response to the show had been phenomenal – Braden was fielding numerous offers and enquiries from the industry attendees, and would continue to do so for days to come – and negotiations with Island Def Jam had advanced to their final stages; the rest of the band were already toasting their deal at the roof bar of the Tribeca Grand hotel. "I assured him 'Dude there are no problems, tomorrow we are going up into the Island Def Jam offices and sign the deal and pop some Cristal!'," Braden laughs.

"Dave's a tough guy," Ronnie said, "but he's also got emotions. You don't think he's taking the blows, but he is. I think that was the first time we ever saw one of the band be emotional."[16]

Straight after the CMJ show, the heavy final negotiations with Island Def Jam began, sealed the following day at Lyor Cohen's house. It was here that Reynolds really stepped up to the plate. "This was the best record deal I've ever negotiated – before them and since," he says. "I was a young lawyer and nervous I would miss something. So I argued everything. I read every book, talked to every lawyer, read articles online, did anything I could to make sure every 't' was crossed and 'i' dotted. I think it was my third record deal and this one meant everything – I negotiated literally every provision of the contract, which I've since learned lawyers don't do. I fought for things that Heath Kudler in [Island Def Jam] Business Affairs kept saying 'Nobody argues this provision'. In the end, business affairs still couldn't sign off on a few things I thought that the band deserved, but I finally got the changes. The final negotiations ended with me in Lyor Cohen's kitchen finishing the last details on a napkin. We then joined the band and all toasted. Lyor was a great label president for The Killers – fantastic and supportive. I love that guy."*

Rumours abounded of a seven-figure deal for numerous albums from The Killers. Braden Merrick is wary of revealing exact figures. "It was

---

* Cohen would become a vehement fighter for the band, as Brandon would recall: "[He was] just so gung-ho about us. In meetings he would be like 'I'm going to burn this building down for The Killers'." Source: *The Sunday Times*, Dan Cairns, May 24, 2004.

a good deal, let's say that. Put it this way – we could have gotten one of the biggest deals known to man but we made a responsible deal so it allowed us to develop properly and have more control. The band got living expenses, a van fund, equipment fund, an album fund and an execution advance for signing the deal." "The multi-figure advance, it was a big advance at the time," says Reynolds, "but it was a lot more about the back-end. We fought harder for good back-end terms, and they paid off for us."

However much they got, it was enough security for them all to quit their day jobs and become full-time Killers. Finally the curse that had hung over the frustrated muso parties at Ronnie's house was broken. Vegas was on the musical map.

And over the coming months, fate would conspire to try to wipe the Killers straight off it again.

★ ★ ★

Over the sex capital of America, the sky was burning. Step outside onto the filthy streets of Chatsworth, California, and the ash rained down like thick black snow. Rising from the bush fires that circled the entire San Fernando Valley, virtually shutting the town off from the world as if in punishment for its sins, the ash settled on the Lamborghinis of the porno producers who shot reel upon reel of skin-flick there by the hour, and on the musicians venturing out of Cornerstone Studios between takes to breathe in the hot, acrid air and wonder if the flames would swallow the town whole. "[The fire] ended up catching up in the mountains," Brandon said, of the 90,000 acres of woodland that went up around Chatsworth that October. "The ash was everywhere. We'd come out of the studio and the cars would have ash on them. We didn't have to evacuate the town or anything but it actually got close."[17]

By luck or providence, the fires never reached the studio – owned by Fleetwood Mac and where mixer Mark Needham was resident – where The Killers, Jeff Saltzman and Braden holed up for several weeks to complete work on the band's debut album. They'd been so pleased with the demo session, they'd decided to keep many of those versions for the finished album, but needed to complete six more songs to give them enough to choose from for the record. The sessions were a success; besides putting the finishing touches to several tracks for the album, including the addition of the Sweet Inspirations gospel choir to 'All These Things That I've Done'*, they also wrote and finished four new ones, including 'Change My Mind', 'Believe Me Natalie' and 'Andy, You're A Star'. The album was really starting to come into focus.

The brush fires weren't the only life-threatening event that struck the Killers studio. When Ronnie took to the kit to record the drums for 'Believe Me Natalie', for a second it seemed like he was playing the beat of his life. The ground shook, the rumble was deafening; Ronnie was thrown off his stool by the sheer force of it. "There was an earthquake," he said. "I was so busy playing drums at the time that I didn't really notice it that much. It happened so fast and it just felt like something just jumped from the ceiling to the floor. Fortunately there wasn't much damage to our equipment. But we got it all on video and we can sit back and watch it any time we like."[18] "When I came out of the booth everyone was freaking out. The same take made it onto the album."[19]

As before, the songwriting in the studio in California was purely instinctive. "I don't put too much thought into it," Brandon said, "it takes the fun out of it. If it's a good song it's a good song. A lot of people pick things apart, but if it's catchy, that's a great thing. And if the lyrics are great, that's even better. There's people that worry and want to know exactly where the bass should be in the mix and if the drums are lined up and if that all technically sounds great. No, it's 'Does it sound good or doesn't it?' The other stuff doesn't matter."[20]

And the music they were recording sounded good, even though the Auto-Tune used on Brandon's voice, he'd decide later, lost a little of his vulnerability and humanity. Once they'd finished tracking at Cornerstone, the band took the finished songs to London, where the legendary Alan Moulder had agreed to complete the mixes at Eden Studios in Chiswick – the band had plumped for Moulder thanks to his links with The Smiths, Depeche Mode and Smashing Pumpkins and

---

* The choir included Cissy Houston, mother of Whitney.

had been impressed by his work on Nine Inch Nails' *The Fragile* album. Here, they found a fresh source of competition. "We were all sitting around," Braden recalls, "and we had Zane Lowe's MTV2 show on and it premiered this 'Take Me Out' video by Franz Ferdinand. We were all freaking out thinking 'We gotta be better than this.'"

Picking the final 11 songs that would make up the running order of the album was tough. By now the band had amassed a large number of songs, roughly recorded, enough for several albums of material. "I don't have many regrets," Dave said, "although one thing I daydream about sometimes is that I feel like there should have been one more album before [the debut album], because we had quite a few songs that we threw away. Probably around 50. I feel that some of those are sentimental favourites for me, and a lot of them are just on four-track. So knowing that some of those may never see the light of day, I kind of wish we made another one... Well, we definitely had a lot of songs to pick from for that album."[21]

So the record they emerged with, inevitably, was a world-beater.

The first half of *Hot Fuss*, as it would eventually be named, would be considered among the best of any debut ever made. Opening with 'Jenny Was A Friend Of Mine' – sacrificing the narrative thread of the murder trilogy in favour of a punchy, seditious and cinematic introduction to their world – the band fired all of their big guns from the off. 'Mr. Brightside' acted as the launch pad and warp engine of the album, the original demo version pumped to full pulsing power during the Cornerstone sessions and Moulder's mixing until it glistened and gleamed like the pure pop diamond it was. The song now sounded not only like The Killers' ticket to the top table of 21st-century alternative rock, easily matching the sizzling class of The Strokes' 'Last Nite' or The White Stripes' 'Seven Nation Army', but like one of the greatest indie hits ever written.*

In keeping with the more billowing moments of The Cure, Depeche Mode, Duran Duran and Suede, these two tracks gave *Hot*

---

* As it would eventually be voted, topping XFM's listener-voted chart of the best songs of the decade in 2009, beating Arctic Monkeys' 'I Bet You Look Good On The Dancefloor' and Kings Of Leon's 'Sex On Fire'.

Fuss a desperate, pained and anguished tone, glazed with a sense of nobility from Brandon's crisp, high-pitched vocals. 'Smile Like You Mean It' formed a plateau, a calming interlude of nostalgic insouciance and dream-like drift between towering melodic powerhouses, but still managed to inject a little urgency and tension into its middle eight, as Brandon's wise and easy-going narrator is struck by the knowledge that the joys of his life were slipping away from him: "Someone is playing a game/In the house that I grew up in/And someone will drive her around/Down the same streets that I did". "Vulnerability was missing in rock," Ronnie would say. "We're not miserable but we're not afraid to sing about shit like that."[22]

Breather over, *Hot Fuss* shifted back into fifth gear with the disco devastation of 'Somebody Told Me', the album's second sure-fire indie classic, re-recorded at Cornerstone from its original demo form. "I always thought that was a great recording," Dave said. "We had a demo and at the last minute we decided, 'No, we can do better than the demo' and I've always loved the way it turned out."[23]

As if racing through the perfect debut album in under 20 minutes, 'All These Things That I've Done' provided an early finale. Having gained a chiming piano and church organ introduction, a military backbeat and a gospel choir called The Sweet Inspirations on its rising refrain of "I've got soul but I'm not a soldier" during the re-recording sessions, the tune had ballooned into a heart-bursting, hair-raising epic that could give a Gorgon goosebumps. The song would become the defining anthem of the new alt-rock breed fighting back against nu metal, imbuing the scene with that same kind of rootsy credibility that Jack White's re-imagining of the blues also achieved. It would have made a perfect album-closer, but instead here it was, thrown up as the grand edifice at the heart of *Hot Fuss*.

Following such an incredible opening, the latter half of the album inevitably seemed to pale; a series of less immediate tunes that grew in resonance with time. 'Andy, You're A Star', initially, seemed a cranky sort of obsession song, built around Dave's degenerate guitar slashes, twisted synths and Brandon's disquieting vocals, delivered with the blank-hearted malevolence of a stalker watching his prey from the undergrowth. Brandon's story was ultimately unthreatening though, a song about the sports star he admired and envied from afar in eighth grade in Peyton. "It's about a football player from my high school," he'd explain. "Teachers favour the football players and wrestlers. It's made known: these guys are special. In fact, the teachers encouraged the hierarchy, as a lot of them were coaches too. [It's] a song for a loner... the longhairs and the musicians, they would get treated the worst by the sportsmen and coaches. They were always bullied."[24] Yet the tune's bitter, biting tone ("On the field I remember you were incredible/Hey shut up, hey shut up, yeah," Brandon sang, "in a car with a girl/promise me she's not your world") eventually lifted for a chorus of unadulterated adoration, with a hint of distant ownership – "Andy, you're a star/In nobody's eyes but mine," Brandon sang over the elevating wails of the gospel choir. This knotted, gnawing ode to teenage dislocation, this cowed craving for acceptance and popularity, ultimately emerges as a very adult note of redemption.

The song would, perhaps understandably, be mistaken for a gay anthem, but Brandon would later counter that suggestion. "How do you know that Andy isn't, in fact, a girl?" he'd say, then instantly deny that he is. "But that doesn't mean it's a gay song... or certainly not as gay as 'Michael' by Franz Ferdinand. I just write stories, bizarre, weird, entertaining stories, and only sometimes are they autobiographical."[25]

If 'Andy...' was essentially innocent in intent, *Hot Fuss* was about to prove its experience. They'd never admit to it, but it's pretty clear that 'On Top' was The Killers' first sex song. To the cold parp of Numan-esque keyboards, Brandon let loose a lusty tale full of shaking bodies, bumps and grinds, curling cigarettes and coiled exotic passion: "Remember Rio, and get down/Like some other DJ in some other town... In the back, uh huh, I can't crack/We're on top... You really need it, so let go/And let me feed it". The tune built to a similarly frisky climax of flanged guitar and pulsing bass that only the distinctly un-sexy image of indie rock beards could help to dispel. Cue 'Glamorous Indie Rock & Roll'* and its very British-sounding satire of the American

---

* On editions of the album outside the UK and Australia, 'Change Your Mind' took this slot.

indie scene, as epitomised by the Café Roma crowd. "It's about people in Vegas who think they have the authority to be cruel and make people feel uncomfortable for being true to themselves,"[26] Brandon would explain. "We always wanted the bigness. A lot of times people just don't have the ability to write songs like we do and they hide behind the idea that they are underground or indie. But if they could write a song like we can, I think they would in a second."[27]

Employing a thumping Oasis beat, a spacious one-note piano line and Brandon's most Britpop nasal tone, the song didn't travel too well, since it was a song parodying indie rock while conforming precisely to what the UK had considered heartland indie for almost a decade. "In England people love it but don't get it," Brandon said. "In America, we knew they'd get it. If you're indie rock in America, you don't want to be played on the radio, you hate anyone who's signed to a major label, it's ridiculous to write a song, it's ridiculous to write a hook. They're just not capable of doing it so they hide behind that and say 'I'm indie'. Well they're idiots because melody is what makes the world go round. Why wouldn't you want to write a great song?"[28]

This writer played his own part in riling The Killers on this issue. When I interviewed them the following year on tour in Germany, I pointed out the similarity of the song to Shed Seven, a nineties band from Yorkshire who, in the UK, were the very definition of indie rock'n'roll. "I don't think that's what we aspire to be," Mark deadpanned. "I've never heard Shed Seven, but I guarantee we're better than Shed Seven. So I really don't care to talk about Shed Seven any more," snapped Brandon. "It's getting confused in England. Some people get it and some people don't. Some think we're being totally serious and like it and some people think we're being totally serious and realise it'd be cheesy if we're being totally serious. So there's all these different takes on it. It would've taken a different person to write 'Indie Rock & Roll' and be serious."[29] *

---

* The comparison would stick with Brandon; 10 years later when we revisited the feature for an anniversary retrospective, Brandon chuckled, "I've still never heard Shed Seven."

But what of the people, without a shred of irony, waving their lighters along to it at gigs? "We don't mean it like that," Brandon said. "It's kinda sad for the people who don't get it. I feel bad when I watch them, but there's always been songs like that. People get married to 'Every Breath You Take'." "Ronald Reagan used 'Born In The USA'," Mark added. Were they patronising their audience? "No," Dave argued, "that would be underestimating the audience. Music has always been that way, it's always been tongue-in-cheek." "We wrote the song and if they take it the wrong way, that's their fault,"[30] Brandon said. "Not a moment in my life has been spent trying to be indie. I feel like I have to put a memo out: look at the lyrics! It's ironic!"[31]

In America, perhaps so as not to offend the indie community, the track was replaced with 'Change Your Mind', an upbeat thumper of a pop tune more in the vein of fellow Britpop crooners Gene, built around nifty riffs on guitar and synth. It cast Brandon as a tragic figure racked with insecurity, expecting rejection from a girl but clinging on to the scrap of hope that he might be able to bring her around: "If the answer is no, can I change your mind?" A cracking tune that would become a cultish live favourite, it didn't, however, have the dynamic impact of 'Glamorous Indie Rock & Roll', and it would be the UK and Australian version that early fans would consider definitive.

The pounding drug-disco tragedy of 'Believe Me Natalie' wiped the smirk from the face of *Hot Fuss* in time for an edgy final push for the prize. 'Midnight Show', the opening scene of the murder trilogy now shunted to the closing credits, raced past in a flurry of murderous funk-punk adrenalin and finished with a burst of crackling picture house strings, ready for the happy ending. 'Everything Will Be Alright' sounded for all the world like one of Coleridge's icy pleasure domes; a hazy psychedelic finale reminiscent of prog rock lullabies like 10CC's 'I'm Not In Love' or Procol Harum's 'A Whiter Shade Of Pale'. Its misty, blissed-out mood was attained by heavy studio trickery: Brandon's voice was warped into a drowsy marshmallow fuzz and Ronnie's sparse, treated percussion was rendered practically electronic, while Dave's guitars wafted glacially through a Beatledelic chug on course for one of his finest solos. "I don't like simple Ramones power chords," he'd say of this amorphous, stately squeal that brought to mind Mick Ronson's seminal work on Bowie's *The Rise And Fall Of Ziggy Stardust And The Spiders From Mars*. "I prefer chords that have more flavour. Solos aren't necessarily in a lot of songs, but I'd like to do more of them on our second album. I thought we cut back a bit too much on *Hot Fuss*. I really like the solo in 'Everything Will Be Alright'. It's not one that people probably listen to because it's not a single, but that's the one I'm most proud of."[32]

The lyric was just as intangible as the song, an upbeat, airy tangle of images – toy dolls, suitcases, "dreamy eyes" – that gave the vague sense of closure on the agonies, lusts and crimes that had come before. It enhanced the surreal *Sgt. Pepper's…* feel, and the storybook slant to *Hot Fuss*; here was an elaborate catalogue of semi-fictions laid out like scenes and chapters in an ensemble revue. *Hot Fuss* was part Raymond Chandler, part Morrissey, part Scorsese, part Simon Le Bon, part Michael Alig, part David Copperfield. With such imagination, character, ambition and melodic clout behind it, it couldn't help but stand out in the early noughties ocean of Brooklyn funk-punk acts, Antipodean pub rock and Strokes clones.

In the warmth of a padded sound booth, the band listened back to the record, and nodded. It wouldn't be long now before the world knew what this feverish fuss was all about.

★ ★ ★

In November, The Killers signed another deal, this time covering Europe with Mercury Records. In announcing the deal, Ben Durling at Lizard King was firm in laying out the band's priorities. "The UK is the key territory for the band and they already have momentum here, so their US label are happy to let the plot develop in the UK before anywhere else."[33]

To that end, hiring Ryan Pardey as tour manager[*], The Killers set about touring the UK in earnest. Their first extended jaunt was that November in support of indie stalwarts British Sea Power. "We'd heard

---

[*] On later, bigger tours, Ryan would act as the merch guy for the band.

'Jenny ...' on an *NME* giveaway, and our booking agent Ross Warnock had sent us some other Killers tracks to listen to for a potential support band," says BSP guitarist Martin Noble. "They sounded like a northern English band to us. Hints of New Order, Morrissey and eighties synth pop. Not particularly cutting edge or cool like The Yeah Yeah Yeahs, but neither were we, and we thought they'd go down well with our fans so we agreed and just had to hope they weren't dicks. Fortunately they were lovely guys. Ronnie was obviously the most gregarious. Big warm welcomes from everyone every single day. Brandon was relatively chatty too, and had this excited nervous energy about him. Mark was a lovely quiet guy, and Dave, the enigma, seemed like an extraterrestrial in the form of Marc Bolan."

Since the venues they were playing were pubs, student unions and small provincial clubs – the Fez in Reading, the Soundhaus in Northampton, Colchester's converted church arts centre – it was a low-rent affair. "A travel day and a show day and a press day and you've got to see a doctor about the cold you have, that was all one day," Ronnie told me. "We cut our teeth on touring for weeks inside a van or a splitter making £110 max, $150. That was our guarantee. We slept two to a room, two rooms, we'd switch it up all the time."

"I have vivid memories of us slumming it in a van," Dave added, "the four of us, you couldn't sleep in it, it's called a splitter, you have the equipment in the back and you sit upfront. You'd have lobby calls of 10 a.m. because you'd actually have to drive to the next town instead of taking the bus to the next town. It was a lot different but it's a good thing we did that first because I was so happy to not have my job and I was enjoying England at the time. The gig I'll never forget is one we did in Lincoln. Our dressing room was in some little girl's bedroom. There was a venue in some guy's house or something and I remember putting my guitar case on a girl's bed and thinking 'This doesn't feel right'. But it was what we were told to do. Her toys were there, her stuffed animals, her Barbie dolls were still out. It was strange."

"That was the Bivouac," says Noble. "Essentially a function room above a big pub. The promoter there, a manic guy called Steve Hawkins, is pretty hands-on and DIY. He constructed a rickety PA stack himself

– he recently lost a finger when it collapsed on his hand. Steve used to put all this camouflage netting up around the place to make it look like a Bivouac, but it looked a bit more like the territorial army HQ. The dressing room was the bedroom of a newborn baby girl, decorated in pinks, teddies and dolls everywhere. The baby was probably downstairs in the pub. I also remember there was a thick fog, and they told us they'd walked up the cobbled streets to the Cathedral and were amazed by the history of the place. Coming from the desert of Las Vegas they said they'd never really seen fog! What The Killers made of all this I've no idea, though they seemed pretty excited to be playing in this strange ancient place. I think they thought they were in Dickensian England, and that the rest of England was covered in cobbles and fog."

Aside from experiencing British weather, this was also the first time The Killers had spent a prolonged length of time living in each other's pockets, and though the label was willing to pay for two rooms for the four of them rather than one this time, a few on-tour habits began to emerge. "Ronnie has a weird thing about fresh air," said Dave. "He almost always has to have a window open. If we're in a car, or a bus, or a hotel room. Almost claustrophobic. For instance, we take turns with who we stay with in a hotel room, and when I'm with Ronnie, he's gotta have a window open. Even if it's the middle of winter. And it kinda bugs me, but I can't really say anything because it's just a weird phobia. And I guess that the weird thing about Mark is that he's grumpy. But he's the nicest one! But he's not a morning person. He's very grumpy, and he's afraid of diseases. All of them."[34]

Brandon has fond memories of the trip, of wandering around Leeds in scarves, enjoying the novelty of the cold. "Our first trip to England was so great. The magic soon wore off a little bit but it was still unforgettable: playing the same clubs in London as Oasis when they started, going around Manchester visiting all the Smiths' sites... I was so used to singing along with Morrissey records in the car, I couldn't stop myself from adopting an English way of expressing my lyrics, even though I'd never even been to Manchester back then."[35]

It was also the point where The Killers began to feel the heat of the media spotlight start to rise. Several magazines took the opportunity to meet up with the band on the tour, and they would begin to hone their responses to some questions that would dog them for several years to come. *Logo* magazine quizzed them on playing in England and their relationship with the UK music scene. "It's been really nice," Brandon said. "We all come from working backgrounds, and it's a luxury to be off and playing in a different country for different people... we feel really fortunate to be able to do this sort of thing and to be received as well as we have been... The UK assimilates music better than the US does... or differently anyway. In the UK, the response has been appreciative and maybe the US doesn't show that appreciation; they enjoy music but it is very much part of the culture for you guys. New music is exposed here more... in England the audience is a little more receptive to newer [music]."[36] Brandon was open about his vaulting chart-bound ambition from the off. "We want to take what bands are doing, bands that are in our vein, to a more mainstream level. We have a lot of the same influences as other bands that are happening now, but we aren't afraid to make a pop song. Nowadays pop songs are only associated with people like Britney Spears or Christina Aguilera, and the rock crowd is afraid to be anywhere near that. But ultimately a good song is a good song, and the word pop is a subjective term."[37]

A major topic of fascination was inevitably their hometown, a place Brandon would later describe as "a 25-year-old single man's dream", but was then keen to play down. "It's a cultural desert," Brandon told *X-Ray* magazine, of Vegas. "It's really not that weird. We don't live in pyramids or anything – and there's a music scene, although it's mainly extremo. It's pretty normal. This band is a way to escape the madness of Vegas. We've all seen friends who've gambled away their money, become alcoholics. It makes you want to go the other way."[38]

From the off, The Killers weren't particularly comfortable with doing press. "If you look around, musicians aren't the funniest, most articulate or outgoing people," said Brandon. "We're mostly shy and have a hard time speaking to people."[39] Nor were they particularly happy with each other at this point: "When we first started touring, it was a complete lifestyle change," Dave recalled. "We got really cranky and hated each other for a little bit."[40]

Yet, as the tour wore on, The Killers became almost as big a draw as the headliners. The venues were packed for their sets, their T-shirts and CDs would sell out, the crowd – real fans, not industry figures any more – would line the barriers, mouthing every word of the songs they'd managed to get hold of. A momentum was building.

"Opening bands in America aren't watched," Brandon added. "[The audience will] be getting drinks and they'll show up late. But when we were with British Sea Power here we got full attention, it was good."[41]

"The Killers show was impressive," Noble says. "They were definitely the strongest support act we'd seen. Even in a function room above a pub in Lincoln they gave it everything. They weren't particularly cool or glamorous back then, but they clearly had some strong tunes. The audience responded well to them on most nights. BSP used to descend into chaos and trash our stage at the end of gigs. I think The Killers liked the ridiculousness and performance of it. I'd like to think it encouraged them to loosen up as the tour went on. Brandon threw himself into it more and more and had this wide-eyed intensity. Ronnie had a bit of Keith Moon cheekiness and would stand up to play the drums occasionally. It was a fun time. All gravy."

The Killers quickly won over the British Sea Power fans. "The first time I remember seeing them play is at Lincoln Bivouac," says BSP fan Kevo. "It was a dark and stormy autumnal night and a couple of us had travelled up from London and got stuck on a one-carriage train somewhere in the Fens... When we eventually got to the venue someone had been to the pick'n'mix section of a sweet shop before the gig and we fed the Killers sherbert flying saucers, which they'd never seen before. It was obvious they had some great tunes even then, and they pretty much immediately won the hearts of the BSP faithful. From that night on, we all made sure we were in the venue in time to see them instead of staying in the pub."

"Near the end of the tour we played a show at Warwick University that Steve Lamacq was broadcasting," says Noble. "The first support, incidentally, were Snowfield, who became Editors. Our travelling fans were clearly enjoying them by now and by that point some were even singing along to 'Mr. Brightside', 'Smile Like You Mean It' and

'Somebody Told Me'. We couldn't get those songs out of our heads either. We'd become infected. I remember a drunken love-in with The Killers – 'You're our favourite new band' we declared to each other, that kind of thing."

The tour bled into the start of December with a one-off show back at the Upstairs @ The Garage venue, a 200-capacity room with far more than its fair share of star quality that night. "We opened for The Dirtbombs," said Ronnie, referring to a garage rock band from the thriving Detroit scene that had already produced The White Stripes, "and we were having a really good time onstage, so much so that The Dirtbombs' manager was giving us the stink-eye. I remember nearly totally mangling Renée Zellweger with my cymbal stand, too. Jack White was there and they were dating at the time. It was such a weird gig."[42] Such was their indie star-drawing capability at this time that, at one early UK show, they came offstage to find an uninvited Peter Doherty taking drugs with a girl in their dressing room.

This early tour finished with a major landmark for The Killers; their first brush with the direct competition. British Sea Power were invited to support The Strokes at the Motorpoint Arena in Cardiff, and as a result BSP managed to sneak The Killers into The Strokes' after-show party at the cavernous Alexandra Palace a few days later. "They clearly loved the occasion and the buzz backstage," Noble recalls. "They weren't big drinkers however, so it was left solely to us to discuss the merits of premium strength beers with John McEnroe."

It was a key moment for the band as, for the first time, it put them in the same room as one of the bands they set out to take on as peers. "Between 1995 and 2000 music was just terrible," said Dave, "it was garbage. I'll just write it off now. We met in 2001 about the time things were starting to get better with bands like The Strokes, but we both felt that there'd really been a void until then."

"That's why we're in a band," said Brandon, "we just think that the world needs more good music. We like to listen to our own music about as much as anything else at the time. We're not afraid to be pop. A lot of indie bands just try and be weird and metal bands just scream but we want to write great pop songs."[43] "We are a great rock band," he'd add, "it's as simple as that. We're as good as The Strokes, Kings Of Leon and The White Stripes."[44]

"There's a movement happening," Brandon would tell me the following year, aligning his band with the new generation of guitar greats, "it's awesome and we're just glad to be a part of it: Franz Ferdinand, The Yeah Yeah Yeahs, us, The Strokes, British Sea Power…"[45]

And just when The Killers were elbowing their place alongside the hottest bands on Earth, mingling with the biggest names in alternative rock, they very nearly became one of rock's most tragic stories…

★ ★ ★

Rushing through the muted aeroplane like a dagger, the siren shook the cabin. A wailing electronic whoop, it froze The Killers, and all of the passengers on their Continental Airlines connecting flight back to Vegas out of Houston. Hearts leapt, pulses rocketed, armrests gripped tight. For a second, nothing happened. The Killers began to laugh among themselves.

Then, the plane fell out of the sky.

"The plane just fucking drops," Brandon said, recalling the sheer panic as the storm-struck plane turned on its side and plunged for what seemed a lifetime. "It felt like we'd hit the ground. People were flying out of their chairs and the noise from all the praying and screaming was unreal. We just thought 'Hey, we're gonna be the one of those bands everyone loves because we're dead.'"[46]

"It was the scariest thing any of us have ever experienced," said Mark. "We really thought the plane was going to crash. Some 13 tornados hit Texas that night. We had a good insurance policy – but that wouldn't have been much use if we were dead."[47] "The plane just dropped," said Ronnie. "Imagine the headlines."[48]

Rolling out of the air pocket that had dropped it 1,000 feet earthward, the plane righted itself and deposited a very shaken Killers at Vegas airport. "They called me immediately when they landed," Braden said, "and said 'We're not flying any more! That's it!' They've since changed their minds due to commitments, obviously."[49] They laughed at the time, but the incident would stay with Brandon for years, making him psychologically terrified of flying. Ultimately, he'd seek therapy for his phobia, and write one of his most stirring songs about it.

Safely back in Vegas and with their album sent off to be mastered, The Killers took a short break for Christmas while plans were laid for the next wave of attack. The year 2003 ended with more plaudits – *The Sunday Times* included 'Mr. Brightside' in its list of the Top 20 songs of the year, stating "'Queen Bitch' met 'Planet Earth' on this astonishing debut tour de force from a Las Vegas band who will be all over 2004 like a rash. Rarely has a cuckold's wallowed-in paranoia been set to such a (forgive the pun) killer tune."[50] And 2004 was gearing up to be a huge year for the band; numerous magazines were tipping them to break big in the coming year. *Spin* magazine listed them among its 25 bands to watch, *The Daily Express* had them nestled alongside The Scissor Sisters and Joss Stone as sure-fire future stars. *NME* featured them in their annual start-of-the-year tip-sheet, the band posed on a light-up eighties dance floor with Brandon sporting a stylish black blazer and white shirt and Ronnie in a neon pink jumper.[*]

Their second blitz on Britain, they decided, would be 'Somebody Told Me'. Set for release on March 15, 2004, it would be a tester of a single to see how much of an appetite the UK had for the band. Lizard King printed up two formats of the single, on CD and 7-inch, the three-track CD[**] boasting the B-sides 'Under The Gun' and a track dedicated to their old gambler and musician friend from Vegas, 'The Ballad Of Michael Valentine'[***]. Recalling Paul McCartney's seventies spin-off Wings – with a touch more rock ballast – a rough-hewn demo version of the track made the single, complete with Brandon's voice cracking and giggling through the higher notes as he told this playful

---

[*] This shoot would cause some hilarity among the band in later years, as Brandon would pore over the shoot and chuckle, "We were all funny looking in this one. I look like a twerp. I'm such a tart! Dave looks good… he looks hungry. He's full now!" "That is one starving kid right there," Dave would add. Source: *NME*, September 24, 2005.

[**] The first 200 copies of which came with a free poster.

[***] The pink vinyl 7-inch version included just 'Somebody Told Me' and 'The Ballad Of Michael Valentine'.

story of a road-tripping gambler lothario in a "new suit and your black tie" who "plays with stars", picks up "soul sisters" and "black-eyed ladies" on his travels from Dallas to New Orleans to Memphis and North Dakota, "although my heart's in Mexico". The night out described in the song was fictional, but giving his hero the panache of antique cinema, Brandon claimed, wasn't even a hint of exaggeration. "He's amazing," he'd say of this tall and charismatic hustler with a penchant for Dickens, Melville and Austen. "He's like something out of a movie. He's a professional gambler who acts as if he's from the fifties, like Brando or something." "A lot of people in Vegas say they're professional gamblers but they actually lose," Mark added. "Others advertise their services as professional gamblers, saying they'll teach you how to play, say, blackjack the best you can."[51]

For 'Somebody…', The Killers needed to make their first ever music video. And there was only one place they could start their band's cinematic adventure: at 'Crystal'. As if the fictional band from New Order's video had sprung out of the screen straight into the Nevada desert, the band headed out into the wilds in February with director Brett Simon to shoot a live performance video in front of a giant screen which, itself, was showing the band performing. "We went out into the desert near LA," Brandon explained. "We shot it in the day in the middle of nowhere and then projected it onto a Jumbotron at night, a big gigantic screen, you know? Then we played in front of it at night as well so you see us in the back in the daytime playing but it's dark and we're playing. It was pretty cool."[52] *

Though the night-time desert setting didn't exactly exude the sweeping desolation perhaps intended – much of the night-time live shots could easily have been filmed in a studio – the video was a fantastic showcase for the band's slick shirt-and-blazer style, deadpan cool and electric live delivery, and also their eye-catching new logo, the band's name formed from dots like Vegas casino lights.

With such a fiery electro-pop tune and a band-defining video to match, it was no wonder the song set fire to the UK. *NME*'s Pete

---

* The band liked the video so much they'd also use it for the US release of the song in May.

Cashmore was suitably enthused in his review: "Franz Ferdinand on space-cakes and a seven-figure jackpot high, is what 'Somebody Told Me' (Lizard King) from Las Vegas bellboys turned rock'n'rollers The Killers sound like," he wrote. "It's jitter-pop with Casio keyboards, glitter-rock flourishes and a Bowie-esque tale of gender-bending boyfriends. Where are the guitars? The bottom of the hotel pool, where they belong."[53]

Meanwhile, led by Zane Lowe, Radio 1 was playing the song 35 times a week. It moved from the specialist shows to playlists, and the singles really started to fly. Realising it was onto a huge hit if it played it right, Lizard King actually quenched the heat around 'Somebody Told Me' with the intention of re-releasing it as a major breakthrough song for the band later down the line. "What I believe happened," Braden explains, "was the label said that Radio 1 and Radio 2 really wanted to cane the song, but they asked them to hold back on it so we made that one disappear and reintroduced it later in the year after the album was out. I think they wanted to test it. We all felt it was such a great song and the fact that Radio 2 wanted to play it... that was the mainstream Tesco of the world and we didn't want to go into that arena just yet, we wanted to build an equal fanbase and didn't want to alienate any of our journalist relationships by going into there. We wanted to build it."

With the radio fever quelled for the time being, 'Somebody Told Me' sold 10,000 copies and hit the UK charts at a relatively modest number 28. But on the tour to promote it there was no hiding the Killersmania breaking out. Flying into the UK on February 13 for a warm-up support slot with Jet at the Hammersmith Palais and their own headline show at the ICA in London[*], they then returned to Vegas for a family and friends show at the Ice House Lounge, then flew back to Leeds to start a tour playing as support to the similarly pop-leaning indie act Stellastarr★ from NYC. From that opening night at the Cockpit, The Killers simply stole the tour. The clubs would be rammed full for The Killers' opening set,

---

[*] After which Mark raced to the Camden Barfly club to DJ under the name DJ Perfect Storm.

then half deserted for the headliners. It was clear the band could easily headline those same venues the next chance they got.

Wending down the country through the bigger clubs – the Manchester Hop & Grape, the Sheffield Leadmill, Camden's sizeable Electric Ballroom – the band broke off from the tour to record a session for Zane Lowe at Radio 1 and to play a one-off support slot at the Shepherd's Bush Empire for Gary Numan. They didn't meet the dark lord of goth-pop, though. "I just remember Gary Numan not giving a shit," Ronnie said. "Pretty funny. I don't think he said two words to us."[54] They did, however, run into Alan Moulder for the first time since he'd finished mixing the album. Alan pointed to the slavering crowds excitedly. "He was saying, 'Well, it worked! We did it!'" Brandon laughed.[55]

The UK leg of the tour finished with shows in Bristol, Portsmouth and Sheffield, amid a flurry of excitable media hype. Brandon was a little dazzled by interviews at first, and group sessions tended to descend into stilted silences as none of The Killers wanted to presume they could step into the role of band spokesman. Hence, Brandon came across as rather curt and repetitive in these interviews, yet to open up on tape. Often he resorted to the bare bones of his story, declaring his love for U2 and Morrissey, and Britrock in general. "We're all into British music," he said. "It's a great compliment to be compared to The Cure or U2. It's weird but a good weird, and I guess it makes sense that British people have latched on to us… I tell people our music is a mix of Duran Duran and The Rolling Stones. Recently I've really got into 'The Chauffeur' and probably before that was 'New Moon On Monday', I love that one… I just really want to be important… I'd really like to be America's answer to U2."[56] He even credited his stagecraft to UK influences. "I guess I can't really help myself. Once we start playing those songs, they're so good, it's easy to just go for it. That's one of the things I've always admired about Morrissey. He owns everyone when he goes onstage. I guess that's what I'm pushing for. I couldn't just stand there and sing."[57]

Questioned on 'Somebody Told Me', he was uncomfortable with being labelled an electro band as a result of the track, and the media's wont for instant pigeonholing. "With that song, the dance comes across and that's the keyboards. Then there are other songs where there's no keyboards because that's the John Lennon side or something. I'm not worried about being pinned on anything, but they wanna say 'This is a dance band' and we really aren't just that."[58] But not as uncomfortable as he would be when later quizzed on the sexually ambiguous nature of the song's chorus line. "I'm not gay," he'd insist, point blank, his interest in playing with androgyny waning under repeated interrogation on the topic. "I can't even be bothered to start any kind of intrigue about it. Bowie could nurture that sort of mystique, but this is an age when everybody knows everything about you in 10 seconds."[59]

With 'Somebody Told Me' causing an almighty stir in Britain, The Killers saw the chance to up the ante for the Stateside release in May, too. A week after their last UK date, they were booked to play two shows on the same day at that year's South By Southwest festival, the week in February when the entire US music industry descends on Austin, Texas, to snort, gorge and gossip their way through gigs by hundreds of that year's array of hotly tipped bands. At an event where every showcase is an orgy of barbecue, margarita and hype, it pays to get noticed. So at one show The Killers got themselves introduced onstage by legendary US comedian David Cross, who claimed, "I'd never heard The Killers before today, but now I'm a fan. I'll definitely be buying their album when it comes out." And at their show at Stubb's BBQ for a *Spin* magazine showcase, they set out to make 'All These Things That I've Done' a full-on festival-stopper.

Somewhere in Austin earlier that day, Braden slammed $800 in cash onto a reverend's desk at a nearby Baptist church and asked him if his gospel choir could learn the "I got soul but I'm not a soldier" refrain for that night's set. A brief 20-minute rehearsal in the church and they'd nailed it. Impressed, Braden booked them a bus to the venue, they had a minute's practice with the band out back of Stubb's and then the choir, in full robes and with instructions just to "give it your best shot", took the stage and brought the house down first time.

Such a simple idea, but its aftershocks were devastating. "The Killers are bona fide rock stars," wrote Joshua Ellis of *CityLife*, reviewing the set. "They sounded better than I'd ever heard them. They even got a local Austin choir to sing with them, for God's sake. The two bands that followed them – The Von Bondies and The Hives – are far more famous but sounded tired by comparison." The band were selected to feature on the prestigious *Music Week* SXSW CD, which highlighted the most promising bands of the festival, and they found themselves nominated for a Diesel-U-Music award at the event.

The Best Rock Act award – voted for by journalists, manager, bands and label reps at the festival – fell to The Killers. As a result, they were heavily promoted by Diesel on a CD and online but, as the crowd of microphones clawed at them demandingly across the velvet rope, it left them cripplingly uncomfortable with the idea of attending award ceremonies at all. "We realised early on," Brandon said, "especially on red carpets, that it was unnatural for us. There have never been four more uncomfortable people on the red carpet, it was so awkward. We realised this was going to do us more harm than good because the interviewers were latching onto the wrong things. It was so uncomfortable. We were more affected in the beginning, but now it's toned down and we made it out pretty much unscathed."[60]

Nonetheless, the US industry started to take serious notice. Which meant that, when a certain Steven Patrick Morrissey hit LA for four nights at the Wiltern theatre without a support act in tow, The Killers' calls were snatched up, first ring.

"It was such a big deal for the band," Braden says. "I remember having several discussions with our agent Kirk Sommer and just saying 'Dude, I know Morrissey is coming to America, does he have support worked out?' We were on the road [with Stellastarr*] so we would have to re-route. Kirk called me up and said 'Hey, I talked to Morrissey's management and sent them the music along with all the press that is happening in England, and find out Morrissey is already a fan and knows the band!' so I said to Kirk 'Let's try and re-route this tour and do one of these shows'. He was doing four shows at the world tournament in LA, he wanted us to do all four shows but we could only do two of them and one in Chicago, which was at the House of Blues, but I'll never forget when I called Brandon and said 'Brandon, I've got some news for you, we are going to have to move some stuff around on the calendar but we are going to be opening up for Morrissey in Los Angeles' and he just fucking shit himself! Oh my God, the band was so excited about that news, to open up for one of their heroes."

Having worshipped him on screen and turntable, had his gushings shunned over a mushroom pizza and attempted a heist on his comeback album, Brandon's wildest dreams of sharing a stage with one of his biggest heroes was about to come true; this would be more than a storm in a stolen Spago teacup. Their 25 nationwide US club dates – stretching from Portland to Phoenix and beyond – couldn't go by fast enough, despite daily reminders of how big they were getting. "I'll never forget DC," Braden laughs. "We show up to this club called the Black Cat, which is about 600 capacity, and Stellastarr★ are the headliner. We go on and the place is just totally sold out. By the time we are done there's maybe 60 people left for Stellastarr★. That started to happen all around the country."

At New York's Irving Plaza, a pivotal gig in an influential city, The Killers' breakthrough chances very nearly went up in smoke. Quite literally – Dave would play everything through a classic Fender Hot Rod DeVille amp, a brand prone to spontaneous combustion. "I did have one explode in New York," he said. "We were about three seconds into the second song and the amp just blew up. There were 1,500 people there and New Yorkers can sometimes be a critical crowd, so I had to do something. It was embarrassing because I had to climb over amps while trying to look cool, but thankfully the band that were on after us had a DeVille, so I grabbed it without asking and managed to get back in by the time the next song started. The show had to go on!"[61]

Finally, come April 10 at the Wiltern, Brandon peered out from the stage during their soundcheck and there the great man was, settled out at the mixing desk in silence, watching intently.

"I was very nervous," Brandon admitted. "I wish I'd waved now. I did put on a show for him though."[62] "Apparently he was tapping his foot... He'd bought our single – that's nuts!"[63]

Backstage, things weren't quite so harmonious. All entreaties from the band or famous hangers-on, like Chloë Sevigny and Fran Drescher, there to meet Morrissey, were rebuffed by his manager with a firm "nobody meets Morrissey". Instead, besides a curt greeting in a hallway, Morrissey all but blanked Brandon when he tried to speak to him, reducing him once more to the level of a lowly pizza waiter hassling for face-time. "I was devastated," Brandon said. "I read an interview with him in which he said Marc Bolan, his idol, did the very same thing to him years earlier and it crushed him. So why did he do that to me?"[64] As time went by and his own fame grew, though, Brandon would become more philosophical about the event. "I'll never forget that second – Morrissey knew who I was!"[65] he'd say. "[And] he did mention us onstage, which he never usually does. We cling to that nugget. Morrissey really was unbelievable. Everybody did want to touch him. If our fans felt that way about us, that would be awesome."[66] *

Back on the Stellastarr* tour, the road began to wear them down. *The Sunday Times'* Dan Cairns joined the band in San Francisco nine weeks into the Stellastarr* stint, and found them tour-weary but in bullish, confident mood. "I think of [sleep] more than I ever used to," said Dave, exhausted from heaving his own gear around the country for two months straight. "I'd sleep on this bench right now."[67] As a row broke out over Mark taking an unscheduled toilet break, they admitted to spots of in-fighting: "We lose it every once in a while, some more than others," Dave said, while Brandon was a little more diplomatic about the stresses and struggles of touring the States – "We all had expectations of what this would be and some things are getting met, and some things aren't... America's the market that's the hardest. We have the big dogs behind us, but there are so many bands that do. If you're not Kid Rock, it's going to be really hard."[68]

Brandon also grumbled about the pressures of press and radio interviews. "We're an intelligent band and we have intelligent songs," he said, "and these people who are interviewing us are used to these kids, which we're really not. We have the mentality almost of an underground band, but

---

* This wouldn't be the last time Morrissey would shun The Killers. In 2012, the band would ask their hero to sing with them in New York, only to receive a polite refusal. Morrissey told the *Herald Sun* newspaper, "I find it difficult to be anything other than honest, and this makes me sound like an old crank. I can't say 'Yes' when I mean 'No' – my jaw literally locks. The Killers asked me to sing with them this month in New York, but I'm just not the type. I stick to my own backyard."

they're asking us mainstream questions. That's where we're colliding."[69] It was, it transpired, the expectations of grand rock pronouncements and the fantasy rock star personalities that the media projected upon him that caused Brandon to feel as though he wasn't able to truly be himself, instead playing a part written for him. "People who are on our side call it 'coming out of yourself', when really they want you to fake it," he said. "We need to find a middle ground. A half-fake." "It's as if they want you to be a comedian and an actor,"[70] Dave added.

Brandon's self-belief remained resolutely undulled, however. Asked if The Killers were the best band in the history of Vegas, he replied, "No, we're the best band in the history of the world."[71]

The tour was proving tough, but the endless on-the-road grind from radio session to meet-and-greet to soundcheck to media appointment was brightened by regular firsts, invigorating signs that the band was breaking through. Cairns witnessed one in San Francisco: while they were driving to an acoustic radio session in the band's van, Braden – who'd been told that the influential station K-Rock had been the first US radio station to play 'Somebody Told Me' and tastemaker Aaron Axelsen at Live 105[*] was set to follow suit – checked that it was 12.15 p.m. and turned on the radio just as the song kicked in, the first time The Killers ever heard themselves on the radio.

"I knew we were good, that we had great songs," said Dave. "I just thought, if only we're given a chance, people will respond. And they did. I knew we were as good as any band on the radio, and here we are, on the radio!"[72]

'Somebody Told Me' caught on US radio like the valley brushfires. Within weeks, 55 stations, largely on the West Coast, had the song on rotation, and America woke up to The Killers with a start. The effect was virtually instant; at the Coachella Valley Music And Arts Festival of 2004, playing low on the bill in a sweltering tent[**], they

---

[*] "Sort of the Zane Lowe of America," he explains.

[**] Even in such a lowly slot, Brandon was fittingly deferential, telling the *Las Vegas Review-Journal*, "It is weird doing Coachella before we even have an album out. But it's also an honour."

drew a wild crowd of thousands, blown away by the appearance of the Mount Cavalry Holy Church Choir during 'All These Things That I've Done'. "It worked so well at SXSW," Braden says, "that we thought, 'Okay, here's Coachella, we're trying to impress American radio and the journalists that are here'. So I got a local church choir to come out and sing on that song inside the tent. That show was freaking awesome, even though it was 110 degrees at three o'clock in the afternoon, but it was an amazing experience. We felt we were much bigger in the UK than America and Coachella was really the launching point of our radio story and press story for the band. There were about 2,500 people in this tent, partying."

Brandon, however, only remembered the heat. "Radiohead and The Cure played, which was cool, but the daytime was just miserable," he said. "It was too warm."[73] Little did he know he'd be craving the Coachella climate come the mud bath of Glastonbury.

'Somebody Told Me' was released in the US in May and, though it wouldn't make a huge dent on the charts this time around, it launched The Killers as a serious alternative rock proposition in the US. "Where their demo tracks were muddled, hotchpotch affairs exploring a variety of influences but never settling on a signature sound," wrote the *Las Vegas Mercury*, "their debut single is brimming with confidence and character." Online, fan forums were beginning to spring up dedicated to the band, their devotees referring to themselves as The Victims.

And just as 'Somebody Told Me' was making waves in America, the band prepared to set off a tsunami in Britain.

The UK was about to go on a Killers spree.

Dave Keuning, March 2014

How did you celebrate when Lizard King picked you up for your first record deal?

I don't remember celebrating. I was very happy. None of us quit our jobs. All I knew is they were gonna fly us out for four shows in London. We were all thrilled about that, we thought if that's the only thing that comes of it then we were cool with that. That's more than most bands from Las Vegas get to do. Paid-for flights, paid-for hotel – even if it was at the Columbia, the Columbia was fun. Now I don't think I could go back, but at the time it was fun.

What happened when you were turned away from the stage door at the Barfly?

The Barfly have the smallest backstage in the world, it's like a closet, so I can't totally blame the guy. We had played with the band and I was just trying to go back there to either grab a drink or say hello and wasn't allowed in.

The reaction in the UK caused a whirlwind of press and label interest back home – how did that feel?

It felt amazing because we'd had almost a year or more of these labels not saying yes but not saying no. I was just getting sick of that. But having them all come down and taking us out for dinner, that felt good. That was probably one of the funnest times of my life, it was such a hopeful, optimistic time where we were gonna get signed by one of them and we got to pick. Not that every label gave us a deal, but there were at least four or five to pick from.

What do you remember about the CMJ gig?

I basically had some sort of technical difficulties on the very first song which was 'Jenny Was A Friend Of Mine', and it was an important showcase, a lot riding on it. I thought there was a lot of risk at the time, but it turns out there wasn't a lot of risk at all because they wanted to sign us no matter what. I just didn't wanna go back to Banana Republic so I was pretty shaken up about the whole thing. I had to stop in the middle of the song and the other guys continued to play and it messed with my pedal board. I managed to play the rest of the show without my pedals. As a musician it sucked. We were trying to impress so I was pretty pissed off. I didn't storm off stage, but when we were done I just packed up and left. I didn't wanna talk to anybody.

Were you relieved to find out it was all fine?
I was just thrilled to find out we got a deal, and it didn't matter.

Did you do anything extravagant with your chunk of the money?
Well we didn't get a lot of money up front. I think we got $20,000 a piece to kind of get started. At the time I was broke, so I saved a lot of it and just lived off it. I was pretty good at saving but actually I was hitting rock bottom as far as money goes. I had stretched my money as far as it could go – I even lived with Brandon's parents for a few months in between there. I moved out of my apartment. The last couple of months I lived with a different guy and he didn't pay me rent because he lost it on gambling. I had to move out. It was at the right time because I was basically homeless after living with Brandon's parents, because we went on tour for two years after that.

How do you feel about *Hot Fuss* when you listen back to it now?
I still love it. *Hot Fuss* is still very sentimental to me at least, maybe not the other guys. It's still a strong album and I hear a lot of joy in the songs from when we were making them.

Were there initial frictions within the band on tour?
No, [but] it didn't take long for there to be some friction. It's kind of like moving in with a friend. It never goes as planned but I think it took a while for there to be real friction. We got along pretty well in the early days.

What were your best video experiences on *Hot Fuss*?
I think 'Somebody Told Me' was a fun one. It was in the desert and it was cold, a lot colder than it looks. It was the first big production one we did, so it felt special. I'm getting sick of desert videos now.

Mark Stoermer, April 2014

What can you remember about those first UK shows?
None of us had travelled overseas so it was kinda mind-blowing. We were all wide-eyed and jet-lagged and had never experienced anything like it. You think you're in another universe. It all went by really fast. I remember the very first show at the Dublin Castle, we got up onstage and we had a heckler who said "All right! Show us what you got!" And then we played 'Somebody Told Me' and I think we impressed him – he shut up! The first one was pretty good then the second one – I think at the Metro club – there were, like, two people there. It started to get a little weird, like "Oh, maybe that first one was a good one and that's it". Then there was the magical night at Club Motherfucker above the Garage where you put the bass amp through a little square about 2 × 2ft – it's a really weird way to get in, you come in through a hole because you can't get the equipment onstage any other way. That was the night where there were record execs from the States in the room. We kinda had a bad show at the Metro and it was starting to be like "It was fun while it lasted, we came to England at least", but that show there was the spark, the magic there, and we had one of our best shows ever. Not just at that point, probably ever, even though it was a short 20-minute set. I think everybody was impressed in the room; it felt like everyone knew something was happening. Word got back to the States so when we did CMJ music fest it was almost already a done deal. We had every label in the States that was interested in the room in New York because of the performance in London.

Did you do anything extravagant to celebrate the Island Def Jam deal?
That night? It seemed like we just got to work. That night was the night we went to the Tribeca Grand and I didn't even know it was the Tribeca Grand then. It was our first time in New York, none of us had been to New York – we went to London before we went to New York. That was the night everyone was celebrating in this A&R guy's hotel suite at the top of the Tribeca Grand and Ronnie peed off the balcony

and it landed on a security guard and he ran up the stairs. Ronnie went "I think someone spilled a drink!" After that it felt like we were busy non-stop, but every day something was happening. We didn't have time to enjoy it on some level because it was "We gotta go back to England" or "We gotta go back to America", which was good, that's where we paid our dues really, that first year from the time we got signed onwards. We were busy every day. Sometimes we played 27 shows in a row or something without a day off.

You've said you were getting to know each other on those early tours – what sort of relationships were being formed?
We're all very different people. Dave and Brandon met through an ad and me and Ronnie were picked up through the scene, but none of us went to school together or anything. We were four Musketeers who all knew what the goal was, to be as good as we can and do the best shows that we can and plod along through the shows. I think everybody was dealing with the reality of being on tour for the first time in their own way, but at the same time we were all relatively young and had the energy. It wasn't affecting anyone too badly, we could go on three hours' sleep a night and play to 20 people and still be excited about the next show if there's 50 people. I think we got to know each other that way, for better or for worse.

What can you remember from the British Sea Power tour?
I remember we played Lincoln, which we never went back to ever again, but that was kinda fun. I remember feeling from another time, stepping out of the splitter van, seeing the fog rolling in the streets and some guy who looked like he belonged in the 1800s smoking a pipe on the street corner. I also remember that same gig the bar that we played in was connected to a house, and that's where the owner or manager lived, and the dressing room was in a child's bedroom. There was a little kid's bed and some toys and they put some beer and water in that room for the band. We're sitting in this kid's room waiting to go on! I also remember it was our first experience of the British winter, it being dark and cold and, having never been on tour before, two weeks felt like two months. There

was a point when, even though I was excited about what was going on, I woke up thinking "What am I doing?" Having to get in the splitter van, only getting three hours' sleep a night – I almost had a bit of a freak out, internally. That was when we were sharing rooms, too, we never had any space. It was a shock just to be on tour in general.

How was the Stellastarr★ tour, when you were stealing the show every night?

We almost felt bad for them because half or more than half of the audience was usually there for us, even though they were the headliner technically. We'd play to a full house in England and noticed that when Stellastarr★ went on, sometimes people were leaving. We continued that same tour in the States though, and there was a turnaround again because they were definitely the headliner in America at the time. We were gaining steam over in the UK but then we came back here and it flipped again. That was a fairly long tour, three or four months, but we were glad to get on the bill – it made sense at the time and everyone got along. That's eventually where we got our tour manager from, we kinda stole him.

Ben Durling, May 2014

You first heard the songs via Alex Gilbert?

I was having a meeting with him one day. He'd been in LA and said "There's this band I quite like, The Killers from Vegas" and he played me 'Mr. Brightside'. I heard it and thought "This is amazing", obviously, amazing name, from Vegas, then he played me 'Somebody Told Me'. Alex's boss Christian wasn't interested allegedly so I called up Braden and said "Do you wanna do an EP in the UK?" "Yes". That EP then turned into an album deal for one album for the UK only, a five-year licence. We knew we'd got a coup at the time, getting that for no money. I was managing a band called Longview at the time and working for Lizard King – I'd been there for six months doing some consultancy. This comes along and I went to Lizard King and said "We have to do this" and they went "Okay, this is brilliant, we'll do that", and we did the deal. It was the first thing I'd brought in to be put out on Lizard King. We did the deal, brought them into London for four shows, Monday, Tuesday, Wednesday and Thursday. They stayed at the Columbia, standard. Conor [McNicholas, then *NME* editor] was at the very first show – Rachel [Hendry] was standing next to him and after two songs I remember turning around to her and Rachel giving me two thumbs up. In those days, without the *NME* you were nowhere.

Was it a brave move to sign them without ever seeing them?
I saw a DVD. A friend of mine, Angus Blair, who now works at Global, he was working at Chrysalis publishing at the time, I told him about the band and he managed to get hold of a DVD of a live show in Vegas. They looked like four weird kids, dressed weirdly in a Vegas club playing these brilliant pop songs. So we knew they could play. Because it was just an EP we thought it'd be fine, I didn't need to go all the way out there and wine and dine them and see them play live, let's do it anyway. That first show at the Dublin Castle, we were a bit crossed-fingers, and they weren't great. By the time they were playing Shepherd's Bush Empire 15 months later they still weren't that great, they were just brilliant songs and they did them well enough. Mark just stands there playing bass, Ronnie's always jumping about, they're kinda four weird guys, and Brandon's quite an odd character really. Lovely, but they were quite a hotchpotch of four weird guys from Vegas. It was kind of the *NME* that brought them together, they were the four people that bought the four copies of *NME* in Vegas.

What were they like when you met them?
When we brought them in, that first week I went and met them at the Columbia and we sat in the bar area, they'd literally just got off the plane and I went "Right, this is what you're gonna do this week, this is how we want to do things…" and they just sat there like I was some kind of alien. They didn't say very much, they were really quiet. None of them had really been outside of Vegas, let alone outside of America. Even for that first six months or a year, we spent a lot of time with them because they were here a lot, they never really changed that much. There was a moment

151

about six months into the campaign when there was a slight wobble from the *NME*, like "There's not enough personality here". We had to just get over that and nurse them through it. I remember we went for a pizza in Bayswater that first night and they were four young men who'd never been outside Vegas being completely freaked out by everything.

How did the first EP go?

We put the single out and we got Zane [Lowe] to play it and I remember Lauren Laverne played it on XFM and didn't like it. In those days it really was Radio 1's *The Evening Session* and *NME*, those are your two start points and we felt we had both of them – Conor came to that first show.

At what point could you see it was kicking off?

We went to SXSW the following March and we'd put out 'Mr. Brightside' as an EP and we were going with 'Somebody Told Me', and this was just pre-downloads. They'd already done their deal with Island Def Jam in the US and it was getting loads of specialist play at Radio 1 and XFM and we were like "We need to midweek this inside the Top 30, if we can midweek it at number 25 without proper Radio 1 support, that's the barometer that we're absolutely in the game". Island Def Jam, who had got the band for the rest of the world, knew that we were leading the campaign and were really worried that we were just keeping our fingers crossed. They made a TV ad for 'Somebody Told Me' to be shown on MTV2 that we spent a week arguing with them about, going "Please don't stick this band on a TV ad on the first single, it's the wrong look, you've got to trust us". They booked it in to be run on the Tuesday night the week the record came out – I was with the band in Austin at the time – the midweek came out on the Tuesday morning, it was 23, and they pulled the ad and went "Okay, we trust you". The single went in at 25 and Radio 1 in those days were like "Bosh, the next one goes on". We would've put out 'Mr. Brightside' next, which was an A-list record, and the album followed.

Was it always the plan to re-release those early singles?

Yeah. We felt it was the right thing to do. People had been doing it. The idea then of going back on something, you're making a very limited run to start off with. These days it doesn't matter because people can get it online or stream it. Then, it really was limited so you felt you could control it a little bit more. If you've got a great track and you go with it first you've got to be able to come back with it. As a first release you don't get as much radio play.

What can you remember about the shows?

I remember going to High Wycombe and someone from British Sea Power had broken his arm falling out of a tree because they put lots of foliage everywhere on the stage. He fell out of the tree and broke his arm so they couldn't play that night and The Killers headlined to 120 people in High Wycombe. I went to a few of those shows and it was them starting to find an audience, but it certainly wasn't crazy. The first really great show they did was on Valentine's Day at the ICA. It was their first proper London headline show – 350 tickets – and that was a moment.

How was the Stellastarr* tour?

At the time what was exciting was that it felt like a movement of US acts doing that slightly new wavey sound but trying to write songs, it was a bit more pop, a bit more accessible than perhaps the Detroit thing. Von Bondies and The White Stripes, that was a bit more garage and this felt more accessible and more mainstream. It was still alternative but it felt like it could go places. It felt like a movement and it was exciting. My memory of it is that it started one day and it was just a roller coaster for the best part of two years.

CHAPTER 5

A Dustland Fairytale

In Nottingham, fans besieged their gold minivan, clamouring and clawing to peer inside at these insanely glamorous indie rock'n'roll stars. In Manchester, when they dared to venture to a bar post-gig, they were mobbed like a boy band. "It got to the point it was scary," Braden says. "We were getting crushed, we couldn't even move and we were worried about how the hell we were going to get out of there. People would recognise them and want to talk to them and get an autograph. We just kept hoping that we could replicate this in America."

The gigs sold out in a matter of hours – three nights in London – and each night the fans knew every word. *Top Of The Pops* booked them a slot; the *Newsnight Review* considered them worthy of a segment[*]. The Killers' first UK headline tour in late May 2004 was a bona fide underground phenomenon, on the back of a knock-out musical one-two, The Killers unleashing both barrels at once.

First, on May 24, 'Mr. Brightside' received its first full UK release. The single came in three formats: the gatefold-sleeve red vinyl 7-inch

---

[*] During which noted feminist Germaine Greer called the band "so dreary, so bankrupt, so empty, so predictable, so repetitive, so infantile". The band liked the quote so much they put it in their press biography.

came backed with 'Who Let You Go?' from the original 2003 release, CD1 featured 'Change Your Mind' and CD2 included an Insider remix of 'Somebody Told Me' and an SBN Live Session of 'Midnight Show'. In Europe and America there were several additional remix versions of the track, including one called 'Jacques Lu Cont's Thin White Duke Remix' put together by producer and songwriter Stuart Price, which the band were particularly taken by. The song was accompanied by a monochrome video directed by Brian and Brad Palmer which captured Brandon's trademark look of the period – he'd moved away from blazers and button-down T-shirts to a white tie and waistcoat combination, the immaculately smart outfit offset by his tousled indie rock hairstyle. Style and melody combined to make the video irresistible to MTV2, which announced a week-long exclusive for the video. "We knew straight away that they'd connect very easily with our audience," said the Talent and Artists Relations Manager David Mogendorff. "They are very tuneful and accessible, but also effortlessly cool, which is easier said than done. The album should do really well and it'd be great to see them break into the mainstream consciousness."[1]

The single hit the B-list at Radio 1 and received heavy rotation across the UK, catapulting it to number 10, their first major hit single. Not that this was anywhere near enough to sate Brandon's ravenous competitive impulses. "The day they told us, we were really excited," he'd tell me. "But it's happened so fast it doesn't feel real. Okay, yeah, we had a number 10, but Franz Ferdinand had a Top 3. That's always there."[2]

Second, with 'Mr. Brightside' still lighting up the singles chart, *Hot Fuss* hit the streets, marked by an instore gig at HMV's flagship London store and a Jägermeister-soaked after-show in a basement bar across the street.

Brandon was immensely proud of the album. "I don't know if anybody has any more than what we have right now," he said. "We have a great live show and I can't think of many debut albums that are better than this. I listen to it all the time."[3]

Britain got just as dizzy over the record. "The Killers have made half of the album of the year," wrote *NME*, "after an epoch in thrall to garage rock, they're about to make U2 cool again."[4] "The Killers combine a bag of UK influences from the obscure (Josef K) to the ridiculous (Flock of Seagulls) and end up sounding remarkably fresh and full of youthful swagger," said *The Times*[5], granting the record a full five stars. Released on June 7, as the UK headline tour wound up, it shot to number six on the UK Official Albums Chart and went gold within a month. Suddenly The Killers were the hottest band in the country. A show at the 2,000-capacity Astoria theatre was put on sale for July and swiftly sold out. A few weeks later[*] at Glastonbury 2004, shortly after this writer had dragged them across the muddy site to Lost Vagueness, they drew a stampede of 10,000 fans rushing to the John Peel tent to catch the new band sensation of the weekend, as great a talking point of that year's festival as the headline sets by Paul McCartney[**] or Muse. "Twenty minutes beforehand we were backstage and saw thousands and thousands of people beelining for the New Bands Tent," said Siona Ryan of Lizard King. "I remember Ronnie and Brandon laughing at us afterwards because we were so overwhelmed. The word of mouth had really tipped over."[6]

"That was the best moment I've ever witnessed at a festival," says Ben Durling. "They played the John Peel tent at four-thirty or five o'clock in the afternoon, it was vilely wet and muddy. Rachel Hendry had bought eight pairs of wellies somewhere on her way down and had them in her little car. The splitter had driven right up to the back of the John Peel stage and the band were going 'Do we really have to get out? It's disgusting!' It went Longview, Hope Of The States, The Killers. It was packed when Longview were on and they were obviously thinking 'This is great, we're playing to a packed John Peel tent' and I'm thinking 'This is brilliant for them but these people are all here an hour and a half early to see The Killers. Hope Of The States played and it got busier, and 10 minutes before The Killers went on I remember

---

[*] The band returned to the US to play at a KROQ Weenie Roast and perform a string of club shows in major cities during this time.

[**] Brandon remembers watching Macca's set with a guy called Ronnie from a fellow band called The Black Velvets, with Ronnie calling people "weirdos" for walking away from the set.

pulling down this hessian fence thing at the back of the John Peel tent and there were miles of people outside of the tent. I said to Ronnie 'Have you seen this?' and he went 'Oh my God', because they had no concept of how many people were out there. It was mental, it was proper roadblock. That was as many people as I've ever seen trying to get into the John Peel tent."

The show gave Brandon a rush of confidence and vindication like he'd never known, the addictive throb of stardom. "The first time we played Glastonbury, a light switched on," he said. "Suddenly, there was this reaction of love and adoration that we'd never ever experienced before and I became totally swept up in it all."[7]

Despite being disappointed watching Oasis' headline set at the festival[*], Brandon left Glastonbury, like so many Glasto virgins before him, a little dazed and overwhelmed by the experience. "We're such a young band, so this year was our first time," he said. "But with Oasis and Franz Ferdinand playing, it was a great way to begin. I think everyone's trying to recreate Woodstock when they go to festivals. Fields would be great if you were by yourself but when there's 149,000 of your new best friends there, I don't know..."[8]

Their first foray into Europe a few days later must have been something of a comedown. They'd already played club shows in Amsterdam, Brussels and Hamburg when, for their first *NME* cover feature, this writer joined them in Berlin, staying in the Hotel Agon – a low-rent flop-house with rooms reminiscent of a seventies granny flat. They were playing to an in-the-know crowd of hipsters at Roter Salon, an elegant room in East Berlin with the air of a Weimar Republic-era gentlemen's smoking lounge. In person they were polite but restrained[**]; interviewed as a group they gave up tiny morsels of personal information

---

[*] "I don't like the fact, and I'm just going to be honest here, that Noel isn't writing all the songs any more," he'd say, "that bothers me! And they've always been quiet onstage, but there's something lazy there now, you can't put your finger on it, but you can really feel it. But there is something there. I think [Noel's] got a couple more in him." Source: *NME*, Peter Robinson, August 1, 2004.

[**] The only outburst I saw from the band the whole trip was a hungry Ronnie marching into a room, slapping his stomach and shouting "Fat Ronnie needs feedin'!"

(Dave claimed to be a "lightweight" when it came to drinking, Mark a karaoke addict) but were happier slipping into well-trodden furrows. "If anything we have a kinship to English bands," Brandon said. "The whole British thing isn't a conscious thing. If you look at the music that's come from there, it's been the best music. If we have songs that sound like that, it's nothing but a compliment. People have made a big thing out of it, like I'm singing in a fake accent or something, but it makes sense if you want to write as good songs as Elton John, The Rolling Stones and The Beatles; top that. We love them all the way down the line to T. Rex and Pulp. [But] we didn't walk around in Vegas with fake British accents..." Mark continued his sentence. "... And Union Jack T-shirts..." "...Eating fish and chips..." added Ronnie. "...And reading *NME*," Dave finished.[9]

Having watched Brandon, in a Jimmy Tarbuck golfing jumper, blast out as much showmanship and star quality for this small club show as he had for a festival tent of 10,000, "making these micro-gigs feel like Red Rocks on the Fourth Of July" and "crooning like the darling of the Bellagio", I travelled with the band to Cologne and insisted on interviewing Brandon alone. Here in a store room above the venue, he began to open up. He was excited by the whole experience of appearing on *Top Of The Pops* to play 'Mr. Brightside', right down to having his make-up done by the same woman who had tended to Marc Bolan. He was stunned when I told him that Brixton Academy had a capacity of 5,000 as "We're pencilled in for November".* And the thrill of his rapid rise to stardom bubbled through. "We met Peter Hook's manager the other night and we heard that they really like us," he gushed. "That's an honour because I've always liked them. There's speculation that they had to throw away a couple of songs because they kept sounding like 'Jenny Was A Friend Of Mine' and 'Mr. Brightside'. If that's true, it's awesome."[10]

Away from his bandmates, more personal details began to emerge. "I still feel like I'm going through puberty," he told me. "I still feel like

---

* This show would be downsized to Shepherd's Bush Empire, perhaps because it seemed such a huge leap.

that chubby 13-year-old kid. I'm assuming that when I'm older it'll go away. Onstage, I used to get really scared. Tonight is the first night I've gone two nights in a row without a beer and I'm really proud of that. I started drinking a lot, but now I'm getting out of it – I'm happy." He admitted to crippling self-consciousness – "I don't feel comfortable at the bank or in the store, it sucks" – but his intense, driven nature shone through. "I wanna beat U2," he said. "I wanna have a couple of songs that are in the psyche of people. For whatever reason, you know, 'I Wanna Hold Your Hand' or 'Save A Prayer' or 'Where The Streets Have No Name' or 'This Charming Man'. You just know that song, I'd really like to have one of those, where you know it's that good it's gonna last forever."[11]

He was also more open on the subject of the band's next single, 'All These Things That I've Done'. "I don't wanna say it's autobiographical but it's probably the most real," he confessed. "It's something I identify with but, after it was done, it kinda feels like anybody can. That's why I'm happy with it, I guess. A lot of people are picking it apart, looking for politics in it, but it's really all spiritual. It's uplifting every time we play it. People catch on and probably once a week while we're playing it I'll have a 'moment'. There's something dark in it but when it's done you feel good."[12]

This writer wasn't the only journalist to find Brandon's impenetrable kernel beginning to crack over the summer of 2004. As the rest of the band stuck to revealing snippets of personal trivia – Mark admitted to being nocturnal and liking orange juice over coffee, for example, while Dave claimed to be "aloof" to Brandon's lyrics and owned up to having a secret nickname, but didn't reveal it – Brandon was getting the hang of the frontman's role of baring his soul in interview sessions. In *The Fly* magazine, he admitted to writing lyrics as emotional catharsis: "I think I have a good combination of fiction and non-fiction. It's not like Morrissey opening up his diary! I view things in a very observant fashion, some of the things I sing hurt. But there's celebration too."[13] In *The Independent* he confessed that "I can make myself miserable in minutes with what my mind can conjure up," and to once having run someone over in his car: "I did hit a man with a car once," he said.

essed down in sumptuous surroundings, Paris, 2004. IDOLS/PHOTOSHOT

Brandon as a child, already swathed by lasers.

Brandon at his high school graduation, practicing his distant desert gaze.

The Killers play CMJ Music Marathon 2003, NYC, shortly before Dave's technical difficulties cause him to walk off into the night. FRANK MULLEN/WIREIMAGE

onnie Vannucci Jr. rocks out on the backstreets of Tokyo during the 'Read My Mind' video shoot, January 10, 2007.

Ronnie takes on Tokyo's ultimate drum machine, January 10, 2007. JUN SATO/WIREIMAGE

At the surprisingly sparsely-attended Mean Fiddler show during their first London trip, June 3, 2004. LFI/PHOTOSHOT

The Moustache Years begin; in the studio, July 2006. JAMES LOOKER/NME/IPCSYNDICATION

early appearance on *Later With Jools Holland*, May 2004. ANDRE CSILLAG/REX

king the all-American diner chic look onstage in New York, August 16, 2004. GREG ALLEN/REX

Airing his eagle epaulettes on the Jay Leno show, November 2008. PAUL DRINKWATER/NBCU PHOTO BANK

ptain Keuning and first mate Stoermer at the Coachella Music Festival. MARIO ANZUONI/REUTERS/CORBIS

ndon feels distinctly underdressed onstage with Pet Shop Boys and Lady GaGa at the Brit Awards, February 18, 2009.

Could Brandon *get* more gold? Glastonbury festival, 2007. ANDY WILLSHER/NME/IPC SYNDICATION

"It was dark and he walked in front of me. He broke my windshield, and even when the ambulance came, he didn't get up. Don't worry, I'm sure he's alive and well."[14]

Brandon might have been increasingly willing to discuss his emotional vulnerabilities and near-criminal activities but, unusually, no stories of backstage rock'n'roll hell-raising were forthcoming. They would claim to be the cleanest band in rock, and that really seemed to be the case. "There was always the opportunity," says Braden, "but the band never really partook in any of it. They were pretty clean, we would have the occasional beer and smoke a cigarette, but honestly, it was the cleanest machine in rock. Except for the crew – they were the dirtiest dogs on the planet."

"None of us is really a party animal," Brandon insisted. "I think our friendship is the best way I can contain it. It's what I grew up with, so I know what I need to do... If I see drugs or slutty girls or something, it just might be me who turns away. I don't know if it's just the way I am, saying, 'I'm going to go to bed now,' or if it's from being raised Mormon."[15]

"We get offered drugs all the time," said Ronnie, claiming to be more into herbal cold remedy echinacea, "but we come from Vegas, man. We've seen it all. That shit doesn't surprise us. I think it's pretty rock'n'roll not to do drugs, right?"

"I guarantee I'm better than anybody that does drugs," added Brandon. "Ronnie plays the drums like he does because he's not wasted and we're an awesome live band because of it."[16]

Instead, Brandon claimed he spent his touring downtime trying to counter the constant references to his inherent Britishness by delving deeper into classic Americana in the shape of Bruce Springsteen. He immersed himself in the wandering tales and everyday hardships of *Nebraska* and devoured *Born To Run*, dissected and examined its formulae, worked out what made it roar and how he could make just as great a bellow.

"I just fell in love with his music and it's been a real blessing," Brandon said. "It was like I was 12 years old again listening to The Cars for the first time. See, Bruce always wears his heart on his sleeve, whereas the groups I grew up with, like New Order, were more about being cool and emotionally detached. What struck me most forcefully about him is that I believe what he says. The guy is so incredibly sincere, whatever he sings. And it just hit me – that's what I want to achieve, too. I wanted to create an album that captured chronologically everything important that got me to where I am today."[17]

★ ★ ★

If Brandon was falling back in love with America, the feeling was mutual. 'Mr. Brightside' had been given its first American release in June, and had made just as huge a wave. The band had shot a second video for the US that was the photo negative of the UK version – a wild swirl of colour, drama and vibrancy. To honour the origins of their name once more they'd asked Sophie Muller – director of New Order's 'Crystal' video – to make them a promo set in a Moulin Rouge-style 19th-century bordello. The Killers played the house band, decked out in velvet dress jackets and gold embroidered waistcoats, while Eric Roberts, brother of Julia and an actor best known for portraying scumbags and lowlifes in eighties films such as *The Pope Of Greenwich Village* and *Star 80*, took the role of a bored bordello owner throwing apples to his coterie of wigged and powdered models. The video's very literal interpretation of the lusts and jealousies of the song demanded Brandon undertake his first ever bout of acting, as the plot revolved around his love for one of the bordello girls, played by Polish model Izabella Miko, and the torments he underwent watching her disappear with businessman after businessman.

"We were doing this scene," Brandon recalled, "it's like my first acting ever, and between the takes I'm talking to [Eric] about fame. I told him we went to Graceland and he says, 'It's almost grand isn't it?' And I was like 'Yeah'. And then he smiles and says, 'But it's so fucking white trash'. About Graceland! Who says that? He's evil! He's the devil! Eric was telling me that I will change, but I don't think I'm going to. My dad's still a bellman. I drive a Hyundai with a dent in it. The window's taped up… Another thing he said to me, he said 'Have you fucked a showgirl yet?' And I said 'No'. And he goes, 'You will'. Then Eric says 'It's not as good as you think it is.'"[18]

Just as in the UK, but a hundred times more impressive, 'Mr. Brightside' hit number 10 in the US *Billboard* Chart*, and *Hot Fuss***would follow it into the upper echelons of the chart, peaking at number seven in the US. "The Killers threaten to pry dance rock from the steely grip of hipsterdom and thrust it unrepentantly into the mainstream," wrote *Rolling Stone*'s Jenny Eliscu[19], and her prediction would be proved sensationally accurate. Before it was finished, *Hot Fuss* would sell seven million copies worldwide***, get certified seven-times platinum in the UK after 173 weeks in the UK Albums Chart and become their first UK number one album six months after it was released. The mainstream didn't know what hit it.

Back in July 2004, however, such monumental figures seemed pie in the sky, but they could certainly feel the whirlwind building. On July 8 the band played to a rammed Astoria, gawping up in awe at the endless balcony as the crowd bawled back every word to every track from *Hot Fuss*, plus 'Under The Gun' and 'Who Let You Go' to fill the set to an hour. "It was the biggest place we'd sold out at that point," Brandon said. "The reaction to the record at that show was such a big rush." "I remember thinking: this is where Radiohead played!" Ronnie added.[20]

That weekend, the mania spread to the Oxegen and T in the Park festivals. "T in the Park was unbelievable," says Braden. "I still have photographs from that. There must have been 20,000 people there and some people were already holding up Killers banners and Brandon was just ecstatic." Ronnie has a slightly more skewed memory of the show, though. "I remember a lot of stuff going wrong on that gig," he said. "The keyboard exploded, the drum set was falling apart, the amp blew up. It throws you a little bit, but you need to keep trucking."[21]

---

* The single also made the Top 40 in New Zealand and Australia.

** Released on June 14, the same day the band played on *Jimmy Kimmel Live!* on ABC-TV.

*** *Hot Fuss* has sold an estimated three million copies in the US and two million in the UK.

And truck they would, right across America. On July 15 at the Lo-Fi Café in the Mormon capital of Salt Lake City, The Killers embarked on their first major US and Canada headline tour, playing a total of 56 dates across the country right up to the end of October. At the start, the shows were club gigs in such insalubrious venues as Jack Rabbits in Jacksonville, Mississippi Nights in St. Louis, the T Lounge in El Paso and Smart Bar in Chicago, places where they'd get the occasional bottle thrown by the indie diehards during 'Glamorous Indie Rock & Roll'.* But by September the band were playing theatres, opera houses, pavilions and music halls in Denver, Toronto, Detroit, Memphis and beyond; night by night, week by week, they could feel their stature growing.

The schedule was dense and arduous, but The Killers tackled it heads down, no complaints. They'd only been touring for nine or 10 months so fatigue had yet to set in, and they were ambitious and dedicated to making their band sustainable without the need for a label's support. Every show, they went out there to make a room full of lifelong fans.

"We took a lot of shit doing a 10-week tour where the most we ever got for a gig was $150," Ronnie said. "We did 10 weeks straight without a day off, in the van, loading our own shit and tearing it up. We cut our teeth."[22]

The *Hot Fuss* tour had its ups and downs. Its downs were minimal. In Sacramento** a fan who'd been following them around the country jumped onstage to offer Brandon a freshly prepared noose. "I don't know what she wanted to do with it," he said. "She held it out to me and I don't know if she wanted me to bend over, or put her neck in the noose or what. It kinda upset me."[23] At one point, their sound guy was electrocuted: "Our current sound engineer saved his life," said Brandon. "It was another scary moment for us."

---

* "It's becoming a big mess!" Brandon would say of the reception to the song. "People really think I'm pouring my heart out and I'm not! People got quite aggressive when we played it in America. I really love that one, but everyone keeps taking the piss." Source: *NME*, Peter Robinson, August 1, 2004.
** The location of this event is based on Brandon's memory of it, which may be erroneous – there is no record of The Killers playing in Sacramento on this tour.

And a show supporting The Stills, a major label alt-rock band from Montreal, would unleash a tendency within Brandon he never suspected he had: the press feud. "That band The Stills," he told *NME* in November, "we played a gig with them and… it's just the kind of people they are. I'm not a hippie, but there's no room in music for arrogance. They're all a bit up themselves and they really don't have any right to be!"[24] *

Brandon would repeatedly take digs at the band in interviews, commenting "it could be worse, we could be The Stills,"[25] and eventually expanding on the story. "We opened for them and we felt this negativity," he said. "They're signed to a major label but they have these indie attitudes. They bitch about their label even while it's supporting them. I'm proud that I'm on Island Records. I'm happy that as many people as possible will hear our music. I feel a sense of purpose in what we do. It's good music. If it makes you smile and dance that's okay. If it touches your heart that's even better. But then our music, unlike theirs, isn't just for people who do 'shrooms and wear black Converse. Although, happily, they like it too. You know what it is? The Killers have universal appeal. I hope it never goes away."[26]

The Stills weren't the only 'indie' band to feel the sharp edge of Brandon's tongue, particularly when he was trying to give fresh examples of bands he was sniping at on 'Glamorous Indie Rock & Roll'. As The Killers played with more mid-level bands on tours and at festivals, Brandon began to feel that same negativity at every turn; The Secret Machines particularly came in for a lashing. "I love seeing old pictures of the sixties and seventies of people in bands hanging out and you don't see that any more and I'll tell you why," he fumed, "I've seen it. It's because they're assholes. All of 'em. It is unbelievably rare to meet a nice band… Everyone is an asshole! I don't know why it is, but there's a

---

* In the same interview Brandon would lay into Jack White in the wake of White being arrested for assaulting The Von Bondies' Jason Stollsteimer in a bar brawl in 2004, saying "I've always loved The White Stripes but when you saw the pictures of that kid I felt terrible. You can't help but think that Jack didn't have to hit him that many times!" Source: *NME Yearbook*, Tim Jonze, November 2004.

certain type of band out there that is really scared by us and what we do. A lot of people may not think we're the real deal and they are, perhaps that's it.

"The Secret Machines are total assholes. Oh man, I can't believe them. They are unbelievably juvenile, they're like little kids. We did a gig with them in Portland once where they had to open for us and they were real upset about it. They obviously don't like the idea of supporting us. If you have this mentality where you're the best thing since Pink Floyd, I wouldn't want to open up for The Killers either. Then we had to play a *$2 Bill Show* on MTV with them and when they walked into the room you could just smell it on them. When we were playing they went into our room and took all our beer and took it out on our merchandise guy. That's the thing that makes me most mad. He's our friend and they were antagonising him and we weren't even around. Then they wanted to meet us in a bar..."[27]

Both bands retaliated in the press, calling The Killers "fake"*; Brandon's first press beefs had been launched. And they certainly wouldn't be his last.

The ups of the *Hot Fuss* tour, meanwhile, were monumental. On July 30, The Killers broke off from US legs to make their first trip to Japan for that year's Fuji Rock festival. At a homecoming show at the Las Vegas House of Blues they were pleased to be introduced onstage by Michael Valentine, telling a story of how he and Flowers had been having lunch in an Italian restaurant the week before The Killers had formed, both talking about starting new bands – Valentine relayed how Brandon had said to him, "Michael, you're a talker, I'm a do-er."

Then, on August 21, they briefly revisited their superstar status in the UK, headlining a sold-out Forum and making a legendary appearance

---

* An accusation that Brandon would be at pains to deflect, stating, "It's just too easy for people to think, 'Oh, they're from Vegas so they must be shallow and fake'. But I would say the opposite. We formed a band and did things in the face of everything around us. There was no one like us in Vegas, or even in America. We gambled and that's the only thing that comes from our hometown." Source: Q, Michael Odell, December 2004.

on the outdoor main stage at the V Festival, which turned out to be Glastonbury squared, the band's first experience of playing to a crowd stretching virtually as far as the eye could see. "V was awesome," Brandon said. "The crowds there just blew us away. I don't know what it is about the English but they just seem to be really excited about us. We had no idea we were going to get such a big reaction. We got onstage and the crowd had gone from 2,000 to 16,000! It just blew us away. And I learned that I really like playing in front of a lot of people. It's something I need and I just want more of it now."[28] "A lot of people who work with us were crying!" he added later. "I usually get overwhelmed when I walk out because that's always the best thing when you watch a band. To be on the flip side was pretty incredible."[29]

This UK visit saw them tick off another important first – their debut international magazine cover. Brandon would count the moment he first saw himself on the cover of the *NME* as among his best of this incredible year, "a big deal for us", but his bandmates weren't quite so overjoyed, since Brandon was pictured alone on the front. "We didn't see it until we landed at Heathrow airport and we each bought a copy. Whoever made the decision not to use those group photos, I just want them to know I had to put up with Dave complaining about it for a long time."[30]

Brandon certainly wasn't complaining when he got home to Vegas from one leg of the tour to find that his girlfriend Tana had converted to Mormonism. Instead, he proposed – the couple set a date for March 2005. "I would have married her regardless," Brandon said. "There were no ultimatums, but while I was away she got involved in it." "We'll be demoing new material all that month, but it only takes a day to get married!"[31] "I don't think I'll be very good at planning a wedding," Tana said, "so I'm relieved it's not happening right away. I'm just happy to be getting married."[32]

August also saw the UK release of the third single from *Hot Fuss*, 'All These Things That I've Done', which reinforced The Killers' UK success by hitting number 18 with the help of a joyous video filmed in East London's famous Brick Lane by directors Alexander Hemming and Kristy Gunn. In stark contrast with the classic video for 'Bittersweet

Symphony' by The Verve, in which singer Richard Ashcroft saunters intently down a street barging people aside, here the band strolled through the streets and alleyways heading for the Astoria stage, gathering friends and followers of their cause along the way – grannies, rock kids, a gospel choir, even one *NME* journalist*. Besides cementing their reputation as a US band chiming deeply with UK culture, their intention was to make a happy, uplifting video, which they rarely saw in rock. "I would hope there was more to it than just us walking down the street," Brandon mused. "There is a bit of a message. It's a positive message, that's all I really know. A positive thing going on. I just think the world could use one, so we made one, and it's worked out."[33]

Plans were afoot for a rather less feel-good celluloid experience, meanwhile. As their success had expanded the band's creative possibilities, there was talk of making a film of the murder trilogy songs. Very much at the drawing board stage at this point, the band decided it should be a 25-minute movie inspired by the extended cinematic video to Michael Jackson's 'Thriller', to be filmed around Lake Mead near Las Vegas, and they started throwing around ideas for cast and director. Anton Corbijn, director of the video for U2's 'One', legendary clips for Depeche Mode and Joy Division and photographer of the classic *The Joshua Tree* sleeve, topped a shortlist of directors that also included David Lynch and Michael Moore, while Mischa Barton, Paris Hilton and Kelly Osbourne were the dream actresses to play Jenny. And the murderous protagonist? "Whenever I see it in my head, I see James Spader killing this girl," Brandon said[34], but was open to the idea of Rob Lowe or *The League Of Gentlemen*'s evil circus clown Papa Lazarou.

The ludicrous nature of some of these suggestions shows that, at the time, they'd throw such names around for fun, never believing they'd actually meet any of these characters from page, stage, sleeve and screen.

Within weeks, however, they'd be on the other side of fame's looking glass.

★ ★ ★

* Tim Jonze is one of the earliest additions to the stampede.

The voices outside the bathroom cubicle echoed from the tiles. Their words were ice.

"So Bowie's coming down to the show tonight," said one guy, "just make sure he gets in without any problems and gets to his table."

A pause. Then the other voice spoke.

"*David* Bowie?"

"That's right, just make sure he gets to his table."

Inside his cubicle, Brandon froze. *David* Bowie? Another night playing at New York's Irving Plaza – two nights in early October this time, both sold out – just turned into the most terrifying gig of his life.

"I actually arranged that through a contact that knew Ron Delsener, who is this legendary East Coast concert promoter," says Braden. "He was kind of known as the Bill Graham of the East Coast music scene. I didn't tell the band, I wanted to surprise them, so I had arranged a limo to come and it dropped Bowie and Ron off together. This was maybe a couple of months after he had had his heart attack in Germany, so he was a little bit skinny and he had a great handle bar moustache and a denim corduroy jacket and jeans. He looked very Western and very cool. I set up a special table for them with some champagne at the top of the balcony where you could just look perfectly down at the stage. During The Killers' set, Brandon was looking up there, looking at me, and he realised who it was. He looked like he saw a ghost!"

"We play and I can just see him and I'm sure it was the worst show we've ever played," Brandon said. "I wasn't ready for that. Maybe in a couple of years I will be."[35] "I could see him the entire time. I was fucking dying, cause he's the one for me."[36]

"Bowie was blown away and he was very gracious," Braden continues. "It was a moment for myself because as soon as the show was over I said 'Bowie, would you like to meet the band?' and he said 'Absolutely!'. So I go backstage and I said 'Guys, I know you want your customary 15 minutes to decompress after the show, but, I'd like to bring back somebody to say hello, is that cool?' then they go yeah, sure, no problem. So I go up to Bowie and he grabs my hand, we're holding hands for like 100 feet, and I open up the door and I go 'Guys, please meet Mr David Bowie' and the band shit themselves! It was such a great

169

moment. They all said their hellos, but kept their distance because they were so nervous, he was just like 'Hey guys, I gotta say your *Hot Fuss* record is one of the greatest records I've ever heard. I am such a big fan and I really loved the show', he was totally gracious and giving them all kinds of wonderful compliments. I remember Ron Delsener came in as well, and he is super gregarious and outgoing, he was telling the band at that point 'You guys are going to go into arenas. I know it is going to happen, you will play Madison Square Garden'."

"I went numb," Brandon recalled. "I shook his hand and thought, 'You wrote 'Ashes To Ashes'. You're not supposed to like me. I still have Bowie posters on my wall... He said 'I felt like I just saw the history of rock'n'roll'. I think he was basically saying we rip off every genre."[37]

Mark would count the moment as among the best of the year for the band. "He was like 'Keep up the good work, boys'. I'm not usually star-struck, but his presence..."[38]

Meeting Bowie wasn't the first time The Killers felt as though they were stepping into unreal territory. In September they were asked to appear in Californian teen drama *The O.C.*, playing live in the Bait Shop, a club featured in the series where real-life bands would occasionally play. "If it was The Killers playing some birthday party at the Peach Pit we wouldn't have done it," Ronnie said. "But it was written into the script that The Killers were playing at a club, which is what we already do. We don't want to compromise anything. We're not about to start doing Miller Genuine Draft commercials or anything." The show's Seth Cohen described the band's onscreen performance of 'Mr. Brightside' and 'Smile Like You Mean It' as "awesome" on the show, and US sales rocketed[*] once more. Then, over the course of October, the band began to get invitations to appear on national chat shows that they previously could only have dreamed of – *Late Show With David Letterman, Late Night With Conan O'Brien*. In the UK they were booked to play 'Somebody Told Me' on *The Jonathan Ross Show*, appearing alongside Sarah Michelle Gellar

[*] The band also gave 'Smile Like You Mean It' to an *O.C.* mix album.

and Barbara Windsor, and put in the dressing room next door to the Royal Philharmonic Orchestra. Suddenly, The Killers were mingling with the stars.*

Always a pioneer in musical matters, Bowie opened the floodgates of celebrity Killers fans. Just over a week after the Irving Plaza show, The Killers found themselves, at the headliners' request, supporting the Pixies at the 8,000-capacity Reliant Center in Houston.

A five-date stop-off in mainland Europe, playing in Germany, France, Sweden and the Netherlands, would be brightened by a nod from another hero. Having their picture taken for a newspaper article in the rotting remains of an Eastern bloc military vehicle, shortly before a gig at the Columbia Club, Dave was in a foul mood, grumbling about his pizza slice having whole chillies on it, and how their 16-week world tour was draining him. "What country are we in?" he said. "You could have said we were in Pittsburgh and I wouldn't have known the difference. We've been on the road so long I can't remember what it's like not to be. It's hard work. People often think we're arrogant when we're really just tired."[39] Yet this was only two days after none other than Elton John had invited them onto a French TV show in Paris in order to announce them as his new favourite band.

"We're going to go out for dinner with him as well," Brandon said later. "We're so excited! He has a show in Vegas and he's a big fan and we're big fans of his. When I was 13 I really got the Elton bug and all his seventies hits and stuff were so amazing, so I can't wait. I wouldn't mind buying Elton dinner. We owe him for the music he's given the world." Although Brandon suspected there might have been an ulterior motive to the invitation on Elton's part. "Elton's boyfriend, he kind of looks like Ronnie. I think he has a type and I think Ronnie definitely fits that. It was obvious when we met him. Maybe we should make Ronnie sit next to Elton at dinner. That would be funny."[40]

---

* Clearly eager to sample more of the superstar lifestyle, with three days off after this show, Brandon took the opportunity with Tana to visit Lake Como in Italy, holiday home of George Clooney.

It was as they headed back towards the UK for a short set of dates culminating at Shepherd's Bush Empire in November, though, that they met The Big One.

Dublin, November 11; after a day spent signing Cup-a-Soups, David Hasselhoff pictures, dollar bills and bras – which only Brandon refused to sign as it was still being worn – at an instore session, The Killers' sold-out show at the 1,200-capacity Olympia Theatre had been a rousing success. Entering to the strains of Andy Williams' 'Can't Take My Eyes Off You' and leaving Dublin gasping for more with a storming finale of 'All These Things That I've Done', Brandon had clearly settled into his role as superhuman rock god. "I become something different, definitely," he said. "When I go to a concert I want to be something that I'm not – something extravagant I guess. I don't want to see somebody who looks like my buddy up there. A lot of people who were attractive to me when I was younger were larger-than-life characters."[41] Afterwards, chased down the street by a gaggle of fans, Ronnie and Brandon* ducked into a bar that Siona Ryan from Lizard King knew about.

A little place called Lillie's Bordello. Owned by one Bono Vox.

Commandeering a table, they peered around the bar. And there, across the room, was a small figure in shades. Spotting them, he sent over a round of cocktails the bar had designed especially in his name – Bono's Black Velvets, half a flute of champagne topped with Guinness – and invited them to his table.

"The room was filled up by him," Brandon said. "He's just an incredible man. U2 are the ideal band to us."[42] Although, Brandon admits, "he was pretty drunk"[43], when he draped his arm around Ronnie's shoulders and slurred "Spare us the 'interesting' second album", they took him at his word. "He makes a lot of sense," Brandon said, "He's the king of what we do, so when he says something, you'd better listen. I think they probably appreciate that we have the same zest as they did when they were a young band. Rock'n'roll is about taking it where you can, it's not about restrictions, and even though they're older

---

* Dave and Mark had gone to bed early and would be gutted to hear what had happened in their absence the next day.

now, it's still in them to put up a fight. If a kid handed you a demo tape that had 'Vertigo' on it, you would freak out."[44]

With an offer of a support slot in the bag, The Killers would gush in the press about how you really should meet your heroes. "U2 have stayed relevant because they know what they are," Brandon would say. "They just know that they are gifted, but they're not pretentious. They sing songs that everyone can understand. And Bono's larger than life onstage – I'd love us to grow and stay like that. Even though I also love Duran Duran, I'd rather go more in a U2 direction as they look and act like they're 45 – not like they are still young. Simon Le Bon's highlights and tight jackets are too much. He has kids who are too old to have highlights!"[45] And though the U2 singer wouldn't give them his legendary Bono Talk*, he would be just as complimentary in return. "It's rare to find a band who not only have the music but a lyricist too," Bono said. "I hear The Killers and I get off the phone."[46]

Bono appreciated a young band giving him so much respect in the press, and the two bands would become intrinsically linked. But their next brush with A-list celebrity would be magical in a slightly different manner.

"At Shepherd's Bush, there was one of our first requests from a celebrity to come to the show," Braden recalls. "I remember getting a call from Daniel Radcliffe's manager, saying 'Hey, Daniel really wants to come to the show, can you take care of him?' and I said 'Happily'. So I let the band know that he would be at the show and backstage and wanted to meet them, particularly Brandon, and Brandon was flabbergasted by this because we were all really big *Harry Potter* fans. I met Daniel outside the venue, he had a hoodie on and glasses, which I thought was kind of silly, but then I realised someone had recognised him out on the street and some people started screaming. So I took him in my arm and just walked him through the backstage area and brought him upstairs to hang out. He sat and watched the show and met

---

* "I don't think we're getting it," Brandon would say. "He's scared to give it to us! Could you imagine how good we'd be if we had it? It wouldn't be fair!" Source: *NME*, Barry Nicholson, September 24, 2005.

Brandon and the band. He was young at that time, and very vocal about what bands he liked in the press. I think in the *Guardian* and the *NME* he may have said The Killers were his new favourite band."

When they weren't hanging with their heroes, they were rubbing shoulders with their contemporaries. Back in the US in the run-up to Christmas, the band played a handful of festive indie arena shows – and a couple of acoustic gigs in Universal City for KROQ – alongside the likes of Modest Mouse, Snow Patrol, Muse, Keane, Franz Ferdinand, Interpol, Jimmy Eat World and The Shins. Again, declaring themselves "the least rock'n'roll band in the world"[47], the band were in shutdown: having texted their own driver to complain about his speeding on the road down from Seattle – "Hey Jack, I'd rather get to San Francisco late than dead", Ronnie messaged – they holed up backstage ignoring the fridge full of beer, Brandon subsisting on his regular touring diet of Twinkies and Coca-Cola. "I drink Coke for breakfast, lunch and dinner," Brandon said. "I never have any meal without it."[48]

None of the girls queueing for autographs outside their dressing room in San Francisco's Bill Graham Civic Auditorium[*] were let inside; with all the nooses and bras, the band had been bitten before. "Some of the things young girls come out with knock me on my ass," Brandon said. "We're used to girls just saying 'Take a picture with me!' then this girl gave me this paper bag with a pillow and a mix CD [and a poem made from lyrics of Killers songs] in it and walked off. There have been a couple of people who have got a little scary. There's a girl used to see us at small gigs – she was a really early fan – but now we can't even let her on the bus. People get weird and you have to push them away. But the really scary ones are still in the shadows."[49] [**]

---

[*] This was also the gig where the band were each given a gold Amex card, on which to put whatever expenses they wished from then on.

[**] Ronnie was a little luckier with regard to fan gifts – he loved one present of a toy Animal from *The Muppets* so much he virtually slept with it. "Animal is one of my idols and inspirations for drumming, so I put that in a special mementos case under my bed." Source: *NME*, Elizabeth Goodman, May 7, 2005.

The rest of the bands on the bill were like the anti-Stills, however. Interpol led the band onstage, Franz Ferdinand stood watching from the wings as, in uniform red velvet blazers, The Killers expanded to fill these vast venues. Indie was getting friendlier towards The Killers. And so it would prove, after a trip to Australia for their first set of shows there and a pair of New Year gigs, when the band was booked to headline the annual *NME* Awards tour of 2005, a prestigious UK tour showcasing the best new bands of the year. Their tourmates for the month-long string of shows would be The Kaiser Chiefs, Bloc Party and The Futureheads. "I can't think of a better way to start 2005 than with an *NME* tour," Brandon said. "I'm really excited. I just hope everyone's friendly…"[50]

★ ★ ★

The Killers that ended 2004 were a very different band from the one that started it. They'd toured the world, played 260 gigs in a year, become the sensation of the festival season, sold almost a million records, been burned out by the road and shocked by strange fans, and met many of their biggest heroes. They'd toured the UK numerous times and become so assimilated into its culture that Brandon was now saying 'tomato' in a British accent and singing songs by The Streets in precise Mike Skinner patois. They'd seen their audience grow from hardline indie fans to include what Mark would describe as "12-year-old girls, a guy in a Metallica T-shirt and 40-year-old men".[51] They received the ultimate accolade from the hometown scene that had once been so sniffy about them when *CityLife*'s Jeff Inman wrote that "The Killers [have] achieved the dream, they did what every Vegas band strives for: they topped Slaughter".

And, most of all, from touring the world in rattling bunks in tiny vans and still blasting out performances worthy of private jet-toting megastars, they'd realised they were built to last. "I think we're all realising how big this thing is now," Brandon said. "I think we all realise how important our second record will be. How this madness isn't going to end."[52]

They'd already begun writing songs for the follow-up to *Hot Fuss*. Songs provisionally called 'Uncle Jonny' and 'It's Only Natural' were taking shape during soundcheck jams, the latter described by an *NME* writer who heard them play it in the soundcheck at *The Jonathan Ross Show* as "a slow, sensitive balled… a far more melodramatic Killers than we've heard before". Its lyrics at this point went, "It's only natural for you to want to swim with me". They also had a handful of other tracks slowly making their way onto tape. "We have three songs already," Brandon said of the on-the-road demos in December. "'Daddy's Eyes', 'It's Only Natural' and 'I Won't Let You Down'*. It's going to be a more organic album. Keyboards are still going to be there on some tracks but it will sound different. I suppose it's just a maturing process. We're learning what to do and what not to do and we're hard workers, so this album will be far better than *Hot Fuss*. I'm hoping it will be out in November [2005]."[53] Elsewhere, Brandon claimed that the plan for album two was to make a record that was "a little more soulful, with gospel singers. We really want to work with Eno."[54]

"That's one thing that's been a real nuisance," Dave added. "We've not had proper time to write new songs like we used to in the garage. Back then we would all get together every day after work and play a song three hours straight and get it almost finished in one day. Now we get 30 minutes here and there at the very most." There was another new song that Dave particularly liked too, then called 'Higher And Higher'. "[It's] the biggest chorus ever written… good enough to keep me in the band for another 10 years."[55]

The Killers also ended the year with the promise of plaudits. Having missed out on the Shortlist award in the US earlier that year and a smattering of MTV Video awards for which they were nominated, they picked up a total of three nominations for the Grammys, for Best Rock Album, Best Rock Song for 'Somebody Told Me' and, for the same song, Best Rock Performance By A Duo Or Group With Vocal.

"I was coming out of the shower," Ronnie said, "and my wife came busting in. 'You're nominated for a Grammy!' It was like nine in the

---

* A lost song.

morning, and I thought that was crazy, I was like 'No way'."[56] "It's blowing my mind, man. You grow up hearing about the Grammys, and you call your friends to watch the Grammys and they come over. That's the one night you don't do your homework."[57]

The day after the nomination announcements, The Killers flew back home to Vegas where they attended the *Billboard* Music Awards, sitting out in the crowd watching the winners gush, no doubt thinking 'Soon it will be us'. Yet, with glory at his fingertips, Brandon's rounding up of 2004 in interviews displayed just how far he still wanted to go. "It's been a small victory," he said. "We can't say a big one until we've conquered America."[58]

In the back of his mind, he knew his victories were about to get super-sized.

Mark Stoermer, April 2014

What were the most memorable shows from the *Hot Fuss* period?
Glastonbury, where we came out to that one I knew something was happening – I think we all did. That was going from every nightclub, club, club, club – it was good, 200 people, 300 people, people starting to know the songs, that was impressive enough. But that's when we walked out and it seemed like there were 20,000 people, which was like playing to Wembley then. Everybody knew every song. That was like "something's different here". Then we'd go back to the States and nobody would know anything.

Did you find yourself in any sticky situations being swamped by fans in the UK?
Not really, maybe I kinda did my own thing and put off the unapproachable vibe that works for me in that respect!

Were you particularly impressed by meeting your heroes?
There's only been a few times when I've ever been star-struck, maybe three times. Bowie was one of them, that was in the early days when he came to the Bowery Ballroom. I remember going backstage and kind of being shoved aside, even though we needed to be onstage in 10 minutes, but then it was like "Oh, it's David Bowie, I'm okay with that!" We all knew David Bowie was there so we all played probably one of the worst shows of our lives because we were all nervous. Something went wrong with the keyboard too, it was playing half a step off. Most people, maybe they don't know, but Bowie knows when something's a half step off!

With your image as the cleanest band in rock'n'roll in its formative stage, was there any revelry on those early tours?
Probably the crew more than the band. We have a crew that rivals the most debaucherous stories of Led Zeppelin, probably. But the band, people can say what they want but we've been about the music and working. Maybe that's why we've been doing it 10 years, because we don't have too much fun but we have fun playing music.

Were there any real pinch-yourself moments?

There was a time when we supported U2 when we were at their hotel. Hanging out with U2, and some members of Pearl Jam were around, and it was in the early days and I'd say to myself "We're just hanging out with Bono…" Although I've always known he's just a guy, if I could've told my 14 or 15-year-old self, he wouldn't believe it.

Dave Keuning, March 2014

What were the high and low points of the *Hot Fuss* tour?

There were a lot of high points. The low point was maybe one time in Japan, in Hiroshima, where we did a show for 50 people. It was kind of weird, at six at night in a shopping mall. As soon as the album was finished we did October of '03 to June of '04 – that's almost nine months of touring without *Hot Fuss* being out. So as soon as *Hot Fuss* came out we played Glastonbury and a lot of great shows and everything changed then. The first two Glastonbury shows were pretty amazing. The first one, we were in a tent that people were spilling out of. That was when I began to be very optimistic about our future. It didn't happen as quick as that in America.

Was that what you expected international success to be?

Maybe not expected, but maybe always dreamed. Early in our career, that was amazing.

Were you really the cleanest band in rock'n'roll?

We went out and drank and stuff, we looked clean at the time compared to The Libertines. They were all about drugs and letting everyone know they did drugs. All that *NME* cared about was any band that did drugs. It was kind of ridiculous. I don't care if people do drugs or not but you can't be big just because you're doing drugs. I think we were just being compared to bands at the time like The Libertines – compared to them we were angels I guess, but that doesn't mean we didn't dabble here and there.

Would you often storm off when things went wrong?
That wasn't happening that often. I don't remember storming off. I mentioned storming off once when we were done playing in New York. I never, ever stormed off during a show. I may have walked offstage and someone thought I was mad, but it's not fair to say I stormed off a lot. Any band is gonna have tension, we were around each other a lot.

Your relationship with Cara Cross began around this time – how did you meet?
I don't really wanna say much about that. You know, she's the mother of my child. It's a bit complicated.

Did your on-off relationship affect your mood on the road?
It's hard being away from any relationship, that goes without saying.

CHAPTER 6

This River Is Wild

"That was arguably the greatest tour of that whole album campaign because it was, to us at the time, four of the hottest bands – Kaisers, Futureheads, Bloc Party, Killers. It was totally sold out and we got mayhem from the audience. It just felt really important to the bands on the tour. There was a friendly competitive nature about the shows, all the bands talking like 'I am really gonna give it good to you tonight' – this friendly camaraderie of wanting to give the best show and outdo one another each night. The coverage was great in the magazines and that tour really sent shockwaves back to America."

– Braden Merrick

The one thing Ricky Wilson – singer with The Kaiser Chiefs and now judge on primetime TV talent show *The Voice* UK – remembers most about the *NME* Awards tour of 2005 is Whitey's Tiegate. "Brandon put [Kaisers guitarist] Whitey's white tie in the tomato soup," he says, a glint of mischief in his eye. "We were at catering and for some reason everyone was on one table but there was another table that just had Whitey sitting next to Brandon. We all looked away and when we looked back Whitey had a white tie on and the end of it was covered in tomato soup. We all looked round and Whitey looked at Brandon and went 'What the fuck did you do that for?' Brandon was like 'What?' Whitey was going 'You took my tie and dipped it in the soup!' We were all like, 'What a fucking dickhead!'" Was this some hidden prankster demon leaping forth from the Killers frontman? Not quite. "It was about five years later," Ricky says, "that Whitey said 'Nah, I spilt soup down my tie'."

The Killers that Ricky met on the *NME* tour were driven, but not exactly playful. One journalist who'd visited them on their two-week Christmas break – their first fortnight at home in 13 months – wrote of a band on edge, an increasingly "snarky" Dave refusing to give Brandon a lift back to the city after a photo shoot at a neon graveyard of old Vegas signs on the outskirts of town, and Brandon calling after him, "Fucking asshole, I don't have a car!"[1]

"There are times when you do get sick of each other," Brandon said by way of explanation, "but not as much as most people. I think we all get along really well... I'm so tired. Your time off goes by so quickly. They think they're being so gracious by giving you two weeks off, but you really spend it all catching up on bills and keeping up on trying to sort out your car or whatever. You turn around and it's time to go again." "We've had such a crazy schedule," Mark added, "going back and forth and all the flying and changing time zones and being in LA one day and London the next..."[2]

"I've had a few breakdowns," Dave admitted. "I've lost it on occasion. If, say, we've argued over soundcheck, or if a show hasn't gone well, or there are days when I feel that nobody wants my opinion, that I don't count any more... that's when I snap. I shout, scream, storm off. But it's never anything serious. It's not like I'm going nuts or anything."[3]

Dave, to be fair, probably had it worst of the group. In his absence, his apartment building had been knocked down, so he was essentially homeless, forced to rent hotel rooms for the duration of his break. This was fine on nights when rooms in the mid-level Stratosphere hotel went for $49 a night, but when a convention hit town on his third night back and the price shot up to $350 a night, it was hard to bear, even for a near-million-selling rock star. "I can't afford $350 for one day," he grumbled. "I had to move out. It's just getting too hard to live like this."[4] Brandon had the luxury of his old fan-flat: "I still have posters on my walls," he grinned, "Morrissey, David Bowie, The Beatles, the Stones, so it's really weird to be in the situation we're in."[5]

Back home, Brandon had a relaxing schedule. He'd wake up each day to *USA Today* newspaper and a spin of Nick Cave's 'There She Goes, My Beautiful World' – "It knocked me off my feet, it's so good, it's like Elvis-style gospel"[6] – then he'd read from *The Complete Stories Of Truman Capote* and check out The Killers' website to fume about people claiming they have a wannabe-Oasis attitude. In the evening he'd hit the Strip to play the penny slots or check out a horror movie. "I enjoy the thrill of being scared, particularly when it affects you for days afterwards. It's invigorating."[7]

Fame was sitting uneasily with Brandon; it simply wasn't what he'd expected it to be. Sure, he was being lusted over in *Cosmo Girl* magazine's Hot For 2005 list, but he wasn't constantly being watched any more than his natural paranoia on the matter led him to believe[*], and he wasn't being mobbed, other than being stopped at a cinema in Henderson by a fan asking "What are you doing here?" "Even though we're doing pretty well now, nobody walks up to us on the street," he said.[8]

In fact, it was the surreptitious nature of fame that rankled him. "I welcome the attention. In fact, I enjoy it. It's early on just now, so maybe in 10 years I won't enjoy it so much, but right now I'm sucking it all up. The downside to all that is that I have to be on guard all the time. For example, I went to see a movie with my cousin in Las Vegas and I noticed a couple of people filming me on their mobile phones. I wasn't being Brandon Flowers From The Killers any more. When they're getting me onstage that's fine, but outside of that, when you're just doing what you're doing… you know, you walk differently, you carry yourself differently from when you're onstage. That, I don't like."[9]

It was also a more stylish Killers than the world had seen before. Ever since their emergence the band had been a photographer's dream,

---

[*] "I always feel as though someone is staring at me," Brandon would say. "It means I won't do certain things. I wouldn't just sit here naked after a shower, for example. I guess being in a band is a way of trying to turn that paranoia into a positive thing." Source: *The Times*, Amber Cowan, January 8, 2005.

turning up to every shoot in ever more swish and fashionable garb. Their photo sessions were becoming more like fashion shoots, with members wearing evening suits, tuxedos and immaculate blazer-and-tie combinations even in the most inhospitable locations – out in the desert or in the wilds of Eastern Europe. Photographers began hiring exotic backdrops for their pictures; banqueting scenes, bordellos, Fifties diners complete with antique crooner microphones for Brandon to wield like a drive-in heartthrob. Slowly, designer names would creep into the picture captions, detailing which label each member was sporting and the cost of the article in question. This aspect of the band, at this point, was entirely in Brandon's control.

"The Strokes did it in a way where it looked like they weren't trying," he said, "but with bands like us and Franz – it's obvious we're trying! But I feel more comfortable dressed like that. Whether you're in a band or not, it brings attention and I like that."[10] "You'll always hear bands saying that it's all about the music and they're right of course. But the way you look is a big part of it too. When someone mentions The Beatles to me, the first thing I think of is these cool grey suits and those boots. Iconic imagery has always been a big deal to me."[11] "It's important to look good. Great music is great music, but image is priceless. I'm not saying I'm in this position because I'm good looking but it certainly helps."[12]

"We feel better in suits," Dave added. "I don't know if I play better, it depends if the sleeves are tight. But I feel good in a suit and I think playing in a T-shirt and jeans is just lazy. I don't think what we do is that extravagant. We don't spend hours in the dressing room. This is stuff that only takes 30 seconds to put on."[13]

By the end of 2005 the band would be doing entirely fashion-based features in *The Sunday Times Style* and *The Guardian Weekend* magazines, picking £1,000 golden Alexander McQueen jackets and Paul Smith suits, £700 Burberry trench coats and £350 Louis Vuitton shoes from racks, being described by fashion writers as touting "a dandyish Dior style" and looking like "a Savile Row Zorro" as Brandon would waltz around photo studios in a green velvet drape coat, scarlet silk scarves and pinstriped trousers, singing into a lizard-head umbrella. Brandon would be cajoled into admitting his fashion icons were Bowie "and Duran Duran when they didn't look like pirates" and giving fashion tips: "I'm a big fan of stripes. I'd say 70 per cent of the stuff I own is striped. My favourite is an orange and blue polo shirt, but it has a green collar. Throw a blue blazer over that and you're set. I've always said that I wouldn't be doing our music justice if I performed in a T-shirt and ripped-up jeans."[14] *

With *GQ* and *Nylon* on the phone offering shoots in top designer clothes, the band realised they were beginning to influence the style of their contemporaries, but their own wardrobes were still essentially made up of the dressy but affordable wares of H&M and Topman, which they'd raid on their visits to Britain. Then an *NME* writer asked them if they were "a Topman band" and they knew it was time to up their game. So, in January of 2005, the band began to reach out to major designers, pitching themselves as a great showcase for their more flamboyant stage wear. And it all started with a now-legendary pink leather jacket.

"We did *Saturday Night Live* in New York in January '05," Braden recalls, "and as far as doing mainstream stuff, that is probably one of the coolest, biggest things you can do. We knew we had to do something special on the stage. Every artist has their own journey, and The Killers always had this vision of wearing the suits, almost like they were going to work and had better dress up for it. The more financing we got and the wares we got, we were contacted by designers and the band could afford it, frankly. So around those points in '05 we had a little bit of cash in our pocket and we could go out and experiment more and try new things. We contacted Hedi Slimane, who was the head designer of

---

* Ronnie was rather less fashion-conscious in these pieces, picking outfits he likened to "Steve Martin in *Three Amigos*" and describing his perfect rock star look as "a good pair of jeans and a good-fitting T-shirt, but one that has room to breathe. And the jeans should be tight but comfortable. I will not disclose how often I wash [my Diesel jeans]. But once they smell once, they adapt. I hate make-up. I hate styling products. It's like a dog getting washed for the first time." Source: *The Guardian Weekend*, Laura Barton, October 2005.

Christian Dior, and he had designed this pink leather jacket for Brandon, like a sport coat, so Brandon wore that on *Saturday Night Live*."

"It kind of sums up our band in a nutshell," Brandon said. "I think we'd have to dip into the old Elton and Liberace wardrobes to top that one. I'm not going to tell you how much it was, but it still hurts, I'll tell you that."[15]

The jacket was a scream on *SNL* on January 15, but didn't go down quite as well the following week, at one of the first *NME* tour dates in Scotland. At the Glasgow Academy the crowd got so rowdy that a full pint of lager hit Brandon mid-song and the gig had to be cut short. "It went all over my keyboard," Brandon said, "and the problem is that electronics and beer don't mix. So we were forced to stop the show. I've got a couple of backup keyboards now."[16] *

"First song in someone lobs a pint, it lands on Brandon's keyboard and it doesn't work," Ben Durling recalls. "They stop, it's pretty crucial to the set. There was a side door and under the stage was the dressing room. So I ran in by this side door – there's 2,500 people out there waiting for them to come back on and their perception would be that there's a mountain of technicians and roadies, but I opened the door and you've got Brandon with a hairdryer and Ronnie holding the keyboard, trying to get it to work. Everyone else stood there going 'What the fuck do we do?'"

Despite the lager-flinging, Brandon had a soft spot for Scotland. "My last name, Flowers, is a Scottish name," he said. "I've looked up my family tree and it dates back to Scotland. So I've probably still got an Uncle Jimmy in somewhere like Loch Ness."[17] So the band were particularly touched when they read in the newspapers while there of the death of a 14-year-old girl called Jodi Jones, whose boyfriend of the same age was that day, January 21, convicted of brutally murdering her in woods near her home in Dalkeith. "I was watching it on the news when we were in Glasgow," Brandon said.

---

* The jacket would see a lot of on-tour action in 2005, until Brandon had sweated so much in it that "it ended up a weird purple colour. Rock'n'roll is very hard on your clothes, you know." Source: *The Sunday Times Style*, Simon Mills, October 9, 2005.

"This teenage kid asked his girlfriend to come to his house and he was waiting in the woods on the way to his house. It was dark and he just brought her in there and cut her up."[18] "It affected me deeply," he explained, "and got me to thinking about how awful it must feel to be the parent of a missing child, how powerless a person must feel in such a dreadful situation… seeing those news stories got me to thinking about the powerlessness and frustration that must come from losing a child like that."[19] The sadness he felt over Jodi's death* inspired him to begin work on a new tune imagining the torment of the parent of a missing child.

Entitled 'Where Is She? (Soft Surrender)', they worked the song up in the extended soundchecks they requested each day to work on new material, and would start playing the song live almost immediately**, premiering it at Nottingham Rock City just two days later. "As long as we had a melody and an arrangement for a song," Brandon would say about their early-period tendency to play new material as soon as they wrote it, "I'd just let it out."[20] A semi-reggae tune with an itchy, insistent bassline, it told the story of police investigating a missing girl, of the tearful parents being informed under the gaze of a protagonist who was possibly the murderer himself. Brandon had distinct plans for recording it: "I want to fill the studio with pictures of her and her killer. It will give the song the most amazing atmosphere."[21]

Little did he know then, the song would never make it to tape. Long before recording sessions for the second album began, news emerged of the origins of the song and there was upset among the Scottish community. Brandon released a statement on the issue: "I'd hate to cause offence or further hurt," he said. "The song is not a direct portrayal of that one story, though – there's no way on Earth I could ever possibly pretend to know what it must actually feel like to suffer such a thing,

---

* Brandon would also claim that Jodi had seen The Killers play live, but since she was murdered in June 2003, this would have been impossible.

** Alongside, according to some reports, another new song, a weaving stomp of a tune called 'Sweet Talk'.

and I wouldn't presume to appropriate any other individual's feelings for a song." The song was quietly dropped.[*]

★ ★ ★

As the tour moved southwards, the trademark pink jacket caused less of a stir. Instead, the fireworks came from the shows[**] and the friendly competition between the bands. "It was a really good time," says Ricky Wilson. "During that tour Ronnie spent most of his time in our dressing room, not in their dressing room. We come from the same world so it's not a million miles away. You get each other, no matter what town you're from. They were blowing up. We were first on and just enjoying the ride. It was weird seeing how big they were getting. That band, or maybe just Brandon, are all about ambition. In the last 20 years I think they're the most ambitious act in the world. Brandon is fucking driven and what he's more concerned about than anything is legacy. He really wants legacy, which is admirable. I've learned a lot from that. He wants people to respect what he's done and not think it's flimflam or pop. Even though his heart lies very much in pop."

The Killers got plenty of respect on the *NME* tour. The academy-sized shows sold out, *Hot Fuss* hit number one in the charts as a result of the renewed interest and a re-release of 'Somebody Told Me' – a song Brandon now described as "'Rio' with chest hair"[22] – reached number three, that magic number that Franz Ferdinand had made such a mental

---

[*] "I felt really bad," Brandon said of the song in 2006. "Before I was in The Killers, I would have been able to write that song and nobody would have known. But it came from a good place. If I never would have said anything about it, nobody would ever have known and maybe that song would be on *Sam's Town* right now. It's a great song. It's a shame." Source: *The Observer*, Craig McLean, September 24, 2006.

[**] The Killers were becoming increasingly confident on these bigger stages, to the point where they'd risk seguing from 'On Top' into a cover of Pink Floyd's 'Time'.

target for Brandon*. All tickets for the London show at Brixton Academy were snapped up in three hours, so fast that they added another show of their own at the same venue for the following week and, when that sold out in an hour, a matinee show on top of that. "I said 'Look, we'll save more money on the promoter fees, and you'll make more money if you think you can do two shows in one day. It's what The Beatles used to do," says Braden.

The sense of indie tribes coming together on the *NME* tour heartened The Killers. "It's predominantly our crowd so that's not bad," Brandon said. "If it wasn't the *NME* tour it would be all our crowd. I guess it's good for us because we're hopefully winning Futureheads and Bloc Party and Kaiser Chiefs fans over."[23] "It doesn't hurt to have a competitive streak. Lennon and McCartney's competitiveness fuelled their greatest songs.

"When you meet a new band in the UK, you're sharing a bill. 'Hey, you're a musician too? Nice to meet you'," Ronnie added. "It's different in Las Vegas. 'Oh, you're in The Killers? Are you a fag? Are you wearing eyeliner?' You just get static in the States."[24] "Bands want to pick fights with us," Brandon said. "We're not New York cool, we are proud to have a pop element to us."[25]

The shows were phenomenal: "We're more raw, more brutal onstage," Brandon said, "when we connect with the audience and they connect with us amazing things happen... through all the touring we've done we've learned how to make a live show that really works".[26] The road was gruelling: "Sleeping on the floor – most nights I sleep in a little coffin bunk on the floor of the bus – the bus jerking around, nine other guys around you at all times, the lack of privacy, every time you look up seeing someone's ass sticking out of a bunk, so many things. But you get used to it."[27] Brandon even admitted to laundry issues. "We run out

---

* 'Somebody Told Me''s second UK release came in two CD formats and on 12-inch, backed across the formats with a variety of remixes and one new track, 'Show You How', a ragged-yet-grandiose ballroom slow-dance about a lover dumping his girlfriend by answer phone message, which opened with a crackly recording of Brandon singing the song onto Dave's answering machine.

of underwear and don't end up having time to wash them," he said. "The last tour, the last month, I was just turning my socks inside out and wearing no underwear."[28]

But The Killers ploughed through, discussing the pros and cons of the previous night's show in each pre-gig band huddle that had become their warm-up routine[*] and watching a DVD of Metallica's *Some Kind Of Monster* on the tourbus to see how not to be a functional group. "We'll never be like that," said Brandon. "They were rock gods and then they ruined it. They were the biggest band for such a long time and they've been pampered so much that they act like little girls now."[29]

Headlining these bigger shows, ironically, eased Brandon's inherent performance anxiety. "I'm getting better at not being myself because I'm not the most secure person in the world, on a night when we play a bad gig I'm very conscious if someone walks out of the room or laughs. It's strange – the bigger the place we play, the more comfortable I feel."[30]

On the day of the final show on the tour, at Brixton Academy on February 9, the band also attended the Brit Awards, where they were nominated for Best International Album and International Breakthrough Act. That they won neither irked Dave into a rather ill-advised post-Awards outburst. "Those pansies The Scissor Sisters got Best International Group[**]," he snarled, clearly unaware of the blatant homophobia in his words, "we were robbed by a bunch of fairy boys." Still, the gig at Brixton Academy was a riot, ending with all of the bands onstage for 'All These Things That I've Done', a fitting send-off for these adopted quasi-Brits as they prepared to fly back to the States to play at the Grammys on February 13. Here, Dave was only a little more diplomatic – "I'll sleep at night as long as we don't lose to Hoobastank," he said, but again the band won none of the awards they were up for, coming away only with the praise of host Jay Z, who announced them his favourite act of the night.

---

[*] "We all join together in a circle before we go onstage," Brandon said of the band's pre-gig routine. "Even our feet touch. It's kind of like a soccer coach talking to the kids."

[**] The Scissor Sisters actually beat The Killers in the Best International Album category.

"The Grammys were a really exciting time because all of a sudden your parents are calling you up for tickets," Braden says. "We stayed up at the Hollywood Roosevelt, and we flew in my family members and got them seats. Once you're in the Grammy Awards you're kind of locked in the building for about eight hours, and you're not really sure when your award category is going to come up. But naturally, we lost those categories – on one hand we were bummed, but on the other hand, it was a cool thing to not actually win because it kept our credibility with our early indie fanbase. Once you win a Grammy, in this country all of a sudden a really mainstream culture latches on to you and the loyal core audience thinks 'Well, that's it for this band, so I'll move on to something else' – that's the mentality. So what it did is it put the mainstream media onto us, but we had a strategy of wanting to keep it cool."

The Killers didn't keep their cool on the night. Bruised from the experience and with tongues duly sharpened, the band laid into Velvet Revolver for "getting votes based on who they are". Clearly, the band felt more appreciated by fans, industry and peers on this side of the pond.

Indeed, when the band returned to play their second Brixton show, the guest list was visible from the moon. "Those first couple of gigs in Brixton the guest list was pretty insane," Braden remembers. "I got calls from Noel Gallagher, Adam Clayton, some of the U2 camp, I had to usher them backstage to meet the band. I have a photograph somewhere where it was just members of U2 and Oasis, maybe The Verve, and they were all just mingling with the band. It was so cool. Brandon's biggest heroes are the U2 guys and the Oasis guys so for him to just be backstage having a beverage with these guys and talking, it was just a moment – the things you dream about can come true. That was a moment, those Brixton shows, where we knew we had definitely made it, when your peers and people you dream about are showing up at the gigs."

"I finally got to meet Noel Gallagher at Brixton Academy and he was cool," Dave said. "He's quite short and a little less mouthy than I expected. Do I rate him as a guitarist? I see both sides. But he's better than basic. People should write a song like 'Don't Look Back In Anger' or come up with a riff as good as 'Champagne Supernova' – then come back and say something."[31]

Noel would also be pictured with his arm around Brandon on the cover of the *NME* following the *NME* Awards that same week. At last, The Killers broke their awards ceremony duck, picking up Best International Band, Best Dressed and Sexiest Man. "We're very excited to win this award," went Brandon's first ever acceptance speech. "This band is comprised of three boys who weren't afraid to dream big, and one gentle giant."

Back-slapping over and back at their table, however, the band were shocked to find they had spawned a doppelgänger.

"We were at the *NME* Awards," says Braden, "and The Bravery were playing. The *NME* had asked us to play but we couldn't play due to scheduling conflicts so The Bravery ended up playing, which was a new signing to Island Records, to the same A&R man, our A&R man. I remember the band sitting at the table and Brandon was like 'Who is this band?' and there was an *NME* journalist nearby. All of a sudden, in the next couple of days, this story comes out in *NME* saying Brandon was slagging The Bravery. So it started a little bit of a rivalry with the band. I think The Bravery benefited from it quite a bit because they were just getting going and here is this band that people seem to respect and really love and all of a sudden Brandon is talking about this band."

Affronted by the idea his band were already being ripped off and copied by his own label and using the same press officer, and his growing confidence in taking swipes at rival acts in the press perhaps bolstered by meeting Noel Gallagher – the undisputed king of the witty band diss – Brandon went to town on The Bravery. "They're signed because we're a band," he told MTV News. "I've heard rumours about [members of] that band being in a different kind of band, and how can you defend that? How can you say 'My heart really belongs to what I do now' but you used to be in a ska band? I can see The Strokes play or Franz Ferdinand play and it's real, and I haven't gotten that from The Bravery. I think people will see through them."[32]

Within weeks, The Bravery's singer, Sam Endicott, fought back. "The poor guy, he's scared, I feel bad talking about him because it's like hitting a girl, it's like picking on a guy in a wheelchair," he said on San

Francisco's Live 105/KITS-FM station, then turned his ire upon Mark. "There's the one who's, like, nine feet tall. He looks like a little Dutch girl with a beard, but like a nine-foot-tall Dutch girl, like a mutant radioactive Dutch girl."

Later, Bravery guitarist, Michael Zakarin, weighed in on MTV. "If you have seen them live, they are incredibly boring," he said. "You remember what they used to look like? Then people started comparing them to us and suddenly they got a stylist. And Brandon frosted his hair and he's buying the cute pink jacket."[33]

Sniffing a Blur vs Oasis-style spat, the press weighed in. *Spin* pointed out that Ronnie's old band Attaboy Skip were a ska band too, and *The Times'* Bob Stanley mused "this hot fuss will run until they kiss and make up at an MTV Awards do, with both groups teaming up to back Britney, Kylie or Kate Moss. Authenticity doesn't come into it when the accountant is but a few yards away."

Unfounded rumours abounded that The Killers had kicked The Bravery off tours, and the question began to be slotted into every interview, journalists keen to stoke the fires of animosity between The Killers and their very first offspring. For Brandon though, the issue was simply one of respect. He'd always been at pains to acknowledge and pay tribute to the bands that had inspired him and, now that he was influencing other bands, all he got was sneers and abuse in return. "People compare The Bravery to The Killers and The Bravery are offended," Brandon said when it was one of a thousand questions sent in by fans for an *NME* interview, cooling his boots a little on the issue. "I took offence to that. I mean, we sold them our van, they use our press people… we've done nothing but open doors for them. That's all we're saying – they could have been more gracious about that."[34] "I haven't really got a problem with them. I just don't understand why they are so offended to be compared to us. I just think they should acknowledge that we were before them, and that helped them get where they are. I'd just like a little respect from them, that's all."[35]

"I've never actually said anything bad about anyone who didn't deserve it but occasionally it is brought on by jealousy," he'd add later. "When I hear a good song, it really does piss me off. But as far as The

Bravery goes… to me The Bravery just aren't real. I've heard that the keyboard parts are all pre-programmed, and that the singer can't reach the high notes on 'An Honest Mistake'. I can reach those high notes."[36] "To me," he continued elsewhere, "our A&R guy is *our* A&R guy, and I want all his affection and all his attention. I don't like it when he signs anybody else, and he signed them. Nothing against them, but The Killers deserve it more. It bothers me. At first I didn't want to hurt anybody's feelings, but it just developed a life of its own. But, y'know, I'll live."[37]

There was also a rather less publicised spat between Brandon and mainstream blues singer John Mayer. When asked by *Rolling Stone* which song he'd expect to hear if he went to hell, he picked Mayer's 'Daughters', unable to properly explain why he hated it so much. Mayer's response was sharp, and magnanimous. "The Killers' lead singer doesn't like me," he wrote in his *Esquire* column, "but he can eat it. I think he has some great tunes."[38] *

Of greater concern was what Brandon perceived to be a lawsuit building from Matt Norcross. "This guy who was in my band a long time ago is trying to sue us," Brandon told MTV in March. "We wrote 'Mr. Brightside' a long, long time ago, when we had a different drummer. He had nothing to do with it, but his wife is a lawyer, so she just sent a letter to our lawyer. Wow. You always hear about people coming out of the woodwork once you get big, but this is – wow."[39]

The whole lawsuit affair was, it turned out, a misunderstanding. Plans were afoot for an extended collector's edition of *Hot Fuss* and the suggestion had come up of including the demo version of 'Mr. Brightside' as a bonus track, which Norcross had drummed on. "[The Killers' representatives] came to me with an offer, and we went back and forth with a couple of negotiations," said Norcross. "It didn't go well, and the deal fell through… I sure as hell never sued them. I never filed a lawsuit. I also never claimed that I wrote 'Mr. Brightside.' I worked on 'Mr. Brightside,' but the song was there when they came to me. There were no drums to it, so I put my drum parts on it and gave them my

---

* Brandon and Mayer later met, made up and became friends.

input. I guess I just wanted a little bit more credit for what I had done… The whole thing really got blown out of proportion, it could have been handled a lot better."[40]

"I think we heard about it in the press first," says Braden, "and we were like 'What the hell?' and scratching our heads. I think the word on the street was that he had claimed that he had written 'Mr. Brightside', which was 100 per cent not true to my knowledge, and then it was pretty much just left in the hands of their lawyer and the story and the lawsuit went away. It could have been a rumour!"

Other salacious rumours began circulating around The Killers that spring too, seriously out-of-character rumours around alleged events in a bar on their four-date post-*NME* Awards tour of Japan. Internet word had spread that the band had gone on a drunken rampage with the daughter of a local ambassador and Japanese pop star Ringo Sheena and indecently exposed themselves, supposedly draping their genitals over the shoulders of unsuspecting women in the Park Hyatt hotel bar. "Our new answer to that question is 'Yeah, so?'" said Ronnie[41], who actually had, the previous year, shown a picture of himself flashing his penis in the shower to a waiter during a *Q* interview.

"I've not heard that one before, and it is of course nonsense," Brandon said. "But a story like that won't do us any harm. Controversy is never a bad thing."[42] "[But] we aren't that brave yet."[43]

That minor irritation swatted away, The Killers turned their attention back to chipping away at conquering America. And there, they had far bigger flies to fry…

★ ★ ★

The roar of the crowd at the Moore Theatre in Seattle had barely died when the call came through to Braden's cellphone.

"Braden, it's Paul McGuinness," said a voice full of the authority that comes with managing the biggest band in the world. "We're playing across town at the KeyArena, there's an after-show, the boys would love to have you along. I'll send a black van in 20 minutes, there'll be laminates waiting when you get here."

The spring US tour had started well – two nights at the Fillmore in San Francisco, two nights at the Wiltern LG Theatre in LA, thrilled crowds lapping up every tune, even the new track 'Stereo Of Lies'*. Now they were going to get a glimpse of how the bigger half gigged.

"I get the band ready," says Braden, "the black van shows up, we get ushered into this sold-out arena and Bono is singing, the crowd is screaming. We're in the pit and he just sort of looks down at Brandon and gives him a wink and then they go into four more hits and the show's over. We're just looking around going 'Oh my God this is insane.' We all get loaded into a van to the after party at the Hilton hotel in downtown Seattle and there's all this security and we get ushered into a freight elevator. When me and the band walk into the elevator, guess who is in the elevator? Bono, every member of U2, every member of Kings Of Leon, Pearl Jam, Bill Gates from Microsoft, the mayor of Seattle and Gary Payton, from the Seattle Supersonics. All up in the same lift! We start going up 30 or so floors and we all look around like, 'Man if this elevator breaks down, here goes half of the music industry, right down the toilet'.

"The party was awesome. We were all hanging out, I'm talking to Paul McGuinness, I'm meeting my manager hero and Bono came up and said one funny thing. Me and Mark and Brandon were sitting around having some red wine, and Bono didn't realise the band had a manager, so for about two minutes I couldn't stand Bono after his comment – he comes up to us and goes 'Hey guys, if you need anyone to break kneecaps for you, Paul sitting over there is your man'. I kind of look at Bono and give him a look and he goes 'Oh, it looks like you've already got someone who can break kneecaps, sorry about that!'

"One of Mark's idols is Eddie Vedder from Pearl Jam and he was over there in the corner drinking wine and Mark was so nervous he

---

* 'Stereo Of Lies' would remain unrecorded; only live bootlegs of the track exist. Built around the repeated line "Matthew has got, a big idea/And he's gonna take it out on me", it was about the Norcross 'lawsuit', which may explain why it was never recorded: "I can't talk about this one much because it's about the person who is suing us," Brandon said in 2005, "but let's just say it's an angry song, and it also taps into all the feelings we've experienced in the past few years." Source: *Q*, Nick Duerden, July 2005.

wouldn't go over and talk to him. I walked him over and made an introduction and all of a sudden they were talking for hours, so that made me really happy. And then we met them again in Chicago[*]. We had a sold-out show at the Riviera Theatre and I had arranged a car for U2 and management to come to the Riviera and I set them up this really nice luxury box seat."

"That U2 party," adds Dave, "the first people there were us and Bill Gates. The show has just ended and we got over there and it was just Bill Gates and his wife standing around a table of food and drinks, it was almost awkward. We just walked in like 'Hi, hello richest man in the world.' We had to say hello, it was just us. He was really nice, he knew who we were. It was bizarre. Then the party filled up and Pearl Jam were there and Kings Of Leon and lots of other normal people too."

Peeks behind U2's scene inspired The Killers to think bigger. Brandon was unhappy with the video for the next single from *Hot Fuss*, 'Smile Like You Mean It' – directed by Chris Hopewell, it further cemented the band's links to the UK by casting them as monochrome ghosts drifting through scenes in an average English home; birthday parties, funerals, Christmases. "It's very English-looking," Brandon said. "It goes through the story of a house over a 20-year period of time. It's got a sentimental feel about it, but I don't really love the video, I'm really not too happy with it. But what can you do? I mean, they're releasing the song as a rock single, and it's the least rocking song we have. It's a mid-tempo song."Released on April 4 in the US and May 2 in the UK[**], the song reached number 11 in the UK and 15 in the States. Great, but not great enough.

---

[*] This was on May 11, two weeks after the first party.

[**] The track was backed on a translucent pink 7-inch vinyl with a cover of the Vietnam country hit 'Ruby, Don't Take Your Love To Town', which the band had recorded in one day for a UK radio session. "It was thrown together really fast," Dave explained, "I just was messing around doing those country licks and they said, 'Keep that on there'. We didn't really have time to try anything else." Source: *Ultimate Guitar*, Steven Rosen, November 14, 2012. On the CD version was a new song called 'Get Trashed', a desolate drinking ballad recorded in the warped, ragged no-fi style of the most desolate moments of Pink Floyd's *The Wall* – as if the whole band, racked with jealousy and stomachs burning, were drunk in a skip.

Irked at not being in complete control of their visual aesthetic, The Killers pressed on with their plans for the murder trilogy film. Island had given the project the green light and they'd sent out feelers to James Spader to see if he'd be interested in starring; the hope was to have the film ready for the next Sundance Festival. And in the meantime, when the next video treatment came up, they'd settle for nothing but the best, someone they'd admired for as long as they could remember as "a genius with his pictures and film":[44] Anton Corbijn.

Getting Corbijn to agree to direct the US version of the video for 'All These Things That I've Done' was a coup, since it was his first video for two years. "They are a great bunch of guys with a long-term vision," said Anton of his reasons for deciding to work with them. "The song is just fantastic and we tried to make it into a pretty bizarre story for the video."[45] Bizarre indeed; Corbijn's treatment, shot in his trademark black and white in the three acres of neon graveyard which were becoming a favourite location for the band, was a quasi-Western story starring The Killers as trench-coated Mexican bandidos, complete with bushy moustaches for Brandon and Dave, as they battled a group of female assassins with boomerangs called The Killersluts. Their action-packed stand-offs were intercut with scenes of Brandon as a cheating husband, the band falling from the sky, or one memorable snippet where Brandon rides a small donkey on a dwarf's porch. "The whole thing was [Anton's] idea," Brandon said, "and there's still some things I don't understand. Like the donkey, I don't understand what that scene's about at all."[46] *

When the cameras stopped rolling, The Killers stayed in their surreal fantasy dimension. "I get a call from Elton's tour manager," Braden recalls, "and he basically says to me, 'Elton wants to meet you and the band tonight, can you do that? He's performing at the Colosseum in Vegas, it's a sold-out show, we'll set you up in a really nice seating area to watch the show and Elton would also like to have dinner with you in his top-floor penthouse at Caesars Palace, please call me back and let me know if that can happen'. So I turn to the guys and go 'What

---

* Despite the crazy video, the single peaked at only number 74 on the *Billboard* Hot 100 Chart.

are you doing tonight?' 'Well I was just going to spend time with my girlfriend.' And I just said, 'Well is there any way we can make this happen?' 'Okay, what have you got?' 'Elton John wants you to come and see him perform live tonight at the Colosseum, and then he wants us to come up to his top-floor suite at Caesars Palace above the Strip and have dinner with him, are you cool with that?' 'Err yes! What am I going to wear?'

"So we go back to the hotel or our individual homes to get dressed up, send for car service, we go watch the show – it was a great show, nothing but hits. Then we get ushered up to the top floor of Caesars Palace, we sit down and have dinner with Elton and he was the most gracious, funny man we all had met. I mean, he was playing all the new records, he was playing new Bloc Party, Broken Social Scene, he was talking about each band, and at the dinner was Baz Luhrmann, which blew Brandon's mind because he was such a huge fan of [*Moulin Rouge*] – it was the inspiration for the 'Mr. Brightside' video. Elton's cracking jokes, talking about music and I remember asking Elton 'Why do you do this? It's obviously not the money' and he just said – this is some of the best advice the band ever got – 'If I don't create every day I will die'. That spoke volumes to me and the band."

The invites round to Elton's suite would keep coming. "He is just the nicest man," Brandon would say, "and people forget how important he is, how many lives he's soundtracked. And when it comes to new music, he's more on the ball than anyone I know."[47] "He's from the era of glamour, real bands and real people writing songs and I think we remind him of how he used to be. We're from Las Vegas, so we always thought of playing live as a bigger thing than just playing music. Putting on a good show is in our blood."[48] At one meeting, Elton would try to wangle himself an invitation to Brandon's forthcoming wedding. "It's in October, right?" Elton said. "If it is I'll be here in Vegas." In the event, Elton's invite never dropped onto his rhinestone doormat.

Brandon's amazement at meeting his musical heroes didn't seem to diminish with the constant bombardment, however. "We've met Elton John, Bono, David Bowie and Noel Gallagher so far," he said. "Two years ago these people were musicians that we admired, but now they know who we are and appreciate our music. It's pretty surreal."[49] "For them to have even heard of my band, let alone say that they like it, solidifies everything for me."[50] "You have to get your mind past who they are. They're still people, after all, and Elton is practically a friend now."[51]

Inspired by seeing the top end of the music business at first hand, as their US tour entered its fourth month of rapturously received theatre shows and the outdoor festival season approached, The Killers decided to up their Stateside game. "The agent and the band and I came up with this idea about 'Hey, let's see if we can do a mini, new music version of Glastonbury on our own,'" Braden says. "So we rolled up into this venue called the Merriweather Post Pavilion, which is just outside of Washington D.C., and we had put Maximo Park, Louis XIV, Keane and The Killers on the bill. The place had a 22,000-seat capacity and we sold it out! We had all the radio stations in the area presenting or involved with that show, on D.C. 101, which is the huge alternative station in that market. I remember sitting out on that stage, watching the band play and the crowd just losing their minds. The band were having such a good show – I just started crying, because I was just like 'We're doing it, we made it, we've worked so hard.' In America, to me, that show was *the* moment."

A few weeks later, they'd play the real-life Glastonbury for the second time. And their journey would once more skirt perilously close to disaster.

Mark Stoermer, April 2014

How was the *NME* tour?
I remember the first show of the tour we flew in from America and went right onstage because we had a show the day before in America. We were in Newcastle or something, somewhere north, so we flew in from America, got another plane and went straight to the gig. You're playing in a daze. The last gig at Brixton was pretty fun. There was a general feeling that something was happening with all of the bands at the time and it was exciting that we felt that this was the Class of 2005. Our tour manager, who we stole from Stellastarr*, became Kaiser Chiefs' tour manager too!

What are your favourite experiences of making videos during this period?
In general I don't love making videos. Sometimes I like them when they're done, I like the idea of being in one, but you learn quickly that you're sitting around all day to do 10 seconds [of footage]. You also learn quickly that they tell you to show up at 8 a.m. and you don't to anything until 3 p.m., usually. The one with Anton Corbijn was fun, although the beginning of my back injury was during that shoot. I remember being really stiff and in pain during that one, but other than that it was fun working with Anton Corbijn, and we did it in Las Vegas.

What was the root of your back problem?
It was just a freak thing, bending over to pick something up in my house and then I couldn't stand for three days, and we had the video shoot on the third day and I was still recovering.

Dave Keuning, March 2014

How did you feel when Brandon would have digs at other bands?
I didn't like it and some of those bands I liked. As soon as he said one bad thing, they loved it and would get him to say another bad thing. The press is like that. He was fearless and confident and wanted to say whatever –

I respect him for that but I didn't necessarily agree with everything he was saying. I wasn't really a fan of The Bravery but I liked their song 'An Honest Mistake', I didn't have a problem with them, I sure as heck didn't want to get in a fight with them. There was no reason to.

CHAPTER 7

Smile Like You Mean It

"Last year exposed us to many people who weren't familiar with our music. We owe a lot to that... Walking out and seeing thousands of people gathered to see us play was totally unexpected."[1]

"[Last year] was a really exciting time, a turning point for us. We didn't know how much England liked us!"[2]

– Brandon, pre-Glastonbury 2005

A t a Fleet Services cash register, halfway down the M3 towards Somerset, Dave paid for his slice of pizza and his drink, his mind wandering. Nerves were addling the entire band that day – Glastonbury was a major show and every decision seemed crucial. Dave had been edgy that morning anyway after a late night up watching basketball, but the journey from the Cumberland Hotel in Marble Arch had been particularly fraught. Mark had been late, Ronnie overexcited about the show and Brandon already dressed for the stage in shimmering mascara and a mint-white dinner jacket. They stopped off to look at the backdrop for the stage – a recreation of the *Hot Fuss* album sleeve that Brandon had described as a disaster – and, amid rumours of flooding and electrical failures on site that made Dave wonder if it was even worth heading down to the festival at all, they'd spent a hefty portion of the drive so far locked deep in discussion over the set list, and which of the many new songs Brandon had pieced together on the road they'd play at the festival.

"Brandon was always writing on the road," Braden says. "We had got him a tape machine, a multi-track tape recorder, and he had a bass and a guitar in the back of the bus and he started writing.* I remember we were in Boston and we got on the bus and he was like 'Hey, I gotta play something for you' and he played this song called 'For Reasons Unknown', which was a little bit slower than it would end up.** I thought 'What a great chorus and melody'. So he was really prolific at that time and live they started to reveal things like the song 'Bones' in their sets."

"To keep us from going nuts," Brandon had said, "playing the same songs for two years straight, we've taken it upon ourselves to write new songs and try them out on the road. For Glastonbury I would expect to hear one or two new ones. We decide on the day of the show."[3] But the discussions had been way too intense for Dave – "If we talk any more about which new number we're doing tonight," he said, "I'm going to fucking kill everyone on the bus."[4]

Instead, between renditions of Beautiful South songs from Brandon and his brother Shane, the band had talked about what they should wear for their appearance at Live 8 the following week; Brandon suggested a uniform of cream white. They resolutely avoided the big question mark hanging over the gig – whether or not they should have headlined. Kylie Minogue, booked for the Saturday night headline set on the Pyramid Stage, had been forced to cancel due to her treatment for breast cancer, and as the second band on the bill, The Killers had been offered her slot. On reflection, though, the band turned it down.

"Next year would be better," Brandon explained. "We want to feel that we grew and accomplished more later. There's nowhere to go from

---

* The band would also plug Dave's guitar and Brandon's keyboard into portable speakers in the bus in order to write together.
** Brandon would later claim he wrote the song on Louis XIV's bus.

headlining the world's biggest festival."[5] "Maybe in 2015, if we never have another hit, we'll look back and think, 'Fuck, we should've said yes', but hopefully we'll be able to headline it in a couple of years, when we've earned it."[6] *

With all of these concerns whirling through his head, Dave wandered back out to the service station parking lot.

No bus.

He stared at the empty parking space where his tourbus should have been waiting. Definitely no bus. He checked his pockets – his phone was still on the bus lounge table where he'd been sitting watching Sky News 10 minutes earlier. He felt in his pockets; the coins there made a terrifyingly sparse jangle.

He didn't panic, there was a simple solution to being left behind at a service station halfway to Glastonbury. He'd just find a phone and use his remaining change to phone Braden's office in the US.

Answerphone.

Now, he began to panic.

"One minute I'm watching an item on Sky News, the next I'm begging for money," Dave said.[7] Reduced from rock star to hobo in minutes, he asked eight people for spare change before anyone gave him enough cash to phone the band's on-site sound guy to get a message to the bus, which was by now an hour down the road without him. When the tour manager got the call he asked everyone on the bus to hide anything that Dave might want to throw at anyone. "We went back an hour," Brandon said. "It was a big ordeal. It set us back three hours. I was watching *Caddyshack* so I didn't notice he wasn't there."[8]

When they got back to Fleet to pick him up, Dave was remarkably chilled about the situation: "He seemed to get through it okay," Brandon recalled. "He usually throws fits but he did all right."[9] He had his frustration further allayed by a stop-off at Stonehenge, where Ronnie jumped the fence to dance in the restricted land and hugged a couple of Swedish girls before Stonehenge security chased him off the site and back to the bus, where he suddenly announced he felt ill and

---

* Coldplay eventually took Kylie's slot at the festival that year.

threw up in the toilet. An eventful journey ended when the bus pulled up a hundred yards behind the Pyramid Stage in a lake of mud, just in time for the band to squelch their way on to the stage to play for a mammoth 100,000 people. "It's a far cry from the Dublin Castle," Brandon chuckled. "In just over a year and a half, we've come such a long way. I was probably more nervous to play for the hundred people there than I will be for the 100,000 tonight."[10]

The show was a stormer, despite Brandon's practised new move – leaving his rhinestone-covered keyboard stand* to jump onto the drum riser to stop 'Glamorous Indie Rock & Roll' halfway through for dramatic effect – falling flat. It also saw the UK premiere of a new song they'd been trying out on the road, 'All The Pretty Faces'. Brandon had called the song "the future of The Killers" onstage at the KROQ Weenie Roast in May; "That song is a lot heavier, but it's very exciting," he'd say. "I think it could be better still, but that's the great thing about taking it out on the road, we can gauge people's reactions to it."[11] The song was heavy indeed, a dark metallic beast with glimmers of The Cure, surging with the desperation of a love turned sour. "Help me out, I need it, I don't feel like loving you no more," Brandon yelped, before hinting at the disorientation he'd been experiencing in the wake of *Hot Fuss* – "I spent two long years in a strange strange land, well how did it happen?"

The song could be taken to refer to Brandon's troubled position on groupies, considering lines like "All the pretty faces ringing out, well I just can't go to bed" and "You shake and you bleed while I sing my song". Early in 2005 Brandon would admit to being tempted by the parade of girls on offer but never succumbing, and his sexual morals were made clear when he was questioned on his view about Janet Jackson's famed 'wardrobe malfunction' during the Super Bowl Halftime Show in 2004. "People say it was an over-the-top reaction," he said of the furore around the 'nipple slip', "but they're the biggest

---

* "We sent away for these rhinestones and I super-glued them on," he said of the bejazzled stage decoration. "I didn't think of Liberace. I just wanted to put things on my keyboard." Source: *Spin*, Marc Spitz, February 2005.

stars in the world and a lot of young kids were watching. The world's become more corrupt. Young girls' skirts are getting shorter and it's wrong. People that kids look up to shouldn't act like that. Morals are going to pot and that has a lot to do with popular music. We're trying to bring back something a little more innocent."[12]

Still, Brandon wrestled with his inner rock'n'roll demons. "I'm trying to find the ideal place," he said. "And I'm still looking. I'm starting to get more comfortable with it. I'm a man and I'm attracted to women. You read about, and you have that fascination with, the drugs. There's a certain level that we're kinda expected to debaucherise [sic], I guess! It's expected of us, almost."[13] "It's difficult, though. I mean, I grew up reading all these stories about David Bowie getting loaded in the seventies, and it all sounded so great. Now I'm confronted with it almost every day. At one point in each day, there's going to be some dude in a new town who's going to approach me and offer me something illegal, telling me how great it is. It can get hard to deal with."[14]

"It bothers me that I'd be more credible to certain people if I had a drug problem," he'd muse. "Why? That's bullshit. I'm not interested in drugs because I've seen what they can do. Take Brian Wilson. I don't want to be like him. What does it matter today that he wrote 'Good Vibrations'? The man goes around talking to himself."[15]

Five days after Glastonbury, The Killers got their first sniff of the stadium. The European leg of U2's Vertigo tour was notable for its array of cool indie support acts – Franz Ferdinand, The Thrills, Kaiser Chiefs and even The Bravery played at various shows across the continent. The Killers' turn came at the Cardiff Millennium Stadium on June 29, an overwhelming experience for Brandon – he prepared for the gig by practising singing the high notes of 'Pride (In The Name Of Love)' in case Bono asked him onstage for it and, finding he couldn't, opted to be simply "a good student" instead.

The band would support U2 twice more in 2005, in Chorzow, Poland, and the Amsterdam Arena, but not before Brandon would be pictured on the cover of the *NME* alongside Bono and Razorlight's Johnny Borrell as the faces of Live 8. "The three greatest bands on the planet?" Bono would joke with them during the shoot, when he wasn't calling Jay Z to urgently get more hip-hop on the bill, "Well the three greatest bands in the room…"[16] A global event involving 10 simultaneous outdoor shows around the world on July 2 organised by Live Aid originator Bob Geldof to tie in with the G8 summit being held in Scotland, the aim of Live 8 was to highlight the issue of crippling debts inflicted upon developing nations. The Killers were booked to play one song, 'All These Things That I've Done' – although the song's 'I've got soul' refrain was slipped into songs by both Coldplay and Robbie Williams at the same show. "We're playing because it's a way for us to get involved without getting political," Brandon said on the day. "We're going to go up there as humans, not as The Killers. We want to go up and feel like we're responsible for helping people without getting all political. Once you get political, you're in a whole new area. And we're not there yet. I don't know if we ever will be."[17]

"People today are coming together as a family," Brandon said as The Killers took to the stage in Hyde Park to play to a crowd of 200,000 and a TV audience estimated at 3 billion, the biggest televised gig ever held, "because our brothers and sisters in Africa need our help, so let's change their worlds." Sure enough, the band wore matching ice-white suits. "The first thing I thought about was the outfits," said Brandon. "Much more so than what songs we would be playing. I saw those white wristbands and decided that we'd go all white. Unfortunately it turned out other acts had the same idea. Madonna came on before us and stole the show as far as white clothes were concerned."[18]

The superstar hook-ups would keep coming. At that year's T in the Park festival Brandon was invited onstage with New Order to sing 'Crystal' and, returning for more theatre dates and festivals in the US, the band would play alongside Weezer and Pixies at that year's Lollapalooza in Chicago. In a break from these dates, Brandon and Tana flew to Hawaii to get married in a private ceremony solely for family and friends, Brandon clad in a white Lindeberg tuxedo. The couple enjoyed four days on the island before Brandon hit the road again.

Around this string of dates leading up to the Reading & Leeds festival, the band often spoke of closing the book on *Hot Fuss* and of R&L being "our big goodbye". Though they dreamed of The Killers lasting 20 years or more[*], they'd been on the road virtually non-stop for two years solid, played over 300 gigs to over three million people and achieved everything they'd hoped from the debut album, which was fast approaching its four millionth sale that summer. The tactic of re-releasing singles had paid major dividends for them, so a new sky-blue vinyl US deluxe edition of the album emerged in the summer, featuring extra tracks – 'The Ballad Of Michael Valentine', 'Glamorous Indie Rock & Roll' and a new recording of 'Under The Gun'. In the UK, the record was well on the way to achieving 173 weeks in the Albums Chart. It was a monster that refused to die.

Plus, the strain was showing. Ronnie's first thought every morning was of hugging his wife and mowing his lawn. Brandon was so homesick he was beginning to miss his Hyundai. Mark was keen to spend time with his girlfriend, a violinist in an Irish punk covers act called Darby O'Gill & The Little People, and had been mildly burned by the road when a couple were arrested for trying to steal his $4,500 Fender bass. When *NME*'s Barry Nicolson met up with the band at the Video Music Awards in Miami in August[**] – Brandon clad in another tuxedo to pick up the award for Best New Artist In A Video from their four nominations – he found them visibly exhausted. An ego-boosted Brandon was predicting that they'd be away for a year to make the most important album of their lives.[***] Mark wandered blankly through their

---

[*] In one interview Dave optimistically hoped they'd last 50 years, to which Brandon replied "He'll be, like, 80 years old by then. Though having said that, that might be about the time I slip down to the Strip and start crooning in one of those hotels. As long as I'm still singing I'd do that in a heartbeat." Source: *The Guardian Guide*, January 22, 2005.

[**] Eric Roberts from ABC's *Less Than Perfect* joined them onstage for their performance of 'Mr. Brightside' at the VMAs.

[***] "Brandon's ego has definitely gone up," Dave said elsewhere. "And he loves what's happening to us. We all do, of course, but Brandon – well, Brandon more." Source: Q, Nick Duerden, July 2005.

photo shoot on Miami Beach in Duran Duran-style suits* as if he barely knew where he was. And most stressed of all, Dave was clamouring for a flight home to deal with what he'd refer to as "relationship problems" with a girl he'd been seeing. It would be some years before these problems were explained – around this time his on-off girlfriend, Cara Cross, gave birth to his son, Kyler.

"There were times when everybody wanted a break," Braden says, "like 'Can I please stay home for a couple of weeks?' but then we'd all get itchy feet and go 'When's the next tour?' With every band, if you're out on the road for two months at a time, away from your loved ones and family and friends, there'll be times when it got stressful and it was very tiring. People would hardly get any sleep and it can have an effect on you. But I've never worked with a band since then that worked that hard, and wanted to work. That's part of the reason why this whole thing was really successful: the band wanted to work."

What's more, their thoughts were racing on album two. The plans for the murder film were shelved as "we want to make a new album first and it'd be weird if we make a film with songs on it from the first album. It might be strange."[19] And, with four months set aside for writing at the end of 2005 and recording sessions already booked for January 2006, with Flood pencilled in as producer**, the ideas for the record were gradually taking shape.

"We've got tons of ideas and songs, but we won't put it out until it's great,"[20] Brandon said, still promising a more organic album in the summer of 2006. "We don't want to be 'that [synth] band' forever. We'll let someone else be that."[21]

"The new songs are a lot more organic," he added. "There are a lot more organs and pianos. A lot of it is very rocky. We're trying some new things out, trying to find the right balance. But it all depends on what you've got. If you've got three or four obvious singles then it'll keep the momentum going, and help people connect. If we can have

---

* Aside from Ronnie, who wore a comedy tuxedo.

** "I'm so honoured," Brandon said. "He's produced most of my favourite albums, and I don't think that can be a coincidence." Source: Planet Sound.

one or two songs on every record that remind people of something in their lives it'll help our music last forever. And that's what I really want."[22] "Our next dream is to be important – to have a couple of songs that live forever, like 'Roxanne' by The Police and 'I Wanna Hold Your Hand' by The Beatles. You know those songs when you're eight but you don't know why. I'd be happy with that."[23]

"The first record is good and focused but perhaps a little too cold, because it was so young and taken from demos," Ronnie said. "It's a little stiff in parts. Especially lyrically. We've become better as a band and I think we're really going to hone in on that part of it." Brandon: 'We've already grown, so even if we write similar songs there's going to be a difference. People have reinvented themselves and still been strong without falling off too far. That's the key. The Beatles and U2 did it and Bowie's done it about five times... We're excited about having hits but we want more. That's the exciting part – knowing there's going to be another one."[24]

In the running for the next Killers stone-cold classic were a number of new songs. Without asking the approval of his family[*], Brandon had written 'Uncle Jonny Took Cocaine' inspired by his real-life uncle Jonny and his paranoid episodes. "I wanted this to sound like it could have come off *Lust For Life* by Iggy Pop," Brandon explained[25], claiming he loved the title but was worried about familial retribution. "There's a real inspirational feeling by the end of the song, I think. You're pulling for Jonny. That's a good thing, having faith in people."[26]

Other tracks in the frame included 'I'm Talking To You', which Brandon described as "our Oasis rip-off song, especially the guitar line. It could rescue their career. It's about talking to yourself and figuring out life's big problems all on your own"[27][**], 'Higher And Higher' which Brandon saw as "the next 'All These Things That I've Done', only better. People love songs with momentum, and the chorus will give people something to scream about"[28] and 'Daddy's Eyes'. "This is

[*] Although originally he hoped his uncle Jonny would play guitar on the track.
[**] The Killers would never release a song called 'I'm Talking To You'; it's possible that it was a working title for 'Sweet Talk'.

211

about a father telling his son that he has cheated on his mother and is going to leave home," Brandon said of the track, a scuzzy lo-fi rhumba with a widescreen prog solo section reminiscent of Pink Floyd, "but explaining that it isn't his son's fault. It's not from personal experience, but everyone will be able to relate to it. This will make people cry, trust me."[29]

"There's another one called 'Where The White Boys Dance' which is everyone's favourite," he added. "It makes me feel dirty. I'd probably describe it as being like 'Somebody Told Me' soaked in blood. It sounds a little like Talking Heads in that it's got a lot of different parts but a very repetitive rhythm. I love it."[30]

Planning to call the album *Make You Feel Dirty* – since that was the intended effect these songs would have on the listener – they were well aware of the pressure to follow up a huge smash like *Hot Fuss*. "We've got a monkey on our back because we've sold about four million records, and that's very tough to beat," said Brandon. "It's fuelled something in me. I want to come back and make an even bigger splash."[31] "When you are a kid you dream about having people wanting to touch you, now I want to touch people. I dream of making another album as good as the first one, but also making it more important."[32] "Anyone who thinks we are a one-hit wonder," he concluded, "will think again. This album might just be incredible."[33]

The Killers waved goodbye to *Hot Fuss* with a succession of rock'n'roll list-ticking. The traffic was so bad between London and Reading on the day of their show that they hired their first helicopter to reach the festival in time for their set. After heading back to the US – on a flight Brandon was certain would crash since everything had been going so well – they played their first festival headline set alongside Oasis and Pixies at the inaugural Across The Narrows event in Brooklyn and also ticked off a gig at the Joint in Vegas' Hard Rock Hotel, where Brandon had first seen Oasis, although they were hardly greeted like returning heroes. "People in Vegas just gawp at us, eyes wide, mouths open," Ronnie said. "It's a smaller town than you'd think. We're still playing to a bunch of fucking people we knew in English class who still don't like us."[34] "When we go back to Vegas it's not like they get the red carpet out or anything," Dave added. "People are bitter. They assume we live in LA and they bitch about us in the papers out there. Some of them knew us or were in a band with us back in the day and they've been against us from day one."[35]

Then, once their live engagements were completed and they were settled back in Vegas for writing sessions in a rehearsal room behind a strip bar – between nights out at the Beauty Bar and the Art Bar downtown, and various house parties to try to re-integrate into the local scene – Brandon fulfilled one of his biggest dreams on November 5, singing onstage with U2 at the MGM Grand Garden Arena in Paradise, Vegas, in a very glamorous blue velvet overcoat and gold brooch, giving it his all through a broad beaming grin.

"We were all sitting around at an after-show," he said, "and we were all pretty drunk. Bono leant over and said 'Come along to our soundcheck tomorrow', and I was like 'Yeah, he was drunk, he'll forget about it'. But sure enough, the next day, I got a phone call saying 'Soundcheck's at five, don't be late'. So I got to this empty arena and Bono said to me 'We were thinking of playing 'In A Little While' tonight, I know it's your favourite song, do you wanna sing it with us?' I mean, it was amazing."[36]

As the year wound to a close bathed in glory – *Spin* would name The Killers its Band Of The Year and picture Brandon on the cover seated on a throne and holding a gold crown – behind the scenes the first serious tribulations were brewing. The band's relationship with Braden had broken down towards the end of the two-year *Hot Fuss* touring schedule, and Merrick was replaced as manager by Robert Reynolds. The circumstances behind this shift would have legal and personal recriminations for everyone involved.

Neither party is at liberty to discuss the details today, but in his $16 million breach-of-contract lawsuit filed in February 2006 Braden claimed that Reynolds, having initially charged a hefty 15 per cent of the band's gross income for his legal services, had then convinced the band to transfer the management role to him. Reynolds refuted these accusations vehemently, stating he always only charged the standard five per cent, and in court papers The Killers' camp would claim that Robert became manager only following his best efforts to convince Merrick to do what it took for him to keep his job.

Settlement negotiations concerning Merrick's removal from the management postion got under way before the lawsuit was filed at U.S. District Court in Las Vegas on February 21, surprising Reynolds and the band. "The only statement the band would like to make at this time is that the claims alleged by Mr Merrick are absolutely meritless and we intend to defend this action vigorously," Reynolds commented. "He was an absentee manager," added the band's new lawyer Michael Guido. "He breached his agreement and his fiduciary duties."

Braden's position was that his four-year contract for 15 per cent of The Killers' gross income, signed on April 8, 2003, still had two years to run when he was fired, and there were payment issues. "As soon as [Merrick] made them superstars they decided to stop paying him," said Howard King, representing Merrick and his company, From The Future. "He's entitled to a percentage of their income for his services as a manager and a producer." "At the time they fired him, they had not paid him much of what they owed him," King said later. "In fact, they're holding $2.5 million dollars, which is what they calculate he was owed to the day he was fired."

The legal wrangles would continue for years to come, Merrick pursuing his claim and, in 2009, the band counter-suing Braden for "multi-million-dollar damages in missed concerts and lost touring revenues, and via the bungling of merchandising and promotional opportunities". The court papers from the counter-claim and a subsequent case against Merrick, which The Killers brought before the California Labor Commission, cast light on the band's position, claiming Merrick was "an incompetent manager who abandoned his clients... at a critical juncture of their careers", who "failed or refused to perform the most rudimentary functions required by his Management Agreement". "Merrick was incommunicado when The Killers needed him most," the papers stated. "On countless occasions, Merrick could not be reached by The Killers, their business manager, attorney, and numerous third parties, to address critical business matters," the papers read. "Rather than the required performance, Merrick offered various excuses for his unavailability, including that his cellular phone seemed to be perpetually out of 'juice' or 'misplaced'."

Citing examples of unobtained visas, misinformation, flight mix-ups and lack of communication that led to shows in Switzerland, Austin and Japan being cancelled, videos running over budget, merchandise designs going unapproved, and finance and promotional activities being fumbled, the claims all added up to a deep-seated lack of trust developing between the two parties. An email to Merrick from an unnamed band member was quoted: "People are becoming frustrated because you're not communicating with them. Now people are blowing me up looking for answers. I'll respond and help for half of your commission. Sound good? What's the deal? We need you to be completetly [sic] available at all times for us or anyone needing timely answers. I'm getting calls or emails from all ends re the tour and that only tells me that you aren't doing a sufficient job organising the tour. From what I'm told, we are losing opportunities by the hour. Why am I getting calls or emails? Apparently I'm the only one that will call or write them back. Please communicate with the team. You must do this!"

Braden's "unresponsiveness" was put down to "double dealing", the band suggesting that Braden was also working as a consultant for Island Def Jam, The Killers' label, with whom the papers claim the band had "an adversarial relationship".

When relations reached breaking point, The Killers' case stated, Braden was even given an opportunity to correct his position and stay manager simply by replying to a "notice of breach" letter with assurances that his breaches would be cured. According to the papers, no such reply ever arrived.

The Killers' suit made no reference to Merrick's claims about non-payment by the band – and, it should be noted, Braden has gone on to successfully manage bands and labels to this day as president of Bright Antenna Records. Ultimately both suits would be dropped in October 2009. Though a ruling by the California Labor Commission found in favour of the band, meaning they actually owed Braden nothing, the Killers camp settled on undisclosed terms to put the whole difficult period to rest.

Back in 2005 and even with this sort of stress weighing on his mind, Brandon was pleased to be home. "We were on tour for two years," he explained, "and all of our fantasies about Europe and Japan and those places became reality. And at the end of it all, when we went home, it made me realise how much in love I was with America, how much I missed Nevada. Absence made the heart grow fonder."[37]

And so he set about making a record in celebration. The Killers' American odyssey.

Ben Durling, May 2014

Did you see any of the fan madness?

Yeah, on the *NME* tour they did a signing at HMV in the middle of Glasgow; there were 600 kids queuing all day, and afterwards we had a car to take us back to the venue. All these kids had come round the back of the HMV and someone held the door open and the four members of the band, myself and Braden ran through these people, jumped in and they were all banging, girls pressing themselves up against the car. It was absolute chaos.

What can you remember about the bigger shows?

Live 8 was the biggest thing. That was the most ridiculous afternoon. There was an artist backstage bit behind the main stage and we turned up. Brandon had borrowed the choir from another act for the gospel bit and decided they were all going to wear white so they all had to go out and find white clothes on the day. The backstage area was Brad Pitt, David Beckham, Paul McCartney, Scarlett Johansson, Madonna, Snoop – it was fucking chaos, everywhere you turn is some über A-lister, it was ridiculous. The band get one song and you were allowed onto the stage as an artist's guest for the band before and the band you're there to watch. They had one song and 10 minutes; it was like a school battle of the bands but to 100,000 people and beamed all over the world. These things are always very unglamorous when you actually get there.

How did they change over the time you worked with them?

I don't think they did really. They got used to staying in nice hotels and Dave certainly liked the ladies. Dave was the one that embraced the female attention the most, I think. Brandon got drunk occasionally – Mark didn't, Mark never drank. We'd spend hours trying to convince him to drink a bottle of lager, literally putting it in front of him and going "Come on!" They kept it all away from people. When we signed them they came over and part of that first trip, after one of the shows, we took them to a Greek restaurant, all got drunk and smashed plates everywhere, that was quite funny. But they weren't ever wild-wild. They just kept themselves to themselves enough for it to never get out of control. They lived it but they were always quite quiet. Ronnie was the real personality but they all had their moments.

How do you look back at the success of the record now?
From a personal point of view it gave me a career as an A&R person and for a couple of years afterwards, because it happened so quickly and it was so massive, it almost blurs your perception of the industry. Five years on, the currency of being involved with it dwindles and dwindles. Ten years later it's kind of irrelevant in a way in terms of my career. But I look back and think how lucky we were to be involved with it.

What impact did the success have on Lizard King?
It was just a weird phenomenon and the aftermath of it was that Martin Heath, who owned 50 per cent of Lizard King – he was ex of Rhythm King, Betty Boo, S-Express – and his partner Dominic Hardisty, who was an accountant, did a deal with Lyor Cohen at Warner in the US. But actually what [Lyor] got was the Lizard King name, Martin Heath and nothing else. He didn't get any of the catalogue and he didn't get any of the people that actually worked on *Hot Fuss* and brought it in. So me and the marketing girl, Siona Ryan, we ran the whole campaign with Dom, writing all the cheques and checking all the numbers. Martin was off in America and when it was all done me and Siona went off and did a label deal with Sony, with Rob Stringer and Ged Doherty. So Lyor thought he was getting this hot British label and actually he didn't quite get what he thought he was getting. And Martin went off and signed a lot of things that didn't work. We didn't sign anything else to Lizard King. We worked on The Killers for 16 or 17 months until they played Reading, a co-headline with the Pixies in 2005. The minute that was done, September 1, we started our label with Sony and left that whole thing.

Was it frustrating not to have The Killers for further records?
Yeah, it was. We tried. Universal had done the deal with them for everything else, five albums in the US and the next four in the UK. That deal was done at CMJ in 2003. We'd worked 'Mr. Brightside' for two and a half months, which is why it got all that heat; Island Def Jam did that deal and then it's "You're never going to be involved on album two". I actually got offered a job to work at Mercury, which is where it went through in the UK, but I turned that down to go and do a label deal through Sony.

CHAPTER 8

Sam's Town

"I love that you know the album by what Brandon's wearing. 'Oh, it's the moustache album, it's the feathers album'. He's quite Elton John about it. How can one man who's so recognisable look so different?"

— Ricky Wilson

Out front, an image of Americana in decay. A decrepit desert trailer home, a bored beauty queen* lounging against its peeling woodwork still in her bikini and winner's sash, a bighorn sheep – the state animal of Nevada – basking on the dry rocks in its shadow. And out back, gunslingers, desperados, freedom fighters for the all-American way. Mark and Ronnie bore full-throated beards, Dave sported a waistcoat with no shirt and Brandon bore the weight of a full bullet-belt.** And a

---

* This was model and singer Felice LaZae.
** "We just put our faith in what [Anton] wanted to do," Brandon said of the artwork. "He listened to the album, had ideas and just ran with it. We were out there during the shooting and he took the pictures of us on the inside of the album that day too. I wasn't sold on it until we put The Killers logo on there and then there was no doubt about it." Source: *Rolling Stone*, November 30, 2006.

moustache that would go down in rock history.*

"Initially they wanted a chic, gypsy look," said Anton Corbijn of his shoot for the cover of The Killers' second album. "Out of those discussions [for the sleeve] came these elements of faded glory."[1]

Faded glory, Wild West kitsch, proud desert desolation. The album was named *Sam's Town* after a Vegas casino built in 1979 by Sam Boyd, which encapsulated the Old West with its wagons embedded in the ceilings and saloon-style drinking dens. When creating a work to honour the land that made him, Brandon wanted it to ooze the traditionalism and gutsiness of Nevada, not the gruesome fleshpot Vegas had become.

"You wouldn't believe where we recorded the album," he'd say. "We were in a place called the Fantasy Tower in the Palms Hotel and Las Vegas right now should have a big sign over it saying 'WELCOME TO SEXTOWN'. It's only interested in attracting sex tourism. It's terrible. It's basically a haven for infidelity and corruption. For me, I wanted to run from the car to the studio and block everything else out. It's fine for us because we live there, but I don't think it would be wise for a band to go out to Vegas to record an album."[2]

"Las Vegas goes through phases. Some years ago, [newsreader] Dan Rather called it a living hell on Earth on US TV and the powers that be decided to clean the Strip up and make it more family-oriented. Suddenly, it was all theme parks, pyramids and lions, and that was popular for a while. But now it's all gone back to sex again. The strip clubs are multiplying. Treasure Island's now called TI, and the pirates are all half-naked women who fight with each other."[3] "It used to be more about families. Now it's just sex. There's trucks driving up and down the Strip carrying billboards with a number to call and have a woman come to your room. That's always existed but now there are asses in your face."[4]

---

* "This is just a phase," he'd explain. "I've never been able to grow a moustache before!"
Source: *The Observer*, Craig McLean, September 24, 2006.

No, *Sam's Town*, recorded between November 2005 and July 2006 at both Studio At The Palms and London's Criterion Studios with Flood and Alan Moulder on the desk*, would represent older, purer American values – hospitality, warmth, love, family and ambition. They premiered many of its tracks at a couple of shows in Vegas, at the Celebrity Theatre on August 23, 2006 and the Empire Ballroom on the 26th** when they brought the desert inside with them: Brandon in 19th-century Wild West lawman garb and his all-American moustache, Dave in his U2-style leather waistcoat, Ronnie and Mark in thrift store clothes, beads and ragged boots, tumbleweed picked by roadies that day and scattered around the stage, fairy lights reflecting the glitz of the city. It was clear that, after three years of being the best British band from America, with their new sound and image The Killers were asserting their heritage, becoming the best American band from America, too.

"I think we're embracing a bit more of our own culture,"[5] Brandon explained. "When people were calling us the best British band from the US, or whatever, it made me cautious, and it made me wonder, especially in my lyrics, what I was trying to achieve and where I was coming from. A lot of people in England identified with our first record, and obviously we don't want only American people to identify with this record, but we have broadened our horizons a bit."[6]

"The success of *Hot Fuss* had been a blessing but it had also brought some questions that they needed answering, and they needed to answer themselves," says Radio 1's Zane Lowe. "'Are we an American band?

---

* With Flood and Moulder's CVs including albums by U2, Depeche Mode and Nine Inch Nails, every member of The Killers had a good reason for picking them to produce the album, but none more than Dave. Since both of the producers had worked on Smashing Pumpkins' magnum opus *Mellon Collie And The Infinite Sadness*, Dave took great pleasure during the studio sessions in probing them to find out about the many songs that had been left off that album, one of his favourites, during breaks when Brandon would head off to lose "a couple of hundred bucks" on blackjack and roulette at the Palms over the entire course of recording.

** They also took these warm-up shows to LA and San Francisco that same week to try *Sam's Town* out in bigger West Coast cities, treating clubs like the Troubadour as the grandest stadium.

We know we're an American band, but can we make American music? Can we make music from the heart and from America?' They knew it would be short term if they were going to be this kind of Eurocentric band because, effectively, they live in America and they're inspired by America every day. You've got to listen to *Hot Fuss* now – it doesn't sound British or European to me but at the time they were just swept up in that moment. They needed to get their own vibe with their next record and I think they were nervous about how it was going to be perceived when they started making that transition. The bands that survive are the ones that aren't afraid of taking transitional risks or putting it all on the line. Otherwise you just get stuck in a moment, you get stuck in the time frame of what you meant to people then. You have to be constantly thinking about evolving."

Brandon was quick to stress, though, that the dusty down-home desert image was just as much of a construct as their dapper previous look. "It's fun – it's all a part of getting ready for a show. Just like it was when it was a more glamorous-looking version of the Killers."[7]

The shows opened the same way as the album. A drumroll as if for a human cannonball, a barrage of showbiz synth dazzle and a curtain-raising guitar cataclysm gave way to an itchy, hectic pop beat, and Brandon once more expounding his outsider status in a low-reaching town. "Nobody ever had a dream round here/But I don't really mind that it's starting to get to me… I've got this energy beneath my feet/ Like something underground's gonna come up and carry me," he sang, his voice broader and more tremulous and dramatic than on *Hot Fuss*. "This time around I wanted my singing voice to sound like the way I actually talk," he said. "I didn't do that on the first album… This time I wanted to sound more like someone who comes from the Mojave desert, which is where I'm actually from."[8] "I think [my voice] sounds better," he continued, "but that could just be because I've been singing every day for the past three years. I love it. We didn't use too many vocal effects. On the first album, we used Auto-Tune, and I didn't even realise what was going on with these machines and the computer. I was adamant about not using it this time. You really hear what my voice sounds like, for the first time."[9]

Though Brandon* took time to snipe at his critics, home and abroad – "I'm sick of all my judges, so scared of what they'll find" – the album's title track and opening number was a blazing blast of positivity and personal assertion. "I took a shuttle on a shockwave ride," he sang of the roller coaster years on the *Hot Fuss* tour**, and stressed his determination not to give up until his greatest ambitions for the band were fulfilled: "I know that I can make it as long as somebody takes me home every now and then". But most important were his salutations to his Americanism – the references to his brother's Fourth of July birth date and his grandmother's Dixie funeral***, and a revealing point where he considers the dichotomy of his UK/US standing and decides there's "running through my veins, an American masquerade". Yet, as the tune slowed to a Vegas circus waltz, the song reached a point of defiant resolution, acknowledging the band's cultural position as a pop colossus straddling London and Vegas – "I see London, I see Sam's Town".

"We had a real confidence because of the success of *Hot Fuss*, so we thought we'd take advantage of it," Brandon said. "We didn't want to make a shy album. We wanted to keep going and keep building on this. We wanted to come back unashamedly and this [song] was the perfect way of sounding confident and strong. Everybody puts their tails between their legs when they make their second album, but we wanted to come out all guns blazing and that's what *Sam's Town* sounds like. The way The Beatles had landmarks like *Abbey Road* and 'Penny Lane';

---

* Brandon would write all of the band's lyrics, which always came after the music was written and often just the day before recording. "Sometimes you have one line and you can base a whole song around it," he said of his technique. Source: Playmusic, Robert Collins, April 2005.

** This also may have been a reference to the *NME* tour of 2005, which was sponsored by hair product manufacturer Shockwaves, hence the reference to "people on the pen pull the trigger for accolades".

*** His grandmother's funeral was Brandon's first experience of death among his loved ones, and by 2006 it was weighing on his mind: "I'm getting older, my parents are getting older. My mom had bad health problems. You just start thinking: my mom's gonna die one day. Ha ha! I'd never thought about that." Source: *The Observer*, Craig McLean, September 24, 2006.

I wanted to do that for Las Vegas. We're proud of where we're from and it marks a period of our lives."[10]

At which point the album gave its belated welcome in the form of 'Enterlude'; Brandon, solo at the keyboard, turning on his Vegas bellhop charm like the old days – "We hope you enjoy your stay/It's good to have you with us, even if it's just for the day… outside the sun is shining, seems like Heaven ain't far away". "We were recording in a hotel casino," Brandon explained, "and I was messing around on a piano. Next to me was a room key-card that said 'We hope you enjoy your stay' on it, and it all just took off from there. The melody came from a dream. I have musical dreams, but I rarely remember them. This is the only time I've been able to remember one. It sounds ridiculous but it was Kurt Cobain on a ship, in the clouds! He was singing this melody and I remember thinking he sounded like Bob Dylan, so that made it even weirder."[11]

Already The Killers' new raft of influences was evident – not so much Oasis, Pulp, New Order and Duran Duran any more, more U2, Springsteen, Tom Petty, Dire Straits and ELO. Not necessarily US acts, but bands that certainly captured the enormity of the wide open spaces of Nevada. "There's a line… that talks about 'burning down the highway skyline' that's all about Vegas," Brandon said. "In the UK, the sky always seems so small because everything's built on this small island. Where we live there's this wide open desert with this skyline that's just… inspiring."[12]

That line, and its breathtaking sense of endless horizon, was the centre point of the track that whooshed in overhead like an Area 51 spacecraft, spluttering an Earth-quaking guitar chucka-chucka and spewing supersonic riffs. This was the blinding glitter-storm of 'When You Were Young', the first single from the album, released on September 18 and destined to be the band's biggest UK hit to date, reaching number two, and hitting number 14 in the *Billboard* Hot 100[*].

"We knew right away this would be a single," Brandon said. "We had the record label breathing down our necks. They were worried that

---

[*] Although the song would make number one on the US Modern Rock Tracks Chart.

we wouldn't write another 'Somebody Told Me' – and we didn't want
to, so they were really worried. One day we were just messing around
and this chord progression came about and I had the Jesus line, so it felt
all right. I remember driving home after we made a rough recording
and I slept a little easier ever since that night."[13]

While recording the album, the band sought out opinion and
advice from trusted friends, musicians and media movers. British
Sea Power's Martin Noble was invited down to hear the record and
Radio 1's Zane Lowe remembers being struck by the lightning bolt
of 'When You Were Young' at Criterion Studios. "They asked me
to come down and listen to some songs, which is something I don't
often do," he says. "I just feel like that process is precious and you
have got to be really careful if you go down there and that process
is still happening. But I went down and I was listening, and all their
music sounded amazing and they said, 'What do you think could be
our next single?' and I said, 'I don't really hear anything, necessarily
– they're all good singles but nothing is going to knock me away'.
And they said, 'Well, we're working on a track upstairs, you should
come hear that but it's not finished, it's being mixed now'. So I went
upstairs and met Alan Moulder and he played me 'When You Were
Young' and I remember just being so blown away by that record.
I said, 'Oh my God, guys, this is it. This is the one. It's unbelievable!'
And they were all looking at me and they were mocking me! I said,
'You've got to make sure that you keep it really organic, don't go
too glossy or electronic or any of that stuff. Just keep it really rootsy
and Springsteen-y'. And I look up and Alan Moulder's looking at me
like, 'Who the fuck are you?' Like, 'Shut up! Thanks, man, thanks,
now get out'. The look on his face was just, 'Really? Is that what
you think? Thanks a lot, thanks for nothing'. It was so embarrassing
– it was one of those moments when you get carried away in the
experience and you forget your place."

'When You Were Young' was real heartland rock, oozing the power
and passion of Springsteen's 'Thunder Road' and 'Born To Run', the
most American The Killers could possibly get, although the video was
shot in Tlayacapan, Mexico by director Carlos Reygadas.

Starring Sonia Couoh and Gustavo Sánchez Parra as a young married couple almost torn apart when the husband cheats*, it picked out the theme of trust, faithfulness and temptation from the lyric, which imagined a heartbroken woman "waiting on some beautiful boy to save you from you old ways" and her suave, sweet-talking paramour who's ultimately tempted to stray: "The Devil's water it aint so sweet/You don't have to drink right now/But you can dip your feet every once in a little while". But there was more going on here. "The Devil's water" was as much temptation to alcohol as lust: "It can be difficult," Brandon said of his attempts to stick to Mormonism's no-alcohol tenet. "I'm only human but I get through it pretty good. If I drink, it's just beer. I never did much of anything else."[14] And the religious references were inherent in the song, another method Brandon used to ground himself and the record in his roots.

"The song's about the idea that saviours can come in different forms, that's a lot of it,"[15] he explained. "There's a line I sing, 'He doesn't look a thing like Jesus'. That's about growing up in a religion where Jesus is considered a saviour and also realising people can be saviours, too, whether they're your wife, your best friend or your next-door neighbour. He can come in other human forms. Mormonism is a Christian religion, but the biggest thing is we believe we know where we're going when we die. It's not just about Heaven and Hell. The Bible says we're all made in God's image but we believe that literally – that God is a man. Other religions have always shied away from embracing that particular concept, but we don't: we really think God's a dude. I've always been a believer. It's always been a big part of my life even when I was young. There's always been that push and pull of living in Sin City and believing in God. And now it's become absolutely incredible, after all that's happened to us."[16]

The theological overtones, here and throughout the album, mirrored a shift in Brandon's perspective, away from rock'n'roll towards religion. "I still hadn't chosen which path I was going to go down," he said of this decisive period in his life. "Was I going to go Ziggy Stardust

* The Killers play the couple's wedding band in a flashback.

or Mormonism? I made my decision and once that was solidified it's become very easy for me."[17] Within a year, Brandon would give up cigarettes and alcohol for good

Hence, *Sam's Town* could be seen as an exploration of Brandon's internal struggle with religion, and his ultimately choosing the holier path. So frequent were the religious references in the record that renowned music writer Nick Kent would describe *Sam's Town* as the first Mormon concept album while Brandon himself would call it a "spiritual autobiography". "I can't ever escape my Mormon roots," he'd say. "Even on the first album, *Hot Fuss*, it informed songs like 'All These Things That I've Done'."[18]

Yet this wasn't an angle the entire band could share. "We're all very different personalities," Mark would say. "Brandon's the only Mormon among us, but he keeps it personal. It's an influence on his life so it comes through in his lyrics sometimes, but not in an overt or preachy way."[19]

From there, the gigs and the album diverged. The shows delved into familiar old territory, while the record strived for even greater glories. 'Higher And Higher' had grown acoustic guitars to add a hint of Johnny Cash and Talking Heads and "make it feel like the desert"[20] and morphed over the studio months into 'Bling (Confessions Of A King)', a song about Brandon's father giving up his alcoholism and turning to religion, as viewed through the metaphor of an epic struggle through a desert landscape, determined to reach salvation. Opening with a sizzling synth that sounded exactly like waking up, parched and hungover, on a roadside with "the sun… beating down my neck", it plunged first into recrimination, its scorching stomp and sunbeam melodies soundtracking lines seeped with self-hate: "I ran with the devil, left a trail of excuses". The song's driving pulse was drenched with the promise of redemption, though, and its protagonist set off on an arduous personal journey, "my vision slipping in and out of focus… I'm pushing on for that horizon… the wind blowing against my face", encouraged by some unseen saviour – "I offer you survival… stand up, poor and tired but more than this". As the tune expanded into a climax of euphoric release, the anguished journeyman, at the last moment and against the odds, reaches his goal – "higher and higher… we're gonna make it out of the fire".

"I guess it's like a medal for my father," said Brandon. "It's glorifying the person who does a great job raising his kids, just going to work every day. A lot of people in bands write about the working stiffs. I wanted to make something that was the opposite, because that's what my family is and I'm proud of it. My dad is 64 years old, he raised six kids and now he's got 20 grandkids and I guess that's what the ending of the song is about. When you see him playing with his grandkids he's a happy man."

'Bling (Confessions Of A King)' was the first of several tracks on *Sam's Town* that seemed destined to challenge 'All These Things That I've Done' as The Killers' most rousing and uplifting song, while 'For Reasons Unknown' looked to be a new, Americanised take on 'Smile Like You Mean It' and "a good bridge to *Hot Fuss*"[21]. Another song that was, rumour has it, inspired by Brandon's family – in this case his paternal grandmother's struggle with Alzheimer's disease – it was a fittingly disorientating affair. It drifted in on atonal mis-harmonies, one voice* a dead, deep undertone to Brandon's line, and saw the band swapping instruments, Brandon on bass and Mark on guitar. The result was a refreshing rock roar about the act of decaying: "I look a little bit older," Brandon trembled, inhabiting some frail future self, "my heart, it don't beat the way it used to/And my eyes don't recognise you no more". If 'For Reasons Unknown' was a true family story, it sounded like a heady celebration of a crumbling life, not a tragedy.

'Read My Mind' began life as a tune called 'Little Angela', a runt of a rock love song the band weren't keen on the feel of, and intended for a B-side. Then, in the studio, it took on a life of its own thanks to the production duo. "One cool thing about Alan [Moulder] and Flood," Brandon said, "is that, even though it was intended to be a B-side, it was taken very seriously. So we're playing the song and, looking through the glass into the control room, I could tell Alan was upset. When Alan and Flood argued, they'd go out into the hall, and it really felt like Mom and Dad were fighting. I heard Alan say, 'We're trying to make 'Peggy

---

* Possibly Mark's.

Sue' [into] 'With Or Without You', which came as a blow because he was basically saying my lyrics weren't good enough."[22]

Moulder came back with an idea. What if they slowed the song down, got Ronnie to play a disco beat, changed the keyboard and guitar parts but kept the chord structure intact. Brandon fought for his keyboard part, but over a few hours, 'Little Angela' morphed into 'Read My Mind'. "I started singing melodies, and in two hours it was a whole different song," Brandon said. "I think it's the best song we've ever written."[23] "It has a hymn-like spirituality and there's a story, it's what you strive for in a song."[24]

"When you change a song so drastically," Dave added, "at first you don't know if you're supposed to like it or not. You're like, 'Is this right?' But each passing day we knew it was pretty special."[25] A Kurt Cobain-influenced solo was recorded first take* and 'Read My Mind' blossomed into an airy, glacial, synth-led pop chug that Brandon knew his new friend, Neil Tennant of the Pet Shop Boys, would approve of**, even though Tennant had been outspoken about his dislike for Brandon's new look of facial hair and Rolling Stones 'Some Girls' T-shirt. "When I see someone like Brandon Flowers who has the appetite, and possibly the talent and looks, to be a star, I find that enthralling," Tennant had said. "I'm worried, though – and I hope he's reading this – that he's grown a beard. It means he's saying, 'I'm not pop. I mean more than that'."[26] In reaction to Tennant's criticisms, Brandon would later collect all of his beard trimmings in a plastic bag he kept among his toiletries, with the intention of presenting it to Tennant when it was full.

The lyric to 'Read My Mind' was one of Brandon's most convoluted yet, largely due to a chorus full of surreal images of trapezes, broken wrists, trampolines and loaded guns, lashed to references to restless hearts, promised lands, good old days and chosen ones – what Brandon would call "a bunch of clichés that are dying and that were good to have

---

* Dave tried a further take on the solo on 'Read My Mind' but the band preferred his first.
** He would indeed, to the extent that, having seen them play at Brixton Academy that November, the Pet Shop Boys would remix 'Read My Mind' as 'Pet Shop Boys' Stars Are Blazing Mix' for the B-side of the single release of the song.

around. In 50 years I don't think you're gonna look back at 2006 and say 'the good old days'. But when you talk about the good old days [of] the fifties, there really was something good about it. Whereas right now it's like we're creeping closer and closer to hell!"[27]

Weaved into these strange, incongruous words, however, were hints of the album's over-arching themes: the struggle to maintain faith both personal and spiritual, grand ambitions to be "breaking out of this two-star town" and a Killers world soaked in magic. The filthy narcotic grind of 'Uncle Jonny', Brandon's itchy portrait of drug addiction and the delusions his own uncle endured*, brought the album back down to earth with a sharp, albeit hopeful** jolt, but the first operatic blast of 'Bones' saw it lift off again, into the glistening world of sex. His synths twinkling like the stars he was driving his girl to the beach to watch, Brandon's seemingly ecstatic ode to bone-on-bone love-making in the surf had been given new life by swathes of horns since its first incarnation as 'It's Only Natural'. "I'd been kicking that song around for two years," Brandon said. "I loved it to death, but it was old, and I thought it might end up as a B-side. But Mark had this idea to put brass on it, and it just brought it back to life. The trumpets reminded me of Oingo Boingo – growing up, I was a big fan, still am."[28] The brass part was added by Mark's childhood jazz ensemble friend Tommy Marth, a larger-than-life saxophonist who'd soon become a regular player with the band.

But bristling beneath the brass of 'Bones' was a darkness worthy of the murder trilogy. "It's a romance," Brandon said of the song, "it's sweet, but twisted in some ways."[29] And how. "I don't really like you," Brandon's soulless anti-hero confessed, giving his sexual entreaties a manipulative edge that even he himself finds upsetting: "The thunder speaks for the sky and on the cold, wet dirt I cry". He fights off doubts and voices – "It's gone to the dogs in my mind," Brandon wailed

---

* "He's heard the song and he's happy to be immortalised," Brandon would say in October, "because he's a rocker, he's always got a Zeppelin shirt on." Source: *NME*, October 4, 2006.
** "Jonny, I got faith in you man," Brandon sang, "it's gonna be all right".

desperately in a tense gap between choruses, "I always hear them when the dead of night comes calling to save me from this fight". The dichotomy leaves the impression of a disturbed, emotionless individual begging for intimacy but ultimately rejected. Only the horns* sing of consummation.

With a more ponderous tone, built around funereal bone-yard percussion, a wiry guitar line, a mournful bass throb and dolorous piano, 'My List' tackled similar themes of yearning. "Let me wrap myself around you," Brandon sang to a lover, perhaps as he prepared to head off on tour, "do you ever think of me?... I'll take your picture when I go." It's a poignant portrait of a couple struggling through tough times, but characteristically for *Sam's Town* the song's climactic refrain of "don't give the ghost up and clench your fist" was a torrent of hope and belief. "It's our attempt at a ballad," Brandon said. "It's for my wife. I wanted people to believe it like I believe when I hear something I love. I want that on every song, but this one has a moment that you never know if it's going to happen again – we just got lucky. This is me. We didn't have many vocal tracks so this is the closest to what I sound like in the shower."[30]

The bombastic closing segment of 'My List' and the equally potent prog intro to 'This River Is Wild' touched on more of the band's classic rock influences. "The eighties thing, it's a small part of what we make up. We're influenced by so many bands – Pink Floyd, The Who, seventies bands too."[31] The overblown pomp and circumstance of 'This River...', combined with its pure pop melodies reminiscent of Strawberry Switchblade or Blondie, split fans on first listen. "It's a strange one," Brandon chuckled, "some people already hate it; some people like it, but the ones who love it are die-hard. I love it! If ever there's been a musical journey this is it. When I listen to it I don't want it to end. Each chorus is different, that's untypical of us, so it's our shot at doing something different."[32]

Lyrically, according to Brandon, it was the most literal song on the record, telling the story of how he desperately needed to escape Nephi as a teenager, his failings to fit in and his pull towards the circus lights as

---

* Inspired by Mark's youthful trumpet playing.

they passed through town. Characters flitted through the scenes – the man in red prodding him out into the big wide world, the put-upon runaway Adam – giving the song a sense of Springsteen's blue-collar storytelling as if to emphasise the restrictions of small-town life that Brandon felt around his throat, pushing him away into the rapids of rock'n'roll. A deluge of personal honesty, it's no wonder many found it overwhelming.

The honesty kept coming. "One of the most personal songs on there is 'Why Do I Keep Counting?'," Brandon would say, "which is all about my phobia of flying. It's something that's become a real problem for me since we got successful. But I feel as though, if I talk about it in interviews, it lessens the chances of my fears actually happening. Like, I've talked about it, so it would have to be a huge coincidence for it to actually happen to me. Does that make sense? It seems more improbable than if I didn't talk about my fears of what might happen. That's why I've been seeing a psychiatrist, once a week for the last few months. To talk about my fear."[33] "Basically it's a bargain with God. I have a big problem with flying and the first thing I do if there's something wrong is I pray. Just bargaining, "I'll be good if you let me live!""[34]

Flying was only one of the fears Brandon had begun to have therapy to rid himself of; he'd also been terrified of the number 621 ever since the ouija board of his youth had told him he'd die on his birthday, which is 6/21 in the US date system. He avoided driving on June 21* and recalled having to fly into the UK to play Glastonbury on that day the previous year. "That was a real mess. It's stupid, it's not a way to live… You're growing up and you're not afraid of anything. You just exist and have fun and have no worries. I've been given this great position to be in. I feel really lucky. It's almost too good to be true. That started making me feel like it's inevitable that something really bad's gonna happen."[35]

Brandon was convinced he could sense bad things approaching – "persuasions", he called them. And it didn't help when paranoid, and slightly batty, pop legends would remind him of his in-air mortality

---

* Or, indeed, at 21 minutes past six, morning or night.

either. "One time we happened to be on the same flight as Brian Wilson," he recalled, "and just before we take off he says, 'If this thing goes down over the Atlantic it'll be the end of all of our lives!' He just shouted it out! I was like, 'Oh shit! Thank you!' He's crazy."[36]

Each of his sessions with his therapist would be recorded so that he could play it back to himself to calm him on flights, and it's this inner monologue that Brandon seemed to recite in the song's pensive opening mantra, asking God if he has a determined number of days left to live and begging for this not to be his last: "There's a plane and I am flying/There's a mountain waiting for me...Will I live to have some children?... Help me get down/If I only knew the answer/I wouldn't be bothering you, Father". The song itself soared, emulating the sky-scraping sounds of 'Heroes' and Electric Light Orchestra's angelic sci-fi harmonies. "It was very difficult to get the band to sound the way we do on this," Brandon claimed of this chest-bursting celestial sparkler, "but it was time well spent because it became a real explosion. It's a bit ELO, a bit Bowie and it's the climax of the album – it ends with the gong."[37]

Sam's Town closed with an epilogue. 'Exitlude', a piano and acoustic farewell "to send you on your way" that summed up the redemptive intention of the album in two lines – "We've seen it all, bonfires of trust, flash floods of pain/It doesn't really matter, don't you worry, it'll all work out" – and revived the welcoming refrain from 'Enterlude' as a stoic goodbye chant, "We hope you enjoyed your stay". The plan was to emulate the feeling of belonging and familiarity instilled by the theme tune to another Sam's bar. "I grew up on *Cheers*," Brandon laughed at the time. "I was with Woody Harrelson the other night and I told him what an effect *Cheers* had on my life! I felt so ridiculous! I didn't want to be melancholic, so I think the beauty of the 'Exitlude' is there's sadness to it but it's not over. You want to go back to Sam's Town and I do too."[38]

In the UK, we quickly did. That edition of the album contained a coda in the form of 'Where The White Boys Dance'. A funky, disco-led tune with a whale-heavy bassline, ominous piano and Brandon in frail vocal mode as he lays out a finely sketched scene of sexual betrayal and revenge. A couple hug on a dark, deserted street; the woman smells infidelity on him. She heads home, pours a bitter whiskey and calls a friend to plot a night of retribution in clubland's sleaziest fleshpots. The song's closing storm of guitars is full of angry passion, the darkest side of disco.

★ ★ ★

When Brandon got the finished album home, he'd spend hours shut in his car in the garage listening to it, convinced it was one of the best albums in 20 years. "For me, this is the album," he'd gush in the first burst of press, pre-release. "I feel totally empowered by singing it. Even my voice itself, it's not as affected any more, it's not quite so... created. There's a spiritual element to the music that wasn't there before, there's something a little bit more... real about it... This album will be a springboard for us to do whatever the hell we wanna do. We want every album to be more exciting than the one that came before it. We want every album to be a new debut."[39] "There's something to be said about a song that's so catchy that the first time you hear it, you love it," he added. "But there's something more long-lasting about these new songs."[40]

"There's nothing that touches this album," he told MTV, "and that sounds like I'm being cocky, but I'm just so excited."[41] "This," he would tell *Entertainment Weekly*, "is the album that will keep rock'n'roll afloat."

So confident was Brandon in his new album, he now felt The Killers were ready for that Glastonbury Pyramid Stage headline slot they'd turned down in 2005. "We would love to take *Sam's Town* to Glastonbury, to the Pyramid, next year," he told *NME*. "Michael Eavis hasn't asked us yet, but I think they generally start asking people in the next couple of months, so I'm hoping we get the call real soon. It would be amazing to go back there."[42] He even likened his new album to the other rumoured Glastonbury 2007 headliners. "With *Sam's Town* I was trying to write a song like the Arctic Monkeys and of course it's nothing like them. It turned out to be this big boisterous thing. But that's cool. It's actually a good tactic, I guess."[43]

His enthusiasm for what he considered a world-beating classic record boosted his self-belief and cockiness through the roof. In interviews he claimed it as a far better representation of American culture than that of the numerous emo and college rock bands he saw cluttering up the charts and award ceremonies – a trend he considered little better than a disease. "All those bands, Fall Out Boy, Panic! At The Disco, they're only influenced by each other," he argued. "Each other and Blink-182. How can that be a good thing?... You don't realise what you could be getting yourself into with Fall Out Boy, and what kind of impact it could have in a way that you don't really want. Culturally, if it gets as big as it is in America, it could change an entire generation of people growing up here. Emo, whatever you want to call it, is dangerous. We don't wanna dislike anyone, and we've never met Fall Out Boy, but there's a creature inside me that wants to beat all those bands to death. They just all go into the happy emo funnel and everyone loves 'em without thinking. 'Oh, Fall Out Boy likes you? Fuck! I'm gonna go buy your CD!'"[44]

There was history to this particular beef. Back in September of 2005, in explaining the minutiae of his feud with The Bravery, Brandon had made a passing comment in *NME* about how he was frustrated that the same A&R man at Island, Rob Stevenson, had signed them, meaning that The Killers were no longer getting his full attention. "Now he's just signed Fall Out Boy," he said, "which means more of his attention will go to them that should have gone to The Killers."[45]

In response, Pete Wentz of Fall Out Boy posted a blog on his band's official site falloutboyrock.com that took a brief but catty snipe at The Killers. "It's funny the way you talk about sharing an A&R guy like it matters," Wentz wrote. "It's too bad you wrote a couple of good songs, otherwise it'd be that much easier to write you off." Emo internet message boards grabbed hold of the post, with commenters wondering if this meant that The Killers were being ignored by Island since these new signings. A few days later, Wentz struck again. In a post on fuelledbyramen.com, celebrating rising Vegas emo-pop band Panic! At The Disco, he wrote, "I hope none of THE OTHER Las Vegas BANDs get jealous that there is another gem out in the middle of the desert. F---ing wasting my time on FLOWERS." And Wentz wasn't done. In April 2006, he tried to call a truce on this so-far very one-sided war of words (Brandon, by this point, had yet to pass comment) by inviting Flowers out for a sushi dinner. "The whole thing has never been like, 'Meet me at the bike racks after school!'" he said. "And since the whole thing started, we've had a whole bunch of near-misses, where we'll show up at a party after he left or something like that. So now I'd just like to make peace. I'd like to go out to dinner with Brandon, because I think he'd be an interesting dude to eat with. But I don't think he would go out to dinner with me. We'll go to Nobu or something like that. I'll get the rock shrimp, some California rolls, perhaps a little spicy tuna."[46]

Judging by his outburst in the *NME* in June, Brandon wasn't hungry. Naturally, Wentz was asked for his response. "Honestly, I like Brandon a lot from what I've read in interviews," Wentz said, now deep in tongue-in-cheek make-up mode. "He's sharp. I don't think people would take as much notice if he wasn't. I respect that. I kinda like how he called Fall Out Boy 'dangerous'. It felt like how Ice called Maverick 'dangerous' in *Top Gun*. The whole thing kind of feels like one of those D.A.R.E. commercials. I kind of think of it this way: How could you feel like a superhero if you didn't have an arch-nemesis?" Wentz did take issue with Brandon's claim that they hadn't met by June, however. "We met a couple of times," he said. "I think they maybe tried to order drinks from us at the [MTV] Video Music Awards, because they thought we were waiters. The drummer was really nice though. Besides, we get Brandon's family and friends into Fall Out Boy shows when we play his hometown. It must be very 'dangerous'. I believe they came to the show in Salt Lake City, but I did not meet them. They were on the list, though."

The spat didn't stop Brandon unleashing further emo tongue-lashings. "You have Green Day and 'American Idiot'," he said in October. "Where do they film their DVD? In England. A bunch of kids screaming 'I don't want to be an American idiot'. I saw it as a very negative thing towards Americans. It really lit a fire in me. You have the right to say what you want to say and what you want to write about, and I'm sure they meant it in the same way that Bruce Springsteen meant 'Born In The USA' and it was taken wrongly, but I was really offended when

I saw them do that. I just thought it was really cheap, to go to a place like England or Germany and sing that song – those kids aren't taking it the same way that he meant it. And [Billie Joe Armstrong] knew it. People need to see that, really, there are the nicest people in the world here! I don't know if our album makes you realise that. But I hope it's from a more positive place."[47]

Naturally, the press latched on to such a high-profile diss, too, and Green Day fans were enraged. "It has caused a lot of unnecessary drama," Brandon said of his comment. "I said it a long time ago; I don't know how it crept up. It wasn't taken out of context, really. The point was, if they're so punk rock, why don't they make their DVD in Washington, D.C., instead of in England with a bunch of English kids singing 'I don't want to be an American idiot'? Do it in front of the White House or something."[48] But he was also somewhat repentant. "I came out with a big mouth," he said. "And I feel bad for my band, because they've got nothing to do with it."[49]

While Brandon was taking all this heat from the emo fraternity, more all-American rock heroes flocked to make a connection to this patriotic new Killers. At the MTV Video Music Awards show at New York's Radio City Music Hall on August 31 they were introduced onstage by none other than Axl Rose from Guns N' Roses, an unlikely new fan you might think. "It was an honour," Brandon explained. "A few days before it happened, we met him at a party in LA after our gig at the Troubadour. And he wasn't sure if he'd make it to New York. The reason, he said, was that he'd 'just come back from London, where they had all these black cabs, and I just can't wrap my head around it'. He's a strange man, but he's cool."[50] *

The warm-up shows in Vegas, LA and San Francisco, however, suffered some technical difficulties and were received coolly; it wasn't until September 8 when The Killers gave the new material its UK

---

* Axl was far from the most celebrated man to show his support for The Killers in 2006 – back in January they'd played a one-off show at the Consumer Electrics Convention at the Pure nightclub in Caesars Palace for MTV and Microsoft, where it's rumoured that Bill Gates enjoyed their performance.

premiere at the Empress Ballroom in Blackpool that they felt it had gone over well. "We played our new songs in Vegas first and we got a really lukewarm reaction," Brandon recalled. "We had to come over here, to Blackpool, to get the boost of confidence we needed. The love we get here in Britain is like nowhere else."[51]

Then, when the reviews began to trickle in, Brandon came down to Earth, hard. If it wasn't annoying enough that most of the writers were focusing more on his facial hair than his band's music, opinion on *Sam's Town* was polarised. Some, certainly in the UK, were glowing. Q awarded the album a notable four stars out of five, praising its bold Americanisms of Main Streets and highway skylines and calling it "frequently terrific and a much, much better record than its predecessor... in thrall to seventies new wave, eighties indie, Pulp's *Different Class* and The Strokes' *Is This It*... Brandon Flowers has discovered Bruce Springsteen of late. It shows."[52] *The Observer*'s Dan Martin awarded the record a full five stars and, in her review, *NME*'s Krissi Murison backtracked on a sniffy live pasting she'd handed the band early on to hear the first album's brilliance blazing through *Sam's Town*: "The pink blazers may have been ritualistically burnt in favour of five o'clock shadows and oil-stained denim," she argued, "but the Boss' influences are – save a couple of piano-belted rock'n'roll numbers near the end – fairly cosmetic... *Sam's Town* is clearly the same band of Anglo-maniacs who brought metrosexuality mainstream with *Hot Fuss*. They've just scrubbed off their make-up, beefed up the vocals and found the turbo-charge button on their tune-making machine."[53]

The Killers had been sensations in the UK with *Hot Fuss*, of course, and were receiving merited appreciation as a result. In the US, though, where they weren't quite such a cultural phenomenon, the backlash was in full effect. One particular review, from *Rolling Stone*'s Rob Sheffield, cut Brandon to the quick. "Why is ['When You Were Young'] the single?" he wrote. "Because it's the closest thing to a good song on the album. All over *Sam's Town*, the Killers leave no pompous arena cliché untweaked in their quest to rewrite *Born To Run* – even though one of the reasons Springsteen's a genius is that he's never tried to rewrite *Born To Run* himself."[54]

"[It] brought everything crashing down around me," Brandon admitted years later. "I was shattered. Critics underestimate their power, because we overestimate the critics. Some guy I'm assuming is this great music aficionado has just said my album is a piece of shit. He said the only thing that resembles a good song is 'When You Were Young'. I spent months and months trying to overcome that review. It ended up being a gift, because it made me a better frontman, but I still go onstage thinking there's somebody like him who's about to review the show, and it still makes me self-conscious."[55] * "We came out and we're wearing suits and there's glitz," he'd add, philosophically. "Definitely they saw that as being contrived. I understand that."[56]

"We almost blew it with *Sam's Town*," Dave would say, stony faced, then laugh. "I'm joking of course. We love *Sam's Town*, and we'll never apologise for it. We're not the kind of band that makes the same songs over and over again. If that's what you want, go listen to somebody else."[57]

In this crushed mood, looking down the touring schedule for *Sam's Town* – 161 shows, including 30 festivals, stretching over 15 months, 28 countries and five continents, many of them covered in two separate legs (and boy, that meant a lot of flying) – you can understand Brandon Flowers feeling daunted. His new devotion to Mormonism meant that being away from his family was more of a wrench this time; his brother Shane, after all, had turned down a place on the PGA golfing circuit, where their cousin, Craig Barlow, had made his name, because it would have meant spending far too much time away from the strong family bond that Mormonism prizes so much. So Brandon made plans with the band to allow him to bring his wife and any future children on the road with him, thereby trying to align his religion with the on-the-road lifestyle.

"With any religion there's dos and don'ts," he argued. "A lot of people think polygamy is involved [in Mormonism], and it's not. [Or that] you can't drink Coke – that we think we're gonna go to hell if

---

* Ironically, in December 2009 *Rolling Stone* would vote *Sam's Town* as the most underrated album of the decade.

we drink Pepsi. You're not supposed to drink alcohol. I try not to. Bob Dylan said it best – you can't be Jewish and be cool. And you can't be a Mormon and be cool! But I'm trying my best!"[58]

Brandon might also have been disheartened that the first string of dates on the *Sam's Town* tour would retread familiar ground. The same theatres they'd played in the US with *Hot Fuss*, the same medium-sized clubs in mainland Europe and the same UK Academies they'd sold out 18 months earlier, only this time they'd sold out three nights at Brixton Academy rather than two. Glaring at the booking for the smaller theatre venue at New York's Madison Square Garden, knowing that his dream venue was so painfully close, must have smarted a touch. This tentative toe-dip back into touring was standard practice among successful bands returning with their second album, reminding their fans that they still exist by restating their previous standing, then lunging for the next rung up. But it must have felt a little like treading water, and all added to the incredibly slow promotional cycle that Brandon felt was stifling The Killers.

"The Smiths released two albums a year, plus singles and fresh B-sides," he mused. "That's just incredible to me. Look at the volume of product Bowie released just between 1970 and 1975: I don't know if we'll ever make that many records! Nowadays, it seems impossible to have a successful career without these long gaps between releases. *Sam's Town* is being released two years and four months after our first one because of all these other commitments, and I truly believe this kind of schedule is holding us back creatively. We've just got to adjust to it.

"At the same time, I understand the record company's viewpoint. They're a huge conglomerate, they don't want to lose money, and they don't know for sure if we're ever going to write a hit again. Right now, they reckon *Sam's Town* has four potential hit singles and they want to milk it for all it's worth. And we feel we can accommodate them. Out of all the new bands that have gotten big lately, there hasn't been one that can be sophisticated and fun and catchy, rock, pop and oddball, and still make it into the big leagues. And that's what we're trying to achieve. Still, it's really hard because record companies aren't used to dealing with smart bands wanting to be successful on their own terms."[59]

Their experiences within the music industry had affected the rest of the band – Dave particularly was amazed by the incompetence he'd seen at record labels. "I don't know if industry people are actually shitty, but they are dumb," he said. "I've seen some of the dumbest decisions being made. I'm just like 'Wow, this person makes $100,000 a year?' And it takes two years for the person above them to figure out how dumb they are and fire them. But they all get fired in the end. Unless they've actually done something successful with one band, like Poison."[60]

Yet Brandon, more than his bandmates, was hell-bent on success; he swore he wouldn't stop working until *Sam's Town* was as successful as the band's debut. And there was plenty to boost him and the band for the slog ahead. First, on its October 2 release, *Sam's Town* shot to number one in the UK charts[*] and number two on the *Billboard* Chart – a bona fide sensation, selling over half a million copies in those two countries alone in its first week on sale. By the end of the year this figure would be more like 1.6 million sales worldwide as the album inched towards eventually matching the five million sales that *Hot Fuss* had already achieved by then.

Meanwhile 'Bones', the second single from the album, gave the band more of a cinematic glisten. "All of a sudden it just clicked," Brandon explained. "Bones, brass, Tim Burton!"[61] The call went out to this dark movie maverick; his agreement came as a shock. "He'd never done a music video, so we didn't think he'd ever say yes, but it all worked out," said Brandon. "It was really exciting. At first we were afraid of him, but he instantly crushes that." "He showed up at the studio unannounced," Ronnie continued, "and the minute he got there, there was a really good vibe. Everyone was getting along, there were a lot of great ideas getting thrown around, and he seemed really happy to see us. When you meet someone like that, when you respect what they've done… we just left everything in his hands. We totally trusted him. We love all

---

[*] With their Lizard King contract expired, The Killers had signed to Mercury Records for the UK.

his films. He hasn't asked us to cameo in the *Sweeney Todd* movie he's making though."[62]

The finished video was a triumph.* Using Burton's trademark skeletons as a motif, it featured The Killers playing in front of the screen at the West Wind Las Vegas drive-in theatre, showing scenes from movies such as *Jason And The Argonauts*, *The Creature From The Black Lagoon* and *Lolita*. Interspersed was freshly filmed black-and-white footage of a couple – Michael Steger and Devon Aoki – who stripped off their skin to re-enact classic scenes of beach-side romance from *10* and *From Here To Eternity* in skeletal form. By the end of the video the drive-in viewers and the band were skeletons too; the promo ended with the band, reduced to bones, falling apart in a desert playground. Witty, irreverent and arty, the video helped push the single, released on November 27, to number 15 in the UK and 21 in the US**.

What's more, The Killers were having fun back on the road. As those first couple of legs of the tour around Europe and the US wore on, Brandon saw more and more appreciation of the new songs in the eyes and maws of the front rows. "There's not a day that goes by that I don't see, looking into the audience, the songs growing on them more and more," he grinned, recalling how the band were even enjoying the mistakes. "We were in Vegas, and Dave messed up on the first five songs. On 'When You Were Young' he broke a string. He was hitting wrong notes – I don't know where he was. I walked over to him and asked him if he'd be joining us on the next song."[63]

Great new music was already flooding out of them, too. When the tour hit London they hooked up in person, for the first time, with producer Stuart Price, aka Jacques Lu Cont, who'd had great success working on Madonna's *Confessions On A Dance Floor* album in 2005 and had impressed The Killers with his 'Thin White Duke Remix' of 'Mr. Brightside', a mix which had opened up whole new electro possibilities for the band. "I didn't really know who he was," Brandon would admit later. "Actually I was familiar with [Price's bands] Zoot Woman and

---

* It would win Best Video at the *NME* Awards in 2007.
** Backed on various formats by 'Where The White Boys Dance' and 'Daddy's Eyes'.

Les Rhythmes Digitales, but I didn't know that was him. I remember when we were recording *Hot Fuss* we always liked that song 'Living In A Magazine', but we just had no idea who it was."[64]

He'd soon learn. Price had dinner with the band, then they all repaired to his home studio. "The first thing I saw was a picture of a David Bowie album sleeve," Brandon said. "Then there was a portrait of Brian Eno and Roxy Music. I knew we'd found the right man."[65] Sure enough, a new song seemed to fall out of the band within two hours. "We just clicked," Dave said. "He had passion and great ideas. We could just tell it was gonna work out. We went back to his apartment and I started playing him [an] intro... and immediately he had an enthusiasm and ideas that seemed to fit."[66] Led with glacial synths, lashed with freeway reverb and pulsing with rampant dance-floor electronics, this instant new track found The Killers really delving into the pop territory of their beloved Pet Shop Boys for the first time. They titled it 'Human' and set it aside for album three.

Meanwhile, there were a host of award nominations for the Grammys and the Brits[*] and those three sold-out gigs at Brixton meant only one thing. In some territories – the UK, Mexico, some major cities in the US and South America – The Killers were ready for the next step up: arenas.

So come Christmas, there was plenty of reason to celebrate. Only Mark bought his bandmates a present each – everyone got a Beatles songbook in the hope that they would inspire backstage singalongs. "I thought we could all learn to play Beatles songs together,"[67] he said. "I had this vision that we'd learn these songs on the road and sing them backstage. That didn't happen. I never even saw anyone carrying their book around."[68] [**]

---

[*] They'd pick up Best International Group and Best International Album at the Brits in 2007, although the nominations meant less and less to the band as time went on. "It's something that you dream about," Brandon said about these Grammy nominations, "but Milli Vanilli got a Grammy. So it's hard to decide whether you're happy or not." Source: *Rolling Stone*, February 9, 2006.

[**] That Christmas, Ronnie had an odd present for his wife – he shaved off his new handlebar moustache for her since it was already showing signs of grey, to the extent he had to dye it black.

Instead, the Killers decided to give their entire fanbase a gift. When the UK tour hit Newcastle, the day before the gig the band donned their best Christmas jumpers – and a multi-coloured Xmas poncho for Brandon – dressed their crew up as snowmen, gnarly smoking elves and gigantic roadie Santa Clauses, and organised for a full Thanksgiving dinner to be served to their full entourage. This was the home-video style promo clip for 'A Great Big Sled', The Killers' first Christmas single. Released in aid of Product Red – the charity headed by Bono and Californian activist Bobby Shriver to fight AIDS in Africa – it was a traditional lightweight affair given a Killers highway rock twist, complete with "ho-ho ho"s, strings and sleigh bells and featuring guest vocals from Toni Halliday of nineties goth-pop band Curve. Lyrically it explored the loss of the youthful innocence of Christmas; full of images of action toys, robots and snowmen, it found Brandon yowling "I wanna roll around like a kid in the snow", recapturing the festive excitement of childhood. He was living proof, he declared, that such youthful exuberance can last into adulthood (as every child's mother wishes), but lamented that others have become lustful and cynical as they've grown – "The boys are all grown up/And they're working their fingers to the bone/They go around chasing them girls on the weekend... how on Earth did we get so mixed up?"

"We'd always talked about doing a Christmas song," Brandon explained. "There have been some great ones. John Lennon. Tom Petty... those are amazing Christmas songs and we figured it was about time people had another good one, you know? So we wrote 'A Great Big Sled'. I realise now that I should probably have called it 'A Great Big Sleigh', because that's what Santa rides, but it doesn't sound very Christmassy at all. It sounds like you're going on a killing spree!... No matter what we do, it doesn't even matter how much of ourselves or how much of our guts we put into something, people still try and take it as a laugh, y'know? Saying that we're cheesy or whatever. At least, that's how it feels. Life would be miserable if we went around listening to what everyone said about us and taking ourselves too seriously. So fuck it – here's our Christmas song."[69]

"People are trying to make out like it's a gimmick or something," Mark added, "like we're going for Christmas number one. It's download-only so it's not even eligible. And Christmas number one isn't a big deal where we're from. We just thought it'd be fun."[70]

Despite being download-only, 'A Great Big Sled' still charted at number 54 in the US. Although the song was perhaps too nostalgic, moralistic and considered, rather than celebratory and trite, to become a Christmas standard alongside the greats of Slade and Shakin' Stevens, it was fun enough to launch an annual Killers charity Christmas song tradition.

"We are tightrope-walking, skydiving wizards," said Brandon as a Christmas message to the readers of *NME*, "and the difference between the wizard and the magician is that the wizard's magic is real; it's not an illusion. Merry Christmas."[71]

And as the new year would prove, The Killers onstage would become real showbiz wizards.

★ ★ ★

At Wembley, flowers filled the stage. Not just the Flowers owning stage-front, welcoming the sold-out crowd of 9,000 to *Sam's Town* from behind his keyboard front desk, hoping they all enjoy their stay, expressing his pleasure at having them with him. No, real flowers, wrapped in coils across the amps at the back of the stage, combining with the bunting hanging from the lighting rig, the velvet curtains framing the stage and the glitter cannons bursting from the wings to make our short stay a dramatic and dazzling one. From the off, the show was a spectacle; a screen spread across the front of the stage showed hand-held black-and-white footage of desertscapes, Vegas signs, album artwork and parades of lights while operatic orchestral bombast built up to the big reveal. Ticker-tape explosions, strobes and smoke, the screen dropped to reveal Brandon poised in Olympian pose on his monitor, dressed in his finest Wild West gent garb, and *Sam's Town* burst into blazing life.

The Killers, new Vegas princes of the arena world, had truly arrived.

Elegant, enormous and with the buzz of a family reunion to celebrate prodigal sons coming good, the *Sam's Town* arena show marked a major milestone in The Killers' rise. The band had expanded to include Ted Sablay playing additional guitar and keyboards*, finally drawn into The Killers live fold, and the set was neatly enclosed by the conceit. *Sam's Town* gave way to Brandon's solo 'Enterlude' and from there the show flowed like pure pop punch at a coming-of-age party, *Hot Fuss* and *Sam's Town* tracks mingling fluidly, 'When You Were Young' and 'Bones' discarded early and hits like 'Somebody Told Me', 'Smile Like You Mean It' and 'Mr. Brightside' dropped like buzz-bombs into the jubilant crowd. Then, come the encore, between 'My List' and 'For Reasons Unknown', sat a surprising cover – Joy Division's 'Shadowplay', a dense, brooding, ponderous track that Anton Corbijn had asked them, during the shoot for the *Sam's Town* cover, to record for the closing credits for his planned biopic about the life of Ian Curtis, *Control*. The band had liked the ominous downbeat drone of their version so much that it became a staple of the *Sam's Town* shows and beyond, a squirming black churn giving depth and deviousness to their otherwise sparkling sets. It made for a hefty leap to the gospel heights of 'All These Things That I've Done', and a final 'Exitlude' made for a fond farewell from this memorable vacation. We'd sure as heck hurry back to Sam's Town.

It was this show, with variations – changing set lists, surprise covers of Bowie's 'Rock 'n' Roll With Me' or Frankie Valli's 'Can't Take My Eyes Off You', the introduction of a sign saying 'WELCOME' across the back of the stage – that The Killers took around the world throughout 2007. They'd already taken it to Japan for three dates in January and hooked it on to the Big Day Out touring festival in Australia and New Zealand, headlined by Tool and Muse. Now they prepared to attune it for the theatres of Europe, the vast sheds of America and Canada, high-end festival slots throughout the summer and delves into uncharted territories – Brazil, Argentina, Chile, South Africa.

---

* Percussionist Rob Whited also joined the band's live setup.

Along the way, 2007 would throw up regular life landmarks to remind them that their stated ambition to be the biggest band in the world was well on track.* In February, 'Read My Mind' hit the UK number 15 spot**, backed over various formats with numerous dance remixes of the song (including the Pet Shop Boys version) and accompanied by a Diane Martel video of the band miming the song at various iconic locations in Tokyo during their January Japan tour, dancing with a Japanese Elvis impersonator and schoolchildren, and riding a variety of unusual bikes around the backstreets of Shibuya – penny-farthings, a recumbent bike and a bicycle with ram's horns for handlebars. Ronnie taught a fluffy cartoon character to clean his teeth before cuddling up to sleep in a capsule hotel, Dave played toy guitars in video arcades and became a traffic cop for a day, Mark looked glum in a full kimono and geisha make-up. This was The Killers at their most playful and approachable since the clip for 'A Great Big Sled', an arena rock band forcing themselves to remain human.

When they hit London on February 9 to play 'When You Were Young' at the Brit Awards, they also headed to Abbey Road Studios, walking in Beatles footsteps to record a stripped-down set for a TV documentary series called *Live From Abbey Road*. Their three-song set consisted of 'Sam's Town', 'When You Were Young' and a cover of Dire Straits' 'Romeo And Juliet', a song they'd originally hoped to record with Razorlight's Johnny Borrell, since Brandon was a huge fan of their latest album. A homage to a stone-cold AOR classic, their heartfelt, piano-adorned version aligned them with the upper echelons of platinum rock. Particularly when performed within such hallowed walls. It was clearly an emotional moment for Brandon. "You know what I would change about this moment?" he said to camera, taking a moment to glance back at his band. "Nothing."

---

* "We set out to be like U2 and conquer the world," Dave said in 2005. "We think they're the biggest band in the world and we'd like to take their place when they retire." Source: *Total Guitar*, Henry Yates, June 2005.
** 'Read My Mind' reached number 62 in America.

Come April, following US shows as huge as the LA Staples Center and the RIMAC Arena in San Diego, The Killers took those few vital steps into the main arena at Madison Square Garden, New York City, for a show that would be described as seminal and which, in another tiny triumph, even won over the frosty *Rolling Stone* magazine. "The Vegas quartet's maligned new album *Sam's Town* might pack more unfortunate big-rock bombast than its New Wave debut *Hot Fuss*," its reviewer wrote, "but it shares a generous hook quotient and a Vegas-y talent for crowd-pleasing. Before a frothy crowd, the Killers proved they've become a tight live band."[72]

June was 2007's cruellest month. The single release of 'For Reasons Unknown' on June 25 – backed by their Abbey Road recording of 'Romeo And Juliet' and promoted with a low-budget video of a very stilted Killers in front of green screen desert footage, leaning against plastic cactuses or looking terrified on slow horses – marked their lowest chart position of the campaign, reaching only number 53 in the UK and failing to make an impact in America. Brandon would put this down to a reluctance to promote a fourth single from the album, claiming they wished they'd never released 'Bones' as a single.[*]

Plus, the Glastonbury headline slot they'd dreamed of and aspired to for so long proved a disaster. As expected, the weather had turned the site into a quagmire, but Glastonbury veterans weren't put off by this. Instead, a new eventuality was the tightening of sound restrictions; meter readings at the perimeter of the site automatically reduced the Pyramid Stage volume when they broke the regulated barrier, so headline sets by both Arctic Monkeys and The Killers were rendered virtually inaudible to much of the huge crowds gathered to watch them.

"That was awful, it really was," Brandon said. "There's nothing we could do about it. Because that happened I'm sure they're going to be more cautious at all the festivals to make sure it doesn't happen again. Our sound engineer is actually a really loud sound engineer, so I'm sure

---

[*] The band would also release 'Shadowplay' as a download-only single on October 9; it too would make little chart impact.

it was more frustrating for him. He's from Birmingham and he plays us pretty loud."[73]

"We could tell it was vastly underpowered," Dave added. "It could have been better in that respect. We were a little bit gutted. You have so many thousand people, you should be able to send them home after hearing a pulverising sound, and that wasn't the case. It was disappointing."[74]

Things weren't much better backstage, according to Ronnie. "Poorly run," he complained. "For a prestigious festival that everybody's on about, it could have been much better organised. We didn't even have a bathroom backstage. Who's the guy that runs it? Eavis, right. Three words: running water, toilet. It was still a great gig. When it comes down to it, it's not about us and our dressing rooms. It's about sharing a moment with people. And that's what happened at T in the Park a couple of weeks later: everything was hitting on all cylinders. That was something to tell the grandkids. That was a great day."[75]

Indeed, July brought nothing but blessings. They'd credit their T in the Park gig on July 7 as among the best they'd ever played, and when Brandon got back to Vegas a few days later it was to a cornucopia of joys. His first son, Ammon, was born on July 14, named after a missionary for *The Book Of Mormon* and son of King Mosiah in the religion.

"It was wonderful attending the birth," he said. "They say a man doesn't become a father until the baby is born, whereas a woman is a mother as soon as she's pregnant. I guess that is true. I was sympathetic to my wife and excited about having a baby, but it didn't hit me until he was born. That was the greatest day of my life."[76]

Over the coming years, fatherhood would become a primary driving force for Brandon. "I think I always knew that I would have kids," he'd say, "but I didn't understand that I could love my kids the way that I love 'em. I didn't know there was room for that. You love your wife, your family, but it's different with your kids. I didn't know I could be so selfless. I would do anything for my kids. Anything. I guess everybody goes through it."[77]

After a month off the road for Brandon to get acquainted with his son, the band returned to headline that year's V Festival before winding the tour through a fourth leg of major US shows and rounding it off in Australia in November with two nights at Melbourne's Rod Laver Arena. They ended this mammoth jaunt homesick, frazzled and exhausted, but more secure. Sure, there'd been bumps, huffs and catty critics, but the *Sam's Town* tour had consolidated The Killers as a major global concern and also proved to the band themselves that, as four guys in a bus, they can survive the sort of year-and-a-half-long tours that the likes of U2 undertake with every album. Their niggles and grumbles, in effect, had made them stronger. They knew to vary the soft drinks from day to day to spice the rider up a little, they knew to give Dave a little breathing space when the red mist hit him, they knew not to hassle Brandon to stay at the after parties when all he wanted to do since he gave up alcohol was get back to his hotel and write music. "I'm as healthy as a horse," he'd say. "Drinking definitely conflicted with what I was raised to believe and what I want to teach my children to believe. When I think about the pain that came with it, it's a no-brainer. Music has taken the place of drinking for me. I write songs in a hotel room at 2 a.m. rather than go to a party. Now I'm even more excited about getting to that keyboard in the hotel room."[78]

They'd spent the tour writing new material, putting together pieces and snippets in Vegas, Panama, London, Budapest, but none was yet recorded. So as the tour wound down and they headed back to Vegas to start writing individually, making their own demos and emailing them to each other via Logic, they set a marker of their success in the earth with their first compilation album. Inspired by classic compilations such as The Smiths' *Hatful Of Hollow*, Oasis' *The Masterplan* and Nirvana's *Incesticide*, *Sawdust*, released on November 9[*] in the final week of the tour, brought together all of the best B-sides, live sessions, oddities and remixes from the previous three years. "There are things that are seen as uncool, but that everyone loves," Brandon said in defence of some of their more guilty pleasure cover songs. "Secretly, even cool people love them too. There was no shame in covering Dire Straits or Kenny

---

[*] It made an impressive number 12 in the US *Billboard* Chart and number seven in the UK and would sell a total of one million copies worldwide.

Rogers on *Sawdust*. In fact maybe it was courageous. We're here to break down those barriers. Just get into it or get over it! We need to have more fun. Otherwise it's not worth it. Anyway, a strange melting pot of influences is very American, isn't it? I guess we are a strange, confused group."[79]

Alongside tracks such as 'Romeo And Juliet', 'Who Let You Go?', 'Shadowplay' and 'All The Pretty Faces', there were some fresh curios. In the summer, when the tour had hit New York, the band had hooked up with another hero of theirs to add vocals to a song they'd recorded during the *Sam's Town* sessions but never quite finished. The song was 'Tranquilize', a sick, scratchy, seditious drawl of a tune pitched midway between Smashing Pumpkins and The Velvet Underground. Broiling with tension and urgency, Brandon giving his best Thin White Duke warbles to lines such as "drown in the dark or we could go sailing on the sea", it built to a string-swathed chorus release redolent of Ziggy at his most dramatic and tragic. And the guest vocalist joining Brandon on this ode to paranoia, medication and faith with its child choirs, its visions of acid rain, bogeymen and Cain and Abel, its "pestilence, pills and pride"? None other than Lou Reed.

"We were scared at first," Brandon said of the two days they spent recording with Lou in NYC, where Dave had already recorded the full backing track for Reed to add his own vocals and guitar parts to. "He does get a little bit of satisfaction in that. He really melted the ice. He showed Ronnie t'ai chi. I sat at a piano and showed him that the chord progression to 'I Will Survive' is the same as 'Perfect Day'. He laughed. He broke down. He's really a nice guy."[80]

For Dave particularly, as a huge fan of Reed's *Transformer* album, watching Reed write his lyric – "Money talks when people need shoes and socks" – was a moving moment; it would be a shame that the planned performance of 'Tranquilize' and one Lou song on *Saturday Night Live* would be thwarted by the Writers Guild Of America strike. Nonetheless the song was released as a single in October* alongside a plush video by Anthony Mandler, who'd also directed the video

---

* The single hit an impressive number 13 in the UK.

for 'When You Were Young', which played on the spooky mood of the song, the sense of being plagued by spectres and voices. The band conduct a séance as if to contact the spirit of Lou Reed, who haunts the video from behind a grand piano. The final scene was particularly eerie as Brandon became possessed by Lou, singing Lou's lines straight back at him.

Unfortunately, *Sawdust* wouldn't contain 'A Great Big Sled' or the second of The Killers' annual Christmas songs, which came out that same month, 'Don't Shoot Me Santa'. This time the festive Killers went down a more novelty route for their Xmas single, mingling their emotive rock with a fifties-style Wall Of Sound tune imagining a scenario where a psychopathic Santa Claus was threatening to kill Brandon for being a very bad boy – he'd been "killing just for fun", targeting the teasing kids on his street. This was a justice-dealing Santa played by a heavily bearded, spoken-word Ryan Pardey both on the record and in the video, in which he'd kidnapped Brandon out in the desert, tied him up with tinsel and was preparing his vengeful grave until the rest of the band came to rescue him. They'd even made special Brandon and Santa Punch and Judy puppets, the comedy nature of which may well have helped the song break into the UK Top 40 that Christmas.

Pardey wasn't completely absent from *Sawdust*, however. Once the track-listing had finished, listeners who stuck around discovered a secret, unlisted track dedicated to Pardey called 'Questions With The Captain' on the end of the CD. An oom-pah song lasting barely a minute, it was clearly a touring in-joke set to tape: "His beard is long and red/And his hat stays on his head/And he asks us all the questions and we know all the answers", the band sang. But *Sawdust* held far greater revelations for the band themselves. Several of the tracks – 'Leave The Bourbon On The Shelf', 'Sweet Talk', 'Under The Gun' and 'Glamorous Indie Rock & Roll' – had undergone fresh studio polishes in the autumn of 2007, and one of the production hands helping out was Stuart Price. Price had also helped produce 'Don't Shoot Me Santa', which had given The Killers' sound an extra pinch of sparkle. And he had, of course, helped give birth to the rave rock miracle that was 'Human'.

"We learned a lot from him without even meeting him because of what he did to 'Mr. Brightside'," Brandon would say. "He's very musical. People talk about using the recording gear as an instrument and making it sing and he's really able-bodied when it comes to that."[81]

It all gave The Killers an idea. After all, did they want to be human? Or did they want to be dancers?

Mark Stoermer, April 2014

As the *Sam's Town* material came together on the road, was there the specific intention to make a more American record?
No. At some point it became clear that that was starting to be the vibe Brandon was feeling. He was getting into Bruce Springsteen and Tom Petty and things like that. It didn't all happen at once but it was probably more when we got off the tour it started to have a little bit of that direction when we were writing together. 'When You Were Young' was one of those songs that everybody contributed to, it was made in a jam session almost. People started saying "Try that, try that", everybody had a little bit of a hand in that. But you could tell by the way the vocals were going, the lyrics and the melody, that Brandon was definitely going towards more of an Americana vibe. I think everybody was on board, but also the way I saw what was happening was a blending of the two worlds. We don't get credit for it, or people say we completely shifted from the new wave, but we had Flood and Moulder involved, the kings of dark alternative, and I thought we were mixing in a little bit of Depeche Mode and there was still a little bit of Bowie in there, but now we're going more rock, more American, but not every song was a drastically different band. We've changed a lot more from then to now. What people focused on a lot was the artwork and the imagery. If you really sit down and listen to *Sam's Town*, I know there's 'When You Were Young' and a couple of others that are pretty different from *Hot Fuss*, but there are still a lot of keyboards in there and you can tell it's the same band. It's not as far as people think because of the black and white photos and the moustache. If we had dressed in Duran Duran jackets on the cover of *Sam's Town* people would've never said anything.

Was there a pressure to follow up the debut?
At that time we felt invincible to some degree. I know Brandon felt the pressure of the follow-up and he has talked about it, but I also know that at that time, every day it felt like we could do no wrong. It started to get where the press would say things like that but that wasn't fazing us too much, at least we wouldn't talk about it too much. It felt like "Yeah,

we're gonna make another record and it's gonna be as good as *Hot Fuss*."
Maybe in the back of our minds we were like "It is a big album to
follow up", maybe we were cocky but it wasn't that scary. Looking back
it could've totally broke us. Although some people view *Sam's Town* as
a failure or a drastic departure, I think that you can speculate all day but
if we'd made "Hot Fuss 2" it might've been worse for us. For The Killers
fans it's the favourite one. Not for everyone but a lot of Killers fans
mention that one. I think *Sam's Town* has a lot more weight, it's deeper.
But they're different; *Hot Fuss* is fresh, it's a brand new band and it has
great pop songs on it, but in retrospect *Sam's Town* is appreciated a lot
more than it was when it came out. It was still pretty big, it still went to
number one in England and sold platinum in America.

**What can you remember about the first set of arena shows on
the *Sam's Town* tour?**
I remember when we played Wembley Arena, we filmed it and never did
anything with it because we don't have the audio. It felt good but after
playing festivals it's not that crazy, although it's still exciting and it's like
"These people are just here for us". It was getting in front of the festival
crowds that were the first really terrifying moments, when there's 30,000
people out there. That prepares you for the arena shows because there's
only 10,000 now! But we still had great gigs. To this day I get nervous and
I used to get really nervous then; I probably had stage fright. I'd always
internalise it but I'd go through the whole show hoping I didn't hit the
wrong note. I was over-thinking it but it was due to anxiety, probably.

Dave Keuning, March 2014

**The writing of *Sam's Town* was completed in a room behind a
strip bar – how was that?**
We rented space behind a strip bar in Vegas, it was just a cheap place to
jam. We didn't really frequent that strip club but I guess we were still by it.
I had a lot of mixed feelings on [*Sam's Town*]. I feel like some people in
the band overreacted to everybody telling us we sounded English so then

they wanted us to turn around and show we sounded American. I never thought that was really necessary, I think it's important to be yourself. We have all these influences in us, whether they be English or American. The press didn't help either, when they said 'When You Were Young' sounded American, all the rest sounded American. I don't think that's accurate. The recording was all done at the Palms Hotel. We spent a lot more time on it than *Hot Fuss*. That's not always a good thing. A lot of second album pressure on that one. We knew we didn't have jobs any more, we had the money and support. We took a lot more time to get drum sounds and guitar sounds and arrange songs and write lyrics. Everything took a lot longer. It was good and bad, I guess, to have extra time. When you have extra time you have the chance to change your mind about stuff or get sick of a song because you've been working on it for months already.

Why would you invite industry friends into the studio to hear the record in the making?
I guess occasionally we still take people's advice. I think we were really concerned with the second album – we wanted to gauge people's reactions to it.

Why did *Sam's Town* become such a fan favourite?
It's got some good songs on it, and I think the fans were more unforgiving than the average listener with the changes we made. We lost some people from *Hot Fuss*. Maybe we picked them up again later, I'll never know. Some people were open to the change and others weren't. Some people like it better than *Hot Fuss*. There's some gems on there but it's more of a grower. *Hot Fuss* was more instantly accessible; *Sam's Town* you have to listen to it over and over. It took longer – we're just very fortunate we had at least one hit off of it, that being 'When You Were Young', and 'Read My Mind' was a decent single, too. Had we not had that then it really could have backfired on us.

How did you feel about stepping up to arenas?
That was a great tour, it was very memorable. On *Hot Fuss* we got to play some bigger shows, but from then on out the big shows were the

norm. It was awesome. We really packed it in, that schedule was brutally unforgiving. There was probably more friction on *Sam's Town* than *Hot Fuss* because of how much we toured. We wanted the success. It was very important to us that our second album was successful, so we were willing to do any press schedule. Even if it was four months long, which it was, pretty much without a trip home. This is the kind of stuff record labels love to hear that you would do, but now I wouldn't be caught dead doing a schedule like that, because that's crazy. T in the Park and Oxegen, those were pretty amazing shows. The Blackpool show was memorable too, it was the first one of the *Sam's Town* tour.

How about the legendarily nightmarish Glastonbury?
The funny thing about that show is that everybody asked us later about it being a nightmare show, but we didn't know there were sound problems onstage. I remember enjoying it and then days later hearing rumours. That's too bad people couldn't hear because I was having fun onstage.

What was it like recording with Lou Reed?
It was cool, I wasn't super involved with him but he was there. The first day when I was there we kind of arranged it together. I remember he was a cool guy, likeable guy, good to talk to. I didn't have a lot of one-on-one with him.

Were you used to working with superstars by then?
It's still startling the first time you're meeting someone like that, someone like Lou Reed. But slowly we've done a lot of stuff like that, so in some way I was getting used to it.

CHAPTER 9

Day & Age

"America is raising a generation of dancers."

— Quote attributed to Hunter S. Thompson

"I'm not saying this is some kind of 'pamphlet for my generation', but you always try to capture your surroundings and what's going on right now. So it needs to be universal. There are questions asked. I think it's implied in the songs that I feel what we're losing is… humanity. The way we now connect with each other through electronics, we're missing out on hugs and kisses… that's part of it. We don't seem to be as… romantic. And that's important."

— Brandon Flowers, 2008[1]

And so the beats flew through the air. Down the wires, through the exchanges, onto screens on the other side of the world. For the first four months of 2008, The Killers cast their music into the ether.

It was a modernist process, conducted blink-eyed. Once the songs the individual Killers had pieced together by email and Logic were fully formed, the band would meet in the studio they'd built for themselves in a unit secured with four large brass locks in a business park at the downtown end of the Vegas Strip, hemmed in by noodle restaurants and computing shops. A studio with no clocks but instead a goat's head

261

hoisted like a hunting trophy over the entrance hall. A studio they named, after the motto on the Nevada state flag, Battle Born.

"It was called Battle Born right away," Dave told me, "and there was debate about whether or not to put a sign outside. I said no we shouldn't do that, and I was right because we've already had some fans come find us. One guy found us from China and we haven't even played China yet. This guy figured out where the studio was and if we'd had a sign out it'd just draw that much more attention. It's not in a great neighbourhood either. That's why it's got several bolts on it and lots of security. It looks like we're ready for battle – it's got four padlocks, it's got bars on the outside."[2]

There the songs took final shape, then bleeped and whirred away into a world of electronic mystery. A click of a mouse and they were in London, sparking around the home studio machinery of Stuart Price, hired to produce The Killers' third album remotely, under orders to make it dance.

"It's not contrived in any way," Brandon would argue on the new electronic sounds that were emerging. "I kind of woke up one day and it was like… you can try and chase U2, or… it just didn't seem natural. I mean, I think we still can be the biggest band in the world but maybe we were falling into traps – getting the producers and photographers U2 had. That's unhealthy. This is more instinctive."[3]

The choice of Price to produce made perfect sense to The Killers. They'd made their huge desert-epic rock record, now it was time for them to move on from Flood and Alan Moulder, try to push themselves into challenging and unfamiliar areas, to leap the chasm of stagnation. And Price was an accomplished multi-instrumentalist with bright pop vision. "We're the same age, and our connection was really immediate," Brandon said of Price's rejuvenating influence, "we definitely share a likeness as far as musicality goes… There were a lot of cool challenges with that – how we do make a cool record that's as dancey as hell, but have a live band play it? We went through several different ways of doing that."[4]

Brandon found the method of putting together demos for the tracks by email invigorating too. "It made it real fresh, I think. It was almost like pre-production was under way as soon as we hit 'send' on an idea. He'd send something back, and we'd all fight about it, or embrace about it, and then we met for a month and sealed the deal. I just read this article on that new Eno and Byrne record. They did exactly what we did. They emailed the whole thing, and then got together for two weeks and finished it. They beat us to the punch. We thought we were gonna be, you know, matadors."[5]

"It's convenient," Dave added. "Even when people live in the same town, you spend time apart. But if you get a song idea at home, you can just email it. You don't have to leave your house. And they can hear it, they can play on it if they want to, they can mess around with it. And then when you're in the same room, you have a head start on what the song is."[6]

Convenience had become a major factor in The Killers' decisions by now; they deeply enjoyed these few months of home-time, even though it served to highlight their dislocation from their Vegas friends. "We've travelled more than most people will in their whole lives," Mark said. "The biggest downside is always being gone, never being able to have a grounding where you can either maintain relationships or create new ones. It's hard to make new friends. Over time, more and more people come around that have ulterior motives. I wouldn't have suspected that before, and it kind of hardens you a little bit. Our friends now are in their thirties and living some kind of normal life, and it's as if we're in a time warp, you feel like you're stuck in your early twenties doing this. When you come off tour it's hard not to talk about it and people can't relate. They think you just want to talk about yourself, but that is your life. And in general it does create this separation between people who do what you do, and those who don't, and the only people we really know who are doing what we do is each other. And that might be the bond between us: the common experience that only we know."[7]

But the successes of *Hot Fuss* and *Sam's Town* had meant they could afford a little home luxury, to build elaborate nests. Brandon had gone for a family home in his old stamping ground of Henderson, a functional beast of a car and a plot of land out in the desert where he hoped to build a home outside which he could raise the gigantic neon sign he'd bought from the Frontier Hotel, a monumental slab of old Vegas. Here, he dreamed of a future enjoying the pleasures of family fatherhood. "It's awesome. [My son] just started walking, and holding his hand while he's walking in a public park is so cool! We're like any other bumbling parents doing our best. I look around and it's a miracle that all these people you see walking around every day have gone through that process and made it. It is, it's a miracle!"[8]

Not that having a child had killed the romance in Brandon's marriage, he claimed. "I do consider myself to be romantic. I know the right time to send flowers. Sometimes it's not on the calendar and it's not about Valentine's Day – it's knowing when to do it. Now, of course, a romantic evening is all about getting the baby to bed early. That's when the romance begins."[9]

Dave, splitting his time between Vegas and San Diego where his girlfriend, Cara, lived with his son, had indulged in something closer to a rock star's pad. His penthouse apartment in a gated community was surrounded by tennis courts and swimming pools, had a 1979 Pontiac Firebird Trans Am in the garage – the car with a firebird painted on the bonnet made famous by the *Smokey And The Bandit* movie[*] – a huge pool table, a full-sized Pac Man arcade machine and a Ronnie Wood print on the wall. His fridge was stocked solely with tequila and champagne, and his walls lined with Killers posters and *Star Wars* memorabilia he'd been collecting – models and light sabres – fuelling his ambition to one day go into space: "I'd like to go to the moon, or far enough to see the Earth with me not on it."[10] [**] The apartment was dotted with mementos of his travels; a model of the Liberty Bell he'd bought in Philadelphia, a rock that had been left by his bed in Toronto[***] and the original four-track recorder that he and Brandon had made the first demo of 'Mr. Brightside' on. "When I cleaned out my storage

---

[*] Dave enjoyed driving his Firebird around town playing eighties heavy metal tapes on its antique tape deck because it was "part of the experience".

[**] One *NME* interviewer claimed that Dave was by now fluent in Klingon.

[***] "I didn't know what it was but I took it to remind me of a time when I was so happy," he explained. Source: Q, Laura Barton, March 2009.

space," he said, "I noticed this tape in a pile of dust. It was the first version of 'Mr. Brightside'."[11]

Ronnie was going down a more ecological route; as well as a place out in the mountains of Utah, he was buying a plot near his parents' house on which to build an eco house heavy on solar panels and insulation, constructed from reclaimed timbers from a railway yard. But Mark had splashed out on a few similar indulgences to Dave. He kept a Rolls-Royce he'd bought on eBay in his garage – "It wasn't as expensive as you'd think it would be," he said, "but I don't really get the chance to drive it"[12] – and had built a home studio in a house decorated with cuckoo clocks and in colours inspired by his favourite Picasso painting. By the end of 2008 his library room of books, DVDs and CDs would be a plush, red velvet Lynchian nightmare of a place, and a picture of the band with Bill Clinton, snapped at a rally for Barack Obama in the summer, would proudly adorn his fridge. Above his record collection, he'd also hang a quotation from mythology expert Joseph Campbell. "He's one of my biggest influences," Mark explained. "He got me interested in religious symbolism, and the idea that heaven and hell are to be experienced right here, that religion comes from the same place as dreams and art, the unconscious, and is a reflection of deep psychic truth. I believe in a higher power but not an afterlife."[13]

It was in such plush surroundings that the songs for The Killers' third album, *Day & Age*, took shape, Elton, Lou and Bowie the benchmarks to aim for. The Killers played their parts, emailed them to Price and got a call back with his comments. Once the songs were virtually complete, Price and the band convened at Battle Born in May to add the final touches, recording right through until September.* The various members had different takes on working with Price. "He's able to give us sounds we want and give us sounds we've never heard. It's really inspiring,"[14] said Brandon, while Dave had mixed feelings about the process, believing his guitar parts weren't given the time and prominence they sometimes deserved.

"It was quite different," he said. "Stuart works really fast and he's really good at what he does and sometimes it was almost too fast. I would play

---

* Additional work was done at Olympic Studios in London.

a guitar part and sometimes he would piece it together. I enjoyed it but it was good and bad. Sometimes he'd say, 'This time, try playing on one string on this take'. I'd try a part on one string just to go along with it and it was in there. Sometimes these parts are mixed low so you can't really hear it but I did a lot of weird stuff like that on *Day & Age*... I felt a little bad 'cause some people were like, 'Oh, I don't hear the guitar as much on this record'. Even though it was technically all over the place – there was guitar all over the place – it was subtler and atmospheric."[15]

Working six days a week, 12 hours a day, *Day & Age* came together smoothly. "It was maybe the least stressful album we've made," said Mark. "I think we know what we're doing now."[16] Dave had certainly developed a method of recording his solos that worked for him, making only five or six passes at his section before nailing or dropping it. "With solos," he explained, "if you think about them too much, they become sterile, they lose the life and the spark they should have. I always think solos should sound like the player is just playing, not like he's performing this piece of music he's written out."[17]

It was only as Brandon wrote his last-minute lyrics that a major theme of the album emerged, and an ironic one, considering the way the record was written. "I'm not the first person to think that there's something we're losing out on with these fucking phones and computers and so on," Brandon would rant. "We're all going to get ear cancer or something. The human connection, which can be as simple as this, we're losing out on it. I think about my son and how I want to teach him the things my father taught me. It could be something as simple as waving to people. Nowadays you freak people out if you say 'hi' to them. So I do it as much as I can because I really want to hang on to it. I wanna say 'howdy!'"[18] "[I do it] just to watch the reactions. There's always a breath, for a second, while they look at you. 'Why did he say hi to me?'... We came up in small towns, they're holding on to it more in those places. I grew up watching my dad wave to every car that drove by. Little things like that, you don't see that any more. You don't know what someone's going to invent next to make our lives easier, and that's awesome, but at the same time, we are losing some basic human functions on the way. I bring up romance and devotion, things like that. It's sad that it's old fashioned. It's sad that that seems strange to people who are coming of age now."[19]

★ ★ ★

Listening back to the album they came out of Battle Born with in September, the first two tracks nailed Brandon's theme from the off. "Console me in my darkest hour," he pleaded as the album opened with blasts of Dire Straits horns, Fleetwood Mac tinkles and the sultry AOR funk moods of Roxy Music and *Young Americans*, the sort of zipless sensuality that came to encapsulate eighties albums by Eric Clapton, George Harrison or Billy Joel. This was 'Losing Touch', an ode to dislocated lovers betraying each other behind their backs and lying to each other's faces: "You go run and tell your friends I'm losing touch/ Fill their heads with rumours of impending doom… an allegiance dead and gone". Though the chorus exploded with pure Killers glamour rock, Brandon would claim as much sonic dislocation with the song as its main characters did from one another. "'Losing Touch' is one of my favourites," he said, "that one's so good it doesn't feel like it's our song! It's just so concise; it's really mature songwriting. Everything in it does what it's supposed to."[20]

The most notable stylistic shift for the band here was the introduction of saxophones, played by Mark's old high-school friend Tommy Marth, a move that some old-school fans felt marked a step too far into the MOR mainstream. "Most of the things that we do, we never realise it's going to cause any kind of commotion," Brandon mused. "We just thought, 'This is great! It's a little bit Roxy Music, it's a little bit sleazy'. And then all of a sudden people made a big deal out of it. The saxophone is the moustache of this record."[21]

Dave would claim the saxophones had been Mark's idea, but a good one. They brought a little of the Motown spice they'd admired about some of Bowie's albums, and made the whole record sound more fun. "We're open to the use of all instruments," he said. "We really didn't realise how big of a decision we were making at the time. We were just like, 'Let's have a sax, it'll be cool.' I like how it turned out."[22]

Then, continuing the concept of mankind losing its physical, intellectual and emotional connection with itself – becoming mere user agreement clickers fluent in textspeak and Javascript but forgetting the language of the heart – came 'Human'. After the murder stories, teenage lusts and revenge fantasies of *Hot Fuss*, and *Sam's Town*'s celebrations of faith, family and the Nevada skyline, 'Human' found Brandon striving for real meaning in his words, unpeeling the next layer of philosophy and faith* from the kernel of his ideas. There was real poetry here, as he tried to express his concerns for humanity's spiritual centre: "My sign is vital, my hands are cold… there is no message we're receiving/Let me know is your heart still beating?"

Brandon had stressed and obsessed over the lyrics for the new album, delaying its completion as he sweated over the words, and the maturing style of 'Human' reflected his improvement, inspired by his recent readings of *Fear And Loathing In Las Vegas* and Jack Kerouac's *On The Road*. "[I'm] very self-conscious," he admitted. "I've said it before. I feel inadequate. But at the same time I think I am getting better at it. Because I'm such a fan of great lyricists, it's difficult. Being American, I don't have the vocabulary of a Morrissey… It's not just being an American. The books were there, I just didn't read them… When it comes to the music, a lot of times your initial response is best. But with lyrics it's more difficult."[23] Kerouac's grand opera of American life had quite an impact on Brandon, giving him a new slant on the bitterness and beauty of his homeland. "It's been a whole new world for me… It was exciting,"[24] he said. "Reading generally opens you up. America's so big and… the way he painted Denver and San Francisco and New Mexico, it's so romantic."[25]

"Brandon takes the lyrics really seriously because he knows that everyone's going to analyse what he's saying," Dave added. "He takes it way more seriously than I would if I were the lyrics-writer. He forces himself to go over everything with a fine-tooth comb. And I can't argue with the results. I think the lyrics on this album are great."[26]

---

* Hence references to "devotion", "grace and virtue" and seeking answers "on my knees".

Brandon agreed. "It's selfish, almost, because I know I'm going to be singing the songs, and I want them to be fun to sing. So sometimes there's a heartbeat, a flow to them. [I've got] more rhythm than most people, I think. It's difficult to do that, because you also want to tell a story and have people believe it. Pound for pound, I think this is the best I've ever done, this album."[27]

It was ironic, then, that it would be 'Human''s pivotal line that would draw Brandon more lyrical flak than he'd ever encountered before. The line "Are we human? Or are we dancer?", referencing Hunter S. Thompson's quote about the youth of America being taught to simply re-enact pre-ordained patterns of consumerist consumption, voting and self-absorption, was widely mocked for being ungrammatical. "I guess it bothers people that it's not grammatically correct, but I think I'm allowed to do whatever I want," Brandon argued when questioned on the line. "I say that it's a mild social statement, and that's all I'm gonna say."[28] "I think [Hunter S. Thompson] was frustrated," he continued, "and for me it's such a colourful comment, I just took it and ran with it… We're all different. Some people are on one side, some are on the other."[29]

Musically it was a bold departure, Dave's trademark reverb guitar smothered with Price's Pet Shop Boys-esque synthetic strings and sampled beats like dance-floor diamonds – "[It] was probably the hardest one to find a balance to,"[30] Brandon said – but for the band, that's exactly what made the song not only too good to throw away on *Sawdust* but an obvious choice as the album's first single, backed by the pop mariachi of 'A Crippling Blow'.* And for the video, Brandon had just as brazen a look planned. Fee Doran, the designer behind the iconic white jumpsuit that Kylie Minogue wore in her video for 'Can't Get You Out Of My Head' single, had created an equally memorable piece of stage-wear for Brandon; a black tuxedo jacket adorned at the shoulder

---

* Each of the four singles from *Day & Age* came with a sleeve featuring a dot-based painting of one member of the band, designed by Paul Normansell. Dave's face was on the cover of 'Human', Brandon's on 'Spaceman', Ronnie's on 'The World We Live In' and Mark's on 'A Dustland Fairytale'.

and breast pocket with plumes of golden feathers. The outfit, which prompted one *NME* interviewer to suggest that Brandon resembled a "chipmunk emperor", had brothers – one with black feather epaulettes and another in blue with a kind of dripping algae effect – and inspired Colonel Gaddafi to request a similar design from Doran the minute he saw it. "I felt empowered when I put that jacket on," Brandon would tell me later, "that was a ceremony, I loved it."

It was in this outfit that Brandon braved the desert heat for the 'Human' video, the band playing among the mushroom-shaped rock formations of Goblin Valley State Park in Utah, Brandon like the human overlord of the eagles flying overhead, a white tiger lounging at his feet. Nature and technology clashed and fused; in the white hot glare, the song hit number three in the UK on its September 22 release* and number 32 in the US, where it gave The Killers their first taste of the pop charts, hitting number one in *Billboard*'s Hot Dance Club Play Chart on the back of a huge array of club-friendly remixes.

Even better was to come. Descending gloriously from the heavens before shooting off to the horizon came 'Spaceman', a chant-along pop classic that imagined latter-period Roy Orbison hitting warp speed. Among The Killers' most brilliantined pop tunes, 'Spaceman' was the product of Brandon's childhood love of sci-fi movies, David Bowie and his religion; he considered this story of being abducted by aliens, blood typed, installed with a probe, "cut open" and returned to a life of paranoia, night voices and public disbelief as a parable. The "star maker" and "spaceman" perhaps represents God telling humanity to find fulfilment within itself: "The spaceman says 'everybody look down, it's all in your mind'." That said, it could just as easily be a declaration that UFOs don't exist, or simply a bit of fictional fun in homage to Brandon's heroes.

"For 'Spaceman' I was looking for a mixture of 'Space Oddity' and 'Rocket Man',"[31] he chuckled. "There was this playful attitude I discovered about myself that I didn't have before. Sometimes if you listen to 'Spaceman' in the right context, it will break your heart – but

---

* And number one in Spain, Norway and Israel, charting in 16 other countries.

it will also make you laugh too. This album's an escape in a lot of ways, and that's what pop music was for me when I was growing up."[32] "I really enjoyed writing that and becoming extraterrestrial. Somehow I think I can apply it to my life and it still makes sense. I was really pleased with it."[33]

As fun as it might've been, it certainly wasn't accurate. At least, not according to UFO expert Roy Lake, who tore apart Brandon's story, claiming that from his extensive research aliens never returned abductees to their beds. "[They] usually dump them back in the garden or another room in their house," he said. "I even know people who've been taken from their cars and then put back in another car, but I've never heard of people being put back in their beds."[34] He also rubbished the idea that victims would later hear voices from their alien abductors. "A lot of people don't want to talk about abduction because they're scared of being ridiculed, and songs like this don't help. I've seen enough evidence to know there's truth behind stories of alien abduction, but not as it's reported in this stupid song."[35] Lake would have preferred a more realistic abduction account, such as the woman he knew of who'd had eggs removed from her ovaries through her navel in order for the aliens to start a hybrid race.

Then *Day & Age* came down to Earth with a swoosh. If the saxophones of 'Losing Touch' had come as a surprise to diehard fans, heaven knows what they thought of the disco funk bass, sax solos, flamenco guitars, bongos, marimbas and general air of the Miami pool party that made up 'Joy Ride'. The story was lodged firmly in Nevada though, as a couple set out to indulge in a night of sordid pleasures in a world of "desert wind", "rattlesnakes and romance", and casino chips hitting felt. As they meet on a sidewalk, drive to a "pink and dirty neon" motel and make love on the floor – all to "ease my pain" and with the unspoken suggestion of money tucked into a clasp purse – Brandon seemed to view the scene with a sense of cool, but not preachy, detachment. As much as it delved into his fascination with the seedier side of Vegas life – these "highs" that are so morally low, these emotional joyrides conducted with "demons at the door" – as the song reached a brighter plateau he unveiled a greater spiritual joy. "There's something in the distance/A glorious existence/A simple celebration... Reaching for the light/Knowing we can win".

If Brandon was talking about achieving a deeper happiness through a purer life, the billowing orchestral rock epic 'A Dustland Fairytale' was his shining example of family values at their most virtuous. Every inch the Springsteen highway rampage right down to Ronnie's pounding drums and Dave's stirring chord progressions, it proudly told the story of Brandon's parents' 50-year love affair, of the faithfulness in their relationship he so admired and planned to emulate in his own life. "It's about my mom and dad, about them meeting, in 1961," he explained. "'Foolish eyes', that's my mom. 'Slick chrome American prince', that's my dad. They grew up in the same trailer park, they've been together since they were 15."[36] "It's an attempt to come to grips with the fact that they're getting older," he continued. "They're in their mid-sixties, and my dad is my connection to... the pure America."[37]

Determined to give his folks his best, Brandon not only gave them the album's grandest tune but his most elegantly wrought lyrics. He turned them into mythical heroes, the "Cinderella in a party dress" and the boxing "devil wrapping up his hands... getting ready for the showdown", and set them as the solid, reliable core of a shifting, magical landscape that hinted at Coleridge: stranded castles in the sky, midnight suns and kingdoms under siege. It cast this everyday romance, begun with "another white trash county kiss" and played out with "blue jean serenades", in the realm of Gods and kings. It was arguably Brandon's finest lyrical achievement to date.

"I think 'Dustland...' is one of my favourites for sure," he'd say. "Lyrically, maybe I'm proud of it. You set out to capture something, and that's difficult to do sometimes. As I get older, I've realised that I want to capture where I'm from and my surroundings. I feel like that's the closest that I've gotten. So hopefully I can beat it."[38] "Musically and lyrically, I think it's pretty imaginative. I'm happy with it."[39]

Like their debut, *Day & Age* was front-loaded. Heavy with major dance-floor hits and stirring epics in its first half, the second half of the album was a chance to have fun and experiment with the possibilities of the band. 'This Is Your Life' was essentially an Afrobeat take on 'Road

To Nowhere'*, lacing the marching drumbeat and tripping bassline of Talking Heads' biggest hit with *Lion King* choirs and trademark Killers synth phasing to tell another story of rising above squalor. It centred on Candy and Jackie, two characters – prostitutes again, perhaps, like the ones Brandon saw advertised all across Vegas these days – living lives of danger, paranoia and loneliness on "Track Street", dodging cops, mingling with strangers and queuing for benefits "where the blood just barely dried". "Wait for something better," he told these women, "the sky is full of dreams but you don't know how to fly". Once again, he painted purity of heart and soul as the ultimate fulfilment, and hope the unquenchable light. It was a naïvely sanguine slant on the sort of existence Brandon could know nothing about, but his intentions were honourable.

'I Can't Stay' was equally catchy, and just as throwaway. Full of kettle drums, harps, strings, tropical percussion and a harmonising choir of Brandons swooping and diving around the Latino samba that conjured images of Bob Hope and Bing Crosby rattling maracas in *Road To Rio* or Carmen Miranda taking her *Week-End In Havana*. Built around a bassline reminiscent of Dexys Midnight Runners' 'Come On Eileen', it seemed a fun novelty piece, a chance for Brandon to indulge his more whimsical and obtuse new lyrical leanings: "Exoneration lost his eraser/ But my forgiver found the sun," he sang, bafflingly. And the louche psych pop of 'Neon Tiger' was, as Brandon would admit, an attempt to write their own version of 'Time To Pretend' by MGMT.

"I was trying to write like MGMT and it's nothing like MGMT, it never turns out that way,"[40] he said, admitting that its title and tale of a protagonist "far from the evergreen of old Assam" brought to "the poster town… of gold and glitz" to encourage people to try to "win big" was glaringly literal. "It's about a tiger. I'm not an animal-rights activist, but I was trying to feel what it must be like to be Siegfried and Roy's white tigers. And you can draw parallels between them and

---

* An idea that the band possibly got from hearing 'In The Morning' by Razorlight in 2006, which used the same iconic rhythm on the eponymous album The Killers had been big fans of.

myself, being performers from Las Vegas. I was finding similarities and putting them in song."[41]

Indeed, if Brandon was finding himself in the persona of the tiger who "took to the spotlight like a diamond ring", it was a hunted, fearful and trapped sort of existence he was relating to. "I don't wanna be kept, I don't wanna be caged, I don't wanna be damned, oh hell," he quivered, as if rock stardom were a restrictive bubble full of vipers and temptation and he was prey for fans and critics out to feed on his fame. "They'll strategise and name you, but don't you let them tame you," he told himself, "there's a price on your head, they'll hunt you down and gut you." But, like the proudest of the big cats, he rose above: "You're far too pure and bold/To suffer the strain of the hangman's hold." In his own personal shape-shift fantasy, Brandon made for a noble Simba.

Day & Age finished with its android head held high. Together, 'The World We Live In' and 'Goodnight, Travel Well' proved a graceful finale. The former was a mid-paced synth shimmer in the vein of eighties MOR pop such as late-era ELO, Madonna, Heart and Genesis, coasting on an ethereal lyrical suggestion of a struggle for belonging and acceptance. "I find that if you write too much about what's going on on your block, that doesn't always resonate with everyone," Brandon explained. "It's almost as if there's got to be some vagueness about it. Yet there's always one sentiment that comes through with us: no matter what we set out to do, it ends up having an element of uplift, or transcendence."[42]

The latter, meanwhile, was a very specific lament. That March, Dave had lost his mother to cancer, and Brandon's mother, too, had recently been diagnosed with a brain tumour. "Oh, it's a heartbreaker," Brandon said. "It just rips your guts out. [But she's responding] really well to the chemo and the radiation so far."[43] And so, in Olympic Studios in August, they put the finishing touches to the album's final song, 'Goodnight, Travel Well', a tribute to Dave's mother. A Cure-esque, funereal paean full of dolorous, mournful horns, weeping strings and percussion-like clocks ticking down a life, there was a sense of hopelessness in the face of death: "The unknown distance to the grey beyond stares back at my grieving frame," Brandon croaked, a distant, spectral presence at the heart of the song, "Every word you spoke and everything you said/ Everything you left me rambles in my head/There's nothing I can say, there's nothing I can do now." The only positive note to the track came as the horns and strings lifted like a soul ascending and Brandon gave his final farewell. A heartbreaker indeed.

One song that didn't make the cut was 'A Change Is Coming', the song Brandon had written to celebrate the birth of his son but decided to leave off *Day & Age*, but as with *Sam's Town*, the album came with bonus tracks in various territories. The UK CD edition of the album featured 'A Crippling Blow' as a tacked-on finale, as incongruous a close to the album as 'Where The White Boys Dance' was to *Sam's Town*. In the US and Canada the iTunes downloadable version of the album came with two bonus tracks, 'Tidal Wave' and 'Forget About What I Said', which made for a better coda. 'Tidal Wave' was another story of nefarious Nevada lovers caught in a rush of love and escape, a good girl and a bad boy overwhelmed by the hope and danger of youth, eloping to the "golden West". Even with the addition of some electronically pitched-up backing vocals, Springsteen's touch was heavy on the song, but The Killers gave it a minimalist, ethereal grace and Brandon's tone stopped short of condemning such youthful foolishness and betrayal, remaining wistful and wry. After which, 'Forget About What I Said' acted as a palate cleanser from all the sleaze, tragedy and dislocation of *Day & Age*. Telling of a relationship whose spark has long since gone out – the same couple from 'Tidal Wave', perhaps, a decade or so down the line – it was a catalogue of retributions and rows between lovers who "used to tear it down, but now we just exist... the lights are gone and the party's over". But for all its lists of wrongdoings and late nights out with cellphones turned off, 'Forget...' was a refreshing reset, partly since its title and hookline set out to wipe the album's troubled lyrical slate clean and partly because it harked back to the funk-punk pulses of *Hot Fuss*. A timely reminder of the indie pop throbs at The Killers' heart.

Considering the more electronic approach of *Day & Age* as a natural progression, The Killers were proud of the advances they'd made. "We follow the direction of the songs, which is almost opposite to what a purist might think it should be," Brandon argued, claiming that growing older, gaining experience and getting bored of old styles constantly drove the band onwards. "I guess a purist would say that the music is an exaggeration, or an example of their life. We almost do the opposite – we follow where the songs go. But I guess the songs are coming from us, so it's just where we are. It's just a weird circle. We change. We aren't the same four guys who wrote *Sam's Town* or *Hot Fuss*, and we're doing our best to represent that... Change is inevitable. We're not afraid of sounding the same, but we're also not afraid of embracing what's happening. We just take it and go with it. This could have just as easily been *Sam's Town*, part two. But when we got together, it just wasn't."[44] "It's like looking at *Sam's Town* from Mars."[45]

"This is our heaviest and most light-hearted album at the same time," he said elsewhere. "It's more fun than I've ever had, which is amazing. But then also... I'm getting older too, and seeing things differently. I think I might even be getting smarter. Or at least I'm able to articulate things better. I think it's a well-rounded album, a journey. I'm a sucker for scenes in movies where the strings come in and tell you you're supposed to cry – that stuff gets me. That element's in a lot of our songs. [And] I love mythology. Fantasy is fun. It seems like it's dying..."[46] "It sits well with our other two albums. It's obviously a little more on the pop end of things; it's not quite as masculine as *Sam's Town*, but I like it. 'Spaceman' is such a playful tune, it makes my body do things I've never done before. 'Human' is one of our best recordings so far. I don't think we've made our best album yet, and that makes me happy, to know it's still out there."

"In a lot of ways it reminds me of being akin to a couple of different Bowie records," Ronnie added. "Sometimes I'm thinking *Young Americans*, sometimes I'm thinking *Low*, sometimes I'm thinking... different songs, different albums. We wanted to dig deep and experiment with our style and sound for this album, and I think we've found growth as a band."[47]

Mark also saw the album as fitting into the lineage of Roxy Music and Bowie, "even the Stones when they were pursuing a bigger sound... As long as we make a record and do the best we can, I think our audience is going to get it."[48]

Dave saw the record as a marked improvement in their writing and recording skills and was particularly pleased that, with its disco overtones and world music touches, it would confound people's expectations of what The Killers were as a band. "I do think we enjoy surprising people because everybody thinks they got us figured out," he chuckled. "'Oh they did this!' and then we do *Sam's Town*. Then they go 'Oh they did that!' and then we do *Day & Age*. Everybody thinks they've got us figured out, but we have a lot of influences, all four of us. We have a lot of favourite bands. Brandon and I never said, 'Hey, we're gonna sound like this...' – we just started playing with each other and those are the songs that came out... I think we sound like ourselves, but I think 'ourselves' have a lot of different tastes, and I think with one song at a time, we're showing what we can do. Whenever people try and predict us, they're gonna be disappointed."[49]

"There's a lot more space [on *Day & Age*]," Brandon mused. "I think it's a sign of maturity, and I think it's awesome that we've gotten to that point."[50] "We're about to reach our peak now – I don't think we've reached it yet. I feel like I'm learning more about becoming a better singer, I'm becoming a better songwriter and we're getting better at all the things we do, so it's exciting for me."[51] "There's been more space between albums than last time, and I feel ready. Although – I'm still on a high from *Sam's Town*. And having a baby and everything."[52]

Above all, though, Brandon put the success of the record down to the band's confidence gleaming through. "Three-quarters of the Killers are quite shy individuals," he said. "It's funny, it took the success of selling 12 million records to really show a little bit of the sex appeal, a little bit of the rock 'n' roll. There's a lot more swagger on this album and a lot more grease but it's also playful and fun. We're finally realising we deserve to be here and we're going to do what we want to do, and this is that album. We weren't afraid to make this record. There were things that we were afraid of when we were making the other records."[53]

Even before the record was completed, The Killers wanted to show it off. With barely a handful of US warm-up dates*, they launched themselves on the 2008 festival seasons of Hungary, Germany** and Belgium, not only to play rare tracks from *Sawdust* live for the first time – 'Sweet Talk', 'Under The Gun', 'Tranquilize' and 'Shadowplay' were set mainstays – but also to see what sort of impact 'Spaceman' would have on a large crowd, especially in their welcoming second homeland of Britain. It detonated like an A-bomb. Headlining Reading & Leeds that August with the old *Sam's Town* stage setup (minus the moustache), it held its own against major crowd-pleasers like 'Somebody Told Me' and 'When You Were Young', fans already bawling along word for word to a song the band had played live only 12 times before.

After the disaster of Glastonbury 2007, Reading & Leeds finally saw The Killers hold their own at the top table of alternative rock. Butterflies the size of pigeons in his stomach but revelling in the sound of the 80,000-strong crowd singing his songs back at him, Brandon gave a consummate performance, the sort that cements legends. But even amid the buzz and the rush, the band knew they couldn't let their success go to their heads, couldn't get complacent. There were still challengers. "I'm scared," Brandon said, "because this is where some people start to get comfortable. And I don't want to get there. I'm not too comfortable yet. The thing that's really kept me on my toes is how my mom would always tell me – it's not the best thing for a mother to tell you – but she'd never tell me after I'd lose a soccer game, 'You'll do better next time.' She'd always say, 'There's always somebody better'. There's always someone ahead. For this album, it was Coldplay's 'Viva La Vida'. I could have really done without that song. And Kings of Leon's 'Sex On Fire'. If not for those, we'd be on top of the world."[54]

---

* During various warm-up shows, TV appearances and award show sets, The Killers tried out a few fun cover versions, including 'Bring On The Dancing Horses' by Echo & The Bunnymen and 'Girls Just Want To Have Fun' by Cyndi Lauper.

** Where *Hot Fuss* had been received coolly in Germany, *Sam's Town* had seen the band take off there; now they were headlining the 25,000 capacity Highlands festival.

The world of rock remained a battleground. And The Killers were once again strapping on their battle armour.

★ ★ ★

Two different Killers worlds rolled in convoy down the highways of six continents through 2009. Out front, the party bus; Welcome To The Jungle they called it. Here Dave and Mark, both single and up for fun at this point, raved hard into the night, Dave knocking back champagne and narrowly avoiding trouble. "I'm surprised Dave wasn't on the front of any newspapers," Brandon said after Dave was spotted shirtless and swigging champagne late into the night after the post-awards party at the MTV Awards in Sydney in March. "I did check. He's the animal of our band."[55]

This certainly wasn't the only time Dave's inner monster had crept out in public. British Sea Power's Martin Noble recalls seeing Dave having a rare series of Long Island Iced Teas before a US festival show and freaking out. "Dave was hammered," he said. "Literally falling on the floor during the gig, legless. He'd jump into the audience to have his hair molested, and then get onstage and topple over onto the floor again. A rare moment of unprofessionalism."

Trailing behind – or, on nights like the Sydney MTV after-show, heading back to the hotel when Welcome To The Jungle rolled party-wards – was the family bus, nicknamed James Taylor. Here, children ran amok*, Jonathan Richman and The Modern Lovers** emanated from the bus stereo, fine malt whiskey graced the cupboards*** and Brandon and Ronnie – both married – worked on the new state-of-the-art recording device that Ronnie had had commissioned, specifically for the road.

---

* Or at least they did on the legs that Tana and Ammon joined the tour. "My son and wife usually travel with us when we're touring, although they haven't come this time," Brandon said on the first leg of the UK in 2008. "My son is at a tough age. Before he turned one, he was a good traveller. Now he's really discovered his lungs, and it's not so easy." Source: *Daily Mail*, Adrian Thrills, November 14, 2008.

** Brandon was getting into the proto-punk band around this time.

*** For Ronnie, who was becoming a connoisseur.

He'd planned to use the mobile studio he'd had made to make a covers album during the tour, with each member choosing three songs to give a Killers makeover to. Ronnie's choices were by Tom Waits, Genesis and Rod Stewart.*

The road, for the *Day & Age* tour, was unfeasibly long. Warming up with a *Saturday Night Live* appearance in October 2008 and a couple of Vegas shows at the Wynn casino and the House of Blues, dates were loosely fixed right through until the end of 2010, making for a full two years on tour. Having spent the best part of three years on the road from 2004 to 2007, the band now knew what to expect from extended stretches of touring, and were determined to take more control this time. So besides the separate buses for parties and family, Brandon also insisted on getting approval on all of the onstage photos taken during the shows before they went out to the press, in order to mastermind the band's image throughout. This meant banning the swarms of photographers from each individual media outlet that usually packed their photo-pits and instead allowing only their official on-the-road photographer, Brandon's brother-in-law Torey Mundkowsky, to take pictures of the band live**, which Brandon would look through after the show. Sometimes there would be thousands of shots to approve or dismiss, but Brandon would painstakingly approve or delete every one.

Brandon's lingering insecurity about how he looked onstage would take him as far as studying YouTube footage that fans would post up after each show, dissecting his performance to work out how he could become less stilted, more natural, owning the stage with the fluidity of Jagger or the charisma of Morrissey. Though he'd claim that "something happens to me when I step onstage and I don't know what… there's a veil I put on when I go onstage, I get much more excited"[56], within the certified pop superstar – the man that even his bandmates would admit had developed "a bit of an ego" by this point – there was still the self-questioning student of stagecraft trying not to get found out.

---

* It's uncertain how much, if any, of this album was ever recorded.

** On later tours, rather than have a photographer travelling with them, the band would employ trusted photographers around the world to shoot them, on the same basis.

The show itself was bigger than ever. They could now fill arenas across much of Europe and the US, and the set expanded to fill the caverns. A huge dot matrix screen across the back of the stage counted down to their entrance in movie-footage rings as Dave plucked out the opening notes of 'Human' or 'Spaceman', then exploded with frantic visuals and snippets from videos. "People have been waiting," Dave said, "some of them for hours and hours, and when we finally play that first song, we want it to be a good one and reward them a little bit. It just puts the crowd instantly into a frenzy."[57]

A 'K' of lights now adorned the front of Brandon's keyboard and palm trees lined the back of the stage, more Vegas accoutrements to give the stage a glamorous down-home colour. Screens set within the lighting rig pumped with patterns and symbols, and the show had more dynamics, Brandon sitting solo at a spotlit piano for a stripped-down opening verse of 'Sam's Town' before the song gradually growled into life around him[*].

The tour also saw the band begin to indulge in tiny club gigs for the dedicated fans, around their major shows – in London on the lower-key first leg of the tour in 2008, the day before they played the Royal Albert Hall for the first time, they played at the ornate but minute Bush Hall, capacity only 350.[**]

Brandon got a huge thrill from preparing for these massive shows. "That feeling of getting ready, and knowing the doors are open, it's almost euphoric," he said. "Because I remember waiting in line to see a gig, and running up to the front of the stage like that. And I love watching that happen now; they don't realise it but I'm probably

---

[*] At some early shows on the tour the band would also play an acoustic version of 'Tidal Wave' as a mid-set calmer.

[**] To keep the shows fresh, the Day & Age tour would feature a shifting set list, often opening with 'Human' and 'This Is Your Life' before including crowd-pleasers 'Somebody Told Me' and 'For Reasons Unknown'. The show would then dot tracks from *Day & Age* through the set as well as 'Shadowplay' and occasionally a cover of Nina Simone's 'Don't Let Me Be Misunderstood', ending the main set with 'All These Things That I've Done'. The encore would include 'Jenny Was A Friend Of Mine' and 'When You Were Young'.

watching it from somewhere. It sets the mood. And that's when I realise I've got a job to do."[58]

The stylistic space of the new album gave Brandon some problems initially. "I suffer with that space live," he said. "I'm used to this freight train of a show that we put on, and I can run around. Now all of a sudden, there's breathing room. Dave has this long solo at the end of 'Losing Touch', and I don't know what the hell to do while he's doing it."[59]

Press-wise, the tour had a far more celebratory launch than the tour for *Sam's Town*. Among fans there were mixed feelings about *Day & Age* – support for *Sam's Town* as a modern classic of hyper-charged Americana had grown over the past few years to the point where many believed it surpassed *Hot Fuss* in stature, so it was inevitable that *Day & Age* would split opinion. Some loved the brighter electronic elements while others found them too mainstream and gimmicky, the album patchier than *Sam's Town* and the lyrical fumble in the chorus to 'Human' a little ridiculous. "The best thing about it is watching the turnaround," Brandon said. "I shouldn't do it, but I watch the comments, even on YouTube, and the first comment when a new Killers album comes out is almost bewilderment. It's shocking for people at first, but it's nice to watch them turn around. We kind of win them over every time – it's fun. We have so much faith in [our music], otherwise we wouldn't put it out."[60]

But the reviews for the record suggested that The Killers had already weathered their minor backlash. *Rolling Stone* had come round, anyway: "When the Killers really push the theatrics, they shine," wrote Melissa Maerz, praising the record for its global scope and stratospheric ambition. "Too bad all that drama sometimes weighs down Flowers – he's developed quite a persecution complex… Relax, dude. With imagination like this, you're doing fine."[61]

"Like *Sam's Town*, every track inflates steadily to echoing heights," wrote *Spin*'s Stacey Anderson, "but the band sounds more mindful than grandiose. This is a cohesive record, even though it's peppered with unexpected diversions… when they strip down the wordy solemnity, the Killers can deliver quite a spectacle. They remain fascinated by heartland mythos, but by becoming more comfortable with their glitzy roots, they've actually found the pulse of something more authentic."[62] There were naysayers, naturally – *The Guardian*'s Dave Simpson wrote of the album's "confused, hollow soul" and likened much of it to "a mad rummage through the DJ box in an eighties Essex disco"[63], while Pitchfork's Ryan Dombal called it "The Killers' spitball album, the one where they try everything and see what works while Flowers grasps for a relatable tone"[64]. But in general the media's approach to *Day & Age* was more welcoming than to the bombastic shock of *Sam's Town*, most reviewers chiming with *NME*'s Dan Martin when he wrote "as The Killers strut about rock's premier league, there's plenty to guffaw at. But just as much to admire."[65]

One criticism did hit Brandon hard though. Because of the mixed reaction to 'Joy Ride' among reviewers, he ditched plans for it to be a single. "It's the best-sounding song on there," he said, "but it's really divided people, so it's frustrating, because we thought it would be our conquering song. The sax has given us a little grief we didn't have before, but I like it. I don't think a pop song should be afraid of putting you in a better place."[66]

Instead, to bolster the release of the album on November 18, The Killers put out 'Spaceman' as the more obvious second single.* The song turned out to be a slow-burner; making number 67 in the US for only one week, it wouldn't register in the UK Top 40 until February 2009, but gradually became a major fan favourite and a West Coast radio smash. In LA it would remain the most-played song on several local stations well into 2010. Perhaps the west of America could better relate to being abducted by aliens.

The video for the song was the band's most flamboyant since the US 'Mr. Brightside' promo. Surrounded by weird humanoid alien monsters in silk dresses, Brandon emerged from a hibernation pod in the kind of feathery red spacesuit you might expect to see in an Elton John remake of *Flash Gordon* and scaled a wedding cake-shaped tower topped with the sculpted face of a demon, where a bacchanalian carnival party of

---

* The song was backed on a variety of formats by remixes of the song, 'Tidal Wave' and a whoomp-heavy, dance-floor-friendly cover of Bright Eyes' folk hit 'Four Winds'.

space-age cowboys, clowns, fire-breathers, revolutionaries and freaks was in full swing. Mark and Dave played harps in areas draped with human chandeliers, Brandon sat down for a lone feast watched over by suits of armour and waltzing 25th-century primitives. The concept, from director Ray Tintori, was more like a wild drug cult taking over a field at Glastonbury than a sci-fi abduction movie, but was undeniably one of the more memorable videos of recent years.

It certainly grabbed attention at the right time. *Day & Age* became the third Killers album to reach number one in the UK that November, and also made number six in the *Billboard* Chart.[*] Its early sales of 200,000 in the first week in the UK and virtually the same in the US would balloon over the coming months until sales of the album eventually hit three million worldwide. Receiving the news that all 150,000 tickets for their UK arena tour booked for February 2009 had sold out in just two hours and the album had gone double platinum in Seattle on December 9, Ronnie bellowed the news across a restaurant to his dad at another table. "Double platinum," his dad yelled back, "what does that mean exactly?"

The start of the tour was peppered with bizarre and uplifting moments. In November 2008 Brandon hit the GQ Men Of The Year awards in London to pick up the Most Stylish Man award. "I feel like the stranger at the end of the bar getting bedroom eyes from some exotic temptress – and I'm making sure it's me that she's looking at," he said of winning. "It's pretty surreal... I feel like I become what the songs are. Most people see it as contrived, but it's the opposite. I change; as humans, it's impossible not to. The band have all these experiences and when we get back together we're not the same people, so when we write the songs come out differently. It's much more exciting to see where it's gonna take you, then dress appropriately."[67]

Brandon also got to meet actor Josh Brolin at the ceremony. "I didn't have the guts to tell him what a fan I am of *The Goonies*; [I] didn't think he would appreciate me mentioning *The Goonies*."[68]

---

[*] The album was also number one in Norway, Ireland and Greece, and Top 10 in 12 more countries, making it their most globally reaching album so far.

Later that same visit, after a cover feature interview with *NME*, the band headed off to the Jagz club in Ascot, where a friend of the band had hired a Killers covers act called The Fillers to play at his 50th birthday. The tribute act were stunned when the real-life Ronnie Vannucci invaded the stage to play drums on the final song, 'All These Things That I've Done'.* It was, it turned out, the least Ronnie could do, considering the problems the new album was causing The Fillers. "The new songs are great," said the fake Brandon, "but the one thing we object to is you're costing us money. Now we need a saxophone player! If you start working with a symphony orchestra, we're screwed. We're in this for life now. Our fortunes are tied to theirs."[69]

The Killers got a similar shock themselves at the Royal Albert Hall show on November 3. They knew that the Conservative Party leader and Prime Minister hopeful David Cameron had a private box for the show, all part of his mission to appeal to the youth vote by name-dropping bands like The Smiths, Arctic Monkeys and The Killers into his interviews. But they were more startled when they were cornered post-show by a masked maniac pretending to be a hoary hair-rock legend.

"We were waylaid in the corridor by someone on the way back to the dressing room," Brandon recounted. "It was Paul McCartney and he was wearing an Alice Cooper mask. He was dancing around and then he took it off and introduced himself." The band were understandably speechless. "As a band, we're not very good socially. Words usually fail me in those situations anyway, but that was a particularly weird one. At first, we all just stared at him. What do you say to Paul McCartney? Eventually, we got chatting and he told us that it had been a great show. Meeting a Beatle was daunting. People in Britain know what an important band they were. But when you come from the States that feeling is magnified. They were untouchable."[70]

Mingling with megastars? The Killers must have been pretty blasé about it by now. Just that year they'd recorded 'Joseph, Better You Than Me', their third Christmas single, with their now good friends

---

* He replaced the fake Ronnie whose surname, much to Vannucci's amusement, turned out to be Balls.

Neil Tennant and Elton John. A mid-paced ballad interrupted by Dave shredding like a champion through a gloriously indulgent solo, it found Elton letting rip his ballsiest bawl, Neil draping his iciest disco tones over a verse and Brandon acting as an angelic falsetto figure.

After years of slipping religious subtexts into his songs, this was Brandon's first overt reference to his faith on record, but he tackled it with a knowing smirk. There was a wryness to the track[*]; essentially an open letter to the on-Earth Father of Christ wondering how he dealt with the notoriety, fame and rumours, as well as the difficulties of having his own life and work overshadowed by a far more successful son. Concluding that Joseph did a far better job of fathering the Messiah than Brandon could have done, it was a rather more universal message than the specifics of the song suggested – in essence it was directed at any father of a famous son struggling to maintain their own identity and belief in themselves, and the references to the desert being "a hell of a place to find heaven" could just as easily be aimed at Flowers' own dad. But the Nativity slant gave colour and humanity to an ancient story that many saw couched in the cartoon fog of the fairytale, an approach that only served to rejuvenate interest in Brandon's religion during interviews throughout the *Day & Age* campaign.

"I do wonder if I was some other denomination if they would care as much," he said. "Probably not. Definitely not... It's funny because I go all over the world and I realise the way that people look at religion now, and the direction that it's going. And then I'll write a song like that. But it never occurs to me that people must think I'm fucking crazy, that I believe that Joseph existed... that stuff doesn't cross my mind till later."[71] "I've realised that while it's okay to believe in God in America – pretty much everyone here does – in the UK it makes you

---

[*] Not least in the video, where footage from the Biblical fifties TV series *The Living Christ* was intercut with religious imagery and archive footage; at the line "Forty years lost in the wilderness looking for God", shots of praying disciples were juxtaposed against footage of the Vegas lights as if they were worshiping Sin City, a Bethlehem for the dazzled and damned.

seem a little odd. I'm Mormon, sure, and I'm proud of it, but it's no big deal, right?"[72]

Several interviewers noted that his faith was turning The Killers into a travelling family. "[Mormonism] is slightly different [from other faiths] – we believe in being together forever. Eternity,"[73] Brandon explained. "One of the things about my church is we're very family-oriented, so I grew up with that and right now I'm applying that to my family. Most churches are like that but I guess we have a certain emphasis on it. I think it's been proven that unless people are sitting around having dinner with their families… I think that's happening less and less."[74]

Brandon's family certainly turned out in force for their Christmas show at the WaMu Theatre in Seattle as part of the Deck The Hall Ball radio promo event on December 9, since many of them would barely see him for a year. In January the *Day & Age* tour kicked off in earnest, hitting arenas in Denver, Boston and another date at NYC's Madison Square Garden, since the city had no bigger indoor arena for them to scale up to. Unlike London, where they'd reached the pinnacle of the UK arena circuit by selling out the 20,000 capacity O2, a step up they took in their stride. "This was a big show," Brandon said. "I argued with our booking agent as I didn't feel ready for it until this stage, when I felt we could play [this] arena and do it right."[75]

The UK leg of the tour in February began with a visit to the Brit Awards, where the band failed to win either of the two awards they were nominated for but Brandon did get to present the Pet Shop Boys with their Outstanding Contribution To Music award. "I was faced with a choice at a difficult age," he said at the podium, "13, to be exact, when I found myself having to pick between two fantastic records. Both would eventually have a huge impact on my life but my mother made it very clear that she was only going to give me enough cash for one of those records. So there I was, hovering over my left hand, which contained *Louder Than Bombs* by The Smiths. It's a very great record, 24 tracks, a lot of bang for your buck. And in my right was *Discography* by the Pet Shop Boys, a singles collection, 18 tracks, this was gonna be a tough decision. But it would eventually be Neil Tennant's perfect execution of that devilish right eyebrow raise that secured Pet

Shop Boys' position for the cassette player on that ride home. And thus I was introduced to a new world of sonic landscapes, beats, synthesizers, imagination and sophistication."

In return, Pet Shop Boys invited Brandon onstage to sing 'It's A Sin' during their medley of hits alongside Lady Gaga, and these wouldn't be the last megastars Brandon would sing with that night. From the Brits, the band raced across town to the Shepherd's Bush Empire to play a War Child charity show with fellow Brits losers Coldplay; come the finale, Brandon found himself onstage in the early hours singing 'All These Things That I've Done' with Chris Martin, Gary Barlow and Bono. "It sounded awful," wrote one reviewer, "but it was a camera-phone moment to die for."[76]

In 2009, it seemed that every A-lister wanted a little of Brandon's star quality gracing their stage. As the tour reached the festival season via shows at Coachella and the V Festival in Australia, he found himself invited onstage with Bruce Springsteen at the Pinkpop festival in the Netherlands on May 30 to sing 'Thunder Road'. "He watched us play, watched the whole set," he recalled of this fantasy he'd imagined "easily 150 times" made real. "And on our way back to our dressing room he asked if I wanted to [sing with him], right after we played. It was great. I was dying! I had a perma-grin. [It was] a dream come true."[77] In April, Kanye West posted a photo of himself, Brandon and Jared Leto, the Hollywood actor who also fronts rock band 30 Seconds To Mars, claiming that the trio had collaborated on an impromptu tune at his studio in Hawaii. "I was working on this dope ass song with Jared and Brandon stopped by," West wrote in his blog. "I played them some of the new Jeezy beats and before everybody bounced, Brandon hopped on the keyboard and I hopped on the MPC. Shit was dope."

Any year-long tour by even the most well-adjusted band is a tangle of ups and downs, niggles and kindnesses, frustration and elation. Even with two tour buses to make things more comfortable, The Killers were no exception. They had great fun dressing up in post-apocalyptic *Mad Max* outfits of futuristic leather armour and wielding spiked balls and chains out in the desert for a *Q* magazine photo shoot, Dave 'dressed down' in an 18th-century French general's blazer smeared with battle-grime.

The interview seemed fun, too, with Brandon raving about the way the new Razorlight album reminded him of Dire Straits, his love of junk food and fajitas, standing in the stage heart of U2's Elevation tour as a fan and the time his mother met Muhammad Ali in the Golden Nugget casino, and Dave doing karaoke with the writer, necking Jagermeister and bawling out 'Shout' and 'Everybody Wants To Rule The World' by Tears For Fears.

The band were buoyed by the fabulous news that Brandon would be becoming a father again in the summer – his second son, Gunnar, would be born on July 28 – and a three-week window around the due date was cleared in the tour to make sure he could be at home for the birth. Brandon decided not to halt the tour for too long though. "I have seen interviews with kids whose dads did what I did, and they all seem to be resentful," he considered. "I don't want that. But I also feel like I've been given this opportunity…"[78]

The opportunities were expanding exponentially. That year The Killers had snagged the highly coveted slot on the latest movie in the *Twilight* franchise, *The Twilight Saga: New Moon*. These soundtracks had become lucrative and prestigious for the bands chosen to contribute, and The Killers found themselves supplying songs for the October soundtrack album alongside indie rock luminaries such as Muse, Death Cab for Cutie, Bon Iver and Thom Yorke from Radiohead. The band contributed a suitably stark, chilling and vampiric ode to loneliness and everlasting faithfulness called 'White Demon Love Song', the first song played over the credits. It was a moment that would fix The Killers firmly into the hearts of a new generation of teenage romantics swooning over the swarthy undead.

There was much patriotic optimism, too, around the inauguration of Barack Obama as the first black US President and a beacon of hope to liberal Americans who had seen their country develop an image of dumb imperialist warmongers under George W. Bush. Brandon had often steered well clear of talking about politics before; his only real pronouncement on the subject was back in 2004, when *NME* asked him which he favoured most: Bush, Bin Laden or Blair. "Bush," he declared. "He was harmless before Bin Laden came around. As far as we know. I think the lesser of the evils is Bush. When George Bush first came out I had no problems with him. He was really animated when he spoke. And I would watch some of the speeches and I liked them. But a couple of things got out, especially that he might not have the most extensive vocabulary. And it really hinders him now. He wasn't like that before. Maybe nobody should feel sorry for him, but I do. I feel bad for him because I've really watched this change in him. When he speaks, he's afraid. You English people do that to us! I'd say 'awesome' whereas someone here would say 'brilliant'. It sounds smarter and cooler but really it's just the same thing. So basically he got a case of that."[79]

As a band that had spent some years defending the US against criticisms abroad and proudly rebranding themselves as staunch all-American heroes, the election of Obama was a vindication of their people that gave The Killers hope that the tide of global opinion may be about to turn in America's favour at last, and their inbred belief in the nobility and honour of their homeland might finally come to the fore. No longer, they hoped, would they travel the world a little embarrassed to be American.

"I think about how my sons will grow up only knowing a black president," he said in one interview shortly after the inauguration, welling up as he chose his most significant cultural event of the year. "I can't explain how that's changed America. There's an optimism now that wasn't there for black people."[80] "You can definitely see it changing," he said elsewhere. "Hopefully in a few months, people will see us in a whole new light. Which is all fine, but you've got to realise that it's not really fair to treat people a certain way when the majority aren't represented by a few hundred rich dudes in Washington... [Bush has] not made it any better. This could be the worst that we've ever looked. So it's bound to start looking up. America is a special place, and people have always looked to it as a place of hope, and I think that's still alive. And I believe in it, and I'm proud to be from there. Nobody wants to see their country or people looked at the way we've been looked at recently. You can just feel the itch. People are waiting for a renaissance."

Had he shed the image of being an American writing British-style songs by now? "There are two sides to me. I want to be socially relevant as an American writing songs – but I don't know if that's the kind of songs I write. But I learned to love music from English bands. I think I'd be more devastated if we were hated over here."[81]

The idea of using their platform to make important statements that might help change the world for the better was opening up to the band. In July, they gave 'Goodnight, Travel Well' to a collaborative video made by UNICEF and MTV to highlight the 1.2 million children being sold into the sex trafficking trade each year. "We are deeply shocked and appalled that women and children are forced into such exploitative situations," the band's statement about the video read. "We hope that through MTV's efforts, and this powerful video, millions of people across the world learn about this tragic form of modern-day slavery." The video was a hard-hitting piece – what at first appeared to be a romantic liaison between a woman in a red dress and her paramour in an upmarket hotel was gradually revealed to be a paid encounter; behind the smiles and seduction the woman's life was lived out in a squalid cell between daily beatings. Brandon's line "There's nothing I can say, there's nothing I can do now" rang poignantly over the final slogan "Some things cost more than you realise".

Then, of course, there were the gigs, shows that, according to Brandon, would "take me away. Sometimes you do become a robot, but the best nights are when you just forget and really become a part of the music and the crowds... We've always talked about our career and how we want the steps; there seems to be a pedestal that's waiting for us... This is the time [for us] to step up."[82]

"To play live is the best thing ever," Ronnie said at the time. "Everything leading up to it is kind of a drag sometimes. But as long as we can play live and share that experience – that, for all of us, never gets old. I'm sure there'll come a point in our career where we'll be able to take longer time off. But at the moment we just gotta keep on keepin' on. And the well's not dry yet."[83]

The mania would be captured not at the more obvious open-air setting of their Hard Rock Calling headline show at Hyde Park on

June 26, but instead at a triumphant second stint at the Royal Albert Hall in July, filmed for a DVD release in November by director Mark Romanek. On a tiny stage designed to heighten the sense of euphoric occasion, the band stormed through a set list custom-honed to create the ultimate crowd hysteria. "That's the perfect audience," Dave said, "singing along to every word, knowing the songs, appreciating the non-hit songs, stuff like that. It was a good setting for it, and hopefully that came across in the DVD."[84] Critics certainly thought it did. "Quite possibly the best live album and video since Elvis and his *Aloha From Hawaii* some 36 years ago," wrote Starpulse. "Brandon Flowers doesn't sing: he testifies," enthused *Rolling Stone*. "When Brandon Flowers et al explode into closing number 'When You Were Young' and the fans start to sing (and then jump) along," wrote *Entertainment Weekly*, "it's a wonder those 138-year-old walls stay standing."*

No band opened for The Killers at the Albert Hall; instead, support came from comedian Jimmy Carr. "We played Comic Relief and he was there one night," Brandon would tell me in 2012. "I'd seen his TV show a couple of times and I liked it. So I struck up conversation and he's great, when he comes to Vegas we see him, and here in London." Carr would turn out to be an unlikely inspiration for future songs, as the pair became friends discussing the economic downturn in America, and the music that might come out of it. "We were talking about Bruce Springsteen or something, we thought that somebody was going to make a record like that. It had an impact on me, it definitely found its way into a song like 'Deadlines And Commitments' and a song called 'The Slot Tech' about a slot machine technician who's got a gambling problem. It's seven and a half minutes long and a beautiful story. One day it'll show its face I'm sure. I'm conscious of it – Las Vegas was hit harder than anywhere else. Empty houses, empty shopping malls. They built a whole shopping centre by my house in Henderson that never

---

* The *Live From The Royal Albert Hall* DVD would sell 87,000 copies in the UK alone in its first seven weeks – making it the fourth bestselling music DVD in the UK in 2009 – and a total of half a million to date.

even got occupied by one store. Dead palm trees, dead golf courses, it's a weird time."

Those that met the band on the road in 2009 found them still socially awkward* and Brandon still a jittery, insecure interviewee, but in good spirits. In Verona on June 8, the last show before eight days off, journalist Craig McLean found Ronnie drinking pink champagne and exploring the dankest corners of Verona Arena, an ancient 2,000-capacity open-air amphitheatre, for the dank tunnels where "the Christians would come out... followed by the lions,"[85] and Mark and Dave hanging out with support act and Oscar-nominated Hollywood star Juliette Lewis.

The second the holiday hit, however, The Killers scattered like ants from fire. Mark to Florence to soak in the culture with copies of *Dante's Inferno* and T.S. Eliot under his arm. Dave to San Diego to see his son; Ronnie to the Utah mountains to hang with his wife. And Brandon to Vegas to take his heavily pregnant wife to the movies – their local cinema was showing the 1986 Molly Ringwald teen classic *Pretty In Pink* and he already had tickets and babysitter booked. "I would not be in this band if *Pretty In Pink* didn't exist," he grinned. "Echo & The Bunnymen, New Order, The Smiths and Psychedelic Furs – the music on that soundtrack is the stuff that shaped me."[86]

One sign, there, of the underlying strains on the band. Behind the scenes, offsetting the plus points, the Day & Age tour was probably the most fraught Killers tour to date. The lawsuits flying back and forth between the band and Braden Merrick were in the process of being settled with staggering sums discussed. The Air France disaster that June, when an Airbus A330-203 crashed into the middle of the Atlantic Ocean due to autopilot failure and subsequent mistakes by the crew killing all 216 passengers and 12 crew, was agitating Brandon's fear of flying to a chronic degree, keeping him awake at night and giving him stress-induced cold sores, although this may simply have been a smokescreen

---

* "I usually assume that people don't like us," Brandon told one newspaper during the tour. "I've tried putting myself out there, but we still tend to stay in our own little corner. It's all a bit goofy." Source: *Daily Mail*, November 14, 2009.

for the deep concerns Brandon had about his mother's worsening health in the wake of her brain tumour.

In America, some of the crowds weren't as receptive as the Albert Hall mob. At the Santa Barbara Bowl on September 13 the audience were noticeably apathetic despite the band's best efforts; deeply frustrated, they stormed offstage and headed straight to the James Taylor bus to continue work on a new song they'd been writing that day, a future classic they called 'Runaways'. "We were like, 'Fuck that show, this song is great!'" said Ronnie, and while it was positive for them to channel their anger into a creative outlet, shows like this fed into a deep-seated insecurity about their place and longevity in music; a sense that they were too real, not as superhuman as their rock star heroes had seemed to them.

"Some days I wouldn't want to be anywhere else, and I think that we're doing it perfectly," Brandon said when asked about the band's niche in rock music. "We've had a couple of bumps in the road but I'm really happy with our career. And there are other days where I just get frustrated because I don't know if we have 'that' thing. I'm not sure because, I guess, I'm so close to it. I don't know if we have a Killers sound or not."[87]

Mark was more philosophical. "The world will change around us and either we will adjust to it or not," he said. "But it doesn't worry me. It's a one-in-a-million shot we are where we are; if it only lasts another five years, we'll have had this. It could go away really quickly but we're doing well in a time when it's hard to do well, and we have an audience that I think will be there for a while. I think we're as secure as we can be."[88]

Meanwhile, discussions about the future of the band were becoming more frequent and intense, largely driven by Dave's frustration at being apart from his son as he was reaching a formative age. "Oh, yeah, everyone's proud of being a Killer 24 hours a day," Dave would sneer when asked about the backroom issues. "Well, not all of us are built like that. I've got a kid, so, mystery solved."[89]

"It was non-stop," he'd add later. "I wanted to live a normal life, just for a bit. I felt I needed to be around for at least a year to teach [Kyler] how to ride a bike. So I'm sorry if no one's sympathetic, but fuck you."[90]

When the discussions boiled over into full-blown rows between the Welcome To The Jungle and the James Taylor camps – Dave and Mark demanding time off to rest and spend some serious family time and Brandon and Ronnie itching to keep making music – Brandon's thoughts turned to stepping outside of the band for a while. "When things get really dark in the band. When the arguments get rowdy enough… It would be more adventurous,"[91] he hinted. "Look, here's how it works. We are a machine of four parts. And when some of those parts wear out, you need to give it time. We all have different temperaments for how much we can manage. You need respect. Otherwise you're a band for maybe three years and then explode… We're all in this. We can't make people do things, and, if you're not careful, it does for everybody."[92]

Back and forth. Argument, counter-argument. In the end, destiny dictated.

★ ★ ★

In February of 2010, with the band having just returned from their Christmas break* to begin a new leg of the Day & Age tour in Australia

---

* The Killers' Christmas single for (RED) in 2009 was the brass-smothered mariachi party number '¡Happy Birthday Guadalupe!', also produced by Stuart Price. A more playful and un-traditional tune than 'Joseph, Better You Than Me', it followed the tale of a man waking up on Christmas morning in the bed of a beautiful "Mexican angel", quickly veering from infatuation to fear over the encounter and leaving that night, only to be haunted by regretful memories of her forever. The video starred *Beverly Hills 90210* star Luke Perry as a cowboy searching the desert forlornly for his lost love, and the family they may have had together, as a skeletal mariachi band and flamenco dancers hint at a supernatural slant to the mysterious woman. The track featured indie rockers Wild Light, and The Bronx in their new brass-based guise Mariachi El Bronx: "Bronx and Killers go way back," says Matt Caughthran from The Bronx today, "we were actually signed to Island Def Jam at the exact same time, by the same A&R dude. Although our bands were completely different, there was always a mutual respect and secret kinship between us. When we started Mariachi El Bronx in 2008 The Killers were the first band to take us out on tour. It was awesome to reconnect with the dudes and the positive vibrations manifested themselves sonically into the Christmas single '¡Happy Birthday Guadalupe!'. Viva los Killers!"

before heading to Asia for dates in the Philippines, Singapore, China, Japan and South Korea, news reached them that Brandon's mother was seriously ill, possibly with only a few days left to live. Brandon immediately cancelled the remaining dates on the leg to fly home to be with her. It was the second tour of Asia the band had pulled.

"I don't remember the excuse last time. But this one was a good excuse!" he'd say later. "It was a strange feeling to be in this position – 'I know I'm cancelling it because I feel strongly about being there with my mother. But she may not die'. And I had that weight: 'I'm holding off money and possibly the expansion of the band'. The success of my band in Asia basically was being gambled on this. And I've got three other guys and a whole crew that are depending on this. And I'm just making this decision...' It was just a weird set of pushes and pulls. But she did die during that time I would have been in Asia. So it was the right decision."[93]

Dave saw the stalling of the tour as a natural break, a time for both mourning and recuperation. At his behest, a year's solid hiatus from The Killers was agreed. Unlike the young protagonist of Dave Eggars' novel *You Shall Know Our Velocity!* – who travels the globe distributing an unexpected windfall to worthy recipients and, ultimately, never stops travelling – however, Brandon's world kept spinning and he didn't want to get off.

He had an undeniable urge to honour his mother in the only way he knew how.

By writing.

Mark Stoermer, April 2014

How did the writing of *Day & Age* work?

We had a few months after the *Sam's Town* tour was done and we were all at home, there were emails of demos coming in the mailbox more from Brandon and Ronnie – Ronnie was learning Logic at the time and a little bit advancing his own recordings. We'd send them to Stuart [Price] and they'd come back and Brandon would put something on it and it'd get sent back. I sent a few things to Stuart to join in, but I wasn't very technologically savvy, especially then, so my demos were a lot rougher. We'd never done anything like that before, but that only went on for a couple of months, and with these demos we got together and kinda did it how we used to do it with *Hot Fuss* or *Sam's Town* – get in a circle, go through song ideas, jam them out live, talk about them, arrange them together, maybe record rough versions with a mike in the room and then work on them again. That was stage two of the writing and then Stuart came and he pretty much came for the rest of *Day & Age*, for the writing. They weren't all just written via email, a lot were written in advance, but that's how it started. Stuart's production style is more heavy-handed than anyone else we had previous to that. It was kind of a remixing style because he is a remixer, and at the time we wanted that, but it was different for us. Some of the songs were just a simple rock band when we were playing them and then you'd hear them back and you'd go "Is that the remix?" "No, that's the album version". We always had an electronic element but pretty simple, where Brandon handled that part, but it would be one or two keyboards, it didn't dig into all the other elements to it.

Were you comfortable having your sound manipulated to that degree?

I'm not sure, I think everyone might have been different. I wasn't 100 per cent comfortable but was going with it because [Price] is our Brian Eno. We were searching for someone who hadn't done something, but we're letting someone get in the mix and almost become a fifth band member for the first time. Not because we needed it but because we were gonna see where it took us. I think some of the results were very good and some were okay. I'm not sure if it was better than if we weren't using him, but we did it. I do think that was a big shift in writing in a couple of ways. One, involving someone else, period. Two, the thing with the emails. Writing from then on started to drift more and more to standing around a computer or sending emails versus getting in a circle as a band. The other thing, the electronic element, which was always handled by Brandon in the past, started to go a little bit towards producers, especially with Stuart and then again later with Damian Taylor. Brandon started playing less keyboards and sometimes the producer was the one playing the keyboards or putting it in there, how they do it. That was a big shift and it's kinda never fully gone back, not that it needs to.

What do you think of *Day & Age* now?

I think there's good songs in general across the board, there's even some hidden gems that we don't play any more. The production really works for some songs and kinda works for some others but it probably could have been better. A song like 'Human', I don't think it could've been any other way; if it wasn't for Stuart we wouldn't have had 'Human' and that was a big song for us in Europe and the UK – especially in Europe, I think it was the song that made us break Europe, countries like Spain and Italy and Germany. That song wouldn't be the same without Stuart. But then there were other songs, like 'A Dustland Fairytale' or maybe even 'Spaceman', where the earlier versions were more like a band and he kinda remixed it a little bit, softening it up, the guitars are kinda tiny, the bass is in the background, there's tons of synth, but not necessarily a prominent synth like on *Hot Fuss*, more like layers of background synths.

Was that a darker period for the band?

Everyone was aware that Dave and Brandon lost their mothers at the same time but at the same time *Day & Age* was an effort to make more of an upbeat poppy album, obviously songs like 'Joy Ride' are on there. I thought the vibe going into it, we were going in a kinda Roxy Music direction, almost countering what we did in *Sam's Town*. In general, everybody knew what was going on but it wasn't talked about, we were moving forward and making this upbeat pop record. But then that song ['Goodnight, Travel Well'] maybe represents those underlying feelings. 'A Dustland Fairytale' is a tribute too, but it's more of an epic. So it was there in the middle of that kind of album that had this tropical pop glam feel to it, that was going on and it still came out.

How do you feel about the more flamboyant visual aspect to *Day & Age* – was it over the top or just a bit of fun?
A little bit of both. Some of it was fun, some of it was over the top. I was on board with most of it, but looking back if I could change it, a couple of things weren't my favourite, particularly the 'Spaceman' video. If the band's even in it. We all showed up to get in for one second. I almost felt like the director was making fun of us, that's how I personally felt about that! Now, the look for some of the pictures and for 'Human' and stuff, that's fine – I felt we were doing this Roxy Music-ish thing but in a new way, but then I thought the 'Spaceman' video, "What's going on here, is this a joke?" It's a good song, I'm not dissing the song.

Why did you decide to have the two buses on that tour?
I think that happens to a lot of bands – if you can, why not? We're getting older and when you're 20-something it's different than when you're 30-something. You start to want your space and make it a little bit comfortable, but it's not drastically more comfortable to be honest, it's still a bus that moves in the middle of the night. I think it's mostly the years of being on the road and wanting to have a little bit more space.

Was there also the need for a different sort of touring experience between the married and single members of the band?
Maybe at times in the *Day & Age* tour that was what the thinking was, but the Welcome To The Jungle bus wasn't really the Welcome To The Jungle bus. There were a couple of nights when there were too many people hanging out and after-parties happening on there, but it wasn't really taken advantage of as much as it could've been or people think it would be.

What were the most memorable moments of that tour?
We had more people onstage than ever. This was the point where we were at Stop Making Sense festival, where it builds up. We're at the point where you have 10 extra guys onstage. As a kid, when I would look at other bands I'd always be like "Why do they have 10 people onstage?" That was always a sign that it was almost over. I don't know if it's almost over but I felt a little bit that way. I kind of understood it and liked it because I would prefer to do as much as you can live rather than put everything on tracks if you're gonna have saxophones and bongos and stuff. That was a big change on the tour, but the big shows, the Royal Albert Hall shows, were really good, where we filmed the video. But *Day & Age* is a blur at the moment. We definitely went up another level. *Sam's Town* was the first couple of arena shows, then there were even bigger festival headlines across Europe. That's when we really broke some other countries – we were playing arenas in Spain and Italy, which never happened before, we were playing the clubs.

Why did you start playing club shows between the arena shows?
I can't remember exactly when we did it but it was probably when we started having big shows and possibly a week or two off and wanting to warm up. It's always fun but I always looked at it as kind of a necessity to get ready for the big show. A lot of times I was the one saying "We gotta do a warm-up show". One, it's a chance to go back to your roots and two, even more importantly, it's a way to get the nerves out and make sure that you're tight because playing in front of people, even a small audience, is different from just rehearsing.

Why did the hiatus come about? Were there tensions and rows within the band?
Yeah, we're at 2010, we've gone eight years non-stop Killers every day. Even going back to the Vegas days in the beginning we were doing it almost every day, we were doing four or five hour practices, five or six days a week and we had part-time jobs. So really, it's non-stop until 2010. The breaks that we had between albums were small, a few weeks before we started writing, or maybe a month or two before *Day & Age* in that

period when the emails were floating around. Partly it was that and maybe there was some tension, but it wasn't really discussed I don't think, there weren't any outward fights that I remember about anything. I think there was disagreement of when the next one should happen and how long the next one should be and since we didn't decide, not only was there a break but there came solo projects and that extended it further, I think.

Was it really you and Dave wanting the break versus Ronnie and Brandon wanting to carry on?
It was the case to a point but it's not as simple as it sounds, it never really is. Yes, but there's reasons and it's hard to explain why, and Dave has different reasons than me.

Dave Keuning, March 2014

Was it strange writing and recording *Day & Age* by email?
It wasn't all by email, there was maybe one little thing by email. Most of it went down like this: we got together for a few weeks to write and we made some of the rough recordings ourselves in a day over at Battle Born studios – a lot of the tracks, not all. I know Brandon had emailed a few things, like really rough, just him on vocals and piano, but I don't think that ended up staying. The demos we made in practice, we emailed them to Stuart and he would rework it and send back. But when he came to Vegas we would finalise it together. That was the quickest album we ever made. Stuart works really fast, which I thought was great, he's kind of an engineer and producer in one, he's really fast on the computer. We made the album in about the total of six weeks. Start to finish. Mixing and everything.

How did you feel about taking a swerve into electronica?
I think it's the most different album of them all because of that. *Battle Born* [Killers' fourth album] is more like *Sam's Town* than *Day & Age* by far. I didn't mind it because I'm open to sounding new, like a lot of my favourite bands – Smashing Pumpkins' *Adore* sounds pretty different to *Melon Collie...* So I was open to things like that. I love and hate *Day*

301

& Age. There are some songs I hate on it and some I love. I have mixed feelings about it. I love 'Human', that's a classic song. There's not much guitar on that album but I was open minded to that, I was a team player.

Was it a group decision?

It wasn't really talked about, it was just how it turned out in the mix. Some people came up to me, consoling me about the guitar on *Day & Age* but actually there was a lot of guitar in the album that I play but it's turned down really low. I guess they hear the parts live.

'Goodnight, Travel Well' must have been an emotional song to play for you.

Honestly, no matter what it's about, the music is what gets me. Brandon chose to write a song about people dying so I guess that adds to it. I really liked the song before it had lyrics. I just thought it was a dark song – it's the only song we have like that. I was disappointed more people didn't say they liked it but I think they expect more fun stuff from us. I thought it was a quality song.

Was it a dark period for the band?

Yes and no. Me and Brandon just tried to focus on music. That's what people do in those situations otherwise it will just upset you.

What went on on the Welcome To The Jungle bus?

In my defence I only said that because I was drunk, it's kind of a goofy title. It wasn't like it was complete mayhem every night. It was just me and Mark on one and Ronnie and Brandon on the other. They were doing their own thing. We didn't party every night on our bus. I don't want my ex to think that's what I was doing every night.

Did the Albert Hall shows stand out?

Meeting Paul McCartney at the Royal Albert Hall – he was wearing an Alice Cooper mask when we met him so it was off-putting. We were like "Who is this weirdo in the hallway?" and he took it off and it was Paul McCartney. That doesn't happen every day, that was pretty crazy. One of the differences [on that tour] is that 'Human' opened up a lot of doors in Europe outside of England, in Italy and stuff where we were playing to 20,000 people in an arena where the previous time we could barely find a way to play to a couple of thousand. On *Sam's Town* we were not that big in parts of Europe.

What was the state of the band after this long tour?
I can't think of examples of tension but after the *Sam's Town* tour we said we were gonna take six months off. Not naming names, but they thought it was a big break and we were wasting time. But it felt like a couple of weeks, it felt like it was over immediately. It looks like a lot on paper, but it went by fast, considering we had just toured for four or five years. After a year and a half of touring on *Day & Age*, we went from touring to recording. So after that it was pretty much seven solid years of recording and touring. Maybe some bands don't mind the machine just rolling and going but I couldn't do that, I needed some time off. The only thing I regret is telling people we were taking time off because if we hadn't said, I don't think they would have known. If you tell people it's going to be a few years before the next album they go "Oh nooo" but if you tell them nothing and you're still on the radio a little bit, and you're still out there a little bit, it goes by really fast, then all of a sudden your new song is out.

How was the decision made?
I wasn't the only one that wanted a break. Everybody in our band and in most bands, they all have different things they want, if it's a week off or a year off. Some people wanna play as many songs as possible and some wanna play as little as possible. There was a compromise that I made and a compromise the others made; you can never all agree on a schedule. Other people did solo projects so they weren't bored.

Did you ever consider quitting the band?
It definitely crossed my mind, but not for very long because we worked so hard to get where we are at and that would be a big decision to make. I wouldn't want to do it just because I was upset on the road. It's a decision you want to make when you're not on the road and have time to think long and hard about it.

rk gets in the zone at T In The Park, July 2004. DAN TUFFS/REX

Mark and Brandon brandish their *NME* Award, London, February 17, 2005. BRIAN RASIC/REX

The newly wed Brandon and Tana at the 2005 MTV Video Music Awards in Miami, Florida. KEVIN MAZUR/WIREIMAGE

Dave keeps one eye open for Scissor Sisters coming to steal their MTV Awards, August 28, 2005. PICTURE PERFECT/REX

g Talk in full flight at their debut show at the Vegas Hard Rock Cafe, July 20, 2011. RD/ KABIK/RETNA LTD./CORBIS

Talking over the setlist with the band's tour manager at the Hammerstein Ballroom in NYC, October 24, 2008.

Playing a surprise club show at the Florida Room at the Delano on Miami Beach, October 3, 2009.

tar god Dave Keuning, 2009.

Bang a gong... Ronnie lets loose in his warm-up for the final show of the US leg of the 'Battle Born' tour. SAYRE BERMAN/COR

Beam me up... Alien Brandon roams the Nevada desert during the 'Spaceman' video shoot, January 7, 2009. BEN ROWLAND/THE HELL GATE/CORBIS

e moment Mark's tinnitus kicked in, onstage at Wembley Stadium, June 22. JIM DYSON – THE FA/THE FA VIA GETTY IMAGES

e gang's all here; taking a bow at Madison Square Garden, May 14, 2013. KEVIN MAZUR/WIREIMAGE

Goodnight, travel well - on the road, November 2012. SHANNA FISHER/CORBIS OUTLINE

CHAPTER 10

Losing Touch

"Dave needed to see his kid and rest up. That was just how it worked. And so we ended up going off and doing solo things, and spending our time that way, and that was good, too. It was a good experience. It definitely taught us different ways of thinking about music."

— Brandon Flowers, 2012[1]

"We were joking about [having a Vegas residency], but then we thought 'That's not a bad idea'. Maybe after three albums we'll want to settle down. We'll tour once a year in Europe and the States, then we'll have four months where people come to us. Vegas is a popular place. We could play three nights a week at the Hard Rock. I don't think we'd get fat though. We'd watch what we ate."

— Dave Keuning, 2005[2]

"Who enjoyed the break the most?" Brandon pondered for a second, mentally darting between the disparate lives of The Killers throughout 2010. The soccer, the camping, the wine tasting, the solo records and tours. "It's hard to tell, I had a lot of fun. I did a lot of hiking and I did the solo record, I had a lot of fun doing that. I know Dave stayed with his son in San Diego so I'm sure that was a nice break for him. Ronnie's always having fun. I think I had my share."

What were the best camping trips? "Taking my sons for the first time was really nice. There's just something special about getting out of your town or city and going somewhere remote and even my kids recognise the difference and they appreciate it, they have a little bit more freedom out there. So that was nice, the first time that we set up a tent and did it right. I prefer places with hiking around but the kids are so small we went on small little trails. People don't realise how close to Vegas some of these places are. We saw deer 45 minutes from my front door. The temperature drops 20 degrees, it's nice."*

The Brandon Flowers I found perched nervily on a couch in a backstage dressing room of the Leeds O2 Academy on August 17, 2012 – the fridge bare of alcohol, a table lined with neat rows of bottled water – wasn't so very different from the Brandon I'd first met at Glastonbury 2004. A stare to the middle distance, a tense air, a permanent half-smile. But there was a slight shift in his aura; an excitement to be back on the road with his band, an itch to get the show started, and also a feeling of semi-comfort, as if he'd travelled far since we last met, achieved almost all he'd ever hoped for, but not quite. He was a man on the last haul to the summit, but with the tang of victory on his tongue.

As Dave took a shower in the room next door – occasionally popping his head out to answer any questions pertaining to him – Brandon and I discussed whether any of the band had struggled with the break – "I don't think so, no, they were rejoicing!" – and how

---

* Elsewhere, Brandon would talk at length about his new love of the great outdoors. "I've grown tired of downtown America," he told Craig McLean in 2010, "and that's where you tend to go on days off. So I've started to go to National Parks and campgrounds on days off. And I'm barbecuing. And instead of running on a treadmill, I'm running out in nature. It makes it all worthwhile for me. On the way here we went to Lake Tahoe, and it was just beautiful. Went and did a hike. Jumped in the lake. It's kinda like going back in time. Stuff that it seems like you only see in movies. And it's been a breath of fresh air." Source: *The Telegraph*, Craig McLean, October 12, 2010.

he felt about 'Mr. Brightside' being voted the best song of the decade by the listeners of XFM: "Yeah! It is a great song, but if I believe the good things that they write about us then I have to believe the bad things. I think there might be Strokes songs that are better [but] it's up there". We talked about the rock star extravagances he'd indulged in (which only extended to "a Ford F250 truck that you will never see on the streets of Soho. It's too big! I love driving it, I love that I have the freedom to do that") and the music Brandon had been turned on to in the interim. "I've been listening to the radio a lot," he said. "I got a satellite radio in my car and there's a station called The Bridge I really like and a great new wave station called First Wave. I heard things I've never heard before on that, a Squeeze song called 'Up The Junction', I had no idea. It just floored me. To stumble across something like that when you're 31, I don't know. The Bridge will play anything from Elton John and Jackson Browne but then they'll play new bands that are sort of in that vein, so I heard this band Doss that are really great, they have a song called 'A Little Bit Of Everything' and it's perfect, the lyrics are perfect."

Past the small talk, we traced the various homes and locations where the four Killers had spent their time apart – Dave in San Diego, Ronnie in his new "place in the wine country – I've never been there", Mark in various hotels around the West Coast and Brandon "holding down the fort in Las Vegas [although] they all have places there." Did he ever think about moving out? "I think about it all the time. I'm gripped by some weird fear. I'm so attached to it, I don't know what I would do. I feel like I would lose some of my identity, what would my kids be? They wouldn't be Nevadans and the only things that I know I can give them are some of the things in our area."

Over the coming week I'd sit down with each Killer to look back at their time away, and also reminisce about the few Killers shows that had happened over the course of the hiatus. Between February 2010 and August 2012 they'd reconvened briefly to play sporadic handfuls of shows and festival appearances in Chile, America and Europe, and a date at London's Hard Rock Calling in the summer of 2011 adorned with two fan-friendly gigs at the tiny Scala theatre*. The Scala shows had been the first UK dates in two years, but Brandon – sporting a new GI-style shaved haircut and spending the shows excitedly shadow-boxing the microphone stand, jokingly asking after the crowd's parents and declaring "There isn't a man onstage who's in his twenties, but you guys are still here!" – had insisted they play no new songs on the first of the two nights. "I haven't written all the lyrics yet," he explained. "I used to ad lib words at early Killers shows. What happened? YouTube. You could kinda get away with it before, but now it's different."[3]

But on the second night he pulled out a lyric sheet saying "I don't wanna mess up, these are pretty fresh", and premiered an electronic bar-room rock behemoth called 'The Rising Tide', hinting at the Americana gloss of The Cars and The Psychedelic Furs and full of quasi-religious references to crucifixion, heavenly choirs and "pitchfork tongues". It was, he told the press, one of four or five new songs he claimed were completed for The Killers' fourth album**. It was on YouTube within minutes.

Most memorably, though, The Killers had played a short seven-song set including a rendition of Irving Berlin's patriotic hymn 'God Bless America' at the Salute To The Military concert for US servicemen on July 4, 2010, at the personal request of the Obamas. "Michelle asked us if we'd play their Fourth Of July party on the White House lawn a couple of years ago, really just to celebrate the troops,"[4] Ronnie would say. "We got an official letter on headed note paper to our agency and we didn't know if it was real – we read it and we were like 'What the hell?', I heard Foo Fighters had played the July 4 show the year before so I rang Dave Grohl up and asked him what it was like. He was like 'Dude, that's like the coolest BBQ ever, you've got to do it!'. There's pretty tight security there, lots of restrictions – one of the funniest things was this very prim and proper female security guard who talked us through

---

* "The Killers' songs simply can't be stripped back," I wrote in my *Guardian* review of one of the Scala shows. "'Smile Like You Mean It' and 'Somebody Told Me' burst a room this size clean open."
** Also including 'Runaways'.

all the rules and then when we walked in and it was totally relaxed and all the formalities dropped and Obama was great – we saw her later in plain clothes and she was totally different. I spoke to Obama a little bit, just small talk really. It's organised by USO for people who have served in the forces or for those families whose officers didn't come home – it was one of those moments where you feel very proud and honoured."[5]

"I ended up grabbing Michelle Obama's ass," he recalled. "She's a hugger! And she's unexpectedly tall, so, when we were all being introduced to them, she ended up with her arms over me like this. Which meant that, the way I had positioned myself, suddenly I found I was grabbing her ass."[6]

Their meeting with Obama himself was rather more formal. What did he say to you? "It was small talk," says Dave, "'Have you guys eaten yet? Did you enjoy some food?' I don't do nearly as many meet-and-greets as Obama does but I know what he's going through a little bit and I couldn't help but think that he must do hours and hours a day of just saying hi and pretending to be interested, so I kind of empathise with him, like 'Yeah, I understand, it doesn't have to be a big conversation'. He didn't say he was a fan, I think he'd heard of us and knew who we were."

Did you take any souvenirs from the White House?

"No, I was too worried the Secret Service would be watching me to do that," Dave told me. "I felt honoured to meet the President and play the White House, that's definitely one of my favourite gigs we've ever done."

"I saw a *Book Of Mormon* that looked like it must've been a hundred years old," Brandon chuckled, "and it crossed my mind that I would like to have that." But then stealing it goes against the very ideals of the book you're stealing... I thought there are great old stories of Joseph Smith visiting the White House and I'm sure he brought the President a *Book Of Mormon* when he came, I wonder if that was the one that he brought. That would've been pretty awesome."

There had also been two Killers Christmas songs released during the break. "Our Christmas single with (RED) is one of our traditions as a band," Brandon announced as the 2010 song 'Boots' was posted online on November 30. "We didn't want to let it fall by the wayside just because we're on hiatus; this cause is too important." 'Boots' was arguably the best of the festive songs so far, a stirring epic about family and faith that opened with a sample of George Bailey from *It's A Wonderful Life* praying for guidance, leading into a song of joyful redemption; a lost son who'd "wasted my wishes on Saturday nights", forgiven and welcomed back into a classic Christmas family scene of "cinnamon candles burning, snowball fights outside, smile beneath each nose and above each chin". The song, and the video of a hobo-like figure cleaning himself up to be reunited with his estranged family reflected Brandon's own religious values and family experiences; the errant father seeing the light and realising what's truly important in life.

By contrast, the 2011 single 'The Cowboy's Christmas Ball' was entirely disconnected from The Killers' personal worlds. In the light-hearted vein of 'Don't Shoot Me Santa' it was a throwaway comedy hoedown, its lyrics taken from William Lawrence Chittenden's 1890 poem of the same name that had been turned into songs by cowboys throughout the previous century. A vivid description of a Wild West do-si-do complete with a leader called Windy Billy with "the reputation that comes when a fella shoots", this was the sort of lark that brought out the playful side of the band. Sure enough, come the video shoot they were decked out in colourful *Bonanza* cowboy costumes on a set that looked as though it was left over from *Oklahoma!*, firing obviously fake guns and fighting off a couple of invading sixties retro robot aliens to save Christmas.

The song became a big favourite in the Flowers family household. "We sing theme songs from shows that they watch," Brandon said of his singalongs with his sons, "*Mighty Machines, Curious George*. But 'The Cowboy's Christmas Ball', they love singing that. It's got this really strange old language... it's funny hearing the kids sing all these weird words. If we're in the car, if the Beatles come on, I try to explain [the songs] to them, let them know that this is more important than other things. Or, like, 'This is Elvis, this is The King'."[7]

So even during their designated break, The Killers had never strayed too far from each other. But apart, they were more productive than ever.

★ ★ ★

310

Of the four, Dave seemed to have had the most relaxing hiatus. "San Diego's a nice place to be," he said. "I swam in my pool a lot and went to the beach every once in a while. I bought a lot of guitars, stuff I didn't have, lap steels, pedal steels, mandolins, ukuleles and dobro guitars. I played around the house with that stuff, some of that stuff made it to the [new] album so it wasn't a total waste or anything."

"He thought it'd be fun to go play soccer," Brandon interjected, "football for you, and he didn't realise what he was getting himself into. Some dudes were taking it pretty serious down there in San Diego."

"It was non-stop sprinting," Dave laughed, "not to mention the fact that it was all Mexicans and – not to be racist – they're good. I wasn't expecting either of those things. But it looked fun on TV. I liked the World Cup, I watched that on our year off, and honestly I did have fun, but I was in way above my head. That was just one day. After watching the World Cup I just had it in my head that I at least wanted to try it because I'd never really played soccer one time in my whole life. It was just way harder than I thought it was gonna be and I wasn't that good at it. It was downtown San Diego, surrounded by barbed-wire fence. I remember having second thoughts right then and there, I was like 'Okay, I thought this was gonna be a really friendly league'. When I called I said 'Is this league friendly?' I wanted to be around people who are the same skill level. I think sports are great when you get a bunch of guys who don't know how to play that sport, like baseball or soccer or basketball or whatever. I was over-matched by a lot of inner-city people who actually knew how to play soccer, it was a little bit scary. I tripped entering the field. It was my turn to come in and I fell on the grass. I shot up but anyway, I don't regret it though. I thought it was fun."

The thought of making a solo album did cross Dave's mind over the break[*], but he only dipped into the rock world during 2010. "I wrote some stuff of my own and some of that made it to the [new] record. I played on one song on Brandon's solo project[**]. I did two Christmas

---

[*] He's still considering it today, too.

[**] Dave contributed guitar to 'Welcome To Fabulous Las Vegas' on Brandon's solo album *Flamingo*.

songs during the break, I played on a friend of mine's band called Halloween Town* and another friend of mine's band called Hyena. These are just one-day excursions, I'd get out of the house and go down and play with them for fun because they asked me to. I didn't really want to take on a side-project, I thought that all of a sudden I'd got this break and the point was not to start up another band, I just wanted to have nothing on my schedule for the first time in six years. I'm a little bit like the guy from *Office Space* the movie, who just likes to do nothing every once in a while. I don't like to do nothing all the time, I just value doing nothing and I didn't want to do anything, so I didn't."

What did you miss most about the band?

"Playing shows. If there was one thing I wish I could control it's to do everything a little more balanced, but unfortunately I can't seem to win that battle. It's all or nothing. Once [it] starts up it's full-on touring for two years instead of just playing two weeks and having two weeks off. But I definitely missed playing the shows because I went a long time without."

In creative terms, Mark was perhaps the best prepared for time apart. Towards the end of the Day & Age tour, late in 2009, he'd begun using his spare time in hotels to record ideas for songs of his own on the GarageBand feature of his laptop, playing acoustic guitar or working up from a bass riff, and humming lyrics and melodies into a Dictaphone. He had no intention of releasing the songs, but by the time the tour spluttered to a halt, he was in the zone, and simply continued to write and record demos 'on tour', even though the band was on hiatus. "I pretty much went back and forth between Vegas and San Francisco and Los Angeles," he told me. "I spent a lot of time in hotels even though I was off! But it would be one hotel for two or three weeks instead of a different hotel every night. I would take these mini-vacations because I'd get tired of being in the same place for two weeks, but at the same

---

* "I've got some friends who record in San Diego and my friend Shaun Cornell didn't live that far," he explained. "This band Halloween Town was there and I played a little bit of guitar on two songs on that." Source: *Ultimate Guitar*, Steven Rosen, November 14, 2012.

time I wasn't ready to do any big travelling. So I'd stick to the West Coast and go to a hotel for three weeks and write. I didn't even plan to do an album but as I was writing more I started recording and as I recorded it started becoming almost enough for a record, and it's a pretty short record anyway."

Over 2010, in various hotels, Mark's solid half hour of solo material slowly came together – sometimes he worked alone, sometimes with the aid of the multi-instrumentalist singer from Louis XIV, Jason Hill, and two members of Australian garage rock band Howling Bells, drummer Glenn Moule and guitarist Joel Stein. Mark had spent several months in 2010 producing Howling Bells' third album, *The Loudest Engine*, at Battle Born, when he'd take the band out on the Strip to soak up the Mojave magic, play drums on their covers of Lennon and Doors songs or bring cult movies and Hitchcock classics into the studio for late-night film sessions.* In return, the Bells helped him out on his own album.

"[It was] pretty much an experiment," Mark said. "I wanted to test my limits as a songwriter and see what I could do. Before you knew it, I had 15 or 20 songs, 10 of which I didn't mind people hearing."[8]

"The writing was liberating but a little bit confusing," he said, "not knowing what to do, you don't have anyone to answer to. So I started incorporating friends to be that 'other person', like 'What do you think of this song, what do you think of this…'. At the end of the day it was still all up to me, which was a different kind of pressure but also a freedom at the same time."

A major challenge for such a naturally shy character was finding the confidence in his own voice, a winsome, sonorous tone reminiscent of Elliott Smith. "The vocals were very difficult for me. I've never been a lead singer before. I don't sing covers, I don't get up and do karaoke – I don't really know where my voice is at. When making these songs, I'd hear a melody and I would try to adapt to that range. My voice is

---

* Mark researched hard for his work with Howling Bells, reading autobiographies of producers and Kevin Ryan and Brian Kehew's *Recording The Beatles* to learn how to allow a band space to play live in the studio. He also hunted down a Studer A820 reel-to-reel analogue tape machine at the request of the band.

kind of low, so I have to stay within certain parameters. I had to adapt a certain style to put the melody across. To me, a song works if a singer delivers it, and that doesn't always have to involve highly technical vocal skills. It's all about sincerity and connecting with the lyric. But I can still appreciate a singer like Freddie Mercury."[9]

By the start of 2011, after almost 18 months of roaming after the songs in his head, Mark had done enough wandering, his first solo album was ready to be recorded. Back in Vegas, at his home studio and at Battle Born, *Another Life* took shape – a 10-track collection of lush, loungey, blues folk romances, with the odd dash of electronic disco and orchestral rock, that evoked Springsteen's *Nebraska*, the US alt-Americana of Lambchop and *Nashville Skyline*-era Dylan.

"That's definitely there on those songs," he admitted. "I was pretty late coming to Dylan. Until about four years or so ago, all I knew were his hits; I didn't know the body of work. Then I started really listening to him, and I couldn't stop. For a long time, I listened to Bob Dylan probably every day. Every album, every period – I absorbed it all. Without a doubt, Bob Dylan is one of my biggest influences. Dylan and The Beatles are huge for me. I do listen to other types of music – I love jazz and classical and… even Black Sabbath. But Dylan, yeah, I'm not surprised that you can hear that. *Nashville Skyline* [was] one of the two records that really opened the door for me getting into him – that one and *Desire*. See, I'm more of a music-and-melody guy – I only get into the lyrics once I like everything else. *Desire* and *Nashville Skyline* have wonderful songs. They're very melodic – they're pop songs, really. Once that door was open, that's when I went out and got everything and really dug into what Bob Dylan is all about. I wasn't trying to 'do Dylan' on my record. If it comes through, that's fine, but that wasn't the idea. Lots of people imitate Bob Dylan, but nobody can do what he does. He might not be what people consider a great singer, but he's great at singing his songs."[10]

At first, *Another Life* seemed to dig into the lonesome heart of the touring musician, exposing the flashes of bleakness, exhaustion, disorientation and despondency that had made Mark argue for a Killers hiatus. "Nocturnal living is bringing me down," he crooned on the string-swathed country noir opening track, 'Weary Soul'. "I need some rest before I have a breakdown/When you're alone again and you're your only friend, you have to look within… rest my weary soul, rest my tired mind". "Life goes so quick when you forget to take a look around," he intoned wispishly over the dolorous folk of 'Shadow In A Dream', "the years go by before you realise you're touching the ground… it all has become a shadow in a dream".

As the album went on, its mood lifted. 'Everyone Loves The Girl', draped in graceful slide guitar whines and emulating Dylan's 'Lay Lady Lay', was a sweet ode to a free-thinking and romantically elusive Clark County girl "wandering all over the world and charming everyone she meets" and came accompanied by a tongue-in-cheek video featuring a sixties retro-futurist heroine flying across the country in a jet pack. 'Need A Hand' was a breathless travelling tune, Mark laying out the story of a Masonic Christian setting out to find a partner to share his life's burdens in his best Michael Stipe wobble. The more obtuse 'Amber Bough', meanwhile, was a song of emancipation, with Mark encouraging a young girl to escape the trauma of her "burning house" by climbing down the tree outside her window. Although in its surreal impressionistic verses there were still hints of touring paranoia: "Living in a Hollywood hotel, hanging curtains, scared to death".

After delving into Eurodisco on 'The Way We Were Before' – an escapist pop anthem about a couple running away to the idyllic Italian countryside to fall in love all over again, given a hint of world music and electronica from having been written in a hotel room in Miami* – there was more hotel-based terror in 'The Haunts', a brooding, doomy country ballad about Mark encountering an actual ghost in a Hollywood hotel which staff later told him was indeed haunted. "It was a crazy way to get a song," Mark said. "I was staying

---

* "A melody came to me, and I just had to complete it right there," Mark said of the genesis of the track, which also had a video made of a couple in silver face masks and hoods running through a neon-lit forest. "It was just an instrumental piece that I applied lyrics to later. It uses drum machines and real drums, whereas the other ones have just real drums." Source: musicradar.com, Joe Bosso, November 23, 2011.

at the Chateau Marmont in LA, having weird dreams and watching Kurosawa*. One night I had a ghost encounter and wound up trapped on the balcony, locked out of my room… The place has always had a bit of a reputation, but I didn't expect that. Fantasy and reality came together for me. It was pretty freaky."[11]

Needing light relief from this spooky tale of a séance encounter with a "lady of the night", Mark followed 'The Haunts' with the upbeat country rock of 'No Time', a jaunty, carefree hoedown that found Mark declaring "ain't got no time for heartache, ain't got no time for feeling blue". After which it was back into the doldrums for the existential raga of 'There Is No Is', a lost and confused Stoermer looking to God and "the bottom of the well" for answers and strength in the face of life's disheartening conundrums, before the album closed with a note of philosophical optimism. The title track, a lush strum with hints of sixties psychedelic folk, envisaged an afterlife when "our hearts aren't crippled with pain" where a broken relationship might finally work out.

Another Life fit neatly into the lineage of side-projects from major rock acts; largely acoustic, largely rooted in traditional folk and country, and full of behind-the-scenes anguish; an outlet for fears, woes and frustrations that couldn't find a voice in his main band. Even with the record having taken two years to complete, though, Mark still considered it a curio. Self-releasing via his own St August label, he put the album up on his website, markstoermer.com, for free on November 1, 2011, only releasing CD, vinyl and iTunes versions in January of 2012**.

With Killers writing sessions recommencing in May of 2011, Mark didn't have the time to put together a band and tour the album. "I never was my own frontman because I didn't play any live shows," he said. "I thought about it but by the time it was becoming serious and the record's out … [The Killers] were starting to get back together and we

---

* Akira Kurosawa was one of Japan's most celebrated film directors, making 30 films in a career spanning almost 60 years, including *Seven Samurai*, the inspiration for *The Magnificent Seven*.

** The iTunes format of the album came with two bonus tracks, 'Agni' and 'King Of The Mountain'.

did some shows and we were writing already. I never had time to put together a band or try the live thing. Our big break was really about a year but in that time I was doing other stuff probably 90 per cent of the time."

Of the Killers I sat down with in 2012, Ronnie had perhaps learned the most from his time away from the band. First, he'd discovered the joys of remote living, out in the hills of Utah in Park City. "It's leisurely, it's good living," he grinned. "When I'm not in Vegas it's a nice respite from the heat and everything that is Vegas. It's the complete antithesis of where I grew up. Great food, great people. The town we live in is a small town, they're very educated – it was sort of an older town, now it's more of a younger, educated, progressive-thinking town with an eye towards agriculture, food and wine."

Then he'd gone back to college to complete the BA in percussion that he'd given up at the University of Nevada to join the band, adding new skills to a characteristic straight-backed drumming style that he put down to being whipped by an old drum teacher. "I had, like, two classes to finish," he explained. "When I left school, I was basically done, but I had to complete some courses, which I did. But I made the mistake of keeping taking classes, so maybe next year, I'll have another degree. We'll see what happens. I just do it because it's something to do to keep busy. I'm pretty lazy."[12]

He'd also ventured out of his safety zone musically, collaborating with various members of Mumford & Sons and Noah and the Whale on Mt Desolation (the new side-project of Keane members Tim Rice-Oxley and Jesse Quin) contributing 'drums, guitars and vibes' to 'Midnight Ghost', a funereal country blues ballad.

He'd also, more than Mark, indulged in the frontman role. Once the Killers hiatus had kicked in, Ronnie hadn't been able to turn off his creative taps, and immediately hooked up with his old Expert on October bandmate Taylor Milne to start writing as a duo, Milne on guitar and Ronnie on everything else, even taking on vocal duties. Adopting Ronnie's boxer dog, Archie, as band mascot, they called themselves Big Talk as an ironic joke on the sort of bands that are constantly hyped by the music industry long before any music is heard*, and set about writing an album. "It was sort of an experiment," he said, "I hadn't done anything like that before, it was that stretching of the muscles. With musical endeavours, it feels like you're doing something else, even though it's music."

"I was just bored, man," he said. "You're moving at 100 mph and then all of a sudden someone says, 'Oh let's take a break' and you're like, 'Yeah okay, that sounds good, let's do that', and then two weeks later you've got your thumb up your ass and you have no idea what to do with yourself. You've been making songs and been moving for nearly 10 years and you're like, 'Fuck man, I gotta do something'."[13]

"I don't have any kids and I don't really want to start a family yet. I was feeling creative, like I needed to start something, so I just started doing demos."[14] "I got restless and an old buddy [Taylor Milne] asked if I fancied playing a guitar solo on some songs and it went from there."[15]

So after barely two weeks of serious relaxation time, Ronnie went down to the studio he had set up in his basement and dug out 50 or 60 demos of "pretty solid ideas" he had stacked up, some of which The Killers had heard. These were songs inspired by the music he'd loved as a child – Tom Petty & The Heartbreakers, Boston, Joe Jackson and The Cars. "It's pretty guitar based, which may sound weird a drummer doing that, but I've always loved playing guitar and making rock 'n' roll."[16]

"Throughout everything, we've been good friends," Taylor, who also had a holiday home in Utah, said. "There were no expectations or promises when he called me. We wanted it to be as stress-free as possible."[17]

"I needed to do this," Ronnie told *Spin*. "And now, having done it, it feels like the right thing to do. It all feels very natural... All these really

---

* The project was also given a full name to avoid any conflict with Brandon's solo album. "I could have called it 'Just Ronnie'," Vannucci told *The Sun*, "but even from the early demos, it didn't sound like one dude, it always sounded like a rock band. Plus I'm a drummer, no one knows my name. And calling it Ronnie Vannucci seemed a bit pretentious, especially because Brandon went under his name and people might view it as some sort of competition."

cool leads that you'll hear on the songs are Taylor. We work on things together, but it's his take, so sometimes it's very different. It sounds fresh to me."[18] "I didn't go into this with any grand objective other than to create some good songs and whatever vehicle they wanted to ride in, fine by me. There was no muzzle put on it at all."[19]

Not that Ronnie didn't come up against some resistance in stepping up to the mike. "Nobody wants to hear that the drummer wants to sing – we already have Dave Grohl,"[20] he said. "Every step of the way, it was, 'You're just a drummer and now you think you can sing and play guitar?' My closest friends and colleagues, and even our record label said, 'Why are you doing this?' There were moments where I didn't know if I was going to show anybody these songs. I never really thought I had anything to say. But I do. Taylor helped validate my whole direction. He encouraged me to see these songs through. I got this bug... and my confidence grew and grew. I was on a bit of a tear."[21] "All I wanted to do was just make a record that you can play drunk and have fun with your friends. But now I'm thinking of it a little more seriously than I did before because I have the perspective all of a sudden. Now I think it's like a necessary thing to go in and tap into a different part of your soul or your brain and see what's happening in there."[22]

By November 2010 they were ready to hit Battle Born for two months to record, Grammy-winning Strokes producer Joe Chiccarelli at the desk and Ted Sablay and ex-Weezer bassist and main-man of The Rentals, Matt Sharpe, popping in to help out on bass. "Matt was one of the first people I played the demos for," Ronnie said. "He kept encouraging me, saying 'This doesn't suck as bad as you think it sucks.'"[23]

Besides occasional bass assistance and Taylor taking guitar duties, Ronnie played all of the instruments on the *Big Talk* album, and would often make up the lyrics as he went along while recording some songs, in order to keep the feel of the album fresh. "For Big Talk I had to sort of man all the bases. I wasn't used to doing things myself. It was incredibly freeing, a lot of fun. I had a lot more input."[24] Was the appeal of Big Talk that he was in complete control? "No, I have a fair amount of control, we're all very involved in what we do in The Killers, so it wasn't like I did it to feel more in control. I did it because I think, like all of us, there's a constant yield of ideas or creative energy, or at least there's that energy there and it feels good to have a birthing, a crop. Having done Big Talk, I was able to garner a new respect for the other guys in the band. Having been a bass player, been a guitar player, been a singer, now I really respect these guys, what they do. They make it look so easy! So it was nice for me to have that perspective, that experience of sitting in that chair, wear those shoes."

"Making the *Big Talk* record was pretty fucking leisurely," he said, "because I didn't go in there with any big expectation or even the thought of making a record. I was just exercising. I was in there learning how to sing, play guitar and make songs to completion. With this band [The Killers], I make songs but they're not always complete because I like the idea of what everybody else will do to these ideas that I have and make them into these bigger beasts. With the Big Talk thing, it was nice because I was able to see them through and it was a fun experience."[25]

The music of Big Talk was very much in the vein of The Killers – synth-heavy US guitar rock made for wide-open horizons and heat-hazed freeways. The self-titled album they made that winter opened with a burst of chiming electronic ambient drone, but once the canyon rock guitars of 'Katzenjammer'* kicked in, the arena drums pounded and Ronnie's voice – reminiscent of Bryan Adams, Bon Jovi or John Parr – curled itself around the line "It's not too early for whiskey, it's not too early for smoke", we were deep in classic US rock territory where mulleted men in ripped denim roared about getting out of "this heartbreak town" with a girl boasting "cold steel looks". From the off, *Big Talk* sounded like Ronnie kicking the stand away from a revving Harley and buzzing off into his wildest rock frontman fantasy, with all the fret-licking, monitor-stomping, Cuban-heeled clichés that encompassed.

As 45 minutes of uninhibited dream fulfilment, it was a pretty fun ride. The themes of 'Runaways' may well have been swirling around

---

* German slang for a discordant noise or a hangover.

Ronnie's brain when he sat down to write the album's first single, 'Getaways'*, a disco-tinged melodic rocker in the vein of eighties teen flick tracks like 'St Elmo's Fire (Man In Motion)' or Eric Carmen's 'Hungry Eyes', telling of a girl wanting to escape a controlling and restrictive relationship. As Ronnie would explain, this was one of the album's "love songs that go wrong. That stuff is more interesting than boy meets girl, they fall in love and have a great life together – I like the contrast of a happy sound with a dark message."[26]

It was a thread that ran through the early part of the album; the upbeat Springsteen-esque chug rock of 'Under Water' concerned a drunken deadbeat who'd drunk too deep from the rock'n'roll wellspring and was now drowning, not waving: "Your solid step is losing the stride, we watch you staggering on… once a silhouette, now you're walking that plank". It's possible this was a warning vision of what he might have become himself, Ronnie looking back at the initial Killers explosion, the heady reel it sent the band into and how it could easily have ruined him.

"We were on this nightmare schedule of being everywhere at the same time, or at least that's what it felt like," he said during promotional interviews for *Big Talk*. "We were being pulled around and it was crazy. As a band, we were still getting to know each other, and we were tossed in this centrifuge where we didn't know which end was up and were just trying to get along. We were being introduced to our idols. There were all these girls. There was drugs. It was like, 'What the fuck is going on?' You grow up pretty fast. As long as you have your head screwed on straight, it can be a nice experience, but I can see how a lot of people lose their shit and just totally go off because they don't have a good foundation or they're just naturally wayward. I'm carefully wayward."[27]

As the album took a mellower tone for its mid-section, more refined influences crept in. 'The Next One Living' smacked of Talking Heads, ELO and The Byrds, the track drenched in lush, polished multi-harmonies; 'Replica' unravelled a lyric of a man – a straying husband, perhaps, or a weary hedonist – resorting to the shallow pleasures of

---

* Released May 11, 2011.

321

a hollow relationship to an eighties prom night rock thump*. And the ominous, winsome blues 'No Whiskey', the most downbeat song on the album, was soaked in the sordid grains of Tom Waits. "We were drinking a bottle of whiskey in the studio," Ronnie said. "When I stepped up to sing, for the first time I felt a certain energy coming out. It felt good."[28]

That sot's lament gave way to a brighter corner of the rock'n'roll dream. The footloose 'Girl At Sunrise', a 'Hungry Heart' country rock fantasy of a man "with a ziplock bag and rolled back eyes" who "played a little rough with a thing called love" and "used to run with the girls in the middle of the night". Again, though, there was the sense of being consumed by romance and hedonism, as the protagonist can no longer sleep, he's so obsessed with the long nights he spends with his "girl from sunrise". There was real mischief here, Ronnie gleefully upending the schmaltzy girl-meets-boy classic rock formula with lashings of bleak vistas and unhappy endings. Likewise 'White Dove', a Costello-ish college rock tune about the death of an affair with a party girl who's lost her spark, and 'Living In Pictures', a punk pop nugget about the vacuous nature of the modelling life, or the abyss that the rock band stare into when gazing into the photographer's lens.

The album's closing quarter only slightly eased the pedal from the metal. 'Hunting Season' shared the garage pop air of Albert Hammond, Jr.'s solo work, 'A Fine Time To Need Me' revisited the album's earlier runaway theme with country rock moonshine on its breath and the closing White Stripes blues rock of 'Big Eye', the third single from the album**, was, according to Ronnie "one of those drunkard tales [written] from the perspective of a guy who doesn't

---

* 'Replica' would be the second single from *Big Talk*, released on July 20, 2011 with a video of a woman, seemingly with insomnia, hunting Ronnie down across a desert. When she finally tracked him down to a motel, she found him there with an exact replica of herself; the woman, it transpired, was an android girlfriend that had malfunctioned and gone astray.

** Released on October 14, 2011.

give a shit, who has a problem with the bottle and trouble with a girl."[29] A monologue from a drunk father to his child as he prepares to leave his family behind – "Hey kid, I want you to know that I love you, your momma come looking for me... two will only get you free" – the video to the song took the story a whole step darker. Here, the deadbeat dad, swigging from a beer bottle, locked himself in his running car in the garage and sat back to suck in the fumes, only to be saved from his suicide attempt by angels floating out of the mist. This was Big Talk tearing off their party masks and finally exposing the sourness beneath.

With mixing taking place at Assault & Battery studios in London under the canny eye of Alan Moulder, *Big Talk* hit the streets on July 19, 2011, released on Ronnie's own label, Little Oil, via Epitaph Records, and it caused quite a critical dent. Most reviewers received the record with a mixture of impressed surprise at the talent that had been hidden in the back of The Killers all these years and genuine admiration for the melodies on show. "Not straying far from the synth-rock brand of music the Killers peddle," wrote *Spinner*'s Theo Spielberg, "*Big Talk* throws out epic hooks, anthemic riffs and eighties-style feel-goodery with effortless conviction. At times Vannucci sounds uncannily like bandmate Brandon Flowers. However, he also tries his hand at dirty Spaghetti Western tunes (see 'No Whiskey') as well as Wilco-ish alt-country rock ('Girl At Sunrise') with the same tangible delight of exploration he demonstrates simply by stepping out from behind the drums."[30] "Though *Big Talk* doesn't deviate from the trusted rock-pop path with a few bluesy stepping stones," wrote Alex Young of Consequence Of Sound, "it's a satisfying listen in which this drummer-turned-frontman holds his own incredibly well."[31]

As with Mark, by the time Ronnie's side-project was ready to go The Killers were back working together again. Ronnie didn't let the new writing sessions from May 2011 stop him touring with Big Talk though. With him and Taylor piecing together a full band featuring Tyson Henrie on bass, Alex Stopa on drums and John Spiker of Tenacious D on keyboards and guitar, Big Talk set out for limited dates, making their live debut at the Las Vegas Hard Rock Café on July 20*, their TV debut on *Jimmy Kimmel Live!* on July 25 and playing a small three-date tour of the UK among a smattering of other shows. "I might freeze in front of everybody, but so far it feels good," he joked before the run. "It's really interesting to feel the transition of these preternatural instincts to beat your guitar up like a drum. There's been a bit of an adjustment… I like the butterflies, man. If I knew this was going to be an easy thing, I probably would have been bored with it already and just put it to bed. I like feeling the pressure and the challenge."[32]

He needn't have worried – his UK shows were rapturously received, fans queuing outside the Scala in London from nine in the morning, greeting him with ecstatic chants of his name and singing along with every word. "Everything seems to fit together," wrote *Clash* magazine's Sophie Williams of the final Scala show, "it's like watching a group of friends have a jamming session and a lot of fun."[33]

Their gigs were few and far between, but Big Talk were no casual phase. "Any time [The Killers] aren't working, Big Talk will be working," Taylor said, plans for a second album already in discussion in mid-2011. "He loves playing guitar and you can either sing or you can't. Ronnie can. Big Talk is not a passing thing. We're having too good a time together."[34]

For those dedicated fans of The Killers, however, one solo project dominated the hiatus period, the closest they had to a fourth Killers album by another name. And that project had had the time to fully take wing.

★ ★ ★

What was the strangest thing you did with your time off?

"Probably make a solo record," Brandon said, back in the dressing room at Leeds Academy. "Most people after touring and working that long probably wouldn't have done that. I didn't take time off really. I don't wanna lose it. Creativity, if you don't nurture it and work on

---

* "It's George Burns on lead vocals," he joked to the *Las Vegas Review-Journal* ahead of the show, such was the strain on his voice.

it, it can go away. Even then, it doesn't mean you're gonna keep it just because you work on it either. So keeping on and writing is important to me."

Is there a fear of stopping for a year in case it disappears?

"Yeah. Some people have nice breaks and they come back and have these weird creative resurgences. I love that story of John Lennon taking I don't know how long off and all of a sudden he just felt like 'I'm gonna write again', and he writes 'Jealous Guy' and 'Woman' and shit! So I don't know, I'm sure I'm gonna have some kind of break."

What were the pros and cons of being on the road and recording without the rest of the band?

"There weren't many cons really. The only thing I can think of is that I'm spoiled by these songs that we've acquired. We rarely have bad shows and we're really lucky in that respect. The fans are great and they love these songs and are thankful for these songs. And all of a sudden I'm going out there and it's a little bit like starting over. I did throw a couple of Killers tunes in there to soften the blow but that was also a thrill and it made me perform and sing my butt off and I had a great time. We aren't four guys that grew up together and we have our ups and downs like everybody else, but it's a family, so I do miss sometimes that bond that we have, if you're not together. Nobody else has experienced what we've experienced but us, so I can get another band and they were my friends and I had fun, but they still hadn't been in the trenches like I have."

While Ronnie and Mark had made solo albums from a lack of anything else to do, Brandon's solo spurt had been a mission of honour. The pleasure he was getting from his growing family helped him deal with the grief of losing his mother, but he felt he needed to repay her for everything she'd given him with an album dedicated to her, and to his roots. He'd been writing solidly on the road and had a cache of songs he wanted to finish so, as soon as the *Day & Age* tour wound up, Brandon, driven by his grief, set to writing for four weeks in what he'd call "an explosion of creativity". Within two months of the hiatus beginning, Brandon was in Battle Born with an album's worth of material to record. Between there and Henson Recording Studios in LA, he made *Flamingo* inside a month, helped along by three producers – Stuart Price again, and two men whose work he'd admired for many years. Brendan O'Brien had been a huge name in US rock production for decades, working on many major grunge and funk rock classics such as Red Hot Chili Peppers' *Blood Sugar Sex Magick* and Pearl Jam's *Vs.*, as well as overseeing Bruce Springsteen's 21st-century revitalisation. And Daniel Lanois was an ambient-leaning legend who'd helmed many of Brandon's favourite U2 records.* Now he was fully in charge, he was indulging all of his deepest fanboy fantasies.

He would also make a record that was, thematically, more personal than ever before. A record that pushed *Day & Age*'s concerns of religion, family and hometown pride to their utmost conclusions. A record named after a street where he'd lived, taken his first jobs and met his wife-to-be.** And a record that opened with the chirp of desert crickets, sumptuous steel guitars courtesy of a guesting Dave and a vision of a broken gambler waking up "in the rusted frame, burnt out old de Ville" at sunset and stumbling in a semi-religious fervour to hedonism down "a boulevard of neon encrusted temples, looking for the grace of God in the arms of another stranger". 'Welcome To Fabulous Las Vegas' was Brandon's biggest hymn to his hometown yet, a sparkling synth anthem that twisted the language of his own faith to represent the mystical allure of Vegas; its call girls, cocaine and arenas of black jack, it's dreamers, harlots and sins seen as symbols and idols of Vegas as a religion of the damned, sucking in every lost soul in America. The song's protagonist is an utterly helpless disciple, having dreams about the loving family he left back home as he's handed "catalogues of concubines" in the streets, prays on his knees to "cocaine and lady luck" and cries "hosanna" to the wickedness of the city.

---

* All three producers would play on the record, alongside a revolving cast of players. Darren Beckett, Mike Kezner and Victor Indrizzo shared drumming duties, Herschel Gaer took on the bass and Benji Lysaght played many of the album's guitars.

** "A lot of my life took place on Flamingo," he's quoted as saying. '"It's part of Vegas mythology, and now it's part of my own mythology… That's my 'hood." (Source unknown.)

"I've stopped drinking and smoking completely because I don't want my children to ever see it," he said, referring to his new ultra-clean-living attitude involving banning all alcohol from his house in Henderson and training for two hours every day to keep in shape, something which he felt was his duty to The Killers. "But I understand why my father did what he did. That's the other side of Vegas. It's literally addictive. I have an understanding of where my life could have ended up, the choices I could have made. It's a crazy town and it's something I have to live with every day being here. I like roulette and blackjack, I've bet big on sports. It's a rush. But that feeling when you're losing money, your body knows you did something wrong. When you lose you feel dirty… I understand why it happens and that's why it makes its way into the songs. But I'm lucky enough to have had very strong foundations with my religion from early on. A lot of people can't understand that, especially being Mormon. But I'm thankful for it."[35]

Despite watching his city slide into a hellpit of sex, drugs and desire, his affection for the place never waned. "I understand that it's not a perfect place," he said, "but it is where I'm from, and I just find myself being drawn back to it… There was always the biggest and the best hotel or over-the-top things. Family would be coming in from out of town, and it was such a thrill to be showing them this newly erupting volcano or whatever it was. And I still retain that excitement about those lights."[36] "I love visiting New York City and London and Paris – the romantic element of it – but after a few days or so I yearn for the sky to open up, for the mountains. It's wide open where we live, it really is."[37]

The ambient desert heat-haze of 'Human' hung heavy over *Flamingo* too, notably on the second track, 'Only The Young', a reflective remake of Springsteen's 'Philadelphia' that ruminated on the flagrancies, rebellion, freedom and aimlessness of youth and featured more overt religious phraseology – "Father, thy will be done… redemption keep my covers clean tonight". "There's a lot of religious imagery going through *Flamingo*," Brandon admitted, "maybe I felt free to be more open about it."[38] Certainly here, Christian views on pre-marital sexual abstinence and supplication to one's earthly and heavenly Father were coming through loud and clear.

There was a firm pulse of age-bought wisdom emerging from the almost 30-year-old Flowers, a sense of paternal guidance that had raised its head in tracks such as 'Joy Ride' and 'This Is Your Life' from *Day & Age*. "It's starting to scare me," he said of leaving his twenties behind, "time seems to go faster now than it ever has; I realise I'm not getting it back. I'm starting to take notice of an hour whereas before I never did. I have a real fear of missing out on things with my family… My dad's a kind of classic old handsome dude. I hope I'm headed there. I seem to be. I'm certainly not afraid of the greys. You're never gonna see me dyeing the greys. I already have quite a few."[39]

Perhaps fatherhood had brought on Brandon's protective and moralistic impulses, inspiring him to write songs that acted as modern pop parables, but it was a tendency that continued into 'Hard Enough', a duet with the legendary Jenny Lewis of Rilo Kiley and Jenny and Johnny*. "Some people think that it's best to refrain from the conventions of old-fashioned love," Brandon sang knowingly over a Cars-ian synth country chug, "their hearts are filled with holes and emptiness, they tell themselves that they're too young to settle down". More regretful than the stoic 'Only The Young', 'Hard Enough' was an apology to a girl that the protagonist had failed to commit to as a callow "little boy", the impetuous mistakes he made pictured as a Biblical flood threatening to consume them both.

Come the jauntier, Latin-tinged pop rocker 'Jilted Lovers & Broken Hearts', it was gambling terminology, from craps ("Why did you roll your dice?") to black jack ("You doubled down my direction") and poker ("You're gonna wish you could go back and fold") that acted as the metaphor for ruined romance, Brandon's portrayal of adultery in a relationship that's become a "worn out dream" mingling with his ongoing love/hate affair with Vegas. And having pushed the casino imagery as far as he could, he did the same with religion on 'Playing With Fire', a slinky downbeat jazz club number with Ronnie on drums and the scent of Dire Straits and Chris Rea in the air. This was

---

* 'Hard Enough' was also the first of four co-written songs on *Flamingo*, with Lewis, Lanois and Lysaght all receiving writing credits.

a complex lyric that appeared to flip the album's previous messages of devotion to parents to study the mindset of the rebel child. The song's anti-hero was reaching adulthood ("The holy fountain of youth has been reduced to a drip") and leaving home to follow a path of – possibly criminal* – individuality which he sees, in itself, as a form of religion. "Ten thousand demons hammer down with every footstep," he croons, "ten thousand angels rush the wind against my back/This church of mine may not be recognised by steeple, but that doesn't mean that I will walk without a God".

There's a nobility inherent in the character's "playing with fire" and his dedication to a life away from the security of home; whether in darkness or light he's determined to make it his own way. "I've got this burning belief in salvation and love/ This notion may be naive, but when push comes to shove I will till this ground... this little town, this little house, they seem to be leaning in the wrong direction". Even as a father with deeply entrenched ideas on the importance of family, perhaps Brandon was looking back at his teenage self, the 16-year-old who left Nephi, a place where the biggest event of the summer was the annual Fifties rodeo in July called the Ute Stampede, for Vegas to chase his dreams of stardom. And who, for all the temptations and demons, turned out all right.

Heavy stuff; *Flamingo* needed lightening. 'Was It Something I Said?'** was a synthetic plasti-pop homage to the dance routine in *The Breakfast Club* following the classic Vegas scenario: a couple rush down to a wedding chapel for a spur-of-the-moment wedding, but the chapel is closed and, in a nearby diner the spark of impetuosity has gone from Valentina's eyes. Her desperate paramour, with "church bells ringing in my head", doesn't give up the ghost, though; he gets a casino job to save money to try to win her back, even though she soon shacks up with a "dealer" of cards or drugs.

A flamboyant set-piece, the song centred the album in place and time – Vegas, in youth – and launched an album-lifting trio of pop smackers

---

* "Perhaps this calling is the channel of invention, I will not blush if others see it as a crime".
** Co-written with Daniel Lanois and Jenny Lewis.

to rival any run of tracks on a Killers album. The gloriously effervescent flamenco pop of 'Magdalena' – one of Brandon's catchiest songs yet – was about the annual pilgrimage along the "60 miles of sacred road" from Nogales to Magdalena in Mexico. It's a journey wrought with significance – not just for the blister-footed pilgrims who walk the hard dirt road to ask a miracle of the statue in the church in Magdalena where the journey ends, but because of the country travelled. Nogales is a town split between Arizona and Mexico, its border a hive of drug tunnels and a prime spot for Mexicans to make the deadly dash for America. The pilgrims of Brandon's song, however, are turning their backs on the divisive symbol of mankind's flaws and inhumanities that the border represents and are headed in a more spiritually fulfilling direction, proudly out into "the broken heart of Mexico" towards the statue that "will lift your load" at the church in Magdalena. A statue called San Francisco, a far more welcoming and redemptive edifice than its Californian namesake.

The political subtext of the lyric – its celebration of Mexican pride, spirituality and hardiness – may have been unconsciously applied, since when Brandon spoke of the song he mentioned the pilgrimage as a purely religious undertaking, and one he wanted to try himself. "It's a Catholic ritual," he said, "but do you think they'd be opposed to me giving it a shot?"[40] Yet 'Magdalena' still stood as one of Brandon's most rounded, layered and insightful songs yet.

A similar level of socio-political comment could also be read into 'Crossfire'*, the Americana pop epic that would be the first single from the album on June 21, hitting number eight in the UK and number six on the US Alternative Chart**. Ostensibly an ode of protection and adoration to his wife, Tana, the "heaven" of their marriage was offset against the "hell" they were caught in the crossfire of, arguably referring to the US recession, an economic "storm outside, dark clouds roll their way across town" as "heartache and pain came pouring down like

---

* Again featuring Ronnie on drums.
** 'Crossfire' also reached number 11 on the US Rock Chart and went Top 5 in Ireland and Belgium.

rain". "Vegas has been hit hard by the recession," Brandon said, "and the street I lived on has empty houses on it now. There are deserted shopping malls, too, with dead palm trees and weeds. It's a weird time to live in the city but I've tried to be positive."[41]

Again, the political slant may have been accidental, but the promise of security at the heart of the song was wailed with a heartfelt warmth. Although it was the woman in the relationship that was doing all of the protecting in the video. Oscar-winning actress and star of *Prometheus* Charlize Theron – a fan of the band who'd suggested she appear in the clip and also recommended Australian director Nash Edgerton for the project – played a *Kill Bill*-style action heroine saving Brandon from a series of violent kidnappings at the hands of ninjas, Brandon giving her a wry, apologetic smile each time he's rescued.

Sticking with the topic of personal security and reassurance, the gospel hymnal 'On The Floor' was *Flamingo*'s boldest tribute to Brandon's mother, and the comfort he got from the prayers she taught him. "One of the things I'm most thankful that I got from my mother was that she taught me how to pray," he said. "And that communication that I have every day. And the benefits that I feel like I receive from it. I'm very thankful for that. And so I think that reflecting on that is where that song came from. I was always taught to pray in the morning and at night. Sometimes I'll only do one, but I do notice a difference – whether it's mental or whatever it is, I notice an optimism in my day if I've started with a prayer."[42]

"Religion seems to be dying in society in general," he lamented, "which saddens me as it's something that's always been in my life and I'm thankful for it. I can't help but feel it's directly tied to the kind of people that we are."[43] "I feel more and more alone as a person of faith. It's not just rock stars who aren't cool if they're religious – it's like it's a taboo for any young person to be religious now. If you love someone, and you know that love is real – that's how I feel about God. I've had feelings I can't describe that are unexplainable to me, unless there is a God. But if I say that, people look at me like I'm crazy."[44]

A simple ode to the reassurance of praying and receiving forgiveness – "on the floor, where the rats all come away clean" – 'On The Floor' was a defiant reassertion of Brandon's unwavering faith in the face of such mockery, adorned with a full gospel choir to give it an even churchier feel. But there was a sense of struggle here, too, a feeling that Brandon believed he belonged on the floor, begging for redemption for the swarm of sins swirling in his psyche, itching to come out in his songs. A sense that this sort of righteousness was a kind of smokescreen to the real Brandon Flowers.*

"I definitely have a darker side," he'd confess when discussing the song. "And a more sinister, maybe more sexual, being inside me that I think everybody's got. And I believe that because of what I believe, and because of the way that I was raised, and as I've got older... I've pushed towards being that positive force that I always talk about. That's kind of where I'd rather be. I know it's frowned upon in art to put a muzzle on something, but I definitely do it... So it's a struggle. I wonder if it's legit. But I can't help but go for the good I guess. Especially after having children – I think, what kind of mark do I wanna leave? For the most part, that's the person that I am. I think I'm a positive and optimistic person."[45]

The closing track – the subtle 'Swallow It', recalling Kate Bush's 'Hounds Of Love' era with its plucked harp intro, dramatic phrasing and languid 'Running Up That Hill' drums – seemed to acknowledge such flaws, coming across as a Bono talk to himself, an open letter to the Brandon of *Hot Fuss* on how to handle the sudden onrush of fame. "Instead of slipping through," he reminded himself, "you bit off more, much more than you could chew/You could not swallow it, no baby you're not ready/Slow down and take the time to evolve". As if regretting his early snipes at Fall Out Boy and The Bravery, he admonished himself with the line "We had a lot to learn, table manners and grace, how to wait your turn", and laid out a guide on how to properly conduct yourself in the rock sphere, the rules to which he was now adhering: "Take your medicine and crawl before you walk/ Think it through before you open your mouth to talk/Be an advocate

---

* The iTunes advance copy of the album and the Japanese version included an acoustic country and western version of the song named 'On The Floor 2.0'.

of joy, find a little heart's desire and follow it". Humility, dedication, positivity, reflection, self-belief and grace: released from the pressures of speaking for an entire band, Brandon had closed his solo debut with not just a personal mission statement but his concise methodology for a fulfilled and nourishing life.*

A deluxe edition of the album would come with five bonus tracks, real treasures, some. The country folk 'The Clock Was Tickin'' was Brandon's most rounded and poignant story-song yet, tracing the entire life stories of an unnamed hero and his childhood sweetheart-cum-wife, Jackie Geronimo, a name chosen, no doubt, to reflect the dizzying speed that their lives together would slip away. Before he knew it, our hero's drinking nights were curtailed by five kids and a low-paying job, and a life of fatherhood became grandfatherhood without the spinning clock hands ever seeming to slow. Before he could ever make enough money to retire, the whirlwind country reel of the song had abruptly become a funeral march to his dead wife. "The house is quiet now and everything inside it seems to know she's gone," Brandon sang, his saddest line yet, "There's a picture of you both 16 years old just kissing/ And that clock up on the wall was tickin'". A lament on the brevity and futility of the blue-collar life and the vicious dash of time, the narrative was undoubtedly concocted with his parents' story, and the sadness of his newly widowed father, in mind.

He juxtaposed this storytelling tour de force with an ominous, electro and Shinto-flecked vision of touring life called 'Jacksonville', in which "time seems so slow" and he'd gaze from his "country window" pondering the big existential questions** and dreaming of the simplicities of childhood. The thread of insecurity and loss linking these extra tracks together – a distinct collection from the more reassuring themes of the album proper – continued with the serrated new wave pop of 'I Came Here To Get Over You', a revenge drama about a jilted lover racked with anger over his partner's emotional and sexual betrayals, his head

---

* 'Swallow It' was the second promotional song to be released from *Flamingo*, made available on iTunes on August 24, a week before the album.
** "Where did it go? And where do we come from? And what are we here for?"

full of nightmares of birds picking her cheating innards clean. Although the man's revenge was never made clear, the song smacked of 'Midnight Show''s poisonous obsession and murderous intent.

Ultimately though, the deluxe edition would end with a note of optimism and hope. Amid the amorphous Human League-ish sizzle of 'Right Behind You', a malevolent track haunted by dusky bar-room piano, Brandon cast himself as a quasi-Messiah figure accompanying the subject of the song "Right behind you, in the light of hope/I'll be beside you on that dusty road… cling to the ways of my name". With a final extra track of 'On The Floor 2.0' rounding the edition off, the extended *Flamingo* felt like an hour-long recruitment tape for the new cult of Flowerism.

And it pretty much worked. "I learned that I am very much a perfectionist," he said of the album. "I didn't just want to put something out there. I wanted to make something fantastic and worthwhile."[46] The fans agreed. On its September 3 release, on the back of a plethora of high-profile national TV appearances playing 'Crossfire' in Britain and the US, *Flamingo* hit number one in the UK and number eight in the *Billboard* Chart[*], making Brandon a bona fide superstar in his own right. Its cover art – Brandon alone and smartly attired in a chintzy Vegas hotel room overlooking the Strip – at once asserted its reflective semi-autobiographical nature and a quiet confidence in its success. 'This city,' Brandon seemed to be saying, 'is mine'.

Critics weren't quite so quick to forgive Brandon his solo indulgences. Reviews were decidedly mixed. At the kinder end, *The Guardian*'s Caroline Sullivan deemed it "sporadically likeable, if not exactly lovable" and *Entertainment Weekly*'s Leah Greenblatt noted that "Though the album's Springsteen-of-the-sand-dunes jangle may underwhelm many longtime fans, there are subtler pleasures in hearing Flowers (relatively) stripped of his razzle-dazzle."[47] But elsewhere the brickbats were out. "A soft-rock drive-time radio album that finds Brandon dealing in the

---

[*] *Flamingo* charted in 17 other countries too, as well as reaching number four in the overall European Top 100 Album Chart. It would be certified gold in the UK and Ireland and find its way into Q magazine's albums of the year list.

most clichéd gambling imagery imaginable," wrote Hamish MacBain of the *NME*. "Brandon's solo journey has led him to Journey."[48] "*Flamingo* is an unworthy follow-up [to *Day & Age*], full of treacly power-pop melodies, leaden lyrics, and the depressing suspicion that nothing was left on the cutting-room floor," claimed *The Boston Globe*'s James Reed, arguing that since much of the album was written before the Killers' hiatus began, the album revealed nothing about the man inside the music.

With such a cool press reception and with the next single from the album, 'Only The Young', failing to match 'Crossfire''s runaway success[*], despite its stylish and visually stunning video of Brandon in a Rat Pack suit singing in a black landscape of waterfalls and rings of fire surrounded by elegant flying acrobats[**], it's no wonder Brandon approached the Flamingo Road tour with a certain caution. Unlike Mark and Ronnie he had plenty of time to tour his solo record, almost a year, and he was itching to get back on the road. "The idea of taking a year and a half off from being onstage scares me a little bit. Being on the road is something I've been cultivating. I feel like I've grown a lot, and I'm feeling comfortable onstage. I don't want to lose that."[49]

But uncertain of how Killers fans would respond to a set of largely unknown material and with a third child on the way, due in February 2011, he planned to play smaller club and theatre shows, the biggest around 2,000–5,000 capacity, to test the reaction and have the tour finished by Christmas of 2010.

"For the most part it's like going backwards," Brandon said on August 23, three days into the tour at Chicago's 1,000-capacity Park West club. "It's weird getting these nerves that I haven't had for five or six years. Nerves about playing smaller venues, people not knowing the material…"[50] His edginess was eased somewhat by having a lot

---

[*] A final single from the album, 'Jilted Lovers & Broken Hearts', would fail to chart anywhere on its release on February 21, 2011.

[**] The performers were from the show *Le Rêve* at the Wynn Las Vegas Casino Resort, a Cirque Du Soleil-style spectacular which features diving performances and feats of strength.

of The Killers' production team on the road with him, and several of the musicians who'd played on the album. "Working with Brandon was a lot of fun and quite interesting," recalled bassist Herschel Gaer, noting how Brandon's ceaseless productivity showed no sign of drying up on the Flamingo tour. "He just loves creating. After a show most people in bands want to go out partying or whatnot, but Brandon loves nothing more than getting back on the bus to pull out his keyboard and start bashing away. Every night he'd come up with new material that left me in awe. Even when he's just tinkering around, his melodies and song ideas are like golden water flowing from an endless faucet that never gets shut off. It's just second nature to him and effortless. He's constantly bristling with ideas he needs to get out."[51]

There were a lot of familiar faces in the crowd, too. "Bless 'em, they are devoted," he said of his hardcore fanbase. "I see some of the same faces every night. It's great to have the support and I realise that comes out of the love that they had for the Killers [but] I feel embarrassed to do some of the same [between-song patter each night], even though it's new for 95 per cent of the audience…"[52]

Although these smaller shows consisted almost entirely of new album material*, Brandon dropped in occasional familiar tracks. From The Killers' catalogue he'd perform 'When You Were Young' and at most shows he'd savour a rendition of Elvis' 'Are You Lonesome Tonight?' or Kim Carnes' 'Bette Davis Eyes', claiming "If you don't like this song there's something wrong with you". But it was his surprise covers that brought local colour to his shows. When the initial run of tiny club shows through the US, Britain and continental Europe** had been received well enough by fans and critics to warrant extending the tour

---

* The shows would often open with 'On The Floor', 'Crossfire' and 'Magdalena' and would feature the five-song sequence of 'Was It Something I Said?', 'Hard Enough', 'Losing Touch', 'Swallow It' and 'Playing With Fire'; the rest of the set varied.

** Including a secret set at London's 800-capacity Relentless Garage that Brandon loved so much it was the venue that would spring to mind when planning a post-Wembley Stadium set.

into theatres, academies and ultimately the 2011 summer festivals*, he began dropping musical references into the sets. At the O2 Academy Liverpool on October 14 he played 'Helter Skelter' in honour of local mop-tops The Beatles; at the Stone Pony in Asbury Park, New Jersey on December 1, he covered 'Promised Land' by famed New Jerseyan Bruce Springsteen. There were sporadic guest appearances, too; support act Fran Healy from Travis joined Flowers onstage in Oakland, California to duet on Travis' 'Side' and at the Wiltern Theatre in LA The Police's Andy Summers emerged to accompany Brandon through the 1978 classic 'Roxanne'. Perhaps best of all for fans, with Brandon's appearance at Coachella Festival in April 2011 being so close to Vegas, Dave and Mark made guest appearances to play 'Read My Mind' and 'Mr. Brightside'.

Everything about the Flamingo Road tour smacked of Brandon relaxing into himself, relieved of the responsibilities of fronting a band of brothers. He'd take the stage in an outfit of granddad shirt and waistcoat, a look designed to reflect the maverick spirits of Paul Newman, Marlon Brando and his classic country and western heroes. "I did want to dig into some of the western elements of my influences," he explained. "I grew up hearing Johnny Cash and Elvis from my dad. Stuff I've grown to love now. And so it was nice to explore that. It's all around me in Las Vegas, too. And growing up in Utah there was always a cowboy culture. That's always surrounded me and I always have a little bit of a fondness for it… Especially in popular modern music, [American culture] seems so distant. And especially the meat and potatoes of those songs – the simplicity of those songs is lost now to the beats and the bleeps."[53]

In the few interviews he conducted on the tour, he seemed more open and revealing than ever before. He spoke of how his son called him Cactus on account of his stubble, and the pleasures of taking his boys to a bagel shop each morning for breakfast. "It's amazing how much attention you get from women," he joked. "If you're a guy it's

---

* *Spin* named the Flamingo Road tour one of the best shows of the summer and the must-see gig for the autumn.

weird how much credit you get carrying a kid around. When I have both they act like a dream's just walked through the door."[54] And he talked of his hopes and fears as a solo performer. "I do feel like I'm carrying the Killers torch up there. And I'm bettering myself. And hopefully I become a better frontman and a better performer, hopefully I can apply that to the next Killers record. And we'll just be all the better for it."[55]

"I'm more comfortable now," he added. "Recently I've been thinking maybe it's not a fluke. Maybe I deserve it after all. If I do, I'm not gonna waste it. Man, I want to shoot for the stars."[56]

His deeper self-confidence allowed him to express his religious beliefs more publicly, too. He'd talk of how the closest he had to best friends in Vegas were his golfing buddies from his church, and of his meeting with rising politician Mitt Romney in February of 2011. Romney, a fellow Mormon, had that very month announced his intention to look into an attempt to secure his place as the Republican nominee for the presidential elections in 2012. Romney had a distinct image problem linked to his religion – he'd been mocked for wearing "Mormon underpants" stitched with snippets of scripture and purposely made difficult to remove in order to dissuade potential adulterers. He was as far from garnering the youth vote as it was possible for a candidate to be, and no doubt, as he bought Brandon a lunchtime burger at The Palm in Caesars Palace, he hoped to persuade Flowers off of his political fence to help him appeal to the teen rock crowd. Brandon remained unconvinced. "I could kinda see that coming," he'd say. "It wasn't too surprising. I think he probably sees a little bit of [youth vote] in me. It's understandable. But [The Killers have] always been neutral, so we just kinda stay out of it. None of us is planning any rallies for anybody. I'm sure he's met with a few different people. But I think [Mormonism is] something that definitely made it a little bit easier to reach out to me… I didn't say anything. We didn't talk too much about [policies]. My biggest issue is, I wish we took better care of our [war] veterans. I don't understand why we don't."[57] "There was no monumental secret there that I can divulge. It was just a regular thing… It was early on in his campaign. There was nothing really

338

significant about it. Except we were both Mormon, and ... he was nice."[58]

Brandon wasn't turned off by the idea of a Mormon president though. "It wouldn't hurt any more than anybody else. There's no secret bombshell that's gonna get dropped if he becomes president! Some new law... [But] I don't think you shouldn't vote for him because of his religion. If you're gonna vote for somebody, you should learn about what their views are on things, and pick the guy that you identify with and believe in the most." "I've said it before, but I don't think any president has ever changed anything. My family were poor, we didn't see any change when Clinton came in. Nor when he left. I just don't think it works that way."[59]

"I have an opinion on certain things but I don't feel educated enough to really be weighing in," he'd continue. "One thing I can tell you is from my interpretation and observation of growing up, the left side in America is seen as sort of elitist sometimes. So, even though their ideals are to help poor people more, it's off-putting to the poor guy. I can see why my dad would have said, 'I'm a Republican' without hesitation when really the left side is more in his favour. I'm just coming to grips with all that and absorbing it. I'm definitely not in any place to be preaching either way. I've a foot on both sides, I think."[60]

Ultimately, Brandon knew that his personal actions in the political sphere would speak not just for him but for his band, and he wasn't prepared to speak for them. "We're really careful not to make any sort of political statements," Ronnie said. "We're not that grown up yet! Now we just want to be a good band, maybe when we get older we can be more of a voice. It's kind of hard to be the band that says 'Somebody told me that you had a boyfriend that looks like a girlfriend', and by the way vote for this guy. We all have our individual stances on politics, I think it's really important that we don't use our band as a political thing. But if someone asks us to play a patriotic event we'll play, you know?"[61]

If Brandon refrained from nailing his colours to any political post in 2011, he did feel more at ease with standing up publicly for his beliefs. In 2011, as *South Park* creators Trey Parker and Matt Stone's

Mormon-mocking comedy musical *The Book Of Mormon* opened to rave reviews on Broadway*, the Church of Jesus Christ of Latter-day Saints launched a publicity campaign to help them portray a more human and accessible face. The 'I'm A Mormon' push featured ordinary and high-profile church members – from world squash champion Leilani Rorani, writer and comedian Jenna Kim Jones, pro rugby player Will Hopoate, Olympic medallist Lacey John and basketball pro Paora Winitana – talking to camera about their life and faith, projecting a pride and normality intended to shatter the image of Mormons as outsiders or cultists. Key to the campaign was Brandon's video, showing him at work on *Flamingo* in the studio and featuring Tana and his sons playing together in their Henderson home.

It was a heartfelt and revealing film, Brandon explaining the role that his religion has played in the development of his life and music. He spoke of his love for his family, how lucky he felt having his dream job but how building his family "has surpassed the music now, for me" and how his lyrics had shed the bitter and envious tone of the early days because "I want to be a positive force in the world, I want to uplift people". "There are a lot of connotations that come along with popular music and it's usually very sex driven or money driven," he said to camera. "I realised very early on that that wasn't the road for me, that maybe because of the foundations that were laid in my life, my mom taking me to church, that I wanted to take a different road."

More than anything, though, Brandon used the film to firmly rebuff the suspicious or incredulous questioning he'd been subjected to on his religious beliefs over the years. "A lot of people love to come up to me

* "I haven't seen it," Brandon told me when I asked him about the show. "Those guys say they have an affectionate stance on Mormons. They love them but they make fun of them. But I haven't seen it." The church itself took a healthily proactive stance to being parodied by the *South Park* team, buying adverts in the play-bills in many of the cities the musical played claiming "the book is always better". "My church isn't known for being the savviest of media operators," Brandon said, "but they've put billboards outside and people have converted. I just don't support it. [The writers] say it's even-handed… but the scales are tipped in the other direction." Source: *NME*, Barry Nicholson, June 22, 2013.

and tell me they were raised in a church and they expect there to be this camaraderie of 'Oh, we've outgrown it now, we're smart enough now to not be in it'," he explained. "It started happening so often that it really made me take a look at myself and I realised I was raised in it and there's still a fire burning in there. My name is Brandon Flowers – I'm a father, a husband and I'm a Mormon."

In return for his participation in the campaign, church leaders allowed Brandon to go to Salt Lake City to study their holiest and most protected artefacts, among them an object that particularly pricked Brandon's sense of rock'n'roll legend: a *Book Of Mormon* once owned by Elvis himself. "Elvis wrote 'There can only be one King'," he recalled. "He didn't like being called The King because, to him, Jesus Christ was The King. It was so cool that I got to see that."[62]

His solo outing had been immensely rewarding for Brandon. He'd gained a level of self-confidence in his stagecraft and songwriting that the crutch of The Killers had kept him from developing – he'd thrown off his sticks and run. Besides keeping his creative and performance engines running through the band's hiatus, it gave him the chance to indulge his wish to honour his mother, his fear and love of Las Vegas, and the beliefs and opinions that he'd been uncomfortable attaching to his bandmates. But by the time the I'm A Mormon campaign kicked in, The Killers were back in action. It was time to return to battle, and he'd kept one song back from *Flamingo* that sounded to him like the perfect comeback.

Mark Stoermer, April 2014

Why were you putting your own songs together while on the *Day & Age* tour?

I was experimenting with the laptop and GarageBand for the first time in hotel rooms, partly out of boredom, partly out of experimentation. I'd never really written a lyric before. I started doing a few ideas and that became the beginning of the little solo album I did and put out myself and didn't do any shows for – it took me a year to finish.

You'd also developed an interest in Joseph Campbell and religious symbolism – where did that come from?

One thing leads to another. I remember reading a John Lennon interview in a *Rolling Stone* book and he was talking about Federico Fellini, and that led to Fellini, and when I was doing research on Fellini he spoke about Carl Jung and I got a Carl Jung book. Somehow that led to Joseph Campbell because Joseph Campbell was influenced by Carl Jung. I started watching this whole series of DVDs that I have, which are these lectures that he did in the Eighties, and read *The Hero's Journey*. That's really the lineage of influence, one led to another.

What was it that interested you?

For me, it bridges the gap between science and religion. I believe in science and at the time I was probably cynical of religion, but it made me accept it in a different way. If it's viewed as a mythology with a deeper meaning, it's not literal and in a way every religion can have a truth that can't be explained logically. But Joseph Campbell is a very rational person, too, and doesn't go against the science of the day either.

By this point you were happy to take time apart from the band, booked into different hotels and enjoying your own movie nights – did you need your own space?

Yeah, I've always needed my alone time, growing up and onwards, and it was kind of a shock to be on tour. When I could afford or call the shots to have a bit more space, I took it when I could. But it wasn't necessarily a personal thing, it was just something I needed.

And that bled into making a solo record?
Maybe. When I was writing it on tour a lot of the time I was in the same hotel as everybody else. I'd be in my room, but everybody goes to their room at different times, it wasn't like I was totally avoiding everybody or anything. In a different way it was challenging myself to see what I can do. I think I want to do music regardless of how big it is and taking advantage of the fact that I'm in a position where I don't have to go back to a regular job, so when I'm not doing that job I'm still gonna do music and if it's my little solo album that a hundred people care about, or it's a Killers thing and hundreds of thousands or a million people care about, or whatever it is these days, I'm gonna do it.

Was it instinct, after the Killers tour had ended, to keep "touring" hotels while writing the solo record?
The last break, after *Day & Age*, I would go from Vegas to San Francisco to Los Angeles. I like short breaks, I didn't like long trips. I kinda got tired of a place every two weeks. This time I feel a little bit different, I've been staying in one spot – I don't like going to the airport at all. But at that time it did feel like that, "I wanna keep moving but at my own pace".

How did Howling Bells and Louis XIV get involved?
It was just Jason Hill from Louis XIV who made a studio in Laurel Canyon and that's when I had those demos. In some ways he prompted me to get the record going because he called me up one day and told me "I got this new studio in Laurel Canyon, you should come down and see it, just do a song". That was actually when I had those demos, so it made sense and we did a few songs. A lot of it we didn't complete because he had about five other projects going on and I had to bring it back to Vegas, but that started the beginning of it and I had to figure out how to finish. I ended up finishing in Vegas.

Howling Bells was because they asked me to produce their record. I'd never produced before but I think they knew what they were getting into. It was to come to the studio and get another musician's opinion on the record. We made a record here in Vegas together – it was their record but I produced it. I put my record on hold during that and then talking to two of the guys in Howling Bells, they stayed back and helped me with my record for a few months.

It sounds like you were their Vegas tour guide.
Yeah a little bit, that's how it was the first week or so. They were from Australia and now most of them live in England or Germany. I just took them to the not-as-touristy bars, the local places. I showed them downtown restaurants, normal stuff.

'Weary Soul' sounds like it's about being on tour for too long.
Kind of. It's supposed to have more than one meaning, but it started when I was really jet-lagged coming back from Australia, where I was going to bed at 11 a.m. but only getting three or four hours' sleep, and every night for a week or two it continued, I couldn't go to sleep and then I couldn't stay asleep. I wrote that about that, but it's supposed to touch on the ideas of reincarnation. I'm not sure I believe that but in the song it's maybe thinking about that.

Who's the girl in 'Everyone Loves The Girl'?
It was kind of about friends and a girl that I wasn't really involved with. It's about a circle of friends who were going for the same girl.

Were you single at this point?
Yeah, I was single, out of a five-year relationship at that point. I was in a relationship being on the road and trying to balance that and then as soon as I get home that all fell apart. So you're waiting and waiting to finally have time together and you get time together, it's over. But in some ways I got time to do some soul searching and maybe that's good in hindsight.

'Amber Bough' seems to be an escape song, is that the case?
That also probably has multiple meanings but it came from hearing about a dream of this friend that I have, a girl that I know. We were hanging out

344

in LA at some time, and it's kind of a combination of a trip that I had. It was an old friend, I was getting to know her again, we spent a few days together and at one point she told me a dream and the dream is mixed in with our actual trip. The burning house is straight out of her dream. She never knew it, I wrote that and I haven't spoken to her that much since.

What was the ghost story that inspired 'The Haunts'?
I was at the Chateau Marmont, which sounds exciting because of Lana Del Rey but this was pre-Lana Del Rey. I was up on the top floor and living the Hollywood life because I was in town working with Jason Hill whose studio is just up the road from there. I went out onto the balcony and the doors are wide open, there's no wind, it's the perfect spring day. Then all of a sudden a huge gust of wind comes, the doors shut, the latch locks and the curtains stuck in between the French doors. I'm stuck out on the balcony, kind of a little bit weirded out but whatever. I'm like "Okay, maybe that just happened, the suction from the windows or something, there's probably some physics to it". I call downstairs and I'm getting information, I get the guy from downstairs to come upstairs and get me and when he opens the door he says "Oh, what happened?" "I got locked outside on the balcony, I don't know how". "Oh, don't you know, this hotel's known for hauntings, it's really weird, it doesn't usually happen on the ninth floor but I just got a really weird call next door at the same time". I was like "What was it?" and he gave me a look like "I can't tell you". Later it makes me think, is this guy an aspiring actor and they tell him to do this to build the hype of the hotel? That's what I think now but that night, that inspired the beginning of that.

Did you intend to make the record so varied or did the electropop and Eastern influences develop as you recorded it?
It wasn't intentional but my favourite band is The Beatles and my favourite album is *Revolver*, which kinda goes all over the place too.

CHAPTER 11

Battle Born

The first week back in Battle Born, it looked like the fire had gone out.

For those seven days in May 2011, Ronnie, Mark, Brandon and Dave set up each day and eyeballed each other across their instruments, nothing coming, worrying that the whole thing might be over. It had been more than a year since The Killers had convened to work up anything new together, and the more they tried to push it the less it wanted to come. "We had a couple of days where we were really trying to force something," Dave says, "like 'We're gonna create some magic today'. We were really trying to force it, but we didn't necessarily come up with much on those days."

Then Brandon dropped his bombshell.

"I knew it when I met you, I'm not gonna let you run away," he howled, handing over the crashing chorus he'd been holding close to his chest for this very moment ever since they'd begun writing back in Santa Barbara in 2009. Through the entire *Flamingo* sessions he'd kept it for The Killers, feeling that it was a fiction that would have sat awkwardly alongside the internal confessionals of his solo album and knowing that the chorus line spoke as much to his band's fundamental bond through their downtime as it did to the characters that inhabited it.

This was 'Runaways', the glorious, bombastic pop rattle that traced, from start to dramatic finish, a perfect teenage couple who elope together only for their marriage to be destroyed years later by infidelity and dislocation; a husband and father fleeing his family in the night, full of cold memories and regret, a lifelong runaway. It struck to the core themes of the record they'd come to make and, once they'd expanded it from Brandon's basic idea into a fully fledged Killers creation, it was the song that gelled the band back together.

"That and 'Miss Atomic Bomb' were the backbone of this record. They made me feel we were on the right track,"[1] Brandon said, but he'd eventually become exasperated that people would keep asking him the meaning of such a straightforward and literal song, and frustrated with people reading it as autobiographical. "I'm proud of 'Runaways'," he told me at the Leeds Academy. "I think it was a great statement for the comeback single, but it's got three verses and it's not typical nowadays, so it's kind of a brave song for us to come out with. It's not your typical song that you hear on the radio nowadays. So many people say 'Is it about your wife?' and if you listen to it once you hear that there's a girl in the story and it's a love story, to me it's about the decay of commitment that I see in America. It's not about my fucking wife, listen to the song one time! It's what I see 30-something-year-old people going through. It was just an observation and it made its way into the song."

Watching other people's marriages break up as middle age begins to creep up on them had brought out Brandon's urge to question human morality. "There's a little bit of me in [everything]," he said elsewhere, "it's inevitable that I'm gonna creep my way into these songs. But I am also good at observing what's happening around me. And 'Runaways', that's not some grand statement that I'm here to make. But it is an observation of what I'm seeing every day, and living. It seems to be harder than ever for people to commit to each other. I guess it interests me. What's changed since my parents' generation? Or our grandparents'? Is it better? Or is it worse? You know, I think we're worse than we've ever been. Humans are worse than we've ever been."[2]

"That was exciting, it got us in line," Ronnie said of the song, "the direction felt right."[3] "It had been a few years since we had been in a studio together," Brandon added, "but after a couple of days everything just kind of fell into place. It could have been 10 years ago last night. It didn't feel much different. I don't think any of us have changed that much."[4]

'Miss Atomic Bomb' was the other rocket booster, launching the band on course for album four. Their most faithful homage yet to the epic canyon atmospherics of eighties U2, Meat Loaf and Foreigner, 'Miss Atomic Bomb' initially began life as just a title, a songwriting technique Brandon had taken from Elton and his songwriting partner Bernie Taupin. "It comes from when I met Bernie Taupin for the first time and we were talking about song titles," Brandon told me in Leeds. "He writes song titles first, I'd never heard that, I'd never thought of that. And it makes so much sense because there's so many brilliant Elton John song titles. You go from there. I shortly afterwards saw the title 'Miss Atomic Bomb' and realised that's a fucking great song title. So it was laid out, shortly after meeting Bernie. The danger of it all, I love it."

The image was a provocative one for the people of Nevada. Back in the early days of nuclear weapons in the fifties, the desert outside Vegas was used extensively as a testing site and, with the fallout from the bombs considered far less dangerous than we now know, they became a macabre form of entertainment for the Vegas high-livers. The casino roofs would fill with spectators in sunglasses, clinking cocktails and enjoying the view, or voting in the beauty pageant to decide who would be crowned Miss Atomic Bomb. "They'd have parties," Brandon said. "Give people martinis and sunglasses and wait for it to go off, it's crazy. They'd take school-kids out to designated points in the desert to watch the explosions. My mom went out." The city would come to feel the impact of such misadventures, and Brandon's family was hit harder than many. "Cancer doesn't run in my family," he said, "no grandparents or great-grandparents or anything like that, nobody, and my mom had brain cancer. The trailer park where my family's from, it's in the desert and there's these slabs of concrete left over from where the trailers were. I went there one night and a guy that grew up with my mom and dad was visiting his particular slab. It was really kind of sweet. He was there visiting his sister who had brain cancer, and his wife had died of it. So I instantly thought of the tests."

Once he had the title, a link slowly formed – a Miss for his Mr. "The light kinda went on once I started to sit down and mess around with the idea of 'Miss Atomic Bomb'," he told me. "I thought 'Mr. Brightside' and thought I can marry them. Then it really opened up and laid itself out for me, it was easy to write. And I'm grateful for those, because some of them are not. Obviously I knew the story very well."

So 'Miss Atomic Bomb' became a prequel to 'Mr. Brightside', complete with a cameo from the original song's opening riff as its middle eight, a nod to its meaning. Rather than focusing on the bitter end of the affair, now Brandon zoomed in on the initial rush and passion of the young and innocent new kid in town making out with his teenage temptress to the strains of the radio – "those neon nights, the leather seats, the passage rite, I feel the heat, I see the light". But the song still hinted at the betrayals to come: "You're gonna miss me when I'm gone" Brandon lilted as the relationship began to falter. At points it seemed that Brandon was looking back at this pivotal relationship and singing to his younger self, the new kid in town being taken for a romantic ride – "You've got a foolish heart," he sang, "you took your place but the fall from grace was the hardest part/It feels just like a dagger buried deep in your back… your soul was innocent, she kissed him and she painted it black… talk about being in the wrong place at the wrong time". But there was a wisdom, care and fondness to his reminiscing as though, after singing about the bitterness of the story for so long, this was his chance to lay it to rest.

"It was 11 years ago so I'm obviously over the girl," he said. "It doesn't keep me up at night, that girl, I've moved on, but there is a sense of closure [in the song] in a weird way. 'The dust has settled/My eyes are clear'." He didn't continue the song's quote – "but sometimes in dreams of impact I still hear Miss Atomic Bomb".[*]

---

[*] The song would go on to become a big live favourite, despite the fact that, over the course of the recording of *Battle Born*, one of the five producers advised the band to drop the song from the album. "There you see we've had the positive and negative sides to producers on this record," Brandon said. "A producer can be wrong! And this one was very wrong! That song holds its own. We've played it live and people who don't even know it yet love it." Source: Spotify, Diego Planas Rego, September 17, 2012.

Back in the saddle, The Killers took their time over constructing the songs for the fourth album, relaxing into the process, letting ideas come and only pursuing the ones that really clicked. For the first time they felt that they weren't trying to please or confound anyone with the style of their writing – this was as natural as The Killers could be.

The initial period of uncertainly having passed, they quickly slotted back into their usual roles. "I don't think the dynamic changed that much," Mark said. "Once we got in a room together it was pretty much working how it always has. We'd changed as people and musicians but the core was probably the same. It seemed to work how it's always worked." "For the most part I think it felt familiar to me," Dave added, "like it did eight years ago in Ronnie's garage, except this time around we had air conditioning, it wasn't 120 degrees. We used to practise in Ronnie's garage, this time it was in an air-conditioned studio, like it has been for the last six years."

"We still have the same goals when we get together," Brandon said, "and the same aspirations. We just want to do our best. We don't sit and think about how much time we had off or what anyone else might have been doing. When we're back together, the goal is always the same."[5]

"Even though people had done other things," Ronnie said, "when there's the four of us together there's a certain dynamic and why rock the boat? No one's trying to. We're all aiming for the same target. World domination. You can't let pride get in the way."

Although, having proved himself with the *Big Talk* record, Ronnie did feel a little more respect in terms of songwriting from his bandmates. "Dave said something really nice to me one day that I keep with me – he said 'Look, if you have any ideas for guitar on this one particular song I'm working on, please be my guest'. He'd never said that to me before and I keep that with me; for whatever reason, it's a tiny vindication."

Writing sessions proceeded gradually, interspersed between those 2011 festival dates as a full band or Brandon solo, for Ronnie's album releases and live outings and for Mark to complete his solo album. Brandon also had his hands full with his third son, Henry, born on March 9, another addition to his in-house judging panel. "Kids can always pick the hits," he told *Rolling Stone* "'Crossfire' is my son Ammon's favourite."[6]

351

By October 2011 the solo projects were pretty much wrapped up and writing took precedence, hitting a free-wheel momentum. "We've got a lot of songs and ideas," Mark said in November. "We recorded some things already, and I think some of what we've done could make the new record. I'd say we're still in the middle of the planning process. Optimistically, The Killers should have something by next summer, but on the other hand, it'll be done when it's done. We are working, however, and the band is more or less back together in Vegas. We were spread out for a little while on our hiatus. It'd be good to get something out next year... if all goes right."[7]

The time off had been a calming influence for the band too; few discussions became blazing rows. "I don't like it when we disagree," Brandon said, "because it's a democracy and we have different ideas on things, but it's been pretty positive so far. Everybody's happy that they had the break and we're excited about these songs, it's positive right now. The thing that keeps it fresh is going new places, changing the scenery, and we look forward to that."

"I think it went pretty well," Dave agreed, "it could've been a lot worse. It turned out we didn't argue as much as I thought we were going to, but it's very hard to get everybody on the same page of 'What's the schedule going to be, what songs are we going to play?' Songwriting in general is a give-and-take process, at some point somebody has to say 'No, your idea is not the right one'. It has to be done and nobody likes to hear it. But you're shaping the song and it's got to turn out a certain way for the better."

"Brandon [was the peacemaker]," Ronnie said. "In the last couple of years I think he's had an eye towards peace, and I'm sure it's got to do with getting older and having a family. I enjoy a bit of peace-making myself. Being in a band, if you're around each other all the time and you let an argument go unfinished or unresolved or unsaid and you have this pent up or harboured resentment, things can get weird. We're in a band, there's some shit that needs to be said, there's some arguments, it needs to he followed through. In the past we've held on to it and it's created uncomfortable... little stuff. It doesn't make the harmony there, and harmony is totally invisible. Whoever's making the argument may not be right but at least you're getting their perspective, and it feels good for the other person to get it off their chest. They may have a point. I'd like to think we're a bit more professional now, at least we try to be. It's such a learning process, you grow up fast, realising that if this is what you wanna do you've gotta bend a little bit. You grow, you learn how to understand people and the virtue of patience and trust."

There was little argument about the direction of the record: it would be what it would be, but it would rock more than it sizzled. "We wanted to make a rock record," Dave said. "We discussed it a little bit but even then I still feel like all we really do is get in a room and write the best songs we can, which is what the album is. The styles are all over the place, there's a nice diversity in it, that's what we came up with this time around. It's different every year. The Killers are, in some ways, whatever album is made that year."

There was a concerted effort to consider how the new songs would be performed, however. "When we were writing these songs in a room together, we were definitely looking at how they would translate live," Ronnie said, "how can we custom build these songs to be live songs? That's how we did the record, we tried to play as much live as possible… We were getting ready for it to be complicated, but it was easier than expected."[8] "When we are writing the songs, I do think we now do so with the live show in mind," Brandon agreed. "I think there are a lot of great 'live show' moments on this record, which will make the songs really fun to play on the road. That is one of the things that we weren't thinking about so much at the beginning."[9]

One sticking point was the decision over which producer to hire to make the record. After their contributions to *Flamingo*, Brandon was keen to work with Daniel Lanois and Brendan O'Brien again, and Stuart Price was still highly regarded by the band, a prime choice to continue where *Day & Age* left off. But there was also a desire to push things forward by working with new names. A Canadian called Damian Taylor had impressed them with his groundbreaking work on Prodigy and UNKLE albums as well as Björk's *Volta* and *Biophilia* projects – for the last, a revolutionary app-based release, he designed musical performance systems, which Björk used to write the album in the studio, as well as software for the audiovisual iPad experience. Taylor seemed the perfect name to push The Killers on technologically but, on the other hand, they were also drawn to the classic skills of Steve Lillywhite, a legend of the desk whose name Dave knew from the back of *Achtung Baby* and U2's prime eighties period, while Brandon knew him from Morrissey's solo masterpiece *Vauxhall & I* and countless other slices of rock's proudest heritage.

The choice was tough, and the various producers' schedules made it even tougher – between them they'd worked with Bruce Springsteen, Madonna, Depeche Mode, U2 and Arcade Fire, so they were in huge demand. None were free for a long enough stretch to work exclusively on the album from start to finish. "We're kind of in this phase where we're trying to decide what to do with producers," Mark explained. "There's scheduling and things to think about. There's a couple of producers we have in mind. It's up in the air right now who will produce the album. We have worked with some people, but we'll figure out in the next couple of weeks what we're really going to do. Multiple producers may be involved. We might use some of the tracks that we did with other producers, but we might scrap everything and start all over with somebody new."[10]

Ultimately, as an 'experiment', they went for the many-cooks approach. "Instead of waiting 10 years to cross all those guys off our lists, we just used 'em all on one record," Dave said. "It's not necessarily the right way to do it but it is how we did it for a variety of reasons… it was just curiosity on our part. Like, 'I wonder what Steve Lillywhite would do with this song? I wonder what Stuart Price would do with this song?"[11]

"The five producers on *Battle Born* was basically the product of a scheduling nightmare," Ronnie admitted. "We asked too late, and those guys are sought-after dudes. We just said okay, we'll take you for two weeks, five days, whatever you can do to help us out with this."[12]

"These guys are booked a year in advance with other bands," he continued, "like, 'I'm sorry, we're doing Pearl Jam that month, but I got two weeks here, I can do that'. So that's how we did it, we'd be like, 'Oh fuck, two weeks, okay, we'll go to Nashville for a couple of weeks, bang out a couple of songs and see how it goes'."[13]

"You never know how that's gonna work," Brandon said in July. "The album just starts to present itself after you've written a lot, but we're still kinda banging them out for now." "I was worried about using so many producers because those guys are strong individuals. They all had their own ideas. But it's a testament to us that it's a cohesive record."[14]

A fortnight with one producer here, a month with another there; in Battle Born and at Blackbird Studios in Nashville, the band flitted between producers, discovering the quirks and talents of each. "It was a really fascinating mix of people to have involved," Brandon said, "all working toward this same mysterious goal."[15] As he pieced together 'Runaways' they noticed how Brendan O'Brien would intensely study a song, soak it in and then, with a visible start, click into it. "I don't always know what he's looking for, but he just gets something and then we go there," Brandon explained. "It happens really fast."[16]

Steve Lillywhite, despite being one of the older and more experienced producers on the album, was a more playful, fun presence that the band would describe as "free and youthful, unbelievably youthful". Price and Taylor*, meanwhile, were more computer-centric, much to Brandon's annoyance. "I didn't know what the hell they were doing half the time," he claimed, "they are always typing into the computer and stuff. That frustrates me and they both know it. The old-school guys that are on the boards I can understand; it's a physical thing and you're watching it happen. You can feel it and see it. You can see their fingers moving the levels around. But this new way – they're so fast, and you're looking at all these images on a screen – it just feels very different. So basically we have worked in every way possible on this record. We've gone down every possible avenue."[17]

Perhaps the most rewarding collaboration of the session was with Daniel Lanois; the band visited his "crazy gothic mansion in Silverlake"

---

* Taylor was matched up with Lillywhite as dual producers for a time as their windows crossed.

for a very productive few days of writing, where they "enjoyed just 'sinking in' and letting the song happen."* "Because he's both a great mind and a great musician, he's able to link up with us in ways that maybe other producers don't," said Brandon. "It was the first time we've ever collaborated with another person to write songs. I guess that he sort of takes a more organic, more earthy approach. He's a big proponent of making human sounds with instruments... and really helps us tap into a side that we've explored a little bit on our own, but never put on an actual record before."[18]

"He has kind of a spiritual approach," said Dave. "It's nice to approach something so familiar to us but do so in a different way." "Lanois is more of a wizard," Brandon continued. "He brings this mysterious mojo that I've never seen before. I've never seen anyone as devoted to music; he's like a gypsy, you know? He goes from one thing to another and it's based around music. Also, there are no TVs in that man's house."[19] Lanois was just as complimentary about Brandon: "He is a little genius," he said. "He's a deep soul and a spirit man. I think we've only seen the tip of the iceberg [with 2010's *Flamingo*]."[20]

Their writing sessions in Lanois' LA castle produced a swathe of elegant ballads. A chorus that Brandon had been tinkering with melted into a verse from the band and one of Dave's unifying guitar lines to create 'The Way It Was', 'Here With Me'** and 'Be Still' emerged in the same session and sometimes lightning simply struck. "We sat in a circle eyeballing each other," Brandon said of the writing of 'Heart Of A Girl', "and that song didn't even exist an hour before that recording was made."[21]

Lanois pushed the band into using new studio writing techniques such as jamming without a click track to help them keep time. Four demos were made using this process, despite its disorienting effect on

---

* Some sources have these sessions happening at Battle Born.

** It's probable that 'Here With Me' began life before these sessions, however, since it's credited as written by Brandon and Fran Healy, his support act on sections of the *Flamingo* tour.

the band. "I didn't know what I was playing half the time," Dave said. "I was just following wherever it was going."[22]

In return, Lanois found his work on *Battle Born* inspiring too. On hearing the band play through a song called 'The Rising Tide'*, which they'd written to be premiered at the Hyde Park Hard Rock Calling show in 2011 but left out of the set, Daniel was overcome. "He took off his glasses," said Brandon, "you know how Daniel is, with his glasses and his beard. And his beard was wet with tears, really wet! We were just playing through the song as normal – we couldn't understand why he was crying."[23] It was the saving of the song – 'The Rising Tide' had been discarded due to indecision in the studio, then later rediscovered and brought back from the dead, a fate which several songs destined for the album would undergo.

Battle Born – named for the Civil War origins of Nevada state – increasingly lived up to its name. The piecemeal construction caused delays and discussions that the band couldn't have foreseen, and between studios they threw more songs out than ever before and revisited old ideas with promising results. It would become their most difficult album to make. "I like the idea of a team," Brandon said, "but you have to get the right team and the right dynamic happening."[24] "Maybe it was wrong to go in with five producers on this record," he'd muse later. "Next time, it's gonna be about getting the right guy, and being a bit harder on ourselves."[25]

Perfectionism crept in, too. A conversation he'd had with Flood had stuck in Dave's mind, Flood claiming he could no longer listen to Depeche Mode's *Violator*, which he'd produced, since he could only hear the tiny mistakes, errors in cymbal sounds that no one else could possibly hear. "We just want to avoid that as much as we can," Dave said. "I want to be able to listen to our records and not feel that kind of regret that we didn't do something differently." Brandon concurred. "We just want everyone to be relatively happy with the final product."[26]

Ronnie, on the other hand, thrived on the fly-by-night nature of the sessions. "I love that type of pressure … Because I love spontaneity,

---

* 'The Rising Tide' was the first song to be completed for *Battle Born*.

I love the sort of gun-to-the-head type of take, like, 'Okay, you've got one take to make this happen – do it and make it fucking count'. I love that. I don't like to spend three days on a fucking song. My idea in the recording studio is to spend a day on a song and if you don't have your shit together, you don't have your shit together. Get your shit together, play the fucking song and make it happen and move on. I like that sort of pressure and the guys that we were dealing with operated in the same way. I don't know if everybody else in the band would say that, but I enjoyed the pressure, I enjoyed the challenge."[27]

Snippets of sessions here, chunks of time there; the recording dragged on, much to the concern of Island, which was itching for an album of big pop hits. "There's a little pressure," Dave admitted. "I think sometimes the label's almost nervous to tell us they would rather us sound a certain way, like pop, because they know we'll resist it. We try and write the best songs anyway. We like songs we think will be great on the radio and we try and do that naturally. But at the same time we want to do our own thing. They were unsure about *Hot Fuss* and then after *Hot Fuss* they wanted us to be like that. And they were unsure on *Sam's Town*. You just gotta do what you wanna do and do it good."[28]

On January 4, 2012, having been working on the album on and off for over six months, Brandon appeared on Zane Lowe's show on Radio 1 to announce the album. "It's just whether it's [released in] the summertime or the wintertime," he declared. "It's just exciting getting everyone in the room to make some noise. It's quite a bit louder than with my solo thing, so I've got to get used to that." He went on to claim that the band was intending to "throw a curveball… I think the consensus within the band is to take those things that we've done well and really hone in on that. We don't want to make 'Hot Fuss 2' or 'Sam's Town 2', or 'Day & Age 2'. We'll maybe take all that stuff, the best of all of it and do what we know how to do."[29]

Plans were put in place to unveil the album over the summer festival season, with a string of North American dates and headline slots at festivals including Sziget and V Festival booked. But then, with the album almost finished, a bunch of tracks were scrapped and new ones started from scratch. And once again, Brandon spent a lot of time working on improving his lyrical skills. "Lyrics are something I've been working on," he said. "I'm the first to admit I've been hit-and-miss in that department. But I am trying to get better. Music can be really powerful on its own but when you attach a good story, that's the ultimate, that's what I'm trying to do."[30]

He did feel that he was making real progress, however, building his narratives from stories he'd overhear in parks or restaurants, a chronic eavesdropper. "I'm a more concise lyric-writer," he claimed. "No matter how close to your heart you hold that first record, the lyrics aren't as fully realised as they are now. I've read more books, I've grown, we've had more experiences. And we've played so many live shows that we can't help but be more powerful as a band. So hopefully those things should come through on *Battle Born*."[31] And when he found himself struggling, he turned back to the album's title for inspiration. "I think of it as a call to arms," he explained. "We have a lot of references like that [on the album]. It's like a positive kick in the ass. It's a wake-up call of sorts. Whenever I was struggling for anything lyrically, it helped just to go to that phrase. It can apply to so much more than combat, and it's definitely the thread through this whole record. But there's always this other side to me. It's not just the struggle. It's the 'what-are-we-gonna-do-to-fix-it? And to break through?'"[32] *

In the spring, grief came to hobble the album's progress. On April 23, Tommy Marth, Mark's old saxophone player schoolfriend who had played on *Day & Age* and its subsequent tour, was found dead from a self-inflicted gunshot wound after a battle with depression, aged 33. The news sent the band reeling. "We knew he was volatile," Mark said, "but it wasn't like the signs were all there. He would be a really nice, happy, friendly, creative guy most of the time. Then at the same time, he'd have these moments of anger and despair that didn't make any sense... just totally out of character."[33] "I knew Tommy probably the best. What can you really say? I think in hindsight I knew that he was going through stuff and was disturbed about a lot of things but at

---

* Brandon would also credit films such as *Terminator* and *Blade Runner* as having an effect on the album, since he and Dave were such sci-fi nuts.

the same time he always put on this kind of joker persona. I took it pretty hard."[34]

"He was a crazy motherfucker, but in a great way," Ronnie added. "He would joke about serious stuff, but always throw it into the comic realm. Nobody ever said, 'Tom, you OK, dude?' We wrote a new song a couple of weeks ago, and we were thinking about having him come in to play on that, but it never happened."[35] "My heart just goes out to his family. He was a whip-smart, mega-talented dude who could talk to anybody. He was likeable, y'know? It was a tragedy that he just went, kind of, circling the drain all of a sudden. You never can tell, man... it's not a perfect world for a lot of people."[36]

Brandon was taken aback by the tragedy. "It's just shocking. He's the last person you would think would do that. What's strange is that he's the one who brought light to the backstage area, brought levity when it was a grind."[37]

"I'll never forget that he texted me a few days before saying, 'Hey, if you're in town let's hang out'," Dave recalled. "I said 'No, I'm sorry, I can't. I'm in San Diego.' His response was like 'No worries, Dave. You're a good guy'. That struck me as odd, that he would say something really nice. But he already knew then what he was doing. I wish I could call him but I can't."[38]

★ ★ ★

As the deadline for delivering the album fast approached, the band worked from noon until midnight every weekday, thankful for the lack of clocks in Battle Born Studios. Six weeks before the album absolutely had to go to pressing and with four weeks to go before the V Festival show, with the album still unfinished, the promotional schedule kicked in. On June 7, a movie-style trailer for the album was posted to YouTube to announce the title, 90 seconds of shots of the band picking up instruments and building a dusk bonfire in the desert.[*] A month later,

---

[*] The band had hoped for this to be the first ever trailer for an album, but were beaten to it by a matter of weeks by a promo film for Muse's *The 2nd Law*.

'Runaways' was released online and the band kept an avid eye on the reception, poring over fan comments and media responses.

"We have a guy who does that for us," Ronnie explained. "Between breaks, he'll come in and say, 'Hey, someone's five-year-old daughter really liked it…'" "I will say this," Brandon said. "None of the previous ones have had this kind of reaction. This one seems like, out of the gate, people respond to it more."[39]

"It was hard to pick a first song to lead with," Dave added. "It would be like, 'Well that's what everyone's going to think you sound like, that first song.'"[40] "It was the song that felt more like the right one to start with," Ronnie said. "I don't think we were trying to say anything other than, 'We heard you missed us and now we're back'."[41]

The media gave The Killers a fond welcome back, although some of the reference points some writers found in 'Runaways' were unexpected – Craig McLean of *The Independent*, for instance, likened it to a cross between 'Bette Davis Eyes' and 'Meat Loaf's *Bat Out Of Hell*. Other writers picked out hints of eighties AOR arena bands. "The first single from the first Killers album in four years is an eighties-rock fever dream that's crazily big, even by their grandiose standards," wrote Jon Dolan of *Rolling Stone*, "a Vesuvian gusher of Springsteen mythos, Toto-Journey power hooks and singer Brandon Flowers' unmistakable commitment to unmistakable commitment." *NME*'s Barry Nicolson, meanwhile, heard a band roaring back through *Sam's Town* on a bigger, more precision-tooled hog. "Four years after *Day & Age* saw them dip their toe into dancier waters, The Killers make their grand return with the Killersiest comeback single you could ever hope to hear. If *Day & Age* was a stylistic reaction to the unjust critical kicking their second record took, then 'Runaways' is the sound of the band re-embracing their inner Springsteen."

On July 17, 'Runaways' had its US release, its sleeve indicative of the band's bold return – a gigantic lightning flash in their trademark Vegas lights, hoisted over the Nevada plains. Its video*, opening with a shot

---

* Directed by Warren Fu, the video for 'Runaways' would receive a nomination for Best Video at the Q Awards 2012.

of a starry sky that added *Space Odyssey* import to the track's opening guitar wails, was a live studio performance backed by visuals of the Vegas Strip and a speeding headlit highway. Yet, despite its aura of the grand, triumphant comeback, the song only reached number 78 on the *Billboard* Chart and number seven on the US Alternative Songs Chart. In the UK, where it was released on September 9, it made number 18; respectable but not the deep impact splash they might have hoped for. Still, Brandon wasn't disheartened. "When we play it, it's just huge," he said later. "But it's fine. You don't have to have a smash single for a song to touch people."[42]

The comeback plans, however, remained monumental. A webcast was planned as part of the American Express: Unstaged project, which hooked major bands up with legendary film-makers who would direct a live show to be streamed online. Previous events had matched Jack White with Gary Oldman, Arcade Fire with Terry Gilliam and Duran Duran with David Lynch. For their show at the Paradise Theatre in the Bronx, set for September 18 to tie in with the album's release, The Killers asked to work with a true cinematic legend.

"I've seen the Arcade Fire one and I've seen the Coldplay one," Brandon said. "I thought it was a great idea and I wanted to be a part of it. And the fact that you get this freedom to pick a director – and we were so lucky to have Werner [Herzog] say yes, I mean, he was at the top of the list, and everything kind of fell into place."[43]

Herzog's methodology and intense approach to his work would open the band's eyes to things they hadn't quite realised about themselves; about why, for instance, a vice-free man such as Brandon would want to stay in Sin City. He was, he discovered, feeding from the thrill of the casino dreamers. "He came to Las Vegas and it's in his nature to dig into you a little bit and ask you questions," Brandon told me. "We're just trying to do a trailer for this gig and he keeps asking, and it forced me to finally spit it out. One of the things that came out of me was 'I know it's strange here [in Vegas], I know it's depressing to people, I get that there's a bunch of musicians they say go there to die and people are losing their money, and I think my brain bypasses that. I feed and I thrive off of the energy of that gold rush, the idea of people coming there for that and the neon buzzes. I still feel like a teenager about that stuff."

Herzog himself revelled in the easy-going attitude of The Killers. "I'm rumoured to be some sort of wild guy," Herzog said. "Fact is, I'm clinically sane. I'm trying to find professionals who are, as well, clinically sane as I am. I was drawn to the urgency with which the band wanted to have me and I thought, yes, this is completely new terrain for me. And when I met the band for the first time, I immediately had this connection that I immediately felt, yes, they're good, solid human beings with a strange background, but at the same time, they are absolutely sane and wonderful to work with as professionals. Very, very easy. Yesterday within an hour, we did a short film with them, written, scripted, filmed and edited in less than an hour. And it will be shown for the people out there for the streaming. It's kind of scary. It came very easy, in the end."[44] *

Herzog's webcast was planned to involve 18 cameras and the band playing on a grand proscenium stage flanked with screens showing fans holding up handmade signs bearing their name and hometown, as part of a global communion of Killers fans throughout the show. "Thinking about, I don't know, maybe 10 million people out there around the world, I wanted to do it more interactive," Herzog explained. "All the other concerts were not really responding that much to the audiences out there, so left and right on the stage we'll have two screens and fans have sent in their pictures identifying where they are from, and thousands have come in and they are still streaming in. And while the concert is going on, they will still stream their photos and it will be part of the show, so the audience and the band will see the pictures left and right, and the audience out in the world will see how we are participants. And they

---

* The promotional film followed Brandon, Ronnie and Mark as they drove down the Vegas Strip and out to a mock Wild West town in the desert where they were interviewed by Herzog. Dave, according to a caption in the film "was not to be found" on the day of filming. "He just didn't show up," Brandon said, "he's allowed to do what he wants." Dave eventually came clean. "They probably want me to lie but I was in Hawaii. I planned a vacation and I didn't want to break it." Source: Q, Ben Mitchell, November 1, 2012.

look at each other, the live audience in the theatre is looking at the faces out there of other fans, and the other way around. So I wanted to have it really interactive... for me, get something across that is authentic, that is alive, that brings over the excitement, that brings over the character of the band, and also incorporates the world out there. They are not the receiving end alone; they contribute."[45] "It's a beautiful challenge and I've accepted it," he continued. "It doesn't matter whether I do something for a narrative film structure or a documentary, this is a very specific challenge I am jumping into. And I know with the band out there, I can jump out the window and I don't care if there is rock bottom down there or soft water, I'll just jump with them. And it's going to be fine."[46]

"I think it's a great idea," Ronnie added. "It's so communal. It's bringing the whole world together. And it makes me feel almost emotional about it when he talks about it."[47]

While this spectacular was being meticulously planned, there were further delays to recording. Brandon found himself suffering from a pinched nerve in his back and had to undergo surgery in mid-July to straighten his curved shoulders in order to fix the problem. In fact, the surgery just made rehearsals more painful for him. "They go in and they saw it straight," he explained after the operation. "The doctor went in three different places, with a little camera and everything, and it's supposed to be cool. Anyway, it's worse now than it was before. I can't lift weights, and picking up the kids is hard. Fist-pumping is hard! I had three cortisone shots before I had the surgery – didn't do shit for me! The third was the sorest, it was tightest – the doctor couldn't get into the groove between the bones, he was poking with the needle. Anything above my head with my hand, I feel. I can only use the right arm."

Hence, the journalists who came to Battle Born to interview the band in the summer ahead of the festival dates and the album's release found them furiously racing to finish the record. "It's living up to its title," Ronnie said. "This is our difficult fourth record." "It gets harder as you get older," Brandon stated. "You want to put in the same effort, and find the same focus you had when you knew you didn't want to work at the casino any more. We're working it out."[48]

"We put a certain amount of pressure on ourselves," he continued. "and we have raised the bar as high as we can physically, you know, these four guys together. And so you want to get there again, you want to get over it. And it's nerve-racking, the prospect that you might not get there, that your best days are behind you. It's possible."[49]

As late as August they hadn't even firmed up the track listing. "It could be nine songs," Ronnie claimed. "Or 10. It could be 12. It's always like this. The thing is, we have to follow the most congruent lines. There's a certain natural chaos in the process." "It's always pretty hectic," Dave added. "But it's never been quite like this. Making the album, and rehearsing the new stuff, trying to refresh the old stuff: it's a lot."[50] "Great things tend to come from pushing yourself to the limit like that," Ronnie would say. "It doesn't feel great while you're doing it, but when you get to the top of the hill it's a wonderful feeling."[51]

The journalists also found a band hemmed in by the studio and aching to get back onstage. In one early interview Ronnie joked that he was so desperate to play anywhere that he'd happily play at a 7-Eleven store. Two days later the band received an offer from the chain to play one of their outlets. Ronnie argued in favour of playing, but he was voted down. "I don't think the rest of the guys were into it," he laughed, "but I'd have played for slurpees. It's a kind of band joke that comes from another band, a pop band. I overheard someone saying 'Yeah, well they'd play a 7-Eleven opening'. You just heard this band everywhere. I won't say who it is, just this pop band. I just thought it kind of sounds fun. Don't knock it, there's a free slurpee in it!"[52]

In the event, the comeback show took place on July 19, not in Vegas as had become customary for the band but in North Carolina, at the 1,100 capacity Orange Peel club in Asheville. They premiered four songs from the album, storming onstage to the tune of 'Runaways' as the most brazen introduction to the all-new comeback Killers imaginable, slotting 'The Rising Tide' and 'Miss Atomic Bomb' into the main set and giving the opening of the encore, a spot traditionally held by 'Jenny Was A Friend Of Mine', to a billowing stadium rock behemoth called 'Flesh And Bone', a sign of their sights settling on rock'n'roll's highest echelons. "In some ways you craft songs with the mindset of 'What's our crowd going to be like'," Ronnie explained. "It does mean the stadium aspect comes into it now, as that's basically what we do."[53]

In terms of onstage attire, these were smartly clad but less try-hard shows without any sort of sartorial gimmick. "I wouldn't say we're ditching [the past flamboyance]," Brandon told me. "I still think we're putting on a show, but this time around I don't necessarily feel pulled towards trying something like that. It's just getting more comfortable in my own skin and feeling more confident is somehow taking the place of feathers and pink leather." His famous eagle feather jacket, he revealed, had been donated to the Hard Rock Hotel in Vegas as a permanent exhibit. "It's strange," he'd say, "the better physical shape I get in, the less I care about what suit I'm covering myself up in."[54]

As the five-date warm-up tour moved through Richmond, Vancouver and New York, another new song, the partner-swinging barnyard jig 'From Here On Out', was added to the set and gobbled up heartily by the try-out crowds. Then it was straight back to Battle Born for a final few weeks of tweaking the record before they hit Europe mid-August, destination V.

★ ★ ★

"It takes a while to get your legs back and to get your voice," Brandon said as we sat backstage at the Leeds Academy on August 17.[*] "We were writing and finishing the record and recording right up until it was time to come play, so we really didn't rehearse enough. A lot of these songs play themselves a little bit now, and that's a good thing. They don't belong to us any more. As soon as you fire up 'Brightside' or 'Human' or 'When You Were Young', something happens. I facilitate it but I don't know that I'm totally needed."

I saw it that night, the Academy crowd ecstatic and enthralled by the communal thrill of the music bulging the walls. The immaculate host, Brandon was often overwhelmed by the reception, a mouthpiece and

---

[*] Brandon would admit to having had singing lessons in the run-up to the *Battle Born* tour.

focus point for roaring mass singalongs to 'Human', 'Mr. Brightside' and 'Jenny Was A Friend Of Mine'. The night had the rush of a homecoming show, the crowd so relieved and excited that The Killers hadn't gone for good that the sense of celebration swept the songs along, Brandon acting as ringmaster setting the gospel avalanche of 'All These Things That I've Done' loose for the crowd to ride to their own Yorkshire epiphany. It was a rare night of real rock magic, topped off with a near riot-inducing 'When You Were Young', a song that had gradually become Brandon's favourite to play live.

"We're all proud of our first record," he said, "and some of those songs go down crazy great. But there's something about ['When You Were Young'] that I think… it's unreal that we were able to do it again. I still have that thrill about that song. Like, 'We did it again!' Because there was a lot of pressure on us, and I get that validation every time that we play it. And that must've given me a lot of confidence when making the third record, and from there on."[55]

Brandon would admit to being nervous about The Killers' big comeback though. "You want people to like the record but you never know how they're going to react," he said. "Bands that say they don't care about how their records sell are liars. We've always been honest about wanting success. We didn't grow up in a cool city like New York or London. We grew up in the Nevada desert, so we have a different perspective. Despite the casinos, Las Vegas has a small-town mentality. We came from nothing, and we did things our way. We grafted hard to become big." He was also concerned that the record had been pre-hyped as too much of a balls-out rock'n'roll album. "Our drummer, Ronnie, said we were ditching disco and going back to rock. Now everyone is anticipating this huge rock record, but *Battle Born* isn't quite like that. It's got more guitars, but it's not exactly AC/DC."[56]

Meanwhile, The Killers were happily being swept back into the bizarre world of life on the road. Prior to Leeds they'd played a few dates in Europe, their two tour-bus technique expanded; Dave, Ronnie and Mark still slept in bunks but Brandon now had his own room with a double bed, even though he'd usually never sleep in it. After an hour

367

or so of restlessness he'd get into one of the bunks himself, his "womb". From pure acclimatisation, he always got more sleep there.

Having ensconced themselves deep into the festival headlining circuit, they enjoyed the pinnacle of backstage luxury, too. The band had a dressing room each when they reached Austria's Frequency Festival, a 40,000 capacity event outside Vienna, partly perhaps so that Brandon, who hadn't drunk alcohol for five years by now, could sip Red Bulls to boost his pre-gig nervousness in a separate room from Dave necking shots of Jägermeister or Ronnie's constant sofa drumming, or practise the new falsetto vocal techniques he'd learnt from his tutor during the hiatus.* Or, indeed, so that they had somewhere to host high-profile guests and their entourages. After Frequency, for example, legendary Welsh crooner Tom Jones hooked up with the band, bringing a gaggle of groupies and hangers-on back to The Killers' hotel to party until 1 a.m. and fill Brandon with stories from his tearaway Vegas days.

Their entourage was a little sparser when they reached V. "We had this area backstage at V Festival," Ronnie laughed, "a big private compound full of dressing rooms and a nice rider with top-shelf liquors and fresh fruit and all the sparkling water you could ever want. Everything was great, but we have a small crew. Apparently the other headliners, The Stone Roses, had much more of an entourage. They had two or three hundred people with them and it was like a village back there. We did this interview and it was like 'So where are all your people?' We're like 'What do you mean?' 'How many people are in your crew?' 'Twelve, 13, why? How many in the other crew?' 'There was, like 300 people'. 'Shit, it's a party!' Maybe one day…"

Mark considered the V Festival show a success. "It was pretty good," he said. "We're getting back into the swing of it. We only played two

---

* Brandon's work on his falsetto may well have had something to do with the new inner rivalry he felt with Coldplay, whose singer, Chris Martin, used such a style and who had recently stepped up to the stadium league at that point. In interviews Brandon would talk enviously of Coldplay's incredible light-up wristband idea, which turned entire stadiums into shifting oceans of neon light. "We're a few steps behind Coldplay now," he told me in Leeds. "There's no catching them now. I never felt we were chasing them and I'm not defeated, but they've just taken that."

new songs and they're not really out and the single's just barely getting radio play here."

That was all about to change. After teasing the crowds with those same few new tracks at further European festival headlining slots in Switzerland, Germany, Ireland and Italy, and widely plugging 'Runaways' on promotional TV appearances around them, *Battle Born* went over the top. At a show at London's Roundhouse on September 11, as part of the month-long iTunes Festival where major bands play intimate shows for audiences of prize winners, they boldly opened with 'Flesh And Bone', as did the album that would finally hit the stores a week later, on September 17. It was arguably the most forthright and brazen opening of a Killers album yet; a baroque synth take on a futuristic harpsichord was swathed with ephemeral guitar spook-tones, game console bleeps and swelling strings as Brandon laid out his latest state-of-the-heart address. "I've gone through life white-knuckled," he sang, once more the most honest rock megastar in the business as he owned up to bewilderment, disbelief and confusion at his own success. "They say I'll adjust, God knows I must, but I'm not sure how/This natural selection picked me out to be a dark horse running in a fantasy." And with that entry statement of stardom set adrift, setting Brandon and The Killers' position at the outset as a major global concern with a very human core, the white-knuckle ride kicked in once more.

'Flesh And Bone' opened out into a sheer cinematic epic. Drums pounded like volcanic magma bursts, the synths were virtually Tolkien-esque in scope, electronic beats rattled and echoed like marauding warbots and Dave unleashed guitar lines custom-built to be as "mighty" as possible. "I thought the verse should sound mighty 'cause it's kind of a mighty sounding song."[57] And over it all, Brandon's stout, powerful voice sang of proving oneself without surrender, whether as a hero of state or nation ("Cut from the cloth of a flag that bears the name Battle Born") or as an individual battler through life. The song's defiant roar was peppered with boxing imagery, Brandon casting himself as a focused, unbeatable prize fighter – "I hit like a raging bull, anointed by the blood... they'll call me the contender, they'll listen for the bell, with my face flashing crimson from the fires of hell". This was Brandon channelling his pride in his homeland and his struggle for success through the violent tale of the founding of Nevada and Vegas, picturing swarms of soldiers descending on defenceless valleys or navigating hostile deserts and concluding in a final spoken-word segment that "in this monster land, we are the descendants of giant men". As a man to whom family values were vital, here he expanded his family to include his geographical forefathers, and marked his own place, as a world-beating pop star, in the lineage of noble Nevadan conquerors.

Although it sounded like a Lanois production, 'Flesh And Bone' was virtually complete in the studio with Damian Taylor before Steve Lillywhite arrived at the session to assist and suggested a fascinating twist for the bridge section – a Motown joint. "There's a certain way that I sing a couple of the lines in the song that we were talking about being reminiscent of Motown and Detroit," Brandon explained, "the way that I sing, 'I'm runnin' out of time', and things like that. And so I think that that sparked something in Steve. We had the bridge written and he suggested maybe we try it with a different flavour. And it turned out that way and that's one of the benefits of having a great producer: more ideas."[58]

"It's like a weird left turn to Detroit, but it's awesome!" he continued. "We wouldn't have done that without him… I wanted to do a bridge like Metronomy, but it ended up nothing like them at all!"[59]

Battle Born's audacious opening was shored up by the bright pop rush of 'Runaways', after which the record relaxed into a brace of ballads. 'The Way It Was', a Brendan O'Brien production co-written with Daniel Lanois, was classic AOR drive-in Americana; eighties cinema theme gloss-rock in excelsis. Synths sparkled like diamanté or shimmered like a *Baywatch* sunset, canyon guitars chugged and echoed, and Brandon wailed a sorry tale of a man driving into the night, Elvis on the radio, wondering if his shattered relationship could ever regain its original spark, revisit those "golden nights" of watching airplanes land out at the airport, laid out on a blanket on the hood of his daddy's car. It seemed hopeless – "That paradise is buried in the dust", Brandon declares – and its companion piece, 'Here With Me', shifted perspective from nostalgic melancholia to sheer heartbroken agony. "Don't want your picture on my cellphone, I want you here with me," Brandon crooned, pining for a long-lost lover, the thought of whom pains him so much he runs away when he spots her in restaurants. The sentiment was darker and more racked with emotion but the song was a similar glossy power ballad in the vein of Foreigner, Chicago, Peter Cetera's 'The Glory Of Love' and Fleetwood Mac's 'Tango In The Night'.

"All that stuff is in us," Dave admitted when I put this to him, "it just never had a chance to get out. We're just trying to be ourselves, and we've definitely got some Fleetwood Mac in us, somewhere in there. There's a lot of different influences, that's just what came out this year. There's definitely rock songs on this record but it's not like every song is a rock song, there's three ballads on this album, kinda slow numbers, and I like those, I'm proud of them, I feel like we've never done that right before. We did a little bit with 'Everything Will Be Alright' but these are totally different from that. So we got a chance to get that out there, that we can do that."

Dave remembered 'Here With Me' starting out as a demo from Brandon, and one he immediately thought would be a huge song. "I was like 'Well, we can't let that go to waste. That's just a hit.' So I didn't want to step on the toes of the piano too much... We've never done [a power rock ballad] before... 'Here With Me' [is] a big sounding song. It's in a way risky for us because it doesn't sound like it's even from this decade. We recognise a good song as a good song and it shouldn't matter what style or era it belongs in."[60]

"That's a tender moment in Killers history," Brandon said. "I love our shows, but Killers gigs are like an assault for an hour and a half every night and it would be nice to go on more of a journey."[61] He'd defend the soppiness of these tunes[*] as a long-standing natural trait. "Even when I was very young, I was like that. I don't know who I inherited that from...but I love to tell stories, and it's inevitable that the stories end up having those sentiments. People appreciate that kind of honesty... It's not always cool to be so sentimental, but I am what I am!"[62]

These were shamelessly mainstream songs, too – the closest The Killers had every strayed to the middle of the road. An accidental

---

[*] A regular criticism of the album from reviewers.

swerve, Mark claimed. "I don't think we planned on it. I don't see this as being more mainstream than the last record. We've always wanted to write big songs so to some extent we haven't been afraid of being mainstream if that's where it goes. But we definitely weren't trying to make a mainstream record as far as what's mainstream for now. We've tried to write songs that will be big live or will be big on the radio, or should be on the radio, but we're not trying to follow any pattern or any genre based on what's hot."

"It never bothered us," Brandon added. "I've always loved big songs. I appreciate all types of music but we've always been ambitious, we want to take it as far as we can."

Prime example: 'A Matter Of Time'. One of the songs that was discarded and then revived towards the end of the recording sessions[*], it built from already huge beginnings – Dave's guitars and urgent gang chant backing vocals crashing headlong into a heat-haze synth intro like 'Jenny Was A Friend Of Mine' skydiving into the Grand Canyon – into a sprawling epic akin to this album's 'A Dustland Fairytale' or 'Bling (Confessions Of A King)'. It took in fifties prom rock choruses[**] and edgy murder trilogy verses as it hurtled towards an incendiary stadium rock climax with echoes of 'Mr. Brightside' and 'When You Were Young'.

"You know when archaeologists do these digs and uncover artefacts like bowls and sabre tooth tiger teeth and jawbones?" Ronnie said. "'A Matter Of Time' is us doing that, digging into our history, going back to my garage. We still have that DNA in us and it was cool to find that without looking for it, it gives credit and validity to what we were doing in a hot garage 10 years ago and we're still driven by that."[63]

The lyric slotted right in with Brandon's new preoccupation with dislocated and dysfunctional families, of husbands and boyfriends hitting the dark deserted roads to escape distraught home lives, to try to figure out how their relationships got so broken. As in 'The Way It Was', the car-bound husband of 'A Matter Of Time' thinks back to idyllic

---

[*] 'A Matter Of Time' was the last song to be completed for *Battle Born*.

[**] A reflection of Ronnie's recent interest in Little Richard and classic rock'n'roll.

early days with his partner, when he was "headstrong" and "made just enough hustling tables that summer to take you out", but the faster pace and pounding rhythms gave the track more urgency and the relationship more danger. The man sees his partner in the street "laughing with your girlfriends, not a care in the world, not a burden on your mind" and contrasts this image with life at home where "there's panic in this house and it's bound to surface". Again, hopelessness wins out. "Look at me flailing in the corner," Brandon sang, "here's the towel, go on throw it in... look what's laying at our feet, that's the wreckage of broken dreams". Here was Brandon's vision of the modern malaise of disavowal and marital inconstancy at its most desperate.

"I think that's what's happening in the world right now," he said when I pushed him on why there were so many shattered marriages on the album. "There've always been dysfunctional families and I'm not romanticising past generations to that point where I think that they were perfect. But there's definitely something happening right now, there's been a shift. I don't think I'm the authority on it, I'm just making those observations. Everybody seems to want to see it as progress and I think it's the opposite, I don't understand that."

'Deadlines And Commitments', a last-minute inclusion featuring The Killers' first ever bass solo, formed a central plank of the album. An atmospheric mid-paced rumble that was particularly reminiscent of Fleetwood Mac's 'Tango In The Night', resembling a more sumptuous 'Big Love'*, it found Brandon, amid all the splits and recriminations of *Battle Born*, offering solace and sanctuary to whatever troubled soul needed him. "There is a place, here in this house, where you can stay," he proffered, providing literal security to the subject of the song but also an emotional fulcrum for his millions of listeners. The Killers, and *Battle Born*, was a place they could find comfort and belonging.

Then 'Miss Atomic Bomb' detonated and the album's second half was drenched deep in more of humanity's moral and emotional fall-out.

---

* Although in fact 'Deadlines And Commitments' was inspired by Bob Seger's 'Against The Wind', one of Brandon's favourite songs.

Rousing rediscovered rocker 'The Rising Tide' very nearly didn't make the album[*], but its inclusion played a vital ideological and unifying role.

First of all, it contained the most blatant references to Brandon's religion to fix into place the record's moral compass. The "slates of persuasion… plated in gold" were perhaps the golden plates said to have been discovered by Joseph Smith buried on a hill near Manchester, New York. The "gates… open wide" were arguably those to Heaven and redemption. The deceitful subject of the song joins a church choir to hide their blackened heart and their equally untrustworthy friends plot their social "crucifixion". The rising tide of the title itself could refer to a cleansing Biblical flood or the redemptive cataclysm of the Rapture sweeping this sort of pitchfork-tongued liar into the jaws of Hades. But couched within this language of apocalypse was the bitterest story yet of families set against each other; the subject, dark-hearted and racked with guilt at their hypocritical Christian façade, appeared to be lying their way through a custody hearing: "I was there in the back of the room when you testified/With your pitchfork tongue you lick your lips and lie/We're never going to know how hard you cry/When your petition and your access was denied". This, according to Brandon's vision, was family life at its most vicious, fractured and damnable, the root of humanity's rot.

The album's lingering motif of driving away the heartache – a classic trope of windswept Americana rock – recurred in 'Heart Of A Girl': "A million miles of freedom, a million miles of road/But I still don't know where to start". The sentiment here was warmer and more honourable, though, and tinged with strong, stirring elements of gospel and traditional US country rock[**], it was the album's most successful ballad on account of its subtlety, restraint and intriguing imagery. A straightforward story of a man falling deeply for a girl who gives

---

[*] As previously mentioned, it had been written before the sessions began and was the first song to be finished during recording, only to be dismissed partway through, forgotten and returned to later in the process.

[**] Daniel Lanois played pedal steel guitar on the song, with Dave on slide and lap steel guitar.

him her number – perhaps an autobiographical nod to Tana handing Brandon her cellphone number when they met in the thrift store out on Flamingo Avenue – became something more elemental. Their love, despite the distance of touring, was rendered as grand and enduring as the Nevada mountains or the God that Brandon believes put them there.

On that note of solidity and reliability, it was time for light relief. 'From Here On Out' was two and a half minutes of sheer hoedown fun, an upbeat, catchy country bar-room swingalong, their 'Glory Days'. Not that the lyric was particularly uplifting. It told of another deceitful character who "had us all fooled with your quarterback smile and your crocodile tears", who "had it easy, then he chose the hard way" and for whom "friends are gonna be hard to come by". It's tempting to read this as a venting of The Killers' feelings towards Braden Merrick, but for all its barbs it ended with a shrugged token of forgiveness: "Should our paths ever decide to cross, you may wonder what the trouble cost/That don't matter now, life goes on".

"That's like a new side to us," Brandon said. "It's a breath of fresh air, a short song!" "That track's like a nutrition bar and it's one of our collective favourites," Ronnie added. "All the dudes in the band love this one."[64] The band enjoyed it so much, in fact, they'd repeat its chorus several times when performing it live, revelling in its lightness and joy.

It was a necessary blast of light before the album's dark and righteous closing. 'Be Still' was a firm-chinned hymnal advocating personal constancy and self-belief in the face of whatever life might throw at you – "It's a totally arresting song for me," said Brandon, "you put it on and you go somewhere else for a few minutes."[65] The song went through several incarnations; a plaintive, organic take played by the band alone in the studio was deemed gorgeous, but instead the band plumped for a more electronic version with drum machine and vintage synths to the fore, a more futuristic take. A sign, perhaps, that the band hadn't dismissed the electro leanings of *Day & Age* completely. "No, we've not ditched electronica forever," Dave insisted when I pressed him on it. "I'd like to do one that's all that way, someday. I don't know when the right time is for that, it's too early to say. I don't think we're done with that yet."

The final song, the album's title track, was stouter still. Coming full circle to the epic power rock of 'Flesh And Bone', but bolstered to even grander heights by multi-layered Queen-style vocals[*], it seemed to address America itself, attempt to rouse the nation from its advert-numbed, leisure-dampened cultural slumber and rediscover the great American dream: "You lost faith in the human spirit," Brandon admonished in Steinbeckian tones, "you walk around like a ghost/Your star-spangled heart took a train for the coast". It was a very traditionalist concept of American ideals and gender roles that Brandon expounded here – "your boys have grown soft and your girls have gone wild" – but the proud and forceful nature of the song hammered home the galvanising and inspiring message: "When they break your heart/When they cause your soul to mourn/Remember what I said/Boy, you were battle born".

As with previous Killers albums, various editions of the record came with bonus tracks. An exclusive edition sold by selected retailers included the alternative version of 'Be Still' and a 'Michael Remix' of 'Runaways'. "I was surprised how much I liked it," Dave told me. "I didn't think you could do a good remix of 'Runaways' because it doesn't seem dance-remixable, but I really like what the guy did with it." A deluxe edition of the record, meanwhile, included a remix of 'Flesh And Bone' by Stuart Price under his Jacques Lu Cont guise, alongside two new tracks. 'Carry Me Home' was an electro-pop chug about a character waking up from a period of self-delusion and suffering a breakdown, while the comedic 'Prize Fighter', a co-write between Brandon and Ronnie, was a virtual *Rocky* theme of trumpets and pop bullishness in which Brandon swore to fight to the death for a fantastical goddess so brilliant she was world renowned as an architect, baseball pitcher and tightrope walker, and deserved a knighthood from the Queen of England. A light-hearted coda to a somewhat stern and serious album.

Battle Born – with its glossy production-rock aesthetic, eighties twinkles and shameless summoning of AOR Americana right down to

---

[*] This was a technique which the band developed when recording a cover of The Raspberries' 'Go All The Way' to play over the end credits of Tim Burton's movie *Dark Shadows*.

the airbrushed sleeve of a Mustang roaring down a desert highway in the wake of another mustang of the equine variety – almost dared the critics to despise it. Instead, while several reviewers were wary of its Meat Loaf and soft-rock tendencies, most accepted the record for the ambitious, overblown synth rock behemoth it was. "It's an unashamedly commercial album," wrote Craig McLean in *The Independent*, "and it's Flowers' emphatic, stirring stand against angst, aggro, chaos and the decline of Western civilisation… *Battle Born*'s wide, inclusive melodies are burnished with a golden optimism, and underpinned with an instinctive feel for the grand stadium moment on which the singer has long been focused."[66]

"A thrilling victory of an album," wrote *Q*'s Rob Fitzpatrick. "A testament to spirit and sheer will… an album about injecting a little majesty into the mundane and holding your head high," wrote *Entertainment Weekly*'s Kyle Anderson. "It's a natural progression from the synth-pop of 2008's *Day & Age* through Brandon's desert-diva solo album, and marks the point where The Killers discard 'indie' pretence and go for the arena-rock jugular," I wrote in my own *NME* review of the record.

When talk turned to the record's clear stadium ambition in our interview, Brandon referred back to a comment he made in 2009 which had caused a minor backlash – "I don't mean it in a bad way," he'd told the *Daily Star*, "but I think Kurt Cobain and grunge took the fun out of rock'n'roll."[67] "People misinterpret my emotions towards Nirvana because I've said things about how something happened with grunge that took a little bit of fun out of things," he explained to me. "It's no offence to Nirvana, they were one of the greats obviously, I have no qualms with that. But something died there too and we haven't quite gotten the groove back. It's seen as dirty to be ambitious. What if U2 wasn't ambitious? We wouldn't have that. What a gift that we have from them. Instead of hearing the reason in what I'm saying, [people] just say 'He hates Nirvana, what a dick!' I'm not saying that, I'm saying that the reaction from bands since then has been their approach is different and I think music is suffering a little bit."

The rock world, he argued, was suffering from a certain degree of anti-commercialism. "Guitar bands aren't writing songs," he said.

"Write a fucking song, get over yourself. Get over whatever it is who you're trying to impress and write a song. There aren't any. Where are they? If bands would write better songs [then] dance music cannot compete with a really great rock'n'roll song. There ain't no DJ that's gonna play something that can take 'Mr. Brightside' or 'Don't Look Back In Anger'. Y'know what I mean? Those songs are better than that. I appreciate the dance culture, it's cool. I love bands that are able to blend that stuff, I grew up on Depeche Mode and New Order, but there aren't any bands that are giving it a run for its money."

Elsewhere, Ronnie would expand on this idea. "It seems that 10 or 15 years ago, there was this barrage of great music," he told *Hot Press*. "People were writing really great songs. I'm not talking about hairdos or looks, but people were productive. People were churning out the tunes. Today, it's like, fuck man, it's falling flat. There's really not shit out there. At least in public consciousness, there's only this fucking pop music and then everything else. And then you've got Spotify and iTunes and everything, so you're totally diluting everything. Everything is becoming so disseminated that it's really frustrating and hard to find music. But it's also sort of cool, because you've got this treasure hunt. You know there's great music out there that you've never heard of and all you have to do is get on your computer and, I dunno, see what some asshole in Brooklyn is listening to. And you will eventually find there's a band in Martha's Vineyard doing some great shit or a band out of Bakersfield again. So, it's a double-edged sword. It's a different cat that we need to learn how to skin."[68]

So The Killers felt alone and adrift in a sea of rock mundanity in 2012, but at least they felt true to themselves creatively and critically bulletproof. "We did *Hot Fuss*," Brandon said, "people were calling us Anglophiles. It made us look at ourselves and we made an American record. People said, 'You're full of shit now, what is this?' So we decided to experiment, do a little more pop... then they were like, 'What the hell is this disco shit?' But in among all that, there were always these songs. And I'm not afraid to say that: 'Mr. Brightside', 'Somebody Told Me', 'When You Were Young', 'Bones', 'Human', and 'Spaceman'. Great, great songs. So in the end, we decided to follow the songs."[69]

"We always seem to divide people when we put out a record," he continued. "People who were fans of *Sam's Town* were a little bit displeased with *Day & Age*. We realise that we have so many different roads we can go down and I think we took that into consideration on this album. We also are big fans of *Sam's Town*. So we're trying to combine everything – trying to make ourselves happy and make everybody else happy, too."[70]

Little did Brandon know, he'd soon run up against his ideological opposite face to face, and on camera.

★ ★ ★

As soon as the presenter's flurry of Norwegian gave way to an English name – "Richard Dawkins" – Brandon's lips pursed, his jaw set firm. As the famed atheist shook the hands of the panel and took his seat on the opposite side of the stage from Brandon, the singer stared dead ahead, waiting to have his core beliefs attacked. His appearance on Nordic chat show *Skavlan* had already been somewhat awkward – he'd been baffled by questions about his relationship with classical composers and the range of kindergarten options in Las Vegas and spoken stiltedly about his band's family ties to the city; Ronnie's mother's job as a cocktail waitress at Caesars Palace and his own father's recent retirement from his bellman job at Treasure Island. He successfully dodged a political discussion by calling The Killers "the Switzerland of bands", but gradually talk turned to his religion, with guests including Ulrika Jonsson attempting to fathom the reasoning behind this oddest of creatures; the God-fearing, leather-clad rock star.

"It's difficult because I'm here to promote this band and then I get questions a lot about being a Mormon," he said, "but it's understandable because it's still a very misunderstood religion and people are pretty unfamiliar with it so it's fine." When asked to explain the "beauty of faith" he replied "my mother teaching me to pray, and that I have that communication with my heavenly Father. That's something I turn to on a daily basis... There are answers to questions that my church has that also are very... it's a beautiful thing for me, and I'm happy... I'm very familiar with the origins of my religion. I've read about it. You get to that age where your parents teach you something and you have to decide once you're an adult, you can't just go off of what they said, you have to gain a testimony for yourself and I believe Joseph Smith."

When Dawkins took to the arena, however, Brandon visibly rankled. After a short interview about the basis and philosophy behind his own atheism, Dawkins turned to Brandon. "There is far more beauty in the real understanding of the reality of nature than there is from reading some ancient book, or the reading of some modern book, which is what *The Book Of Mormon* is," he said. "I have to say that when I read *The Book Of Mormon* recently, what impressed me was that this was an obvious fake. This was a 19th-century book written in 16th-century English. 'And it came to pass', 'verily I say unto you'. Things like that. That's not the way people talked in the 19th century – it's a fake. So it's not beautiful, it's a work of charlatanry."

It was an argument Dawkins had levelled at *The Book Of Mormon* previously, and an unfortunate one since, of all the questions hanging over the authenticity of the book, this ignored the fact that the text was claimed to be a translation of a work not originally written in 1830. "The book's been studied and torn apart and looked at," Brandon responded. "I'm not one of the professors that have done it. But to call this man a charlatan, I take offence to it."

"Well he was a convicted charlatan," Dawkins returned, "he was a convicted con-man."

"These are all falsehoods," Brandon rebuffed, "you should do your research."

Dawkins grinned. "Well, I think I have…"

The interview wrapped up a short time later with Brandon having to leave the debate to play his slot with the band, but he left offering to continue the discussion with Dawkins by phone – "I'll give you some true history of the church." That conversation never happened. "I haven't continued our debate, no!" Brandon said. "Nobody's ever going to convince him there's a God. But nobody's ever going to prove that there isn't. Guys like Dawkins argue with priests about whether or not there's an afterlife, but it's about having faith or not having faith."[71]

"I didn't know exactly how it was going to go down. I'd heard about Richard Dawkins before and I'd seen his spiel on Mormonism before, and he just says the same things verbatim. He has it locked down. But he does it with a tenacity that I didn't expect, because he's done it so many times, so that was strange to be receiving that in the flesh, and not watching it on YouTube or something."[72] "I see both sides of it. He sees [religion] as a dangerous thing [with] people that are fanatical, you know... I'm not going to be the one who persuades Richard Dawkins that there's a God, and I knew that. But I tried to at least answer a couple of questions and speak a little bit more. But yeah, he wasn't nice. He wasn't very Christ-like. Which makes sense."[73]

Outside of the Scandinavian TV studios, the world seemed much more welcoming. *Battle Born* became The Killers' fourth successive UK number one album and hit number three on the US *Billboard* Chart and number one on both the Alternative and Rock Album Charts. It would chart well in a total of 26 countries and sell a million copies before the end of 2012, pushing the total Killers album sales so far close to 20 million.

Two more singles would be taken from the album by the end of the year. 'Miss Atomic Bomb', released on October 23 as a digital download, came accompanied by a video directed by the album's aesthetic controller Warren Fu that tied the song ever closer to 'Mr. Brightside' by casting the same actors that had played the in flagrante couple in 'Brightside' to act out a similar scene, purported to be the real story behind the original song rather than just what Mr. Brightside had known about. In a desert trailer a middle-aged man found a mysterious letter pushed under his door, which set him thinking back to the days, told in animation, that he would be distracted from his band's rehearsals by the vision of a ballerina in a window across the street. In the fantasy colours of comic book romances, the pair rode out through the desert on the guy's silver dream machine, shooting stars chasing them towards their ever-calling destiny. But in the dazzle of the city she's ultimately seduced by a glamorous older man on the New Year's Eve that her dejected boyfriend was planning to propose, and the tragic hero retreats to a lonely trailer life, tormented by the memory of the atomic lover he'd lost.

The song would be voted the best of 2012 in a *Rolling Stone* reader's poll and, following that year's (RED) Christmas song on December 4[*], The Killers would put out 'Here With Me' the week before Christmas, promoting it on American TV with a duet with the eventual winner of NBC's third season of *The Voice*, Cassadee Pope.

The 'Here With Me' video had a little more star power behind it, though. Directing his first music promo since 'Bones', Tim Burton helmed the clip and brought in Winona Ryder to play a cinema starlet on whom a teenage boy develops an unhealthy crush. Unable to get any closer to his idol than a "picture on my cellphone", he instead stole a waxwork mannequin of the star and embarked upon a series of romantic dates, relaxing at the beach or slow-dancing in an empty ballroom[**]. Eventually his sense of reality began to crumble; he saw the woman's face on every person in a fast food restaurant, and when he treated his waxwork partner to a candle-lit meal, she became the candle, a wick in her crown lit with a firelighter. Just as the hero lit a wick atop his own head, the waxwork came to life. A very gothi-comic, very Burton sort of love story.

'Here With Me' would be viewed almost seven million times on YouTube, a signifier of *Battle Born*'s vast crossover success. As the band took the record into the arenas of the UK and North America from October right through until Christmas 2012 the new songs were met with roaring receptions and the older tunes prompted scenes of celebration and elation that seemed to elevate them into the realm of true classics. It was here that Brandon's insecurities finally melted away and the band realised they'd really struck notes of depth and emotion with the new album that were resounding globally, and that they had built a canon that could resound through the decades.

---

[*] That year's festive single was a Fleetwood Mac/Chris Rea style electro-rock throb called 'I Feel It In My Bones' that came with another comedy video in which Ryan Pardey reprised his role as the psychopathic, eggnog-pumped Santa Claus from 'Don't Shoot Me Santa' to hunt down The Killers and slaughter them for being on his 'naughty' list, cackling like a cross between St Nicholas and Freddie Krueger. The video featured Ronnie's brother playing a gas station attendant.

[**] These scenes were all filmed in Blackpool during a break in the band's UK arena tour.

"I feel like it's just starting to be acknowledged that we are survivors and that we are actually accomplished,"[74] Brandon said. "Before our time off, I didn't have a grasp on what we'd achieved. Now I understand our impact. I understand what songs like 'Mr. Brightside' mean to people. They will last forever. Hopefully, we've got more to add."[75]

And, having reached the creative heights of their heroes – U2, Depeche Mode, Bruce Springsteen – it was time to walk in their shoes.

A date was fixed, a calendar marked. The Killers' destiny finally let out its piercing call.

And its cry was "Wembley".

Mark Stoermer, April 2014

How were those first writing sessions back with the band?

We got back together and we were speaking of the *Day & Age* process and said we'll get back together like a band again, in a circle. And we tried, but we were almost out of practice of that for more than one reason. For *Day & Age* we veered away from that a little bit and also just not being together for a few years and three of us did solo records. So it was kinda awkward and a lot of noise was being made. We gave up on that quickly and thought "we got to bring in producers", and eventually we got five.

Was that a hangover from writing with Stuart – thinking that producers can have a writing role as well so why not write with as many as possible?

Maybe, it was kind of like opening Pandora's Box once we used Stuart. We'd call up everybody on the Rolodex of famous producers. Don't forget, we made *Hot Fuss* with Jeff Saltzman, who'd never really made a big record before, it was really the band, and even *Sam's Town* with Flood and Moulder, they were producers who'd just let a band be a band, they're not picking up instruments, they're there giving guidance and that's about it.

Who were the best and trickiest producers to work with?

Daniel Lanois was inspiring, he would jump in there and get us jamming again and he kind of brought life back to everything, but we abandoned working with him, I personally think, too soon. He tried to get us to play things over and over and jam, and he would get in there with a guitar, but he'd be pushing the band to do things. We made some pretty cool stuff but we only did that for two or three days with him and when we'd get on a roll with one song, some of the other guys were like "Okay, that's good, let's go in that room with the computer" and even he was like "What are we doing? Let's keep playing! That's good!" He was explaining how U2 made *Achtung Baby* and that's how they did it and that's what everybody supposedly wanted, but we were almost not really listening to Lanois. We were like "We're used to this lane now where you just go in front of the computer once you have a rough idea" instead of just letting things develop organically and, even if it seems kinda hippie, jamming out the song and doing it over and over. He brought that kind of approach and that kind of feel and I think we were actually productive, but we cut it short. We probably could've worked with him longer but we didn't.

How about the other producers?
They've each got their own style. Damian Taylor is really good; he's more along the lines of Stuart but a little bit darker, edgier, but similar. He has a similar talent that comes from the electronic world. Then Brendan O'Brien is old school rock'n'roll but mainstream rock. Amazing musician, guitar player, he plays the organ, but it's very much his way or the highway. I don't know what he does but tell stories. Always about himself.

Were there any memorable co-writing moments with the producers?
With Lanois, a couple of songs. Even though we stopped working with him we ended up using two of the ideas we jammed out in a couple of days, and he was in the room jamming with us on a couple of those. Some of it was lyrics – Brandon went back to Lanois for lyrics, which was a first.

Did the record drag on as a result of working with so many producers?
I believe so, and I think it's a result of over-thinking and a result of having your own studio and dealing with minutiae, not trusting your own instincts. Miraculously the album came out pretty good but the process was a nightmare. We did most of the album in two or three months. Backing up to Brendan O'Brien, we went to Nashville, we recorded five songs in one week, three of those songs are on the album. Then we stopped working with Brendan O'Brien. The rest of the album took six to seven months and six of those months were standing around the

computer nit-picking – "How long should that verse be?" or "Does it need a fourth guitar part on that verse right there?", that kind of stuff. Mixing was happening in January even though the album wasn't done until July. We were listening to 20 mixes at once from five different mixers.

Did you ever think the record just wasn't going to happen?

I never thought it wasn't going to happen but there was a point where I thought "I can't believe I signed up for this"! Out of all the album experiences, this was the worst one by far. We started in May of 2011, finished in July of 2012, although in the beginning we went a month on, month off, because I think Brandon was still on his solo tour. But then from September 2011 until July we're basically doing it non-stop and it kept dragging on and on and we weren't writing new songs, even.

Would you agree that *Battle Born* was a radio-friendly record that truly embraced the mainstream?

You think it did embrace the mainstream? Yes and no. A song like 'Runaways', the first single, the chorus doesn't come in for two minutes. It's not 'Mr. Brightside' or something. Sonically I definitely know what you mean, but not necessarily in terms of pop songs. Definitely 'Here With Me', and I don't necessarily love the mix of that one. I have mixed feelings about that. I know when we got into this we loved big bands, we weren't afraid of being a big band so what's wrong with being a big band, kind of thing. I love a lot of underground music – back in the beginning when I was getting into Nirvana I was buying jazz albums at the same time, I was buying a Nirvana with a John Coltrane or Jimi Hendrix and Charlie Parker at the same time, so my tastes are pretty wide. But with The Killers I've always elected to have big pop songs, not to be afraid to be an arena band because I like pop songs and arena bands too. But there are elements that I personally don't love, but I think that album has good songs.

Was there one eye on Wembley at this point?

Maybe. Wembley was something that I was possibly even bringing up back on *Day & Age*. Personally I felt we could've been doing it by *Day*

& Age – I think we've been overdoing the festival scene, which has been one of my differences with some of the people in the band. I don't think we need to go back to the UK to play every festival, every time. I don't mind going back, but sometimes play a headliner. Well, a headlining show you're spending more money, it's not as guaranteed and all that. I personally don't care, I'd rather be more about the legacy. Now it proves to be true that Wembley Stadium is a gig that we'll talk about for the rest of our lives, but besides a couple of the festivals most of them are forgotten. So I'm more for doing things for the legacy, for ourselves, for the fans. Festivals can be good but I think there can be a point where you're just doing them to do them, because they're asking.

Dave Keuning, March 2014

Was it difficult writing as a band after the break?
It wasn't that difficult, we were just trying to jam with each other again. We came up with a lot of stuff that didn't make the album. We were trying to make music with each other again rather then making demos separately.

Were there concerns that it wouldn't work again?
No, but there was a mystery as to what the material would be, of what *Battle Born* would be. We were trying to make it different from *Day & Age*, a few more guitars, but that was the only direction we had.

Was using multiple producers a mistake?
The number one reason we had multiple producers was because of scheduling on their part; we kind of decided we were gonna make an album and looked for who was available then and there. Daniel Lanois came in for a week and that was fun. We didn't use some of the stuff we did with him, we've still got it. He came to our studio for a bit to play guitar and stuff. We worked with Damian Taylor on some stuff, he was all right, I liked his stuff with Björk. He was probably around the most. Steve Lillywhite came and went – his influence was hit and miss. He's an

odd person, I can't honestly tell you what he did on some of the songs, but he gets credit because he was there. Stuart really helped on 'Miss Atomic Bomb' and 'Carry Me Home'. Most of the blame shouldn't fall on the producers. We just took forever to record it. We didn't have a deadline, which we wanted, but that was kind of a bad thing because we thought we had all the time in the world. It's hard to find the balance when you're not being pushed, or pushed uncomfortably. We threw away songs, we worked at three different studios. One in Nashville, in ours, New York and some in London.

How do you feel about *Battle Born* now?
I really like the diversity of that record – I'm not gonna rank it but I will say I like a lot of the deeper tracks. I like 'From Here On Out' and 'The Rising Tide'. We tried really hard to polish the songs up, maybe too much on some of them. I would have liked it to be a bit rougher looking back. Similar to the *Sam's Town* record, we just worked really hard on arranging and mixing.

CHAPTER 12

Exitlude

"In the Borough of Brent
If the legend is real
Stood a two-headed monster
Made of 23 thousands tons of steel
And they called it Wembley"

– The Killers, 'Wembley Song'

"Pink Floyd, The Animals and Genesis, The Who without the Moon, ELO, INXS, Michael you left us too soon…"

The endless, beaming grin stretched a mile wide across Brandon Flowers' face as he listed the giants of rock and pop in whose footprints he was proudly standing, their pictures flashing up on the huge screen behind him, flanked by two 150-foot Killers lightning bolts.

"The Boss, the Stones, The Man in Black, The Bitch is Back and Fleetwood Mac…"

With a smile that wide, he couldn't resist the odd light-hearted, self-deprecating aside as he ran through the acts that had graced that legendary stage over the decades. "Take That, Bon Jovi, Green Day, I said some shit, but that was the old me," he sang to an image of his pink-jacketed younger self flipping the double bird. "AC/DC,

G n' R," he rapped, "George Michael, stay away from cars". And as the list climaxed with references that proved The Killers' love for Britain and their knowledge of the venue's proud history and heritage – "'66 the winning team, Freddie Mercury and Queen" – it made the moment all the more significant and moving when Brandon gestured to his own band's image flashing onto the screen, and said "After tonight you're gonna put another name on that list".

And the crowd roared like the world's biggest family reunion.

That The Killers had written 'Wembley Song' especially "to celebrate this joyous occasion" of their ascendance to the stadium echelons spoke to how much the night meant to them, and to the veterans of those early Camden pub gigs watching from the stands. It had been a 10-year struggle – years of solid touring and recording, of being lauded and lashed upon the critical scaffold, of overcoming insecurities, homesickness and separations thanks to a steely self-belief, determination and an unwavering focus on world domination. That night they were no longer second-guessing their fans, mimicking their heroes, out to please critics or hiding behind fashion gimmicks; The Killers were entirely their own band, forging their own distinct path. They, and we the watching Victims, felt the immense swell of achievement, relief and celebration that rose from the band that night; that puffed 'All These Things…' as full as a hot air balloon, elevated Dave's spotlit guitar intro to 'Mr. Brightside' into the realm of unforgettable rock legend and made 'When You Were Young' explode from Brandon's chest like an A-bomb from a canyon bed. The little boy gawping in awe of Bono on his brother's bedroom TV had finally broken his way right through the screen.

"'Mr. Brightside' had you scratching your heads when you heard we were from Vegas, but you were positive it was Sheffield or Camden… you took us in like your own, now we're bound by tradition, my how we've grown, from Dave's apartment to Wembley."

And that they spent half of the song paying tribute to the country that had first taken them to its heart, and with a very British wit, served to show just how much they'd grown over the past decade, from world-dazzled bright-eyed kids into confident, well-heeled rock stars. Ronnie was now the fifties rock'n'roll lover, classical composition fan, bike rider and architecture junkie, a man who'd become accustomed to playing in tight cotton boxer shorts onstage because "I like to be held in tight when I perform. Then I peel 'em off and throw 'em at the nearest groupie."[1] The band bon viveur with a taste for fine whiskey, he would be spotted on the *Battle Born* tour clutching bottles of Laphroaig malt, spoke of his plans to take a tasting tour of the Glengoyne Distillery near Killearn in Stirlingshire when he was next in Scotland and necked a shot of $2,500 scotch on NYE 2012. "It was good," he said, "but I'd never pay $2,500 for a shot of scotch. I was in a casino and the owner bought it for me."[2]

"Without wanting to sound like a total cheese-dick," he'd say of the Wembley show, "this gig is the culmination of a lot of hopes and dreams and aspirations. Back in the early days, when we were in my garage playing 'Jenny Was A Friend Of Mine', I remember thinking – I may even have said it out loud – 'We'll play this shit at Wembley Stadium one day'. Now, it's like we get to join that echelon."[3] Yet he was acutely aware of the dangers of getting too wrapped up in the significance of such milestones – "You can go too far down the rabbit hole, thinking about the importance of things, we've got a job to do, and that's to kick asses!"[4] – and the transience of such happiness and success. "I've reached that age when you realise the mortality of everything. I'm 36 and I have all these friends with marriages dissolving. Nothing lasts forever. I'm sort of like 'Fuck, take it day by day because anything can happen. I'm just waiting for the bottom to drop out."[5] "After Wembley," he'd joke, "it'll be back to playing weddings and bah mitzvahs for us."[6]

Mark, meanwhile, had become a more self-assured, cultured and philosophical presence over his decade with The Killers. He'd grown happy with his own space, using his days off to visit museums or settle in with a drink and a movie by Woody Allen, Ingmar Bergman or Fellini. "I feel like I'm out of my shell compared to where I was when I was 16," he'd say, attributing such development to the deep personal connection running through his band. "It's deep, man. You sort of have this suspended adolescence where you're the kids and you've got mom and dad doing your laundry and taking care of you so you bicker about the small things. Just like 'God! Where are the avocados?' I think we're growing out of that a bit."[7]

Mark had certainly come out of his shell enough, in rock star terms, to enquire whether they'd be hiring helicopters to help them beat the traffic around Wembley on show day.* "[We've been] staring at [it] on the calendar ever since it's been booked," he admitted, "one of those first-time-never-done-before kinda things that we don't have too many of these days... We decided not to entirely change the show, because this is the only stadium show on the tour. One day we'll build a stadium-specific production. But I don't want to undersell it... it's going to be like the arena show, but on steroids."[8]

"It was amazing," Mark said of the experience afterwards, "but more of a celebration of the band and the music than a quality show in some ways. For me, it was a really big stage and hard to hear... but it was one of those things that I'm glad we did and crossed off our list."[9]

Of all of the Killers, Dave was still feeling the biggest bumps in the road. Now based in San Diego and commuting to band appointments – "For the record, it's on-off," he said of his ongoing relationship with Kyler's mother, "it's driving me nuts, it's not very fun and I'd rather not talk about it"[10] – he'd expel his frustrations in rock'n'roll behaviour, splashing out on $2,100 1921 Gibson guitars to cheer himself up, drinking a cocktail he'd invented involving Jägermeister, Red Bull and cranberry juice or renting a private plane between dates on the *Battle Born* arena tour** to live out the ultimate rock god fantasy. "I hired a private jet for a couple of days, and that did seem excessive," he said. "Only because I couldn't get the band to do it, and I really wanted to. So I just said 'Screw you, I'll do it myself'. I used it to get home for a couple of days off. I don't regret it. It was a lot of fun [but] let's just say

---

* They wouldn't – the band travelled to Wembley in limousines.
** The tour was global and extensive, taking in a headline slot on the Big Day Out tour in Australia in January 2013, some UK arena dates that were rescheduled after being postponed due to Brandon straining his vocal cords in 2012, and major legs in Europe and North and South America before hitting Wembley.

[it cost] too much. I rented it by the hour, not the day, so the cost is a little less, but it was still ridiculous. But I'm glad I did it."[11]

Success, and the stresses, boredoms and tribulations hidden behind it, had made Dave a double-barrelled rock star. On one hand he'd occasionally play up to the brooding wildman clichés, venting anger on unsuspecting hotel furniture and resenting his image in the press. "I've been let down," he said. "Everyone thinks I'm so aggressive. I've broken a TV or two in hotel rooms but I'm not that bad a person." On the other he would sink into deep emotional grooves: "I do things like buy guitars to make myself feel better. Or maybe play basketball in the back yard by myself. I never have anyone to play with."[12]

He was often torn, just as keen on stardom as privacy. He'd resent half the front row watching Brandon drinking a bottle of water during his greatest guitar god moments onstage, but be thankful he didn't have to do the amount of interviews Brandon did to attain that sort of adoration and attention. He'd appreciate his time away from the rock world but talk with a little regret that he hadn't made his own solo album in the hiatus. "We all have ideas that don't get used for the band," he said. "I've got plenty. Most of them will probably never see the light of day, but I wouldn't mind doing something with some of them. In what context I don't know. I have acoustic songs that I don't do anything with because, to me, doing a song with just vocals and acoustic takes a lot of courage. I'm maybe too shy to put out an album like that."[13]

He'd claim that success hadn't really affected him – "People ask me all the time what it's like to be famous and I just tell them my life's a lot more busy. That's it. I'm pretty much the same person, I just have a lot more to do"[14] – but, almost in the same breath, he would regret the fact that the changing face of music consumption might have stopped his band matching *Appetite For Destruction*. "It's just impossible now," he said of multi-million album sales. "It just doesn't happen to anyone except Katy Perry but to get an album to hit 10 million would blow our minds… There's more stuff to do now. People play video games and watch songs on YouTube or maybe they just listen to the song two times and they never pay for it. It used to be that you had to buy the CD, the vinyl, or the cassette. I remember how precious it was having a vinyl record, the pride of ownership of having that record and the artwork on it – reading the inserts to the lyrics. I would listen to it several times a day. It was such a different experience when I was younger. Now I download things to my iPod and listen to it when I'm on the go. It's just junk food now the way people listen to music."[15]

So it was no surprise that Dave was simultaneously excited and insouciant about Wembley. "People couldn't care less about us in France, and that's just across the water," he'd say dismissively. "We played a festival there on the *Day & Age* tour, and the people in the front row could've drunk tea without spilling a drop. We had just played a major festival in England, so it was humbling to get there and have the crowd be like, 'Yeah, we're French and we don't care!'" Then, in the same interview, he'd alter his tune somewhat. "I don't get nervous for any show but if I think about this one too much, I might. We've seen other bands play there, and we've talked about it in terms of when we might be able to do it ourselves. But I don't think I realised just how big it was. Not too many bands have done it. It's pretty amazing when you think about all the different venues we've played in London. But this is the peak. This is Mount Everest."[16]

There was no question that for Brandon, however, Wembley was the gig he'd been waiting to play all his life. "It'll be one of the biggest stages we've ever been on. There aren't as many bands who've played there as I thought, so it means even more,"[17] he said. "I need to treat it like it's just another gig, but it isn't. This really means something to me. It's an honour."[18]

He'd had big ideas for the show, too. "We've been talking about building some kind of spacecraft for 'Spaceman' for a while, but it never pans out. Maybe one day. We're just gonna do what we do, but a little bigger and a little better. We've never played as well as we are right now; that's exciting."[19]

It was a far more relaxed and rounded Brandon Flowers who took to the Wembley stage than had graced the Dublin Castle or Tramps back in 2003. A Brandon who'd soothed his style to a classic homage to Steve McQueen, Paul Newman and Marlon Brando, and who was content with his wholesome on-the-road routine, using his days off to catch buses to go walk around the nearest national park – "it connects you with something"[20] – and skipping after-shows in favour of a Coke and an early night. "I'm at a point now where I don't even go out any more. On the road, there are times when there's a party that I'm going to want to go to to meet somebody cool, and I'll go. But it gets a little bit boring drinking Coke after a while and you just go back to the bus."[21]

Though backstage onlookers would note Brandon stressing over set lists* and photos and quibbling over the size of his Coke cans or the inadequate padding protecting the band's on-the-road table tennis table, onstage he'd become a consummate, high-spirited showman. He was becoming more playful with and appreciative of his success; his ease of performance and quick wit** would emerge when he dropped a quick tongue-in-cheek verse of The Beatles' 'When I'm Sixty-Four' into The Killers' headline slot at the Isle Of Wight festival, in reference to the island being the chosen retirement destination for the song's protagonist, and his lingering humility shone through when he'd insist in interviews that he remained a long way off the A-list. "I don't feel like a celebrity," he said. "It's never been on the agenda to be a celebrity. When you're coming up you don't realise there's a difference between being famous and being a celebrity. Celebrities do red carpets and go to nightclubs and have their publicists call to inform the press when they're going to be eating at the Ivy. That's never been our agenda. Maybe I'm more famous than I ever thought I would be, I guess. I don't wake up and feel famous. I don't feel any different. I'm thankful for the success and that I get to sing and play music for a living, but I don't think about it too often. I get brought right back to the real world as soon as I go back home. I have three sons and a wife... It keeps my head in the right place."[22]

He'd largely kicked the old habit of sniping at his rock rivals, too; having found a sense of peace with himself, he no longer needed to tread on other bands to feel worthy. "I only did it to hide the fact that I never

---

* Brandon always wanted more new songs on the *Battle Born* tour setlists.
** His bandmates would often credit Brandon with a hidden wit that only they got to see.

felt sufficient," he said. "I never felt I had a sufficient education, yet there I was, going to these thriving metropolises of the world, supposed to entertain people."[23] But then his calming may just have been down to a lack of competition in 2013. "When we were starting out, there was always something coming around, like Hard-Fi, or somebody would come out with something that made you think 'OK, in a couple of records' time, these guys could be big'. I can't think of anybody like that today. But I like The Vaccines and the first Hurts record."[24]

Instead, Brandon reserved his wrath for the rising tide of electronica. "[EDM] had taken over Las Vegas," he grumbled. "Those guys – David Guetta, Deadmau5 – they're the superstars. They're doing residencies at the big casino nightclubs. I've always had a foot in the synth world, so some of that stuff is OK, but… I just don't understand how you can get attached to it. How can it shape you, the way a rock band can shape you? Daft Punk? I've only heard the single ['Get Lucky']. And I totally understand why it's huge. But I'm so sick of people stealing. I'm not trying to pick a fight with Daft Punk, but I hear the Michael Jackson references in the vocal melody and the chord progression and it bugs me. And I'm just so sick of songs about fucking."[25]

And, after all those years, Brandon had finally come to terms with the dichotomy at the very core of his life; the anti-rebellion rock star. "I want to be myself," he argued. "I live my life how I want to. Isn't that the idea of what rock'n'roll is? I am more rock'n'roll than anybody else that you're going to meet."[26]

So this was The Killers that entered their tenth year of international touring in 2013; older, wiser, largely mellower and eternally thankful. To mark their more career-defining shows they'd play club dates straight after the main set, such as the early-hours show of rarities, covers and major hits at the Highbury Garage that I was bundled into through the stage door following their Wembley triumph. "We've done a few gigs recently where afterwards we'll go out and play some shitty 200-capacity bar," Ronnie explained, "and we've been using that to get into the back catalogue. We were playing songs we haven't played for years."[27] "Those are our roots, and we enjoy playing those shows," Brandon added. "It's also about keeping the machine well oiled."[28]

Reaching the stadium league virtually dead-on their 10-year anniversary; this needed a true rock toast. And what better way to hail their arrival than with their first greatest hits compilation, *Direct Hits*, slated for a November 11 release. As on previous tours, the band had been writing for their fifth album while on the road and then demoing up the songs in their breaks back in Vegas, and in July and August of 2013, back at Battle Born, they began working up two new songs to add to the compilation for fan-friendly freshness. One, 'Just Another Girl', was born from a collaboration between Brandon and "my brother" Stuart Price and recorded ad hoc during the tour, wherever the band could grab studio time. "It's The Killers but I don't feel like everybody put their prints on it," Ronnie said of the track. "We're all playing on it, but we had to do things in stages, we were on the road. I cut those drums in fuckin' Cincinnati in a back room, then Stuart processed them. It's not what would happen normally."[29]

'Just Another Girl' would act as the greatest hits' solidifying round-up song, a consolidation of everything The Killers had achieved up to 2013. A fiery melodic rock tune racked with heartache over a girl that, despite his friends' advice to forget her and move on, the hero simply can't forget, it harked back to career-forging tracks like 'Mr. Brightside' and 'Midnight Show' and, when it was released as the second single from the compilation in November, it came with a video that nodded to the entire Killers history. Dressed in Brandon's iconic feather jacket, actress Dianna Agron – famous for her role in American musical-comedy TV series *Glee* – wandered through recreations of a variety of old Killers videos, from the boudoir of 'Mr. Brightside' to the desertscape performance of 'Human' and the Killersluts stand-off from 'All These Things That I've Done'. Slapping on a false moustache to march through the Mexican wedding scene from 'When You Were Young' and Brandon's cartoon-red astronaut suit to recreate 'Spaceman' while cradling a skeleton hand from the 'Bones' video, she wanders past a whole decade of Killers ephemera, be it the giant video screen from 'Somebody Told Me', a living *Sam's Town* sleeve, the blue-robed gospel choir of the original 'All These Things…' clip or the speckled moon of *Day & Age*. A four-minute Killers recap, it would make for an obsessive reference-spotter's wildest dream.

The first new single from the album, 'Shot At The Night'*, meanwhile, pointed the way forward. Having played with French electronic pop pioneers M83 for a few weeks at the start of 2009 on the *Day & Age* tour, the band decided, on the advice of their label Island Records, to invite their main man, Anthony Gonzalez, to produce a new track with them. "We love Anthony," Brandon said. "He's one of the best ping-pong players that I've encountered in my life. I guess in France they teach these things. He also loves a lot of the same music that we do, and so it was great to finally come together and do it."[30]

"There was a mutual thing like, 'Yeah we think he's good. We'll try him out.' It's something we finally agreed with our label on,"[31] said Dave, and Brandon added, "He's one of these new school producers. He's a technical wizard, but you can't discount his musicality. A lot of people do, because of the involvement of computers, but he's a real musician, too. He and Stuart Price may be known for working on the digital side of things, but they're also two of the most musical guys I've ever met."[32]

"We're at that point in the career of the band where we have that licence to sort of play around a little bit," Ronnie added, "do some collaborations with people and make it happen. Who knows what you might stumble on? So I welcome that sort of thing."[33] The song, Ronnie explained, went through several incarnations as they figured out how best to work together. "We're still working on it down in the studio, horsing around," he said in July. "We were sort of at odds with this one song, we didn't really know where to go with it. We did it Anthony's way, stripped it all back, and he sort of gave us another perspective. It sounds really cool. I'm up for taking chances, it's fun to experiment, and it's very much an experiment. It's organic."[34] Ronnie also appreciated Gonzalez's stripped-back approach to their sound. "We

---

* Premiered on nme.com on September 16, 2013, the tenth anniversary of The Killers' debut London gig, ahead of a digital download-only release in November.

can be guilty of making things so ornate, and sometimes that's a bad thing. So I always have conversations with Brandon about working from a smaller palette, simplifying things."[35]

There were hopes that, if the sessions with Gonzalez went well, it could signal the direction for their next album; instead, 'Shot At The Night' was destined to be a one-off collaboration. Taking on the repetitive lyrical imperviousness of electronic music, the song was built around the suggestion of chances waiting to be taken and the possibilities of nocturnal Nevada. "Once in a lifetime," Brandon repeated over the perfect blend of human soft rock and ultra-cool electronic chill, "give me a shot at the night, give me a moment, some kind of mysterious".

"It's a perfect fit for Anthony," Brandon said. "I was in the middle of touring when we recorded it and I think my voice sounds great, and that's something to take into consideration. If you haven't been keeping the cords lubed up it's not the best, so it's made me think about my time off and how I'm going to practise."[36]

With those two new tracks fixed to close *Direct Hits**, originally to be called 'Cream' in contrast to their B-side compilation 'Sawdust'**, it only remained to decide on the rest of the track list. The band decided to include their singles chronologically but omitted 'Bones', 'Tranquilize', 'The World We Live In' and 'Here With Me' in favour of 'The Way It Was'. "That was never a single that maybe should've been a single," Brandon mused. "And I wonder if 'This River Is Wild' should be on there... you're never going to be completely happy. [But] I feel like this puts a lot of things in perspective. When I look at it, I'm really proud of it, but I'm also really excited about evolving and growing. I look at the songs that maybe are my favourites on it, and maybe I'm wondering if I need to conjure up those spirits, if they're still in there."[37]

---

* Plus additional bonus tracks on the deluxe edition: 'Be Still', a Calvin Harris remix of 'When You Were Young' and a demo of 'Mr. Brightside'.

** Brandon's vision of the sleeve of 'Cream' was the Hoover Dam holding back a reservoir of cream.

As *Direct Hits* was fired towards its target*, however, it looked for a moment as if it might be The Killers' final shot.

★ ★ ★

"I'm sick of this," Dave blurted out backstage at an arena a world away from Wembley. "I'm done. The end is in sight. Some people might go, [adopts sarcastic voice] 'Why are you complaining?' But you haven't done what I've done, so you can't relate."[38]

Shanghai, China, October 3, 2013 and, after a solid year on the *Battle Born* tour, Dave was destroyed again. The fact that the Mercedes-Benz Arena was only a third full due to the high price of tickets – up to £128 – and the show falling on a national holiday, plus the news that the restrictive authorities had banned them from playing some of their songs, certainly didn't help. "We've just... toured a shitload... 'Change Your Mind' was on our set lists but we forgot to submit the lyrics, so we're not allowed to play that. And even... cats playing. I was trying to watch a cat playing on YouTube and I couldn't because the site is banned here."[39]

This was the first time the band had ever made it to China, having cancelled all previous shows there, the *Day & Age* dates because Brandon's mother had died. "We talked about starting [the *Battle Born* tour in China] because we missed that tour, but it didn't make any sense routing-wise," said Ronnie. "We're glad to be coming there now though – better late than never... It's exhausting, we've just come off having played for more than a year straight. We're playing better than we ever have before, so that's good. The shows are better than they've ever been."[40]

In China, The Killers were a broken band. Ronnie was as "fried" as Dave and Mark hadn't even made it onto the plane for reasons unknown. Band representatives were citing "personal reasons" for Mark being replaced by session bassist Jake Blanton for the short final string

---

* It hit number six in the UK, number 20 on the US *Billboard* Chart and made dents in 12 other countries worldwide.

of dates running through South-East Asia and culminating in the Palm venue in Dubai; Mark himself claimed he'd injured his back. Even his bandmates weren't certain of the truth, or if Mark's break would turn out to be permanent.

"His back is totally fucked," Ronnie confirmed. "I've spoken with him about it, I don't know how much he wants in the open... I don't want to blow the top on it. But look, being part of this machine is physically and mentally exhausting... If he ever [leaves], that's his decision. I'd hope we'd keep on truckin'. But at the same time, it isn't the same band."[41]

Brandon put his usual brave, smiley face on the situation. "We have our ups and downs," he said. "I hear different stories [about Mark] all the time. He's tired... something physical, something mental. I can't force him to come here. But it's fine, we're getting through. Whatever's happening now [with Stoermer] is going to be fine by the time we make another record."[42] He took his mind off the temporary split with a band visit to the Great Wall Of China* and didn't hold back onstage, throwing his jacket into the crowd at the peak of his performance. "It's an honour that we can draw this many people," he said of the smaller-than-expected crowd, "it's a far cry from Las Vegas. It was a high playing Wembley, but playing an arena is still a rush."[43]

Yet all of The Killers were speaking openly about another lengthy break at the end of the *Battle Born* tour. "[The last hiatus] was a nice little reset," Ronnie said. "After this tour we're going to need another reset because we hit it so hard. It's tough to do, man, it fucks with your mind a little bit. It's not only the physical stress of being here, there and everywhere in a month's time, it does mess with your brain a little bit. You've got to take time to be normal at some point, otherwise you get weird."[44]

The break, he suggested, would be substantial. "I think it will be a little while," he said. "I don't think it will take an unnaturally long time

---

* "It was a ball-buster," Ronnie said of the rather arduous trek that, just two days earlier, Justin Bieber had taken on his security guard's back. "*We* didn't have any bodyguards to carry us..." Source: *NME*, Jamie Fullerton, October 12, 2013.

for us to get together, [but] it's time to take a breather and ground out a little bit. I think everybody is looking forward to putting their feet up for a little while and having some normalcy."[45]

"I'm excited about going home," Brandon agreed. "I'm looking forward to having a normal year. But I'm going to write. I'm going to be filing those diamonds – it's my job."[46] He was also looking forward to "putting my heart and soul" into a second solo album. "I'm definitely going to do another solo record," he promised. "*Flamingo* wasn't just me dipping my toes in the water. I really loved it. It was successful, and that helps, but I love those songs and I miss singing them. It wasn't something I had totally planned on, but I'm always writing songs, and I think – or I hope – that I'm always gonna have that. So what else am I supposed to do with myself?"[47]

Ronnie was also planning to resurrect his Big Talk side project. "I'm already starting it," he said. "I like to keep moving. I love that notion of momentum. I think some of the guys are just going to chill out, keep writing probably, make sure to get some rest."[48] "I'm looking forward to doing it again, if it makes sense. I've got some stuff ready, it just depends on what we end up doing, if we take a break after this or we keep writing. We have a pile of Killers stuff, then there's a pile of game show music and a pile of Big Talk stuff. I show everything to the guys, and whatever sort of sticks, we use."[49]

Their talk of time apart didn't signal a lasting split though; The Killers knew they still had work to do, territories to conquer, hearts to win, masterpieces to make. "We're writing stuff," said Dave. "We're not sure when the next album is coming out or what it'll be, but we always write, even if we're on tour. I don't think it'll be as long... I should stop there."[50]

"We haven't made our *Sgt. Pepper's...* yet," Mark had said earlier in the year. 'We've made good albums and great songs, but that sort of ground-breaking album is the one thing we haven't done."[51] And if Mark was focusing on the band's artistic ambitions, Ronnie still saw the drive to expand live. "To be able to reach this same level, in all these different countries, that would really be something. Like, let's try and do this in America. Let's try and do this around the world. Let U2 be

U2, and let's try to figure out how to connect with large amounts of people in a different way."[52]

Indeed, with a headline slot in the offing at V Festival 2014 and an eighth annual Christmas song, 'Christmas In L.A.', released on December 1, 2013*, the Killers this writer last saw exiting the stage in a fountain of ticker-tape and glitter at the Hammersmith Apollo on November 6, 2013, after a glorious celebratory launch show for *Direct Hits*, seemed more together, enthused and alive as a creative force than ever. A band that had battled through 10 years of fabulous highs and soul-searching lows. Had devoured and confounded their critics at every turn and consistently delighted millions of fans. And had redefined not only what an alternative rock'n'roll band from Las Vegas could achieve but what the Best British Band From America was actually capable of.

The world remains theirs for the slaughtering.

---

* 'Christmas In L.A.' was a mournful country ballad featuring Taylor Goldsmith from US folk rockers Dawes, telling of a lonely struggling actor looking back at the small-town life he'd left behind as he spends the festive period in a deserted Los Angeles. Continuing the band's recent spate of celebrity video cameos, Owen Wilson played the lead in the part-animated clip alongside Harry Dean Stanton as the old-time actor he tries to talk to in a bar.

Mark Stoermer, April 2014

How was Wembley?

It was an important show and I'm glad we did it and it was a milestone. We did set that date early in the tour, or even before the tour, and we all had it in mind. The show itself, for me personally, I couldn't hear anything in the monitors, was kinda freaked out, I was playing watching my fingers. I think we pulled it off and did a pretty good show but it wasn't enjoyable to me. It was enjoyable seeing the audience get into it but I wasn't able to feel the music and be in it. I believed that we needed five days of production rehearsal minimum, I think we did two. We talked about five early on and everyone agreed to that, then it got cut down to do another a gig over here or something. Talking to an acquaintance, Dom from Muse, the drummer, they've done Wembley before us and we were talking about it and he said "You guys have to do at least five days". He explained why and it all made logical sense and I agreed and I brought that to the band and it was on the schedule for a while. Before you know it, agents get involved and then you have two days. With two days, we'd never played on a stage that big and I couldn't hear myself that well, I don't think Brandon really heard himself that well. The other thing is, that's the day I believe my tinnitus really started, which I've never talked about. I have really bad tinnitus now and I think it was from an explosion that happened onstage that made me go deaf for about two seconds during 'Miss Atomic Bomb'. No one informed me that "Y'know that explosion, that cue in the song, it's gonna be a hundred times louder than usual". The next couple of days I had ringing that just wouldn't go away and it's still not going away. I've seen people and they basically say you can't do anything, you can hope that it lessens but there's no real cure for it. All the years of not playing with in-ear monitors I was doing all right, but I think it was that explosion.

How did 'Wembley Song' come about?

That was Brandon's idea. It's pretty impressive, he can write a song pretty quickly when he wants to and he wrote that song a couple of days before. We had to learn that in soundcheck. I was playing with the chords on the ground because it wasn't a simple chord progression, every verse was different.

How was the rest of the tour? Fun, tough, draining?
A little bit of everything, in some ways all of the tours have been that. The worst thing was some of the travelling. We had nightmares travelling in Russia with our own plane and it got grounded there, we thought we were stuck in Russia. Then we thought we were gonna die coming out of Colombia in one of the worst plane flights in our 10 years. We hit really bad turbulence multiple times where everybody on the plane was scared for their life. It happened in the very beginning of our career, then it was okay for the most part, but that was on the level of that one where everybody was really scared. The plane broke down in Europe a couple of times. Once we were delayed 10 hours in Spain. We thought we were doing the rock star thing, leaving the festival and going straight on the plane at two in the morning, and there was a miscommunication, the pilot wasn't even awake. We had to sit there until nine in the morning to wait to leave.

So the private plane wasn't quite the U2 life you expected?
No, it was terrible. I'd have much rather have done a regular commercial flight. And we were doing it with the crew so we had to wait with the crew, so it wasn't just a cool jump-on-the-plane-and-leave.

You missed shows in China towards the end of the tour, was that down to your back problem?
It was that and the tinnitus actually. It was getting really bad and I wanted to see someone and I saw someone there but they can't do that much; I'm still working on getting the proper ear protection, I'm in the process of refining that, trying a couple of different things. By that point it was starting to get painful to even be onstage, and with the way this tour was scheduled there's never a day to get checked out and then practise with maybe a new ear monitor or something, since there's no practices. The back problem started probably all the way back in 2005 but it kinda went away for years. It was aggravated at the beginning of the *Battle*

Born tour and it was coming and going but at that point it was getting pretty bad again, and that combined with the ear, I needed to take a break. Honestly, everything was much longer than they said it was going to be when we started the tour, too. I said "I've already done more than I signed up for and I need to see a doctor about my ears and my back's not getting any better". At the moment it is a little bit better but it's an ongoing thing.

Did it feel odd not being on the Chinese tour?
A little bit but I have no regrets. I would've felt worse doing it. I was looking at the schedule and they were bouncing on everywhere. They were from Singapore working their way back to Japan on a plane every day – some of the flights are six to eight hours – and then they went to Dubai, which is the other way again. The way I was feeling, I looked at the schedule and went "I'm glad I'm not doing that". If I regret anything, I spoke to Dave about it and he mentioned a couple of shows, especially the one in Japan was good, and we'd never really had a good show in Japan. I kinda wish I was there for that but I don't regret that I didn't do that entire tour because I wasn't ready for it, I made the right decision for myself.

Were the same fractures emerging towards the end of the tour? Dave certainly seemed tired of the road by then.
Probably a little bit of that. When we got back together we had a talk about it, that we were gonna do it a certain way with more breaks, that we were never gonna go more than three weeks. And by the time we start adding dates and managers and agents get involved things are going six weeks straight, y'know? And then it's like "Okay, we're already in it". Things got switched on us in the middle of the tour as far as the amount of it. I'm not saying that to complain about workload or anything, this is more of an internal difference. Personally I would tour forever if it was at a pace that I liked, where I still think it's fun to do the show, I can get up there and give my all, I'm not thinking that I'd rather be home. I could do that years and years straight, but everyone has a different threshold, and it's tough finding the balance when you've got four guys. It went

over our threshold in our different ways, but it's not like me and Dave have an alliance – we just happen to be on the same side of that, but for different reasons.

Were there any other issues?
If there's any other issue for me – and I don't know if it's an issue because maybe it's just the way it goes because bands change – but what I was bringing up about the producers from *Day & Age* on, it's a different story if you're touring two years straight and you feel like "This is my record, I love this record, I was in this". That's how it was for *Hot Fuss*, that's how it was for *Sam's Town*. I think for me and Dave a little bit, it started to feel like we weren't as involved. There's a lot of cooks in the kitchen, there's not even room for the four guys in the band sometimes on the record. Of course Brandon's gonna be involved and that's fine, I understand why, because he's the main songwriter and the lead singer, I'm not contesting that. But we have five producers – that's more producers than band members. Something's gonna give, and I think what has given is some creative input or even some say on something as simple as a mix. Then, maybe you don't realise it when it happens, but you get into a tour and you're a year into it, you don't feel as much attachment to this album that you're supposed to be giving your life to. It's a different story back on *Hot Fuss* and *Sam's Town* because it's a four-piece and I felt that these albums are at least a quarter me. *Battle Born* feels like it's 7 per cent me, and not because I didn't try but because there wasn't room.

Have there been any personal issues between the band?
Nothing obvious or overt. I think we're all different personalities, but that's been the same throughout. In some ways if anything our success has amplified each person's personality but everybody's basically the same. But it becomes a little bit strained because it's starts getting to "I don't have to deal with you, I don't have to listen". Back in the day when we disagreed we had to come to a conclusion. Now everyone's ego is inflated and I think that's probably the typical story of a band that's been together 10 years.

How have you changed?
I don't know, it's hard to say. In general I feel the same, I feel the way anyone does as they get older, that you're still growing. I feel a bit older and wiser but at the same time a bit tired and slightly jaded sometimes. But there's good days when I don't feel jaded and you're like "Oh yeah, this is as fun as it used to be". I think that's what happens when you get older. It's the trade-off – you gain a little wisdom but you lose a little of the excitement.

Are you planning on another solo record?
I work on music, I'm kind of going in circles at the moment. I only want to do something if it's fun and it's good, it doesn't necessarily have to be a solo record even. I'm open. I work on music in my back room but if it doesn't feel right I just put it away. I'm always hacking away at something. I'd like to maybe do some kind of tour on my own, even if it's small clubs, and I'd like to do another album, whether it was a side project or another solo album. But I only wanna do it if it feels right. I don't wanna tour the one I did just by itself, unless I make a second one. So if it's right I wanna do something and I'm always working towards something but I don't know what.

Will it be a lengthy break this time?
Well we're kind of on tour anyway, little short tours. There's still 10 gigs in the year. Maybe – Brandon's doing a record, Ronnie's doing a record, we're all getting older. We'll see.

Dave Keuning, March 2014

You hired a plane for some parts of the *Battle Born* tour, was this a step up in your on-the-road indulgences?
I don't think it felt much different to *Day & Age* or *Sam's Town*. That plane was a shitty plane. We had it for less than a week because we had some shows that were hard to fly out of, like Russia and stuff. I hated that plane, I'll never get in that plane again. It was smaller than most

coach seats, the seats wouldn't lean back – it was like an older plane, that's why we could afford to rent it.

How was Wembley?

That was a great moment. Probably a top five Killers moment. I could have been done after that and I would have slept fine. It was such a massive show, to fill it out was pretty special.

Who wrote 'Wembley Song'?

Brandon wrote that, I thought it was goofy. It was a good idea, I was wrong. It was kind of thrown together at the last minute and I thought, "What is this?". [The fans] loved it, it was pretty cool.

What was it like being on the road for so long?

It dragged on for me. It was over a year and a half.

What are the band's plans at the moment?

I can't really comment on what we're doing right now, anything is possible, it's just up in the air. We are on a much needed break and that's all I know. I'm enjoying being at home but I do have an itch to make music, too. I can't predict the future right now. We could make another album or we could enjoy people's solo projects for a few years. I think it was nice to put out the greatest hits until we figure it out.

Any plans to do that solo album?

I'm just not motivated time-wise. I'm totally fine with just being the guitar player in The Killers, that's enough for me. I do have a lot of music piling up that needs using, probably not with The Killers, even if they did like it. I have a lot of different stuff. Just be patient. I'm not really looking to sing, I was totally content just playing guitar. That's all I ever set out to do when I was 14. There isn't that much envy that makes me want to sing – I'm curious about it, it might be fun, but I mostly like playing guitar and writing. I have songs that could have other people's lyrics.

Acknowledgements

It's a rare source of immense satisfaction for the biographer of a band they love when the band in question embraces the project. Such was thankfully the case with *Days & Ages*. For deciding to contribute interviews and corrections to the book, I'd like to thank The Killers and, for their help in making this happen and for additional interviews, many thanks to Robert Reynolds and Rachel Hendry. Special thanks to Braden Merrick for granting me extensive interviews and assistance, and also to Ricky Wilson, Zane Lowe, Martin Noble, Matt Caughthran, Simon Williams, Richard Cassar, Ben Durling, Alex Gilbert, Kate Booker, Ben Ayers, Rob Fitzpatrick and anyone I may have forgotten for granting, arranging or passing on interviews. Thanks to Martin Robinson and *Shortlist* magazine for permission to reprint transcripts from my previous Killers interviews, to my editor, Lucy Beevor, and to the very understanding Chris Charlesworth and David Barraclough at Omnibus Press. Thanks to my agent Isabel Atherton at Creative Authors – to whom, once again, I direct any publishers of fiction who have enjoyed this book – and to my ever-patient and supportive partner, Jane Lancaster, for letting me work through yet another Christmas.

Notes

INTRODUCTION
(Endnotes)
1 *NME,* July 3, 2004
2 ibid.
3 ibid.

CHAPTER ONE
 1 *Clash,* Simon Harper, July 2004
 2 *NME,* Tim Jonze, December 25, 2004
 3 *Spin,* Elizabeth Goodman, November 9, 2004
 4 Q, Laura Barton, March 2009
 5 *Shortlist,* Mark Beaumont, September 2012
 6 Q, Simon Goddard, September 1, 2010
 7 *Entertainment Weekly,* Ray Rahman, August 31, 2012
 8 *Spin,* Marc Spitz, February 2004
 9 *The Observer,* Craig McLean, September 24, 2006
10 Q, Simon Goddard, September 1, 2010
11 *NME,* December 16/23, 2006
12 Q, Nick Duerden, July 2005

13 *Shortlist*, Mark Beaumont, September 2012
14 ibid.
15 Q, Michael Odell, September 2004
16 *The Guardian*, Nick Kent, October 20, 2006
17 ibid.
18 *NME*, Rob Fitzpatrick, January 22, 2005
19 ibid.
20 *Entertainment Weekly*, Ray Rahman, August 31, 2012
21 *The Aquarian Weekly*, Jordana Borensztajn, January 20, 2009
22 *The Sunday Times Style*, January 9, 2005
23 *Spin*, Marc Spitz, February 2005
24 *Hot Press*, Stuart Clark, July 6, 2005
25 *Boyz*, May 20, 2004
26 *NME*, December 25, 2004
27 *The Independent*, Alexia Loundras, June 25, 2004
28 *Boyz*, May 20, 2004
29 Q, Simon Goddard, September 1, 2010
30 *The Independent*, Alexia Loundras, June 25, 2004
31 *Playmusic*, April 2005
32 *The Big Issue*, Dorian Lynskey, January 17, 2005
33 *The Times*, Amber Cowan, January 8, 2005
34 *The Beat*, Alasdair Duncan, 2012
35 Q, Simon Goddard, September 1, 2010
36 Q, Laura Barton, March 2009
37 ibid.
38 *Time Out Chicago*, Brent DiCrescenzo, August 3, 2009
39 ibid.
40 *The Observer*, Craig McLean, September 24, 2006
41 *Boyz*, January 6, 2005
42 *The Big Issue*, Dorian Lynskey, January 17, 2005
43 Q, Laura Barton, March 2009
44 Spotify, Diego Planas Rego, September 17, 2012
45 GQ, August 2005
46 Spotify, Diego Planas Rego, September 17, 2012
47 Q, Simon Goddard, September 1, 2010

48 Q, Laura Barton, March 2009
49 Q, Simon Goddard, September 1, 2010
50 *Playmusic*, Robert Collin, April 2005
51 ibid.
52 Q, Ben Mitchell, November 1, 2012
53 *Rolling Stone*
54 Q, Simon Goddard, September 1, 2010
55 *TV Hits*, May 2005
56 Q, Laura Barton, March 2009
57 Q, Michael Odell, December 2004

CHAPTER TWO
 1 *Guitar World*, February 2009
 2 *NME*, December 16/23, 2006
 3 *Guitar World*, June 2005
 4 Q, Laura Barton, March 2009
 5 *Ultimate Guitar*, Steven Rosen, November 12, 2012
 6 ibid.
 7 *Los Angeles County Register*, Kyle Munson
 8 ibid.
 9 ibid.
10 *Ultimate Guitar*, Steven Rosen, November 12, 2012
11 *Clash*, Simon Harper, March 2004
12 *Ultimate Guitar*, Steven Rosen, November 12, 2012
13 *Clash*, Simon Harper, March 2004
14 *Guitar World*, February 2009
15 *Clash*, Simon Harper, March 2004
16 *Guitar World*, February 2009
17 ibid.
18 *Ultimate Guitar*, Steven Rosen, November 14, 2012
19 *Guitar World*, February 2009
20 *Ultimate Guitar*, Steven Rosen, November 14, 2012
21 *Las Vegas Mercury*, Ted Sablay, July 25, 2002
22 *Total Guitar*, Henry Yates, June 2005
23 *Guitar World*, February 2009

24 *Ultimate Guitar*, Steven Rosen, November 14, 2012
25 *NME*, Gavin Haynes, November 29, 2008
26 popmatters.com, February 11, 2010
27 *The Times*, Amber Cowan, January 8, 2005
28 *Ultimate Guitar*, Steven Rosen, November 14, 2012
29 popmatters.com, February 11, 2010
30 *Las Vegas Sun*, Spencer Patterson, April 16, 2010
31 ibid.
32 ibid.
33 ibid.
34 *Attitude*, Martin Aston, July 2004
35 *Spin*, February 2005
36 *The Killers: Destiny Is Calling Me*, Jarret Keene (Manic D Press, 2006)
37 *Bullit*, Trevor Baker, July 2004
38 *Las Vegas Sun*, Spencer Patterson, April 16, 2010
39 *Bullit*, Trevor Baker, July 2004
40 *Las Vegas Sun*, Spencer Patterson, April 16, 2010
41 ibid.
42 ibid.
43 *The Independent*, Alexia Loundras, June 25, 2004
44 *Clash*, Simon Harper, March 2004
45 *Attitude*, Martin Aston, July 2004
46 *Las Vegas Sun*, Spencer Patterson, April 16, 2010
47 ibid.
48 *NME*, Tim Jonze, January 2004
49 *The Sunday Times Style*, Simon Mills, October 9, 2005
50 *Las Vegas Sun*, Spencer Patterson, April 16, 2010
51 ibid.
52 ibid.
53 ibid.
54 *The Guardian*, Nick Kent, October 20, 2006
55 *The Killers: Destiny Is Calling Me*, Jarret Keene (Manic D Press, 2006)
56 *Las Vegas Sun*, Spencer Patterson, April 16, 2010
57 ibid.
58 ibid.

59 ibid.

60 ibid.

61 ibid.

62 ibid.

63 ibid.

64 *Ultimate Guitar*, Steven Rosen, November 14, 2012

65 *The Observer*, Craig McLean, September 24, 2006

66 *Las Vegas Mercury*, Ted Sablay, July 25, 2002

67 ibid.

68 ibid.

69 *Las Vegas Sun*, Spencer Patterson, April 16, 2010

70 ibid.

71 ibid.

72 ibid.

CHAPTER THREE

1 Q, Laura Barton, March 2009

2 ibid.

3 *Groupie Magazine*, November 12, 2008

4 Spotify, Diego Planas Rego, September 17, 2012

5 ibid.

6 Q, Laura Barton, March 2009

7 ibid.

8 ibid.

9 *Rock Sound*, Pierre Perrone, March 2004

10 *NME*, December 16/23, 2006

11 *NME*, Tim Jonze, December 25, 2004

12 ibid.

13 *NME*, Gavin Haynes, November 29, 2008

14 worldwithoutborders.com

15 *X-Ray*, Amber Cowan, December 2003

16 *Spin*, February 2005

17 ibid.

18 Q, Laura Barton, March 2009

19 *Rhythm*, Roger Hadfield, October 2004

20 *Las Vegas Sun*, Spencer Patterson, April 16, 2010

21 ibid.

22 ibid.

23 *Spin*, February 2005

24 Q, Ben Mitchell, November 1, 2012

25 Q, Laura Barton, March 2009

26 *NME*, July 10, 2004

27 *NME*, March 20, 2004

28 *The Independent*, Alexia Loundras, June 25, 2004

29 *NME*, Gavin Haynes, November 29, 2008

30 Q, Nick Duerden, July 2005

31 *The Observer*, Craig McLean, September 24, 2006

32 *Rhythm*, Roger Hadfield, October 2004

33 *The Killers: Destiny Is Calling Me*, Jarret Keene (Manic D Press, San Francisco, 2006)

34 *NME*, Mark Beaumont, August 17, 2004

35 *The Killers: Destiny Is Calling Me*, Jarret Keene (Manic D Press, 2006)

36 *The Independent*, Alexia Loundras, June 25, 2004

37 *Evening Standard*, David Smyth, August 20, 2004

38 *Daily Mirror*, Gavin Martin, April 29, 2005

39 *Hot Press*, Stuart Clark, July 6, 2005

40 *Playmusic*, Robert Collins, April 2005

41 Q, Laura Barton, March 2009

42 *Ultimate Guitar*, Steven Rosen, November 14, 2012

43 *Spin*, February 2005

44 *Rock Sound*, Pierre Perrone, March 2004

45 *Spin*, Elizabeth Goodman, November 9, 2004

46 ibid.

47 *Attitude*, Martin Aston, July 2004

48 ibid.

49 *NME*, March 20, 2004

50 goldenplec.com, James Hendicott, July 25, 2013

51 *Boyz*, January 6, 2005

52 *NME*, Alex Rayner, March 20, 2004

53 Q, Michael Odell, December 2004

54 *Bullit*, Trevor Baker, July 2004
55 *Ultimate Guitar*, Steven Rosen, November 14, 2012
56 *Hot Press*, Stuart Clark, July 6, 2005
57 ibid.
58 *NME*, Gavin Haynes, November 29, 2008
59 *NME*, September 24, 2005
60 *NME*, Nicole Elyse, September 27, 2003
61 *Las Vegas CityLife*, Jarret Keene, September 3, 2003

CHAPTER FOUR

1 *The Killers: Vagabonds And Victims*, Jimmy Ramsay (Independent Music Press, Shropshire, 2005)
2 Q, Michael Odell, September 2004
3 *Time Out*, Harriet Gibsone, June 18, 2013
4 *Attitude*, Martin Aston, July 2004
5 beat.com.au, Alasdair Duncan, 2012
6 *The Sunday Times Style*, Simon Mills, October 9, 2005
7 *The Sunday Times*, September 7, 2003
8 Q, Simon Goddard, September 1, 2010
9 *Time Out*, Harriet Gibsone, June 18, 2013
10 ibid.
11 *Hot Press*, Stuart Clark, July 6, 2005
12 *NME*, Tim Jonze, September 7, 2003
13 homereviewsconcerts.com, Samantha Hall
14 *NME*, October 4, 2003
15 Q, Laura Barton, March 2009
16 ibid.
17 pollstar.com
18 *The Daily Record*, Rick Fulton, September 3, 2004
19 *Rhythm*, October 2004
20 *Sound Waves*, Nicole Roberge, June 2005
21 popmatters.com, Evan Sawdey, February 11, 2010
22 *Rock Sound*, Pierre Perrone, March 2004
23 *Ultimate Guitar*, Steven Rosen, November 14, 2012
24 *NME*, Alex Rayner, March 20, 2004

25 Q, Nick Duerden, July 2005

26 *Time Out*, Chris Parkin, July 7, 2004

27 *Daily Mirror*, Gavin Martin, April 29, 2005

28 *Big Issue*, Dorian Lynskey, January 17, 2005

29 *NME*, Mark Beaumont, August 5, 2004

30 ibid.

31 Q, Laura Barton, March 2009

32 *Total Guitar*, Henry Yates, June 2005

33 *Music Week*, November 22, 2003

34 Bedlam Society, Simon Becker-Sadava

35 *The Guardian*, Nick Kent, October 20, 2006

36 *Logo*, Liz Starbuck, June 2004

37 ibid.

38 *X-Ray*, Amber Cowan, December 2003

39 *Time Out*, Chris Parkin, July 7, 2004

40 live-magazine.co.uk, Lara Khajetoorians

41 *Clash*, Simon Harper, March 2004

42 *Time Out*, Harriet Gibsone, June 18, 2013

43 *Bullit*, Trevor Baker, July 2004

44 *The Independent*, Alexia Loundras, June 25, 2004

45 *NME*, Mark Beaumont, August 5, 2004

46 *NME*, Tim Jonze, January 2004

47 *The Daily Record*, Rick Fulton, September 3, 2004

48 *Rock Sound*, Pierre Perrone, March 2004

49 *The Killers: Destiny Is Calling Me*, Jarret Keene (Manic D Press, 2006)

50 *The Sunday Times*, December 22, 2003

51 *NME*, March 20, 2004

52 *Clash*, Simon Harper, March 2004

53 *NME*, Pete Cashmore, March 13, 2004

54 *Time Out*, Harriet Gibsone, June 18, 2013

55 ibid.

56 *Clash*, Simon Harper, March 2004

57 ibid.

58 ibid.

59 Q, Michael Odell, December 2004

60 *Ladygunn*, September 17, 2012
61 *Guitar Magazine*, June 2004
62 *NME*, August 27, 2005
63 *The Independent*, Alexia Loundras, June 25, 2004
64 Q, Nick Duerden, July 2005
65 *The Evening Standard*, David Smyth, August 20, 2004
66 Q, Michael Odell, December 2004
67 *The Sunday Times*, Dan Cairns, May 24, 2004
68 ibid.
69 ibid.
70 ibid.
71 ibid.
72 *Guitar World*, February 2009
73 Q, Glastonbury Review, July 2004

CHAPTER FIVE

 1 *Music Week*, April 24, 2004
 2 *NME*, Mark Beaumont, August 5, 2004
 3 *The Fly*, Ian Abraham, June 1, 2004
 4 *NME*, Dan Martin, July 1, 2004
 5 *The Times*, Johnny Dee, June 5, 2004
 6 *Hot Press*, Stuart Clark, July 6, 2005
 7 *The Guardian*, Nick Kent, October 20, 2006
 8 Q, Glastonbury Review, July 2004
 9 *NME*, Mark Beaumont, August 5, 2004
10 ibid.
11 ibid.
12 ibid.
13 *The Fly*, Ian Abraham, June 1, 2004
14 *The Independent*, Alexia Loundras, June 25, 2004
15 *Spin*, Elizabeth Goodman, November 9, 2004
16 *Time Out*, Chris Parkin, February 16, 2005
17 *The Guardian*, Nick Kent, October 20, 2006
18 *Spin*, February 2005
19 *Rolling Stone*, Jenny Eliscu, July 8, 2004

20 *Time Out*, Harriet Gibsone, June 18, 2013

21 *The Daily Record*, July 12, 2013

22 *Playmusic*, Robert Collins, April 2005

23 *NME Yearbook*, Tim Jonze, November 2004

24 ibid.

25 *NME*, Peter Robinson, August 1, 2004

26 *NME*, Rob Fitzpatrick, January 22, 2005

27 ibid.

28 *The Sun*, Jacqui Swift, December 24, 2004

29 *NME Yearbook*, Tim Jonze, November 2004

30 *NME*, September 24, 2005

31 *Daily Mirror*, Gavin Martin, April 29, 2005

32 *Las Vegas CityLife*, Jarret Keene, October 7, 2004

33 *NME*, Peter Robinson, August 1, 2004

34 MTV.com

35 *The Guardian Guide*, Tony Horkins, January 22, 2005

36 *The Killers: Vagabonds And Victims*, Jimmy Ramsay (Independent Music Press, 2005)

37 ibid.

38 *NME*, Tim Jonze, December 25, 2004

39 *The Times*, Amber Cowan, January 8, 2005

40 *Boyz*, January 6, 2005

41 *The Big Issue*, Dorian Lynskey, January 17, 2005

42 *NME*, Tim Jonze, December 25, 2004

43 *Spin*, Marc Spitz, February 2005

44 *NME*, Barry Nicolson, September 25, 2005

45 *The Sun*, Jacqui Swift, December 24, 2004

46 Q, Michael Odell, December 2004

47 *NME*, Rob Fitzpatrick, January 22, 2005

48 ibid.

49 ibid.

50 ibid.

51 Q, Laura Barton, March 2009

52 *NME*, Rob Fitzpatrick, January 22, 2005

53 *The Sun*, Jacqui Swift, December 24, 2004

54 *NME Yearbook*, Tim Jonze, November 2004
55 *The Guardian Guide*, Tony Horkins, January 22, 2005
56 *The Oregonian*
57 *Las Vegas Review-Journal*
58 *NME Yearbook*, Tim Jonze, November 2004

CHAPTER SIX

1 *The Guardian Guide*, Tony Horkins, January 22, 2005
2 ibid.
3 Q, Nick Duerden, July 2005
4 *The Guardian Guide*, Tony Horkins, January 22, 2005
5 ibid.
6 Q, February 2005
7 ibid.
8 *NME*, Rich Pelley, November 13, 2004
9 *NME*, Barry Nicolson, September 24, 2005
10 *NME Yearbook*, Tim Jonze, November 2004
11 *The Sunday Times Style*, Simon Mills, October 9, 2005
12 Q, Nick Duerden, July 2005
13 *Total Guitar*, Henry Yates, June 2005
14 *The Guardian Weekend*, Laura Barton, October 2005
15 *NME*, September 24, 2005
16 *NME Festival Guide 2005*, Rich Pelley
17 *The Daily Record*, Rick Fulton, September 3, 2004
18 *NME*, Elizabeth Goodman, May 7, 2005
19 Killers press statement, 2005
20 *NME*, July 2, 2011
21 Q, Nick Duerden, July 2005
22 Q, January 2005
23 *Playmusic*, Robert Collins, April 2005
24 *Time Out*, Chris Parkin, February 16
25 Q, Michael Odell, December 2004
26 *Leftlion*, Neil Howie
27 ibid.
28 *NME*, Elizabeth Goodman, May 7, 2005

29 *Playmusic*, Robert Collins, April 2005

30 *The Times*, Amber Cowan, January 8, 2005

31 *Total Guitar*, Henry Yates, June 2005

32 MTV News, March 2005

33 MTV, May 5, 2005

34 *NME*, Elizabeth Goodman, May 7, 2005

35 *NME Festival Guide 2005*, Rich Pelley

36 Q, Nick Duerden, July 2005

37 *NME*, Barry Nicolson, September 24, 2005

38 *Esquire*, August 1, 2005

39 MTV News, March 28, 2005

40 *Las Vegas Sun*, Spencer Patterson, April 16, 2010

41 *NME*, Elizabeth Goodman, May 7, 2005

42 Q, Nick Duerden, July 2005

43 *NME*, Elizabeth Goodman, May 7, 2005

44 amplifier.at

45 *The Killers: Vagabonds And Victims*, Jimmy Ramsay (Independent Music Press, 2005)

46 *The Killers: Destiny Is Calling Me*, Jarret Keene (Manic D Press, 2006)

47 *NME*, Barry Nicolson, June 28, 2006

48 *New Woman*, June 2005

49 *TV Hits*, May 2005

50 *Daily Mirror*, Gavin Martin, April 29, 2005

51 Q, Nick Duerden, July 2005

CHAPTER SEVEN

1 *The Sun*, Jacqui Swift, June 24, 2005

2 *NME,* June 25, 2005

3 *The Sun, Jacqui Swift, June 24, 2005*

4 *Q Glastonbury Review*, 2005

5 *NME*, June 25, 2005

6 *NME*, Barry Nicolson, September 24, 2005

7 *Q Glastonbury Review*, 2005

8 Radio 1 interview, quoted in *Contact Music*, June 28, 2005

9 ibid.

10 *Q Glastonbury Review*, 2005
11 *NME*, Barry Nicolson, September 24, 2005
12 *NME Yearbook*, Tim Jonze, November 2004
13 *The Telegraph*, Craig McLean, October 12, 2010
14 *The Guardian*, Nick Kent, October 20, 2006
15 Q, Nick Duerden, July 2005
16 *NME*, July 9, 2005
17 MTV News, James Montgomery, June 22, 2005
18 *The Sunday Times Style*, Simon Mills, October 9, 2005
19 *NME*, August 27, 2005
20 *The Sun*, June 24, 2005
21 MTV News, March 28, 2005
22 *NME Festival Guide 2005*, Rich Pelley
23 *New Woman*, June 2005
24 *Playmusic*, Robert Collins, April 2005
25 Q, Nick Duerden, July 2005
26 *The Observer*, Craig McLean, September 24, 2006
27 Q, Nick Duerden, July 2005
28 ibid.
29 ibid.
30 *NME*, Barry Nicolson, September 24, 2005
31 ibid.
32 *Daily Mirror*, Gavin Martin, April 29, 2005
33 Q, Nick Duerden, July 2005
34 *NME*, December 16/23, 2006
35 *NME*, Barry Nicolson, June 28, 2006
36 ibid.
37 ibid.

CHAPTER EIGHT

1 *The Observer*, Craig McLean, September 24, 2006
2 *NME*, Barry Nicolson, June 28, 2006
3 *The Guardian*, Nick Kent, October 20, 2006
4 Q, Simon Goddard, September 1, 2010
5 *The Observer*, Craig McLean, September 24, 2006

6 *NME*, Barry Nicolson, June 28, 2006

7 *The Observer*, Craig McLean, September 24, 2006

8 *The Guardian*, Nick Kent, October 20, 2006

9 *Rolling Stone*, November 30, 2006

10 *NME*, October 4, 2006

11 ibid.

12 *NME*, Barry Nicolson, June 28, 2006

13 *NME*, October 4, 2006

14 *Daily Mirror*, Gavin Martin, April 29, 2005

15 *NME*, October 4, 2006

16 *The Guardian*, Nick Kent, October 20, 2006

17 Q, Ben Mitchell, November 1, 2012

18 *The Guardian*, Nick Kent, October 20, 2006

19 ibid.

20 *NME*, October 4, 2006

21 ibid.

22 *Rolling Stone*, November 30, 2006

23 ibid.

24 *NME*, October 4, 2006

25 *Ultimate Guitar*, Steven Rosen, November 14, 2012

26 *The Observer*, Craig McLean, September 24, 2006

27 ibid.

28 *Rolling Stone*, November 30, 2006

29 *NME*, October 4, 2006

30 ibid.

31 *Spin*, Marc Spitz, February 2005

32 *NME*, October 4, 2006

33 *NME*, Barry Nicolson, June 28, 2006

34 *NME*, October 4, 2006

35 *The Observer*, Craig McLean, September 24, 2006

36 *The Times*, Craig McLean, June 19, 2009

37 *NME*, October 4, 2006

38 ibid.

39 *NME*, Barry Nicolson, June 28, 2006

40 *Rolling Stone*, November 30, 2006

41 MTV, James Montgomery, May 2, 2006

42 *NME*, December 16/23, 2006

43 thequietus.com, Mark Russell, October 31, 2008

44 *NME*, Barry Nicolson, June 28, 2006

45 *NME*, September 27, 2005

46 MTV, April 21, 2006

47 *The Word*, October 2006

48 *Rolling Stone*, November 30, 2006

49 ibid.

50 ibid.

51 *NME*, December 16/23, 2006

52 Q, October 2006

53 *NME*, September 29, 2006

54 *Rolling Stone*, September 21, 2006

55 *NME*, Barry Nicolson, June 22, 2013

56 *The Times*, Craig McLean, June 19, 2009

57 *Guitar World*, February 2009

58 *The Telegraph*, Craig McLean, October 12, 2010

59 *The Guardian*, Nick Kent, October 20, 2006

60 *Total Guitar*, Henry Yates, June 2005

61 *NME*, December 16/23, 2006

62 ibid.

63 *Rolling Stone*, November 30, 2006

64 *Groupie Magazine*, November 12, 2008

65 *Daily Mail*, Adrian Thrills, November 14, 2008

66 *Guitar World*, February 2009

67 *NME*, December 16/23, 2006

68 Q, Ben Mitchell, November 1, 2012

69 *NME*, December 16/23, 2006

70 ibid.

71 ibid.

72 *Rolling Stone*, Christian Hoard, November 16, 2006

73 *NME*, April 5, 2008

74 ibid.

75 *The Scotsman*, January 16, 2009

76 *Daily Mirror*, Gavin Martin, February 13, 2009

77 *Baby Couture*, December 20, 2010

78 *Daily Mirror*, Gavin Martin, February 13, 2009

79 thequietus.com, Mark Russell, October 31, 2008

80 *Time Out Chicago*, Brent DiCrescenzo, August 3, 2009

81 *NME*, April 5, 2008

CHAPTER NINE

 1 thequietus.com, Mark Russell, October 31, 2008

 2 *Shortlist*, Mark Beaumont, September 2012

 3 thequietus.com, Mark Russell, October 31, 2008

 4 *Groupie Magazine*, November 12, 2008

 5 The A.V. Club, December 30, 2008

 6 ibid.

 7 Q, Laura Barton, March 2009

 8 thequietus.com, Mark Russell, October 31, 2008

 9 *Daily Mirror*, Gavin Martin, February 13, 2009

10 Q, Laura Barton, March 2009

11 ibid.

12 Q, Laura Barton, March 2009

13 ibid.

14 *NME*, April 5, 2008

15 *Ultimate Guitar*, Steven Rosen, November 14, 2012

16 *NME*, Gavin Haynes, November 29

17 *Guitar World*, February 2009

18 *NME*, Gavin Haynes, November 29

19 The A.V. Club, Amanda Petrusich, December 30, 2008

20 thequietus.com, Mark Russell, October 31, 2008

21 *Time Out Chicago*, Brent DiCrescenzo, August 2009

22 The A.V. Club, Amanda Petrusich, December 30, 2008

23 *NME*, Gavin Haynes, November 29, 2008

24 The A.V. Club, Amanda Petrusich, December 30, 2008

25 *NME*, Gavin Haynes, November 29, 2008

26 ibid.

27 The A.V. Club, Amanda Petrusich, December 30, 2008

28 MTV, James Montgomery, June 22, 2005

29 *NME*, Gavin Haynes, November 29, 2008

30 *Groupie Magazine*, November 12, 2008

31 thequietus.com, Mark Russell, October 31, 2008

32 *The Aquarian Weekly*, Jordana Borensztajn, January 20, 2009

33 *Daily Mirror*, Gavin Martin, February 13, 2009

34 *Q*, Laura Barton, March 2009

35 ibid.

36 *The Scotsman*, January 16, 2009

37 thequietus.com, Mark Russell, October 31, 2008

38 radio.com, September 27, 2013

39 *Entertainment Weekly*, Ray Rahman, August 31, 2012

40 thequietus.com, Mark Russell, October 31, 2008

41 *Time Out Chicago*, Brent DiCrescenzo, August 2009

42 thequietus.com, Mark Russell, October 31, 2008

43 *The Telegraph*, Craig McLean, October 12, 2010

44 The A.V. Club, Amanda Petrusich, December 30, 2008

45 *Rolling Stone*, Austin Scaggs, October 2, 2008

46 thequietus.com, Mark Russell, October 31, 2008

47 *Groupie Magazine*, November 12, 2008

48 *NME*, Gavin Haynes, November 29, 2008

49 popmatters.com, Evan Sawdey, February 11, 2010

50 The A.V. Club, Amanda Petrusich, December 30, 2008

51 *NME*, April 5, 2008

52 thequietus.com, Mark Russell, October 31, 2008

53 *The Aquarian Weekly*, Jordana Borensztajn, January 20, 2009

54 *Time Out Chicago*, Brent DiCrescenzo, August 2009

55 The Vine, April 3, 2009

56 *Daily Mail*, Adrian Thrills, November 14, 2008

57 popmatters.com, Evan Sawdey, February 11, 2010

58 *Q*, Laura Barton, March 2009

59 The A.V. Club, Amanda Petrusich, December 30, 2008

60 *The Aquarian Weekly*, Jordana Borensztajn, January 20, 2009

61 *Rolling Stone*, Melissa Maerz, November 27, 2008

62 *Spin*, Stacey Anderson, November 24, 2008

63 *The Guardian*, Dave Simpson, November 21, 2008

64 Pitchfork, Ryan Dombal, December 5, 2008

65 *NME*, Dan Martin, November 19, 2008

66 The Vine, April 3, 2009

67 *GQ*, Craig McLean, October 2008

68 *The Scotsman*, January 16, 2009

69 *NME*, Gavin Haynes, November 29, 2008

70 *Daily Mail*, Adrian Thrills, November 14, 2008

71 Q, Laura Barton, March 2009

72 Q, Nick Duerden, July 2005

73 *The Telegraph*, Craig McLean, October 12, 2010

74 *Time Out*, Jonny Ensall, November 2012

75 *Time Out*, Harriet Gibsone, June 18, 2013

76 *The Telegraph*, Adam Sweeting, February 20, 2009

77 *The Times*, Craig McLean, June 19, 2009

78 ibid.

79 *NME*, Tim Jonze, December 25, 2004

80 *Baby Couture*, December 20, 2010

81 *The Scotsman*, January 16, 2009

82 *The Times*, Craig McLean, June 19, 2009

83 *The Scotsman*, January 16, 2009

84 popmatters.com, Evan Sawdey, February 11, 2010

85 *The Times*, Craig McLean, June 19, 2009

86 ibid.

87 *The Aquarian Weekly*, Jordana Borensztajn, January 20, 2009

88 Q, Laura Barton, March 2009

89 *NME*, Gavin Haynes, August 14, 2012

90 Q, Ben Mitchell, November 1, 2012

91 *Time Out Chicago*, Brent DiCrescenzo, August 2009

92 *NME*, Gavin Haynes, August 14, 2012

93 *The Telegraph*, Craig McLean, October 12, 2010

CHAPTER TEN

1 *NME*, Gavin Haynes, August 14, 2012

2 *Total Guitar*, Henry Yates, June 2005

3 *NME*, July 2, 2011

4 goldenplec.com, James Hendicott, July 25, 2013

5 gigwise.com, Lawrence Poole, June 23, 2011

6 *NME*, Gavin Haynes, August 14, 2012

7 *Entertainment Weekly*, Ray Rahman, August 31, 2012

8 musicradar.com, Joe Bosso, November 23, 2011

9 ibid.

10 ibid.

11 ibid.

12 *Hot Press*, Olaf Tyaransen, July 2, 2013

13 *Time Out Shanghai*, September 1, 2013

14 *Las Vegas Review-Journal*, Jason Bracelin, July 14, 2011

15 gigwise.com, Lawrence Poole, June 23, 2011

16 ibid.

17 *The Salt Lake Tribune*, David Burger, July 15, 2011

18 *Spin*, William Goodman, May 3, 2011

19 *Las Vegas Review-Journal*, Jason Bracelin, July 14, 2011

20 *The Salt Lake Tribune*, David Burger, July 15, 2011

21 *Spin*, William Goodman, May 3, 2011

22 *Time Out Shanghai*, September 1, 2013

23 *Spin*, William Goodman, May 3, 2011

24 goldenplec.com, James Hendicott, July 25, 2013

25 *Hot Press*, Olaf Tyaransen, July 2, 2013

26 *Spin*, William Goodman, May 3, 2011

27 *Hot Press*, Olaf Tyaransen, July 2, 2013

28 *Spin*, William Goodman, May 3, 2011

29 ibid.

30 *Spinner*, Theo Spielberg, July 12, 2011

31 Consequence Of Sound, Alex Young, July 19, 2011

32 *Las Vegas Review-Journal*, Jason Bracelin, July 14, 2011

33 *Clash*, Sophie Williams, October 5, 2011

34 *The Salt Lake Tribune*, David Burger, July 15, 2011

35 *Q*, Simon Goddard, September 1, 2010

36 NPR, Liane Hansen, September 12, 2010

37 The A.V. Club, Amanda Petrusich, December 30, 2008

38 *The Telegraph*, Craig McLean, October 12, 2010

39 Q, Simon Goddard, September 1, 2010

40 ibid.

41 *Daily Mail*, Adrian Thrills, September 14, 2012

42 *The Telegraph*, Craig McLean, October 12, 2010

43 Q, Simon Goddard, September 1, 2010

44 rapgenius.com, source unknown

45 *The Telegraph*, Craig McLean, October 12, 2010

46 NPR, Liane Hansen, September 12, 2010

47 *Entertainment Weekly*, Leah Greenblatt, September 16, 2010

48 *NME*, Hamish MacBain, September 6, 2010

49 *The Globe And Mail*, J. D. Considine, December 6, 2010

50 *The Telegraph*, Craig McLean, October 12, 2010

51 *Ladygunn*, September 17, 2012

52 *The Globe And Mail*, J. D. Considine, December 6, 2010

53 *The Telegraph*, Craig McLean, October 12, 2010

54 Q, Simon Goddard, September 2010

55 *The Telegraph*, Craig McLean, October 12, 2010

56 Q, Simon Goddard, September 2010

57 *The Independent*, Craig McLean, September 9, 2010

58 FL, David Swan, February 13, 2013

59 *NME*, August 14, 2012

60 Q, Ben Mitchell, November 1, 2012

61 goldenplec.com, James Hendicott, July 25, 2013

62 Q, Ben Mitchell, November 1, 2012

CHAPTER ELEVEN

1 *NME*, Gavin Haynes, August 14, 2012

2 *The Independent*, Craig McLean, September 9, 2012

3 Spotify, Diego Planas Rego, September 17, 2012

4 *Ladygunn*, September 17, 2012

5 stereogum.com, T. Cole Rachel, September 25, 2012

6 *Rolling Stone*, April 6, 2011

7 musicradar.com, Joe Bosso, November 23, 2011

8 *Time Out Shanghai*, September 1, 2013

9 stereogum.com, T. Cole Rachel, September 25, 2012

10 musicradar.com, Joe Bosso, November 23, 2011

11 *Ultimate Guitar*, Steven Rosen, November 14, 2012

12 goldenplec.com, James Hendicott, July 25, 2013

13 *Time Out Shanghai*, September 1, 2013

14 *Daily Mail*, Adrian Thrills, September 14, 2012

15 stereogum.com, T. Cole Rachel, September 25, 2012

16 ibid.

17 stereogum.com, T. Cole Rachel, September 25, 2012

18 *Crave*, Johnny Firecloud, September 21, 2012

19 stereogum.com, T. Cole Rachel, September 25, 2012

20 *Entertainment Weekly*, November 12, 2010

21 Spotify, Diego Planas Rego, September 17, 2012

22 stereogum.com, T. Cole Rachel, September 25, 2012

23 *NME*, Gavin Haynes, August 14, 2012

24 stereogum.com, T. Cole Rachel, September 25, 2012

25 *NME*, Barry Nicolson, June 22, 2013

26 stereogum.com, T. Cole Rachel, September 25, 2012

27 *Time Out Shanghai*, September 1, 2013

28 *Ultimate Guitar*, Steven Rosen, November 14, 2012

29 BBC *Newsbeat*, January 4, 2012

30 *NME*, July 2, 2011

31 *Crave*, Johnny Firecloud, September 21, 2012

32 *The Independent*, Craig McLean, September 9, 2012

33 *NME*, Gavin Haynes, August 14, 2012

34 Q, Ben Mitchell, November 1, 2012

35 *Rolling Stone*, Gavin Edwards, June 12, 2012

36 Q, Ben Mitchell, November 1, 2012

37 ibid.

38 ibid.

39 *NME*, Gavin Haynes, August 14, 2012

40 *Ultimate Guitar*, Steven Rosen, November 14, 2012

41 digitalspy.co.uk, Lewis Corner, September 17, 2012

42 radio.com, September 27, 2013

43 *Crave*, Johnny Firecloud, September 21, 2012

44 ibid.

45 ibid.

46 ibid.

47 ibid.

48 *Rolling Stone*, Gavin Edwards, June 12

49 *Crave*, Johnny Firecloud, September 21, 2012

50 *NME*, Gavin Haynes, August 14, 2012

51 Spotify, Diego Planas Rego, September 17, 2012

52 goldenplec.com, James Hendicott, July 25, 2013

53 ibid.

54 *Details*, Jesse Ashlock, October 2012

55 *Entertainment Weekly*, Ray Rahman, August 31, 2012

56 *Daily Mail*, Adrian Thrills, September 14, 2012

57 *Ultimate Guitar*, Steven Rosen, November 14, 2012

58 *Crave*, Johnny Firecloud, September 21, 2012

59 Spotify, Diego Planas Rego, September 17, 2012

60 *Ultimate Guitar*, Steven Rosen, November 14, 2012

61 Spotify, Diego Planas Rego, September 17, 2012

62 *Beat* magazine, Alasdair Duncan

63 Spotify, Diego Planas Rego, September 17, 2012

64 ibid.

65 ibid.

66 *The Independent*, Craig McLean, September 9, 2012

67 *Daily Star*, April 7, 2009

68 *Hot Press*, Olaf Tyaransen, July 2, 2013

69 *NME*, Gavin Haynes, August 14, 2012

70 *Ladygunn*, December 17, 2012

71 *NME*, Barry Nicolson, June 22, 2013

72 FL, David Swan, February 13, 2013

73 *Time Out*, Tommy Ensall, November 2012

74 stereogum.com, T. Cole Rachel, September 25, 2012

75 *Daily Mail*, Adrian Thrills, September 14, 2012

CHAPTER TWELVE

1 Q, Ben Mitchell, November 1, 2012

2 *NME*, Barry Nicolson, June 22, 2013
3 ibid.
4 *Time Out*, Harriet Gibsone, June 18, 2013
5 Q, Ben Mitchell, November 1, 2012
6 *NME*, Barry Nicolson, June 22, 2013
7 Q, Ben Mitchell, November 1, 2012
8 *NME*, Barry Nicolson, June 22, 2013
9 *That's Shanghai*, Monica Liau, September 27, 2013
10 Q, Ben Mitchell, November 1, 2012
11 *NME*, Barry Nicolson, June 22, 2013
12 Q, Ben Mitchell, November 1, 2012
13 *NME*, Barry Nicolson, June 22, 2013
14 *Ladygunn*, December 17, 2012
15 ibid.
16 *NME*, Barry Nicolson, June 22, 2013
17 *Time Out*, Harriet Gibsone, June 18, 2013
18 *NME*, Barry Nicolson, June 22, 2013
19 ibid.
20 *Time Out*, Harriet Gibsone, June 18, 2013
21 *Details*, Jesse Ashlock, October 2012
22 *Ladygunn*, December 17, 2012
23 *NME*, Barry Nicolson, June 22, 2013
24 ibid.
25 ibid.
26 Q, Ben Mitchell, November 1, 2012
27 *NME*, Barry Nicolson, June 22, 2013
28 FL, David Swan, February 13, 2013
29 *NME*, Jamie Fullerton, October 12, 2013
30 radio.com, September 27, 2013
31 Pitchfork, Evan Minsker, August 7, 2013
32 *NME*, September 16, 2013
33 *Time Out Shanghai*, September 1, 2013
34 goldenplec.com, James Hendicott, July 25, 2013
35 *NME*, Barry Nicolson, June 22, 2013
36 *NME*, Jamie Fullerton, October 12, 2013

37 radio.com, September 27, 2013

38 *NME*, Jamie Fullerton, October 12, 2013

39 ibid.

40 *Time Out Shanghai*, September 1, 2013

41 *NME*, Jamie Fullerton, October 12, 2013

42 ibid.

43 ibid.

44 *Time Out Shanghai*, September 1, 2013

45 *The Hollywood Reporter*, Georg Szalai, July 11, 2013

46 *NME*, Jamie Fullerton, October 12, 2013

47 *NME*, Barry Nicolson, June 22, 2013

48 *The Hollywood Reporter*

49 goldenplec.com, James Hendicott, July 25, 2013

50 *NME*, Barry Nicolson, June 22, 2013

51 ibid.

52 ibid.

BY THE SAME AUTHOR

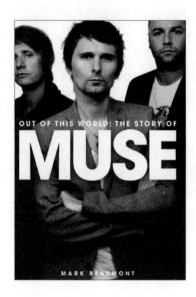

THE STORY OF MUSE
Out Of This World

by Mark Beaumont

From the first time they smashed up all the stage equipment as 16-year-old punk kids, Muse were always a stadium band in waiting, and this new in-depth biography from one of the UK's award-winning music journalists follows their every step on the road to Wembley, with detailed accounts of all four of their studio albums including the million-selling *Black Holes* And *Revelations* and all of the wild nights, theories and falsettos they experienced along the way.

This new edition of Out Of This World has been updated to include the release of Muse's album The Resistance..

Available from **www.omnibuspress.com**

ISBN: 9781849383684
Order No: OP53350

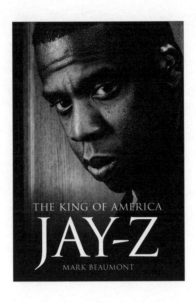

JAY-Z
The King Of America
by Mark Beaumont

A hero for our times, Jay-Z is one of the world's most successful hip hop artists, record producers and entrepreneurs, selling more than 50 million albums globally and winning 13 Grammy Awards.

Mark Beaumont has interviewed Jay-Z and many revealing insights from that encounter inform this no-holds-barred biography of a great American success story, in which musical talent and youthful criminality co-exist alongside some impressively wide-ranging entrepreneurial skills. This fascinating book tells it all, revealing how the good, the bad and the corporate are all part of the incredibly far-reaching Jay-Z legend.

Available from **www.omnibuspress.com**

ISBN: 9781780383170
Order No: OP54527